Business English

A Worktext with Programmed Reinforcement

Third Edition

Business English

A Worktext with Programmed Reinforcement

Third Edition

Keith Slocum

**Department of English
Montclair State College,
Upper Montclair, New Jersey**

GLENCOE/McGRAW-HILL
A Macmillan/McGraw-Hill Company
Mission Hills, California

Copyright © 1985 by ITT Bobbs-Merrill Educational Publishing Company, Inc.,
Copyright © 1981 by The Bobbs-Merrill Company, Inc., Copyright © 1964 by Donald
Publishing Company, Inc.
Copyrights transferred to Glencoe Publishing Company, a division of Macmillan, Inc.

Send all inquiries to:
Glencoe/McGraw-Hill
15319 Chatsworth Street
P.O. Box 9509
Mission Hills, California 91395-9509
Printed in the United States of America

ISBN 0-02-678230-8
    7 90

for Kathleen, Michael, David, Thomas, and Peter

Contents

PREFACE

As an instructor in business English, you know that although the latest advances in computer technology may have altered the ways in which a business person communicates, they have not altered the fact that successful communication depends on a firm grasp of the rules of English and the ability to express oneself clearly and correctly. Indeed, as numerous studies confirm, the ability to communicate is far more important to success in business than is expertise in a particular field. *Business English* has been carefully designed to help your students acquire that ability.

The results of extensive surveys and market research have gone into the writing of this new edition, which has been thoroughly revised, updated, and expanded from the previous edition. Outdated references and allusions to outmoded equipment and business practices have been eliminated. Chapter topics have been reorganized, and treatments have been rewritten to reflect current practice. Chapter exercises have been significantly expanded. New chapters on the parts of speech, composition, and editing and proofreading skills have been added, as have three new appendices. The text itself has been completely redesigned, with a new two-color format to help clarify the presentation. The goal throughout has been to create a complete and flexible text that you can use to give your students a firm foundation in the rules of English grammar combined with extensive practice in the writing and editing skills they will need in business.

The principal focus of *Business English* is on grammar, presented within the traditional framework of the eight parts of speech and in a logical progression preferred by most instructors. Chapter 1 introduces the parts of speech. Chapter 2 introduces the four kinds of sentences and discusses complete sentences, sentence fragments, and run-on sentences. Chapters 3 through 13 present the eight parts of speech. Chapters 15 through 19 treat in systematic detail the correct use of punctuation marks. Chapter 20 presents the rules and conventions covering capitalization, word division, and the presentation of numbers. Chapter 21 lists and discusses 57 groups of words many writers often confuse or misuse.

Each chapter ends with extensive exercises so that your students can apply what they have learned. These exercises draw on typical business situations, language, and format. Before attempting the exercises, students can first check their understanding of the topic in the chapter's Programmed Reinforcement sections, a unique feature of *Business English* designed to give students the chance to reinforce their learning. This proven sequence of study, review, and application in each chapter helps ensure your students' successful mastery of each topic.

Because proofreading and editing are such important skills, beginning with Chapter 2 every chapter asks students to edit examples drawn from various types of business correspondence. Each editing exercise focuses on the subject matter of that chapter: for example, the chapter on nouns affords practice in proofreading for errors in the use of nouns; the chapter on the colon and semicolon presents a memo to edit with special attention to these marks. New to this edition is Chapter 22, which is devoted to proofreading and editing exclusively. Here your students are shown how to use and interpret proofreaders' marks and are given the opportunity to proofread and edit, in typed and printed formats, sentences, paragraphs, letters, a job résumé, and a memorandum report.

Also new to this edition of *Business English* is the inclusion of material on business correspondence. Chapter 14 demonstrates techniques for achieving effective composition and illustrates the seven common characteristics of effective business writing. In addition each chapter from 1 to 21 inclusive contains one or more composition exercises drawing on material covered in that particular lesson so that your students can not only see the chapter material in the text examples but also demonstrate the ability to use it in their own writing.

Moreover, Chapters 14 through 22 also ask your students to compose beyond the sentence level. Students are given the chance to write various types of short business letters and memorandums—orders, complaints, requests, and so forth, finishing with a short recommendation report. Due to the flexible structure of *Business English,* all this composition material is optional. You can ask your students to do all, some, or none of it, depending on the requirements of your class and the needs and abilities of your students.

Rounding out the text, the four appendices at the end present information on the use of the dictionary, helpful spelling rules, business letter formats, and common business abbreviations.

To assist you in leading your students to a full mastery of all the textbook material, a comprehensive Instructor's Guide accompanies *Business English.* The extensive evaluation materials consist of a pretest, individual chapter tests, five unit examinations, and a final examination. Scheduling options, general teaching strategies, chapter-by-chapter teaching suggestions, transparency masters to clarify discussion, supplementary exercises, and complete answer keys are also provided. All these features are described in detail in the Instructor's Guide. *Business English* and its Instructor's Guide combine to give you, the instructor, a complete and effective teaching package you can use to ensure that your students have the skills they will need to become competent members of the business world.

 # ACKNOWLEDGMENTS

I would like to thank the many teachers whose comments at various stages during the preparation of the manuscript helped shape the scope and format of this edition of *Business English.* In particular I wish to thank the following colleagues who reviewed the completed manuscript and provided valuable suggestions for final revision:

Janice A. David, Illinois Central College, East Peoria, Illinois
Carol Engel, Fort Steilacoom Community College, Tacoma, Washington
Mary Link, Carroll County Area Vocational-Technical School, Carrollton, Georgia
Bonnie Scott, Taylor Business Institute, Paramus, New Jersey
Judy B. Shay, Southwestern College, Chula Vista, California

I would also like to acknowledge the editorial support of the people at Bobbs-Merrill, including Dennis Gladhill, acquisitions editor; Sara Black, editorial development coordinator; and especially Diana Francoeur, developmental editor. To all of you my sincere appreciation.

Keith Slocum

INTRODUCTION

The ability to write clearly and correctly has always been a valuable skill in the business world. This is especially true in today's organization, in which modern technology has significantly altered both the way and the extent that business people communicate through writing.

A few years ago, if you wanted to send a message, you probably would dictate it or give a rough copy to an assistant to type and mail. If you preferred, the assistant would type the message, return it to you for possible revisions, then retype and send it. Lengthy letters and reports demanded a great deal of time for typing and retyping. In today's office, however, you could dictate the message by phone into a recording device at the word processing center. There, the operator of a word processor would keyboard it and have the word processor print out hard copies to be mailed or returned to you for possible revision. Any changes could then be keyboarded and incorporated into the original text without the need for complete retyping. Copies of the revised message could be printed at speeds many times faster than anyone could type.

If you wanted to send an interoffice memo, whether to someone in your building or to divisions throughout the country, you might decide to keyboard it yourself at your work station on your personal computer. You could make any revisions on the computer's video display and then transfer the message electronically to the computer terminals of the people for whom the memo is intended. You would not need to use even a single sheet of paper.

Modern technology thus places a premium on your ability to communicate correctly and quickly. Both the increased volume made possible by computer technology and the need to make the technology cost effective by using it to its full potential require today's business person to know and to use correct English automatically.

Remember, the computer can greatly increase your potential efficiency as a writer, but it cannot take your place. You still must *create* the message. You must be sure it is clear, complete, and correct if your reader is to understand the message and act on it. Writing errors such as mistakes in grammar and punctuation, misspelled words, and improper usage will distract and confuse the reader as well as decrease his or her confidence in you and your business. Obviously, your message will be less likely to be successful.

Knowing how to express yourself correctly is not just necessary for writing successful messages. It is important to your personal success and advancement in the business organization. Numerous studies, some of which have gone into the planning of this book, confirm that your ability to communicate, more than your expertise in your particular field, will be the most important factor influencing your success in the business world. No matter how much you know, if you are unable to express it clearly and correctly, your knowledge is lost to others. They will not fully understand you, and they will not fully appreciate you. Indeed, if your writing is marked by common grammatical and spelling errors, others will undervalue your abilities and worth. Hence your opportunity for advancement depends quite heavily on your ability to communicate. The higher you progress in the organization, the more important good communication skills will be.

In short, whether it is your responsibility to write messages yourself or to transcribe those of someone else, your command of English is essential to your success in business. Your study of *Business English* will give you a firm and thorough foundation in the basics of business writing to help you achieve this success.

1

THE PARTS OF SPEECH

NOUNS, PRONOUNS, VERBS, ADJECTIVES, ADVERBS, PREPOSITIONS, CONJUNCTIONS, INTERJECTIONS

Language is the use of words to express ideas and feelings. Sometimes these words are spoken. Sometimes they are written. In either case it is through language that people are able to express thoughts and emotions.

We call the rules of language **grammar.** Grammar is simply a description of the natural pattern of language that people have evolved over many centuries. This does not mean that there is one natural pattern of language. There are many. Each language has its own particular pattern. In English, for example, the words that describe or modify a noun (called **adjectives**) normally appear before the noun. In French they appear after the noun. In English the noun and verb usually appear next to each other. In German a major part of the verb usually appears at the end of the sentence. French, German, and English have their own rules of grammar. So does every other language. To express your ideas clearly and effectively in any of these languages, you need to know these rules of grammar.

In this text, of course, we are concerned with the rules of the English language. Most of these rules apply to both spoken and written English. Others, such as all the rules regarding capitalization and punctuation, are intended specifically for written English. We will be looking at the rules for written English. When you know them, you will automatically know all the appropriate rules for spoken English as well.

When we describe the language, we talk about different classes of words. We categorize these words according to the jobs they perform. These jobs include naming, describing, connecting, and showing action. In English there are eight classes of words. They are the basic building blocks of the English language. We call them the eight parts of speech: **nouns, pronouns, verbs, adjectives, adverbs, prepositions, conjunctions,** and **interjections.**

As you can see from our discussion so far, it is almost impossible to discuss our language without using these terms. So, in this chapter we are going to look briefly at each part of speech. This will help give us an overview of the material we will study in detail in the following chapters.

NOUNS

A noun is the *name* of anything—a person, place, thing, quality, concept, action.

person—Diana, sister, architect
place—Newark, home, outside
thing—computer, book, building
quality—honesty, sincerity, obstinacy
concept—beauty, truth, love
action—writing, speaking, dancing

Nouns are one of the two most important classes of words in the language (verbs are the other). Sentences revolve around nouns because nouns serve as both the subjects and objects of verbs.

The following employment ad contains many different kinds of nouns. All of them have been italicized. Notice that they are all *names* of something. Some of the words that are not italicized may look like nouns. They have not been italicized because they are not being used as nouns. We'll have more to say later about how the same word can be used as more than one part of speech.

Systems *Development* & Systems *Analysis*
Rosemont Cosmetics, fast becoming a significant *force* in the cosmetics/fragrance *industries*, seeks the following *individuals* to advance our automation *efforts* further. If you recognize the *advantages* of *working* in a small shop *environment* and are able to develop strong working *relationships* with user *departments* and key management *staff*, telephone or write us immediately! Excellent verbal communication *skills* are imperative for all *positions*.

PRONOUNS

Pronouns are noun substitutes. They provide both efficiency and variety of expression. Look at this sentence without pronouns:

> Victoria said Victoria needed the pocket calculator Victoria's father had given Victoria if Victoria was going to complete Victoria's accounting assignment on time.

Now look at it with pronouns:

> Victoria said she needed the pocket calculator her father had given her if she was going to complete her accounting assignment on time.

The noun to which a pronoun refers—the noun for which it stands—is its *antecedent*. It is important, of course, that this antecedent be clear to the reader.

Here is a list of some common pronouns:

I	we	some
you	they	none
he	him	anyone
she	her	nobody
it	them	it

VERBS

As we said, the verb is one of the two most important parts of speech. A verb can be either a word or group of words. Usually the verb tells us what the subject *does*. This kind of verb is called an **action verb.** Words like *run, write, see, give, teach, build, talk, throw, enter, express, take* are action verbs.

Often a verb joins, or links, the subject to words that describe it. This kind of verb is called a **state-of-being** or **linking verb.** Here are some common linking verbs: *is, are, am, will be, has been, will have been, were.*

We will discuss verbs in detail in Chapters 6 to 9. Right now it is important to be able to recognize verbs to see whether a sentence is complete—to know whether a statement is really a sentence. Every sentence must have at least one verb and one noun. That's why verbs and nouns are the two most important parts of speech. Look at the following examples. Some have more than one verb. See how verbs are used to make statements, ask questions, or give commands.

 STATEMENTS

Kareem *scores.*
Kathleen *is knitting* a sweater.
The entire staff *should have been notified.*
Ms. Robinson *reprimanded* Tom when he *misplaced* the file.
The computer *is* off line.
It *seems* later than it actually *is.*

 QUESTIONS

Where *were* you?
Where *have* you *been?*
Will this new filing system *be installed* before Mr. Todd *returns* from Miami?

 COMMANDS

Bring me the proposal as soon as you *have completed* it.
Relax, take a deep breath, and *tell* me about the interview.

 PROGRAMMED REINFORCEMENT

Now you are going to reinforce your understanding of what you have just read by working through a carefully chosen sequence of questions and answers.

Programmed Reinforcement is based upon an educational idea called programmed learning. In programmed learning a complex idea is broken down into many small bits of information that you can easily learn one at a time. In this section you are asked a question about one simple bit of information. You write your answer in the space provided. Then you check your answer against the correct answer printed in the book. If your answer is correct, you go on to the next question. If it is wrong, you go over it again to see why. Thus, you don't go on until you are certain that you understand each step. In this way you can move with certainty step by step to a full understanding of the topic.

 WHAT TO DO IN THIS SECTION

Generally you are told to do one of two things in each frame:

1. Where you find blanks, write the missing word or words.
   For example—In studying English grammar we refer to basic classes of words in the language. These words are known as the *parts of speech* .

2. Where you find two or more words in parentheses, circle the correct word.
   For example—In English there are (six, (eight), ten) parts of speech.

Questions or statements are numbered in sequence S1, S2, S3, and so on. The correct response, or answer, to S1 is numbered R1, the correct response to S2 is R2, and so on.

Begin with S1, which appears in the top right-hand frame. Cover the corresponding answer (R1), which appears in the left-hand box of the second frame. Simply follow the frames down the page and onto the next page until you have completed the Programmed Reinforcement section. Then turn to the exercises that are assigned at the end of each Programmed Reinforcement section. These exercises will give you extensive practice in applying the principles you have just learned.

You will not be graded on your work in Programmed Reinforcement. There is nothing to be gained from looking at the correct response before you write in your answer. If you do, you will only be cheating yourself out of valuable practice.

Work through this programmed material carefully. You will then be able to move on to the practice exercises with ease and confidence.

S1 When we study the rules of language, we study _____ _____.

R1 grammar

S2 In studying English grammar we refer to basic classes of words in the language. These words are known as the _____.

R2 parts of speech

S3 There are (six, eight, ten) parts of speech.

R3 eight

S4 Words that name persons, places, things, concepts, qualities, and actions are known as _____.

R4 nouns

S5 Circle the nouns in the following list: office, cruelty, think, thought, truly, truth, Robert

---

R5 office, cruelty, thought, truth, Robert

S6 Underline the nouns in the following sentence: Professor Stanley from the local college is offering classes in business writing on Thursdays.

R6 Professor Stanley, college, classes, writing, Thursdays

S7 A word that can take the place of a noun is a _____ _____.

R7 pronoun

S8 Circle the pronouns in the following list: I, you, very, some, they, five, Mary

---

R8 I, you, some, they

S9 The noun to which a pronoun refers is known as its _____.

R9 antecedent

S10 Circle the pronouns in the following sentences. Draw a line to their antecedents.
a. Madeleine asked her supervisor for details.
b. John told me that his brother was touring the plant.
c. I understand from Carole that her new home computer has its own printer.

R10 a. Madeleine asked her supervisor for details.
b. John told me that his brother was touring the plant.
c. I understand from Carole that her new home computer has its own printer.

S11 A verb is a word that shows (a) action, (b) state of being, (c) either action or state of being.

R11 c

S12 Circle the action verbs in the following list: write, is, composition, compose, learns, walked, will be.

R12 write, compose, learns, walked

S13 Another name for a state-of-being verb is a _____ _____ verb.

R13 linking

S14 Circle the linking verbs in the following list: was, would have been, thought, am, teach.

R14 was, would have been, am

S15 In order to be a sentence, a statement (must have, need not have) at least one verb. A sentence (may, may not) have more than one verb.

R15 must have, may

S16 Which of the following statements do not contain verbs?
a. The home computer market
b. The market is expanding
c. The market in home computers
d. The market has expanded

R16 a, c

S17 Underline the verbs in the following sentences:
1. The text will be published in tomorrow's paper.
2. Greg gave Cindy the package he had been holding.
3. Will you send me a copy of your report when you have finished it?
4. Tell me why you are late.

R17 1. will be published
2. gave, had been holding
3. Will send, have finished
4. Tell, are

Turn to Exercises 1.1 and 1.2.

So far we have looked at the two most important parts of speech, nouns and verbs, and we have also looked at pronouns, which serve as noun substitutes. These three parts of speech are used to form the core of a sentence. The remaining parts of speech are used to add more information.

ADJECTIVES

Adjectives are words that *modify*—describe—nouns or pronouns. They answer questions such as *what kind, how many, which one.* Which of the following adjectives describe your boss? *tall, short, young, old, jovial, successful, incompetent, energetic, demanding, inefficient, unreasonable, fair.*

Adjectives usually come before the nouns and pronouns they modify, but they may follow these words, especially when they are used with linking verbs. In the following real estate ad, all adjectives have been italicized. Here again some of the italicized words may look to you like other parts of speech. They have been italicized because in this passage they are being used as adjectives. Notice that the words *a, an, and the* have all been italicized. As you will learn, these words form a special group of adjectives known as **articles**.

> ***Luxury* Home in *Dramatic Country* Setting**
> *This* stunning *fieldstone* and *cedar* contemporary home is dramatically situated on *three wooded* acres overlooking *the beautiful* Jacksonburg River in *desirable* Woodland Township. Enhanced by *terraced* landscaping, *this outstanding* home affords *four generous* bedrooms, *three marble* bathrooms, *an 18' × 16' artist's* studio, *an enormous stone* fireplace in a *breathtaking* living room with *cathedral* ceiling, and a *heated 38' × 20' in-ground* pool. *A peaceful* retreat with *direct* access to *New Jersey corporate* centers allows you *superb contemporary* living.

ADVERBS

Adverbs modify verbs, adjectives, and other adverbs. They answer such questions as *when, how, where, to what extent.*

Adverbs modifying verbs:

> She typed *quickly* and *accurately.*
> He arrived *late.*
> I put the report *there.*

Adverbs modifying adjectives:

> She is *extremely* conscientious.
> Our equipment is *too* old.
> I am *truly* sorry.

Adverbs modifying adverbs:

> He performs his duties *exceptionally* well.
> She arrived *surprisingly* early.
> The applicant responded *somewhat* nervously to the interviewer's questions.

As the above sentences show, most adverbs end in *ly*.

PREPOSITIONS

Prepositions show the relationship between a noun or noun equivalent (called the *object of the preposition*) and another word in the sentence. The preposition and its object, along with any modifiers, form a **prepositional phrase.** These phrases usually function as adjectives or adverbs. Common prepositions include *at, by, for, from, in, of, to,* and *with*.

prepositional phrase	prepositional phrase	prepositional phrase
p m op	p m m op	p op
at the office	*in* the foreseeable future	*from* New York

p m op	p m op	p m op
by the desk	*of* the mistakes	*with* your approval

p m m op	p m op	m = modifiers
for a few hours	*to* the employees	op = object of the preposition
		p = preposition

We will discuss prepositions in detail in Chapter 12. For the present it is important to recognize prepositional phrases as modifiers and to be able to distinguish them from sentence subjects.

CONJUNCTIONS

Conjunctions connect words or groups of words. The most common conjunctions—including *and, but, or, nor*—are called coordinating conjunctions. They act as connectors between equal (coordinate) parts of sentences. Other conjunctions such as *since, because, if, although, unless, before* are known as subordinating conjunctions. These connectors show a relationship or dependency of one sentence part to another.

Notice the conjunctions in the following sentences:

> Ms. Shurley *and* Mr. Gross were promoted.
> They were promoted, *but* I was not.
> Send your payment *or* we will bill you later.
> I feel disappointed *because* I was not promoted.
> I intend to look for another job *if* I am not promoted soon.

In each of the preceding sentences, the conjunction is placed between the two sentence parts that it connects. However, some conjunctions may be placed at the beginning of a sentence rather than between the sentence parts. For example, we could rewrite the last example this way:

If I am not promoted soon, I intend to look for another job.

 # INTERJECTIONS

An interjection is a word used to show strong feelings or sudden emotions. An interjection usually is followed by an exclamation point or a comma. Because interjections do not contribute to the basic meaning of a sentence, they are seldom used in business writing apart from advertising copy. Look at these examples:

Wow! Look at the quality of this reproduction.
Ouch! I just hit my finger.
Oh, I don't believe that will happen.

 # SUMMING UP

We have now looked at each part of speech. Every sentence must contain at least two of the parts of speech, a noun and a verb. Most sentences contain more. Very few, however, contain all eight. Here's one that does:

Yes, your knowledge of grammar will be very useful and rewarding.

Business English was written to help you attain this knowledge.

 # PROGRAMMED REINFORCEMENT

S18   The two parts of speech that describe or modify other words are called _____ and _____.

R18   adjectives and adverbs

S19   a. _____ modify nouns and pronouns.
b. _____ modify verbs, adjectives, and adverbs.

R19   a. adjectives   b. adverbs

S20   Circle the adjectives in the following list: seven, efficient, the, truly, being, Bob, me, a, happy

---

R20   seven, efficient, the, a, happy

S21   Circle the adjectives in the following sentences and underline the words they modify.
     a. The boss gave me a big raise.
     b. The new secretary is a skilled typist.
     c. The large brown crate contains new office furniture.

R21   a. (The) *boss* gave me (a)(big) *raise.*
     b. (The)(new) *secretary* is (a) (skilled) *typist.*
     c. (The)(large)(brown) *crate* contains (new)(office) *furniture.*

S22   Words that answer such questions as *what kind, how many,* and *which one* are _____.

R22   adjectives

S23   Words that answer questions such as *when, where, how, to what extent* are _____.

R23   adverbs

S24   Adverbs modify _____, _____, and _____.

R24   verbs, adjectives, and adverbs.

S25   Most adverbs end in _____.

R25   ly

S26   Circle the adverbs in the following list: blue, very, sincerely, writing, computer, there, often

R26   very, sincerely, there, often

S27   Circle the adverbs in the following sentences. Draw a line to the words they modify.
     a. She arrived early.
     b. He spoke rapidly and loudly.
     c. We are very unhappy with your product.
     d. She arrived unexpectedly early.

R27   a. She arrived (early)
     b. He spoke (rapidly) and (loudly)
     c. We are (very) unhappy with your product.
     d. She arrived (unexpectedly)(early.)

S28   Words that join noun or pronoun objects to other words in the sentence are called _____.

R28   prepositions

S29   The preposition and its object plus any words that modify that object are known collectively as a _____.

R29   prepositional phrase

S30   Prepositional phrases usually act as what two parts of speech? _____ and _____

R30   adjectives and adverbs

S31   Circle the prepositions in the following list: all, of, with, very, extra, from, to, because

R31   of, with, from, to

S32   Circle the prepositions and underline their objects in the following sentences.
 a. The message is on the desk by the phone.
 b. Most of the errors must be corrected by noon.
 c. In a few days I will be traveling to New York to meet with your representatives at corporate headquarters.

R32   a. The message is ⟨on⟩ the *desk* ⟨by⟩ the *phone.*
 b ⟨Most⟩ ⟨of⟩ the *errors* must be corrected ⟨by⟩ *noon.*
 c. ⟨In⟩ a few *days* I will be traveling ⟨to⟩ *New York* to meet ⟨with⟩ your *repre-sentatives* ⟨at⟩ *corporate headquarters.*

S33   Conjunctions are (a) modifiers, (b) connectors, (c) action words, (d) name words.

R33   b

S34   There are two kinds of conjunctions, coordinating and subordinating. Coordinating conjunctions connect (equal, unequal) parts of sentences.

R34   equal

S35   The words *and, but, or, nor* are (coordinating, sub-ordinating) conjunctions.

R35   coordinating

S36   Conjunctions that show a relationship or dependency of one sentence part to another are called _____.

R36   subordinating

S37   Which of the following are *not* subordinating conjunctions? although, because, but, if, or, since

R37   but, or

S38   Circle the conjunctions in each of the following:
 a. Ray and Bob are eager to accept her offer, but I have reservations.
 b. I feel hurt because of your decision not to attend the luncheon and reception.
 c. Since we have not received payment for more than three months, we will be forced to seek legal action unless you settle your account within seven days.

R38   a. and, but
 b. because, and
 c. Since, unless

S39   A word that shows strong feelings or sudden emotion is a(n) _____.

R39   interjection

S40   An interjection is usually followed by (a) a period, (b) a colon, (c) an exclamation point.

R40   c

S41   Interjections (are, are not) often used in business writing because they (do, do not) contribute greatly to the basic meaning of a sentence.

R41   are not, do not

Turn to Exercises 1.3 to 1.5.

EXERCISE 1·1   NOUNS AND PRONOUNS

Various nouns and pronouns have been italicized in the following sentences. In the blanks provided, identify each italicized word as either a noun (N) or a pronoun (P).

               (1)   (2)

1. Please tell *me* your *schedule*.   1. _____   2. _____

          (3)   (4)   (5) (6)

2. *We* wish to express our *appreciation* for all the *help you*   3. _____   4. _____

have provided.   5. _____   6. _____

           (7)   (8)

3. *Marc O'Dwyer* is our new *representative*.   7. _____   8. _____

    (9)   (10)

4. *I* am confident he will be a *success*.   9. _____   10. _____

             (11)   (12)

5. A good *reputation* cannot be bought; *it* must be earned.   11. _____   12. _____

            (13)   (14)

6. The *supervisor* reprimanded *us* yesterday.   13. _____   14. _____

      (15)   (16) (17)   (18)

7. *She* expects *people who* work for *her* to be conscien-   15. _____   16. _____

tious.   17. _____   18. _____

      (19)   (20)

8. *Anyone* without *knowledge* of at least three computer   19. _____   20. _____

      (21)

languages should not bother to apply.   21. _____

      (22)   (23)

9. *Their* full *cooperation* is expected.   22. _____   23. _____

      (24)   (25)

10. A *pronoun* takes the place of a *noun*.   24. _____   25. _____

EXERCISE 1·2A   VERBS: ACTION AND LINKING

Place a check mark in the spaces provided to indicate whether the underlined verbs in the sentences below are action verbs or linking verbs.

		ACTION	LINKING
1.	I <u>am</u> pleased to meet you.	——	——
2.	Relations between labor and management <u>are</u> much better now.	——	——
3.	Our company <u>manufactures</u> video disks.	——	——
4.	He <u>spoke</u> with their representative.	——	——
5.	We <u>borrowed</u> $100,000 to begin operations.	——	——
6.	The union <u>negotiated</u> a new contract.	——	——
7.	My parents <u>were</u> in town for a visit last week.	——	——
8.	They <u>visited</u> the store.	——	——
9.	The shop <u>is</u> closed.	——	——
10.	<u>Close</u> the door.	——	——

EXERCISE 1·2B   VERBS

Underline the verbs in the sentences below.

1. Our newest computer is compatible with most varieties of software.

2. Supporting statistics are included in the Appendix.

3. This computer features twin disk drive.

4. Will you be staying for dinner?

5. Take your time; then act decisively.

6. They will be arriving later this evening.

7. We need efficiency more than we need economy.

8. Several dozen applicants have already responded to our advertisement, which appeared in Tuesday's paper.

9. Close the door and sit down.

10. The letter has been signed, sealed, and delivered.

EXERCISE 1·3   ADJECTIVES AND ADVERBS

In the spaces provided, identify each of the italicized words in the following sentences as an adjective (ADJ) or an adverb (ADV).

            (1)   (2)

1. The *effective* speaker pronounces words *clearly*.   1. _____   2. _____

            (3)   (4)

2. We need a *knowledgeable* and *articulate* spokesperson   3. _____   4. _____

            (5)

to present our position *effectively*.   5. _____

            (6)   (7)   (8)   (9)

3. The *latest* order was *carefully* printed on *very* *expensive*   6. _____   7. _____

stationery.   8. _____   9. _____

         (10)   (11)   (12)

4. The *newly* installed *bookkeeping* machine *automatically*   10. _____   11. _____

                       (13)

bills, posts, and maintains an *inventory* control.   12. _____   13. _____

        (14)   (15)   (16)

5. *Intelligent* and *enthusiastic* employees are *certainly* an   14. _____   15. _____

asset to any organization.   16. _____

                 (17)   (18)

6. We must change our *advertising* appeal *immediately* or   17. _____   18. _____

        (19)   (20)

we will *surely* lose a *large* portion of the market.   19. _____   20. _____

EXERCISE 1·4   CONJUNCTIONS AND PREPOSITIONAL PHRASES

Each of the sentences below contains one conjunction and one prepositional phrase. Circle the conjunction and underline the prepositional phrase in each sentence.

1. Some of our stock is damaged and outdated.

2. Bob or Ralph will represent us at the conference.

3. Mr. Lewis came to the meeting, but Allan did not.

4. I will consult with my attorney before I sign the contract.

5. Although I am not entirely satisfied with the agreement, I am happy the negotiations have been completed.

6. We will bargain in good faith if you will.

7. Since Bill Robinson resigned last week, we have been without a regional representative.

8. If you want my advice, get out of the stock market.

9. Mail a check for the balance before you forget.

10. Return your payment in the enclosed envelope today because your account is past due.

EXERCISE 1·5A   PARTS OF SPEECH

In each of the following sentences, one word is missing. What part of speech is needed to complete each sentence logically? Write your answers in the spaces provided. Be sure to use all eight parts of speech.

1. The _____ room is locked.   _____

2. Marie's colleagues took _____ to lunch yesterday.   _____

3. Mr. Cosco _____ Mr. Pine will be at the meeting to-morrow.   _____

4. _____! I've been promoted.   _____

5. I'll meet you _____ the lobby.   _____

6. Word processing is a _____ expanding field.   _____

7. Please _____ me the information.   _____

8. Your order _____ processed.   _____

9. The three _____ were unavailable for comment.   _____

10. Luis is taking an evening course in _____.   _____

EXERCISE 1·5B PARTS OF SPEECH

For each word in the sentences below, identify its part of speech. Write your answers in the spaces provided.

    (1)   (2)   (3) (4)   (5)   (6)   (7)   (8)   (9) (10) (11)(12) (13)   (14)

1. Joe quickly wrote and signed the memorandum before he went to an important meeting.

    (1)   (2)   (3)   (4) (5)   (6)   (7)   (8)   (9) (10)   (11)

2. The recent order from the manufacturer was shipped to you yesterday.

    (1)   (2) (3) (4)   (5)   (6)   (7) (8) (9) (10)   (11)   (12)   (13) (14)

3. Although Maria and the accountant returned from the trip early yesterday afternoon, they arrived

  (15) (16)

too late.

1.
1. _____
2. _____
3. _____
4. _____
5. _____
6. _____
7. _____
8. _____
9. _____
10. _____
11. _____
12. _____
13. _____
14. _____

2.
1. _____
2. _____
3. _____
4. _____
5. _____
6. _____
7. _____
8. _____
9. _____
10. _____
11. _____

3.
1. _____
2. _____
3. _____
4. _____
5. _____
6. _____
7. _____
8. _____
9. _____
10. _____
11. _____
12. _____
13. _____
14. _____
15. _____
16. _____

EXERCISE 1·5C   COMPOSITION: THE PARTS OF SPEECH

Compose complete sentences in which you use each of the words below as a noun, an adjective, and a verb.

TYPING

1. (noun) _____

2. (adjective) _____

3. (verb) _____

WORK

1. (noun) _____

2. (adjective) _____

3. (verb) _____

SUPPLY

1. (noun) _____

2. (adjective) _____

3. (verb) _____

2

THE SENTENCE

DEFINITION OF A SENTENCE, THE FOUR BASIC
KINDS OF SENTENCES, SENTENCE FRAGMENTS,
JOINING SENTENCES, RUN-ON SENTENCES

In the first chapter we looked briefly at the building blocks of the English language, the eight parts of speech. In the next 11 chapters we will discuss each of these parts of speech in detail. In this chapter we're going to look at what happens when these words are put together in a grammatically correct fashion—the sentence. It is the sentence, not the word, that is the basic unit of communication in the language, because it is the sentence that expresses a complete thought. This is why we are going to begin our study of grammar with the sentence.

 ## DEFINITION OF A SENTENCE

A **sentence** is a group of words that expresses a complete thought. Every sentence must contain two essential parts:

1. a **subject,** which tells about whom or what we are talking, and
2. a **predicate,** which tells what the subject does.

Every subject consists of a noun or noun equivalent, and every predicate consists of some form of the verb. In other words, every sentence must contain a noun and a verb. We cannot express a complete thought without them. This is why we said in Chapter 1 that nouns and verbs are the two most important parts of speech.

Economists disagree.

This is a sentence. It expresses a complete thought by telling us:

1. Who? *Economists* (the subject)
2. Do what? *disagree* (the predicate)

These three leading economists disagree.

This, too, is a complete sentence. We have merely added some adjectives that describe our subject. They do not change the subject. The subject is still *economists* and the predicate is still *disagree*.

These three leading economists disagree very strongly sometimes.

Again, this is a complete sentence. *These three leading* describes *economists*. *Very strongly sometimes* describes *disagree*. The subject remains *economists*. The predicate remains *disagree*.

In grammar we call the subject and all the words that describe it the **complete subject.** The particular word about which something is said is the **simple subject.** The predicate and all the words that describe it are called the **complete predicate.** The particular word or words that tell us what the subject does is the **simple predicate.**

These three leading economists disagree very strongly sometimes.

RECOGNIZING THE SUBJECT AND PREDICATE

The following examples deal with the simple subject and simple predicate, but, to be brief, we'll simply call them the subject and the predicate.

Whenever you want to find the subject and the predicate of a sentence, just ask yourself two simple questions:

    a. Who or what is the doer of the action? (The subject)
    b. What does the subject do? (The predicate)

For the moment, disregard all other words that merely describe the subject or the predicate.

1. The manager works diligently and effectively.
    a. Who? *Manager* (The subject)
    b. Does what? *Works* (The predicate)
    c. Disregard *diligently* and *effectively.*

2. On Wednesday evening after the banquet, the executives will meet.
    a. Who? *Executives* (The subject)
    b. Do what? *Will meet* (The predicate)
    c. Disregard *On Wednesday evening after the banquet. . . .*

In this sentence the predicate *will meet* consists of more than one word. The word *will* is what is called an *auxiliary verb.* You'll learn more about auxiliary verbs in Chapter 6.

For now, remember that auxiliary verbs are part of the predicate. You'll see the auxiliary verb *can* in two of the following examples.

3. The secretary, after taking dictation, transcribed the notes.
    a. Who? *Secretary* (The subject)
    b. Did what? *Transcribed* (The predicate)
    c. Disregard *after taking dictation . . . the notes.*

4. No one in all this confusion can decide upon a course of action.
    a. Who? *(No) one* (The subject)
    b. Does what? *Can decide* (The predicate)
    c. Disregard all other words.

5. At the top of the résumé is the applicant's name.
    a. What? *Name* (In this sentence the subject comes *after* the predicate.)

    b.   Do what? *Is* (The predicate)
    c.   Disregard all other words.

Would you have located the subject and predicate more easily if the sentence had been written in the more usual subject-before-predicate order: *The applicant's name is at the top of the résumé.* Don't let the predicate-before-subject order fool you. Just rearrange the sentence mentally into the usual subject-before-predicate order.

  6.   Can you mail me the invoice by Friday?

By rearranging this question into an affirmative statement, you can quickly locate the subject and predicate: *You can mail me the invoice by Friday.*

    a.   Who? *You* (The subject)
    b.   Do what? *Can mail* (The predicate)
    c.   Disregard all other words.

  7.   There are two people to see you.

Here again a little rearrangement will make it much easier to find the subject and the predicate: *Two people are there to see you.*

    a.   Who? *People* (The subject)
    b.   Do what? *Are* (The predicate)
    c.   Disregard all other words.

  8.   November and December are our peak sales months.
    a.   What? *November (and) December* (The subject in this case consists of more than one item.)
    b.   Do what? *Are* (The predicate)
    c.   Disregard all other words.

When, as in this example, the subject is composed of two or more items, it is called a **compound subject.** In chemistry a compound is a substance that is composed of two or more elements. In grammar also, the word *compound* shows that something is made up of more than one part.

  9.   Sales last year rose in May and fell in June.
    a.   What? *Sales* (The subject)
    b.   Did what? *Rose . . . fell.* (The predicate in this case consists of more than one action.)
    c.   Disregard all other words.

As you probably guessed, the predicate in this example is called a **compound predicate.**

10.   Stand still!
    a.   Who? *You* (Understood)
    b.   Do what? *Stand*
    c.   Disregard *still*.

What do we mean by *understood?* This is a particular type of sentence—a command. Most commands are short and to the point. The subject of the command is understood to be the person who is addressed.

THE FOUR BASIC KINDS OF SENTENCES

As you have seen, the words in a sentence perform different tasks. We put these words into classes according to the jobs they do and call these classes of words the eight parts of speech. Sentences also perform different tasks and can be classified according to the jobs they do. In English there are four basic kinds of sentences—**statements, questions, commands,** and **exclamations.** All four have been illustrated in the preceding examples.

A **statement** makes an assertion and ends with a period.

> Sales last year rose in May and fell in June.
> The representative is here.

A **question** ends with a question mark.

> Can you mail me the invoice by Friday?
> What optional equipment is available with this model?

A **command** ends with a period; or, if the command is a strong one, it ends with an exclamation point. Remember, the subject in a command is always understood to be *you,* even though *you* normally is not stated outright.

> Please examine your cancelled checks carefully.
> Stand still! (strong command)

In spoken language, the speaker's voice tells you whether the command is a strong one. In writing, the exclamation point serves this purpose.

Stand still! also illustrates the fourth type of sentence, the **exclamatory sentence,** which expresses strong feeling or sudden emotion. Exclamations are followed by exclamation points. Exclamations may not appear as complete sentences because the subject or predicate is usually implied. Use exclamations sparingly in business writing.

> That's fantastic!
> What an incredible coincidence [this is]!
> [There's a] Fire!

PROGRAMMED REINFORCEMENT

	S1 A sentence is a group of words that expresses a complete _____.
R1 thought	**S2** To express a complete thought, every sentence must include (a) someone or something to talk about, (b) something to say about that person or thing, (c) both *a* and *b*.
R2 c	**S3** The _____ of a sentence tells us whom or what we are talking about.
R3 subject	

S4   The subject of a sentence is the _____ of the action.

R4   doer

S5   The _____ of a sentence tells us what the subject does.

R5   predicate

S6   Because every sentence must contain a subject and a predicate, how many essential parts must every sentence have? _____

R6   two

S7   In the sentence **Mark types,** the subject **Mark** answers the question _____, while the predicate **types** answers the question _____ _____.

R7   who; does what

S8   **Able, efficient Mark types quickly and accurately.** The subject is _____; the predicate is _____.

R8   **Mark; types**

S9   **Able, efficient Mark types quickly and accurately.** Circle the words that describe (modify) the subject **Mark.**

R9   **able; efficient**

S10   **Able, efficient Mark types quickly and accurately.** Circle the words that describe (modify) the predicate **types.**

R10   **quickly and accurately**

S11   In the sentence **The supervisor spoke directly and clearly,** the subject _____ answers the question _____; the predicate _____ answers the question _____.

R11   **supervisor,** who; **spoke,** does what

S12   In the same sentence, **The supervisor spoke directly and clearly,** circle the words that should be disregarded in determining the subject and the predicate.

R12   **the; directly and clearly**

S13   **On Tuesday morning after the workshop, the department heads met.** The subject is _____; the predicate is _____.

R13   subject—**heads;** predicate—**met**

S14   **Ms. Lopez, after consulting her notes, approved the request.** Circle the subject and underline the predicate.

R14   subject—**Ms. Lopez;** predicate—**approved**

S15   **No one, in my opinion, can deliver a better sales talk than Ms. Reynolds.** The subject consists of two words, _____ _____, and the predicate here also has two words, _____ _____.

R15   subject—**no one;** predicate—**can deliver**

S16   **In the warehouse are our new office desks.** In this sentence the subject, _____, comes (before, after) the predicate, _____.

R16   **desks;** after; **are**

S17   **Oats and wheat are basic commodities on the market.** The subject in this sentence is _____ and _____. Since there are two parts to the subject, this is called a _____ subject.

R17   **oats; wheat;** compound

S18   **Salaries in our firm rose in the first quarter last year and then leveled off in the second quarter.** In this sentence the predicate is _____ and _____. This is called a _____ predicate because it is composed of more than _____ part.

R18   **rose; leveled;** compound; one

S19   **Sue and Gary typed and filed constantly all morning.** The subject is _____ and _____; the predicate is _____ and _____. Both the subject and the predicate are _____.

R19   **Sue; Gary; typed; filed;** compound

S20   There are four basic kinds of sentences: statements, _____, _____, and _____.

R20   questions, commands, exclamations

S21   **Avoid erasures on typed material.** This sentence is a (command, question). The subject in this sentence is not expressed; rather it is _____.

R21   command; understood

S22   **Report to your supervisor before lunch.** The understood subject is _____.

R22   you

S23   **Where am I?** This sentence is a _____. If we reverse the order of the sentence, it will read: _____ _____? In this order the subject is obviously _____; the predicate is _____.

R23   question; **I am where?; I; am**

S24   **Patent law is a highly specialized field.** This sentence is a _____. It ends with a _____.

R24   statement, period

S25   **That's incredible!** This sentence is an _____. It ends with an _____.

R25   exclamation, exclamation point

S26   Let us review. A sentence is a group of words that contains a _____ and a _____ and expresses a _____.

R26   subject; predicate; complete thought

Turn to Exercise 2.1.

SENTENCE FRAGMENTS

John.

Is that a sentence? Obviously not. It names a subject, *John,* but does not tell what the subject does. It is not a sentence because it contains no predicate and does not express a complete thought. It is a **sentence fragment.**

My colleague John.

Is this a sentence? Again, the answer is no. Our subject is described to us, but we are still not told what he does. We still have no predicate and no complete thought. Remember, a sentence must have both a subject and a predicate and also must express a complete thought. Some careless people write only part of a sentence as though it were a complete sentence. For example: *John Smith, president of our firm. Was invited to the banquet.*
Is either of these parts a complete sentence?

1.   John Smith, president of our firm.
2.   Was invited to the banquet.

No. Neither part is a complete sentence. Part 1 contains a subject but no predicate. Part 2 contains a predicate but no subject. Alone, each part is merely a fragment of a sentence. The careful business writer guards against sentence fragments. To correct sentence fragments like 1 and 2 above is simple. Right: *John Smith, president of our firm, was invited to the banquet.* We now have one sentence that includes a subject and predicate and expresses a complete thought.
Here are some examples of fragments and complete sentences:

> **Fragments:** Our book, the latest, most authoritative work on the subject. Has just been published.
> **Complete Sentence:** Our book, the latest, most authoritative work on the subject, has just been published.
> **Fragments:** The interest rate that we are offering you. Is the lowest you can get anywhere.
> **Complete Sentence:** The interest rate that we are offering you is the lowest you can get anywhere.
> **Fragments:** The committee of which you are a member. Met in secret session.
> **Complete Sentence:** The committee of which you are a member met in secret session.
> **Fragments:** Pat was promoted to the position of regional manager. And was given a thirty percent increase in salary.
> **Complete Sentence:** Pat was promoted to the position of regional manager and was given a thirty percent increase in salary.

This last example contains a compound verb, *was promoted* and *was given,* with the single subject *Pat.* When the second half of the compound verb is written as a sentence, the result is a fragment because it has no subject.

 ## MORE FRAGMENTS

The preceding fragments were easily corrected because they could be joined to form complete sentences. Together they formed sentences that included a subject and a predicate and expressed a complete thought. Sometimes fragments lacking a subject or predicate cannot be so easily corrected. These are fragments involving *phrases*. A **phrase** is a group of related words that do not contain a subject or a predicate. Look at this example:

Wrong: Her book, the latest, most authoritative work on the subject. Now in stock.

Her book, the latest, most authoritative work on the subject contains a subject but no predicate. The phrase *now in stock* doesn't contain a subject or a predicate.

Simply joining these two fragments will not be enough because there will still be no predicate. We need to supply one. We could correct these fragments in several ways:

> **Right:** Her book, the latest, most authoritative work on the subject, is now in stock.
> **Right:** Now in stock, her book is the latest, most authoritative work on the subject.
> **Right:** Her book, now in stock, is the latest, most authoritative work on the subject.

Now look at this example:

Wrong: An innovative course. Designed to improve your communications skills.

An innovative course contains a subject but no predicate. The phrase *designed to improve your communications skills* doesn't contain a subject or a predicate. More words are needed to make these fragments complete sentences. Here are several possibilities:

> **Right:** An innovative course has been designed to improve your communications skills.
> **Right:** An innovative course is now being offered. It is designed to improve your communications skills.
> **Right:** Dynamics of Business Communication is an innovative course. It is designed to improve your communications skills.
> **Right:** Dynamics of Business Communication, an innovative course, is designed to improve your communications skills.

Fragments that have no predicate are frequently used in advertising. You should avoid using them in standard business correspondence. Make sure that your sentences have both a subject and a verb and that they express a complete thought.

PARTICIPLES AS FRAGMENTS

Another type of sentence fragment that you should be careful to avoid seems to have both a subject and a predicate. When you look at it closely, however, you see that it doesn't contain a predicate and doesn't express a complete thought.

> *John, running at full speed.*

Let's test this example to see if it is a sentence.

a. Who? *John* (The subject)
b. Doing what? *Running* (The apparent predicate)
c. Complete thought? No! It leaves us with the question:
   John, running at full speed, did what? This sentence fragment may be completed as follows: *John, running at full speed, fell.*

Now we have a complete sentence.

complete subject

| simple subject | | predicate |

John, running at full speed, fell.

In this example the phrase *running at full speed* serves as an adjective modifying *John*. *Running* itself is called a **participle.**

Participles like *running* can appear by themselves or in phrases in other parts of the sentence. Whatever their position, do not let them fool you into thinking that they are predicates.

> **Right:** Failing to give his employer any notice, Jack suddenly quit his job to work for another company.
> **Wrong:** Failing to give his employer any notice. Jack suddenly quit his job to work for another company.
> **Right:** Sue sped away, leaving Mary standing on the corner.
> **Wrong:** Sue sped away. Leaving Mary standing on the corner.
> **Right:** His body trembling with anger, Mr. Brown told Ralph he was fired.
> **Wrong:** His body trembling with anger. Mr. Brown told Ralph he was fired.

We'll discuss the formation and use of participles in more detail in Chapter 9.

CLAUSES AS FRAGMENTS

The final type of sentence fragment involves the *clause*. A **clause** is a group of related words that contains both a subject and a predicate. A clause does not always express a complete thought, however. Look at this example:

Since the order arrived.

Is this a complete sentence? No! The word *since* limits our thought in such a way that it does not express a complete thought although it contains a subject, *order,* and a predicate, *arrived.* The fragment *Since the order arrived* leaves us up in the air. We want to know: *Since the order arrived,* what happened? We must add something to complete the thought. For example, we might say: *Since the order arrived, we have increased production.*

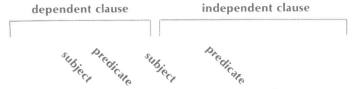

dependent clause   independent clause

Since the order arrived, we have increased production.

In the sentence *Since the order arrived, we have increased production* there are clearly two distinct parts, each of which contains a subject and a predicate. In other words, *Since the order arrived* is a clause, and *we have increased production* is a clause.

A quick inspection of these two clauses shows you that there is an obvious difference between them. *We have increased production* expresses a complete thought; it could stand as a sentence by itself. For this reason it is called an *independent clause.*

In contrast, *Since the order arrived* cannot stand by itself as a sentence. The word *since* makes it *dependent* on the rest of the sentence. For this reason it is called a *dependent clause.* It depends upon the *independent* clause, *we have increased production,* to complete it.

There are many words like *since* that make a thought *dependent* upon a main thought. Here are some other examples:

1.   *Although* we received your order, we could not fill it.

The word *although* makes *Although we received your order* incomplete by itself. It makes it dependent upon the main thought, *we could not fill it*. *Although we received your order* is the dependent clause; *we could not fill it* is the independent clause.

2.   *As soon as* we heard the news, we ran to congratulate you.

As soon as makes *As soon as we heard the news* dependent on *we ran to congratulate you*. *As soon as we heard the news* is the dependent clause; *we ran to congratulate you* is the independent clause.

3.   We felt disappointed *because* we were not promoted.

Here, the dependent part comes last. *Because* makes *because we were not promoted* dependent upon *we felt disappointed*. *Because we were not promoted* is the dependent clause. *We felt disappointed* is the independent clause.

4.   We kept trying *until* it was too late.

Until makes *until it was too late* dependent upon *we kept trying*.

In Chapter 1 you learned that words such as *since, although, as soon as, because,* and *until* are subordinating conjunctions. They begin dependent clauses. Sentences like those above, which are composed of a dependent clause linked to an independent clause, are called **complex sentences.** We will discuss complex sentences further in Chapter 13. The important thing to remember right now is never to write a dependent clause by itself, as though it were a complete sentence. You must connect a dependent clause with an independent clause to form a complete sentence.

1.   **Right:** Although we received your last shipment, we feel it is of such poor quality that we should not pay.
     Wrong: Although we received your last shipment. We feel it is of such poor quality that we should not pay.
2.   **Right:** Though their computer is excellent, their software is inferior.
     Wrong: Though their computer is excellent. Their software is inferior.
3.   **Right:** We were awarded the contract because our bid was the lowest.
     Wrong: We were awarded the contract. Because our bid was the lowest.
4.   **Right:** Because our bid was the lowest, we were awarded the contract.
     Wrong: Because our bid was the lowest. We were awarded the contract.

 PROGRAMMED REINFORCEMENT

S25   A part of a sentence that is written as though it were a complete sentence is called a _____.

R25   fragment

R26   group of related words that do not contain a subject or predicate.

S26   Some fragments involve phrases. A phrase is a _____ _____.

S27   **The efficient typist.** This is a fragment involving a _____. What is needed to make it a complete sentence? (A predicate, A subject)

R27   phrase; A predicate

S28   **Made three copies.** This is another phrase used as a fragment. What is needed to make it a sentence? (A subject, A predicate)

R28   A subject

S29   **The efficient typist. Made three copies.** How would you write these two sentence fragments as one complete sentence? _____

R29   **The efficient typist made three copies.**

S30   What three necessary characteristics of every sentence can be found in **The efficient typist made three copies.** (a) _____; (b) _____; (c) _____

R30   a. subject;
b. predicate;
c. complete thought

S31   A clause must contain a _____ and a _____. The following words are not a clause because they do not contain a _____. . . . **all our offices.**

R31   subject; predicate; predicate

S32   A clause that expresses a complete thought is called an _____ clause.

R32   independent

S33   A clause that does not express a complete thought is called a _____ clause.

R33   dependent

S34   **When we hear from you.** . . . This is a(n) _____ clause because it (does; does not) express a complete thought.

R34   dependent; does not

S35   **We will make our decision.** . . . This is a(n) _____ clause because it (does; does not) express a complete thought.

R35   independent; does

S36   **When we hear from you, we will make our decision.** This sentence contains a _____ clause and an _____ clause. Such a sentence is called a _____ sentence.

R36   dependent; independent; complex

S37   A _____ sentence is a sentence that contains a dependent clause and an independent clause.

R37   complex

S38 **The order was shipped while you were away.** This is a _____ sentence because it contains an _____ clause and a _____ clause. Underline the dependent clause; circle the independent clause.

R38 complex; independent; dependent; **while you were away;** (The order was) (shipped . . .)

S39 **Organizing his thoughts** . . . (is; is not) a clause because it (does; does not) contain a subject and a predicate.

R39 is not; does not

S40 A clause is a group of words that contains a _____ and a _____. A dependent clause is a group of words that contains a _____ and a _____ but does not express a _____ _____.

R40 subject; predicate; subject; predicate; complete thought

S41 An independent clause is a group of words that contains a _____ and a _____ and expresses a _____ _____. An _____ clause can stand by itself as a sentence.

R41 subject; predicate; complete thought; independent

S42 **Since I didn't feel well.** This is a fragment. It has a subject **I** and a predicate **didn't.** Yet one important essential of a sentence is missing. It does not _____ __ _____ _____.

R42 express a complete thought

S43 **Since I didn't feel well, I stayed home from work.** This is a (sentence fragment; complete sentence).

R43 complete sentence

S44 In the above sentence, S43, **Since I didn't feel well** is a _____ clause, and **I stayed home from work** is an _____ _____.

R44 dependent; independent clause

S45 Write the following correctly: **Although our business has increased. Our net profits are substantially the same.**

_____

_____

_____

R45 **Although our business has increased, our net profits are substantially the same.**

S46 Which of the following is correct:
a. **Because automation is increasing. We must reexamine our own methods.**
b. **Because automation is increasing, we must reexamine our own methods.**

R46 b.

Turn to Exercise 2.2.

JOINING SENTENCES

Look at these two sentences:

1. We hope to attend the banquet.
2. We may be detained by business.

You may combine these two sentences into one thought:

3. We hope to attend the banquet, but we may be detained by business.

This combined sentence is better than the first two because it expresses the relationship between the ideas of Sentences 1 and 2 more accurately.

Very often in your writing you will have two such sentences that are so closely related that you will want to combine them into a single sentence. Although some methods of sentence combining are grammatically acceptable, others are not. In this example the two sentences were combined by using a comma and the word *but*. The word *but,* as you know, is a **coordinate conjunction**. So are *and, or, nor,* and *for.*

> The company's profits this year were the highest in our history, and next year's will be even higher.
> You must accept our offer, or you will suffer the consequences.
> I do not seek your support, nor will I accept it.
> Ms. Fletcher received the largest bonus, for she worked the hardest during the year.

We'll study these and other conjunctions in more detail in Chapter 13. For the moment, notice how each of these words, plus a comma, was used to join two separate sentences. In other words, one way of joining two sentences—or two *independent* clauses—is to use both a comma and a coordinate conjunction that expresses their relationship.

Another way to join two statements is to use the *semicolon*. This mark of punctuation should be used only when the two thoughts are very closely related. For example:

> Thank you for your note; it was most timely.
> We cannot send the dies; they are not yet in stock.

Either of these methods is a grammatically correct way to join two sentences to express the relationship between them.

 RUN-ON SENTENCES

A **run-on sentence** is a sentence error that occurs when two separate sentences are written as one. There are two ways a run-on sentence can happen. In the first way, the two sentences are joined only by a comma, without any conjunction.

Wrong: We hope to attend the banquet, we may be detained by business.
Wrong: Thank you for your note, it was most timely.

This joining of two or more independent clauses with only a comma is known as a *comma fault* or *comma splice*. This common error can be easily corrected in one of several ways:

1. Make the two independent clauses two separate sentences.
2. Join the two independent clauses with a comma and a suitable conjunction.
3. If the sense permits, join the two independent clauses with a semicolon.

The second way a run-on sentence can happen is when two statements are joined with no mark of punctuation at all. For example:

Wrong: We hope to attend the banquet we may be detained by business.
Wrong: Thank you for your note it was most timely.

This error, known as a *fused sentence,* can be corrected the same way as the comma fault. The following examples illustrate both right and wrong ways to join sentences.

1.   **Right:** Here is your order. We look forward to your reply.
     Right: Here is your order, and we look forward to your reply.
     Right: Here is your order; we look forward to your reply.
     Wrong: Here is your order we look forward to your reply.
     Wrong: Here is your order, we look forward to your reply.
2.   **Right:** We are new in this field. Our clocks are unmatched in quality.
     Better: We are new in this field, but our clocks are unmatched in quality.
     Wrong: We are new in this field our clocks are unmatched in quality.
     Wrong: We are new in this field, our clocks are unmatched in quality.
3.   **Right:** We must change our advertising appeal. We may lose a large part of our market.
     Better: We must change our advertising appeal, or we may lose a large part of our market.

 # PROGRAMMED REINFORCEMENT

S47   Writing two separate sentences as one sentence is a common sentence error. **We shall attend the meeting we may be detained, however** is a sentence error called a _____-_____ sentence.

R47   run-on

S48   A run-on sentence occurs when _____ separate sentences are written as _____.

R48   two, one

S49   There are two kinds of run-on sentences. The kind in which two sentences are joined by a comma is called a _____ _____. We call the type in which two sentences are joined without any mark of punctuation a _____ _____.

R49   comma fault or comma splice; fused sentence

S50   Correct the following run-on sentence by inserting the conjunction **but: Here is your exam paper, do not start until we tell you.**

R50   **Here is your exam paper, but do not start until we tell you.**

S51   Correct the following run-on sentence by using a period and starting a new sentence: **We must change our bookkeeping practices they are almost obsolete.**

R51   **We must change our bookkeeping practices. They are almost obsolete.**

S52   It (is, is not) permissible to separate two complete sentences by a comma alone. A semicolon may be used when the two sentences are closely allied. Where would you insert the semicolon in this run-on? **Speak carefully before sales executives, they are practical-minded.**

R52   is not; **Speak carefully before sales executives; they are practical-minded.**

Turn to Exercises 2.3 to 2.5.

EXERCISE 2·1A   TYPES OF SENTENCES

In the space to the right of each sentence, write either *S, C, Q,* or *E* to identify the type of sentence. Use the following system: S—statement; C—command; Q—question; E—exclamation.

1. Readers have uniformly expressed their delight with this book. _____

2. We wish to see either Ms. White or Ms. Yu. _____

3. Where did you put the overhead transparencies for this afternoon's meeting? _____

4. What a break! _____

5. Please read, initial, and return the report by noon tomorrow. _____

6. Have you seen the President and his cabinet in session? _____

7. The investment counselor will arrive early and complete her presentation to the seminar participants before noon. _____

8. Just off the main road is a narrow driveway leading to the back entrance. _____

9. Near them sat the two partners of the firm. _____

10. Give it to me this minute! _____

EXERCISE 2·1B   SUBJECT AND PREDICATE

In each of the following sentences, underline the subject with one line; underline the predicate with two lines. Remember to ask yourself two questions: 1) Who or what? (*the subject*); 2) Does what? (*the predicate*). Ignore all other words.

1. I like this book.

2. This book has been sold to over 200,000 readers.

3. Readers have uniformly expressed their delight with this book.

4. Did you enjoy it?

5. Where did you put the overhead transparencies for this afternoon's meeting?

6. Juan and Maria are co-owners of the restaurant.

7. Mr. Gomez and Ms. Jones are in their office.

8. At the stroke of noon the President and his cabinet met in the East Wing.

9. Have you seen the President and his cabinet in session?

10. Neither Mr. Black nor Mr. Alvarado has sent in his reply.

11. We wish to see either Ms. White or Ms. Yu.

12. Neither of them is here.

13. He can keyboard and program expertly.

14. Please read, initial, and return the report by noon tomorrow.

15. Have the contracts been signed and mailed?

16. There is a simple solution to the problem of unfulfilled obligations.

17. An increase in consumer recognition of our product's name is the object of our current promotion campaign.

18. The investment counselor will arrive early and complete her presentation to the seminar participants before noon.

19. Before them stood New York—big and beautiful—with its towering buildings, shimmering rivers, and ribbonlike bridges.

20. Give it to me this minute!

21. Ready to greet the new supervisor was the staff of assistants.

22. Waiting at the airport were the accountant and the lawyer.

23. Near them sat the two partners of the firm.

24. Needed more than economy is efficiency.

25. Just off the main road is a narrow driveway leading to the back entrance.

EXERCISE 2·2A   SENTENCE FRAGMENTS

As you know, a sentence must express a complete thought. Below is a list of expressions. Some of them express complete thoughts. In the space provided, mark C next to these sentences to show that they are complete sentences. The rest of these expressions do not express complete thoughts. Mark F next to these to show that these expressions are sentence fragments.

1. Running down the street at full speed.   1. _____

2. Despite a lack of experience and maturity.   2. _____

3. We agree.   3. _____

4. Night after night, day after day, till they could hardly speak anymore.   4. _____

5. W. O. Roberts, the most noted authority on aerodynamics in recent
        years.   5. _____

6. Reviewing all of the résumés that had been submitted in response to
        the announcement of an opening and selecting those candidates
        who would be contacted for an interview.   6. _____

7. Where are we going?   7. _____

8. After reviewing all the résumés that had been submitted in re-
        sponse to the announcement of an opening, she selected those
        candidates who would be contacted for an interview.   8. _____

9. Although we were certain that she was a fine leader and were willing
        to follow her wherever she would lead.   9. _____

10. When the order arrives and is processed by the receiving department.   10. _____

11. Despite explicit orders to the contrary.   11. _____

12. Nearing the attainment of the production goals set at our last meeting.   12. _____

13. Nearly everyone present, including President Chen and her aides.   13. _____

14. Nearly everyone was present, including President Chen and her aides.   14. _____

15. There is no time for further discussion.   15. _____

16. Despite his long record of service and his promise to make full
        restitution, he was fired.   16. _____

17. Your order was received.   17. _____

18. Forgetting all the instructions the supervisor had given in the
        morning.   18. _____

19. Don't send the letter.   19. _____

20. Where in this entire office?   20. _____

EXERCISE 2·2B   DEPENDENT AND INDEPENDENT CLAUSES

A clause is a group of words with a subject and predicate. A *dependent* clause is one that cannot stand alone as a sentence. An *independent* clause is one that can stand alone.

In each sentence below a group of words is italicized. In the space to the right, write D if it is a dependent clause; write I if it is an independent clause; write N if it is not a clause.

1. I prefer the computer *with the larger display screen.*   1. _____

2. *When a letter is typed,* it is easier to read.   2. _____

3. He led the sales force *because of his ambition.*   3. _____

4. *Because she was ambitious,* she soon impressed her employers.   4. _____

5. *We can offer this guarantee* because of our high quality control.   5. _____

6. *Standing behind each salesperson* is our fine order department.   6. _____

7. *She is an excellent broker* because she knows the market thoroughly.   7. _____

8. *Although we have worked hard,* the end is not yet in sight.   8. _____

9. *Your order was received in time* despite an unexpected delay.   9. _____

10. Because we have years of experience, *we can satisfy all your printing requirements.*   10. _____

11. We will notify you *as soon as the package arrives.*   11. _____

12. *When shopping for a computer,* you should take into account the available software.   12. _____

13. When shopping for a computer, *take into account the available software.*   13. _____

14. *She is an excellent spokesperson for our company* because she is personable and articulate.   14. _____

15. *When you are shopping for a computer,* consider the available software carefully.   15. _____

EXERCISE 2·2C SIMPLE AND COMPLEX SENTENCES

A simple sentence is a sentence made up of one independent clause. A complex sentence is a sentence made up of an independent clause and a dependent clause. In the space to the right of each example, write S if it is a *simple* sentence; write X if it is a *complex* sentence; write F if it is a sentence *fragment*.

1. On the last day in April we will hold our meeting. 1. _____

2. Despite our protests, he entered the primary race for the Senate. 2. _____

3. We will expect delivery as soon as possible. 3. _____

4. We will bill them after the goods are delivered. 4. _____

5. If anything ever sounded as though it were unwise. 5. _____

6. Please try to arrive before ten o'clock to avoid any delay. 6. _____

7. Though you have a prior engagement, won't you try to attend? 7. _____

8. There are several good reasons for our decision and for our un-willingness to participate. 8. _____

9. The merchandise arrived in damaged condition despite the warnings we sent you. 9. _____

10. Do you agree with the commission's report on unemployment? 10. _____

11. Because at present the available software is inadequate for our needs. 11. _____

12. Before the insurance company will pay the claim, their investigator must assess the damages. 12. _____

13. I refuse to become a party to any wrongdoing. 13. _____

14. She was hired although she had limited marketing experience. 14. _____

15. If he's staying, I'm leaving. 15. _____

EXERCISE 2·3   RUN-ON SENTENCES

Some of the following sentences are run-on sentences; others are correct. Wherever there is an error in punctuation or capitalization, cross out the error and write your correction in the space above. If a sentence is entirely correct, mark C in the left-hand margin.

1. Have your representative call, a definite appointment should be made in advance.

2. Perhaps later on we will be willing to do as your representative writes, just now, though, we do not wish to change.

3. Are the letters and articles graded according to difficulty, in our book they are.

4. James Quinn, a man with considerable experience in office planning, will be ready to help you on March 4.

5. At this time, however, we do not wish to change, we are sure you will understand.

6. Tax-free municipal bonds offer the investor a significant tax savings, may we send you our brochure.

7. Won't you please take a few moments of your time to tell us of the improper shipment so that we will be in a position to rush you the correct items.

8. Won't you please take a few moments of your time to tell us the details of the improper shipment, once we have this information, we will be in a position to rush you the correct items.

9. We are making our vacation plans for next summer, we are interested in your booklet describing New England.

10. Try time management, it will bring order to your working day.

EXERCISE 2·4A   SENTENCE FRAGMENTS AND RUN-ON SENTENCES

This exercise asks you to distinguish a complete sentence from a sentence fragment or a run-on sentence. In the space provided, mark C if the expression is a complete sentence; mark F if it is a sentence fragment; and mark R if it is a run-on sentence.

1. Whenever the attorney had a chance to speak.   1. _____

2. Ship the books, we will remit within 30 days.   2. _____

3. Lessons by day, study at night.   3. _____

4. Because of his initiative, and because he had the proper connections.   4. _____

5. What will happen next?   5. _____

6. Continue with your college course, you will graduate with honors.   6. _____

7. Looking around, sizing up the situation, and considering all its
   ramifications.   7. _____

8. Oil, steel, and coal in the right proportions.   8. _____

9. Expect only great things of yourself, and never waver nor doubt
   that they will come true.   9. _____

10. Though Ms. Blake is young, she is not immature.   10. _____

11. Speaking of telephone prices. A new low rate for evening calls is
    now in effect.   11. _____

12. Photocopies are useful for sharing information with others, especially
    in business correspondence.   12. _____

13. Stay late tonight, you will be paid for overtime.   13. _____

14. Please check your accuracy, however speed is essential too.   14. _____

15. Of course we are interested, you would be too.   15. _____

16. We have written twice, please reply at once.   16. _____

17. As soon as the incident was reported, rumors started flying; accord-
    ingly, the President rushed to clarify the issues to the nation.   17. _____

18. Courtesy is contagious, therefore smile often.   18. _____

19. Help!   19. _____

20. We followed the directions, but we couldn't assemble the display
    rack no matter how many different ways we arranged the pieces.   20. _____

21. Many are called few are chosen.   21. _____

22. While the person in the upper tax brackets who invests in municipal
    bonds can realize a significant tax advantage.   22. _____

23. You're fired!   23. _____

24. If we do not receive payment within five days, we will be forced to
    turn your account over to a collection agency.   24. _____

25. No holder of public office shall demand payment or contribution
    from another holder of a public office or position for the campaign
    purposes of any candidate or for the use of any political party.   25. _____

EXERCISE 2·4B   SENTENCE FRAGMENTS AND RUN-ON SENTENCES

This letter contains a number of sentence fragments and run-on sentences. Proofread this letter, crossing out all mistakes and writing in all necessary changes.

Dear Mr. White:

No two people are alike, one person jumps to a conclusion without careful consideration of all available information. Another examines each fact. Checks every claim. Profits from the experience of others, and then makes a decision.

We believe you are the latter type of consumer. A man who has to see for himself before he buys. For this reason we are delighted to offer you a Slick Electric Razor on a free, home-trial basis. Although you may have used another razor all your life. After seven days with the Slick you will never again use your old razor.

So mail the enclosed card today, we will ship your sample Slick Razor by return post.

Sincerely,

EXERCISE 2·5   COMPOSITION: THE SENTENCE

Phone messages are often written in phrases and fragments on preprinted forms. Rewrite the following message as a brief paragraph. Be sure to use complete sentences. Begin your paragraph with "While you were out . . ."

To _Mr. Jacob Zimmerman_
Date _today's date_ Time _1:00 PM._

WHILE YOU WERE OUT

M_s_ _Marla Olivera_
of _Consolidated Services_
Phone _703 - 9062_

TELEPHONED	X	PLEASE CALL	X
CALLED TO SEE YOU		WILL CALL AGAIN	
WANTED TO SEE YOU		RUSH	

Message _received contracts - Has question regarding payment schedule - Must talk with you before 4 P.M._

Mr. Zimmerman,

While you were out, _____

_____

_____

_____

3

Nouns

THE TYPES OF NOUNS, THE CLASSES OF NOUNS, FORMING THE PLURALS OF NOUNS, POSSESSIVE NOUNS

We have seen that every sentence must have a subject and a predicate, and that it must express a complete thought. Because subjects are built around nouns and predicates are built around verbs, nouns and verbs are the two most important parts of speech. They are the essential parts of the sentence.

Because sentences revolve around nouns as the subjects and objects of verbs, we are going to begin our study of the parts of speech with nouns. In business it is important that you know how to write and use the correct forms of nouns. Two forms of the noun, the *plural* and the *possessive,* sometimes pose problems for the writer. These are the two forms we will focus on in this chapter.

As you recall from Chapter 1, nouns are name words. We use them to name persons, places, things, abstract qualities, concepts, and actions. Here are some examples:

Persons—child, typist, Mr. Harris, Martha
Places—lobby, courtroom, Chicago, college
Things—desk, chair, shorthand, stationery
Qualities—dependability, loyalty, initiative, reliability
Concepts—beauty, truth, knowledge, happiness
Actions—walking, typing, supervising, thinking

Nouns are either **concrete** or **abstract. Concrete nouns** name specific things that can be experienced by one of the five senses—things that can be seen, felt, heard, tasted, or smelled. **Abstract nouns** name qualities and concepts. Most nouns are concrete. Because concrete nouns are more precise, specific, and forceful than abstract nouns, they are more effective in business writing than abstract nouns. The good business writer usually prefers concrete nouns to abstract ones.

Nouns can be further divided into two classes: **common nouns** and **proper nouns.** A **common noun** names a general class of people, places, or things. (All nouns naming qualities, actions, and concepts are also common.) A **proper noun** names a specific person, place, or thing. Look at these paired examples:

COMMON NOUN	PROPER NOUN
girl	Maria
country	United States
car	Buick

FORMING THE PLURALS OF NOUNS

Nouns may be either singular or plural.

SINGULAR	PLURAL	SINGULAR	PLURAL
book	books	child	children
secretary	secretaries	alumnus	alumni

Do you know how to spell plural nouns correctly? How do you spell the plural of *attorney?* of *solo?* of *notary public?* of *crisis?* In business you will have to be able to spell these and other plural nouns properly at all times. The following list of rules for forming plurals will guide you.

 RULE 1

To form the plural of *most* nouns, simply add *s.*

cigarette	cigarettes	paper	papers
crowd	crowds	piece	pieces
desk	desks	receipt	receipts
group	groups	town	towns
European	Europeans		

This rule also applies to proper names.

Michael	Michaels	Mrs. Slocum	the Slocums

 RULE 2

To form the plural of a noun that ends in the sound *s, sh, x, z,* or *ch,* add *es.*

box	boxes	glass	glasses
bus	buses	lash	lashes
bush	bushes	lunch	lunches
church	churches	tax	taxes
gas	gases	waltz	waltzes

This rule also applies to proper names.

Mr. Rich	the Riches

 RULE 3

To form the plural of a noun that ends in *y* preceded by a *vowel (a, e, i, o, u),* simply add *s.*

alley	alleys	play	plays
alloy	alloys	survey	surveys
attorney	attorneys	trolley	trolleys
essay	essays	turkey	turkeys
galley	galleys	valley	valleys
money	moneys		

(*monies* is also an acceptable plural form)

RULE 4

To form the plural of a noun that ends in *y* preceded by a *consonant* (any letter other than *a, e, i, o, u*), change the *y* to *i* and add *es*.

accessory	accessories	county	counties
baby	babies	laboratory	laboratories
company	companies	specialty	specialties
country	countries	variety	varieties

Note: Proper names ending in *y* preceded by either a vowel or a consonant add *s* to form the plural.

the Henrys   the Kellys   the Caseys   the McCauleys

 ## RULE 5

To form the plural of a noun that ends in *o* preceded by a *vowel*, merely add *s*.

cameo	cameos	radio	radios
embryo	embryos	ratio	ratios
patio	patios	studio	studios
portfolio	portfolios		

 ## RULE 6

a. To form the plurals of many nouns that end in *o* preceded by a *consonant,* add *es*.

echo	echoes	tomato	tomatoes
embargo	embargoes	veto	vetoes
hero	heroes	volcano	volcanoes
potato	potatoes		

b. To form the plurals of many *musical* terms that end in *o* preceded by a *consonant,* merely add *s*.

alto	altos	piano	pianos
banjo	banjos	solo	solos
concerto	concertos	soprano	sopranos

A few other nouns that end in a consonant plus *o* add only *s* to form the plural.

auto	autos	memento	mementos
casino	casinos	tobacco	tobaccos
dynamo	dynamos	zero	zeros
halo	halos		

 ## RULE 7

To form the plurals of many nouns that end in *f* or *fe*, change the *f* or *fe* to *v* and add *es*.

calf	calves	leaf	leaves
half	halves	life	lives
knife	knives	loaf	loaves

self	selves	wife	wives
shelf	shelves	wolf	wolves
thief	thieves		

Some other nouns ending in *f* or *fe* simply add *s* to form the plural.

bailiff	bailiffs	proof	proofs
belief	beliefs	roof	roofs
chef	chefs	safe	safes
chief	chiefs	staff	staffs
handkerchief	handkerchiefs	tariff	tariffs
plaintiff	plaintiffs		

RULE 8

Certain Old English nouns have irregular plural forms. You should find these words very familiar.

child	children	man	men
foot	feet	mouse	mice
gentleman	gentlemen	ox	oxen
goose	geese	tooth	teeth
louse	lice	woman	women

RULE 9

A number of nouns in English are actually foreign words. These words usually take foreign plural endings. Some of them also have English plural endings. In other words, you may form the plural of these nouns simply by adding *s* or *es*. Both the foreign plural and English plural are considered acceptable. Below is a list of foreign nouns frequently used in business situations. Learn to recognize these words and their plurals. If you are not certain of the exact meaning of any of these words, look them up in your dictionary.

SINGULAR	PLURAL	ENGLISH PLURAL
agendum	agenda	
alumna (female)	alumnae	
alumnus (male)	alumni	
analysis	analyses	
antithesis	antitheses	
appendix	appendices	appendixes
axis	axes	
basis	bases	
crisis	crises	
criterion	criteria	criterions
curriculum	curricula	curriculums
datum	data*	
focus	foci	focuses
formula	formulae	formulas
hypothesis	hypotheses	
index	indices	indexes
maximum	maxima	maximums
medium	media	mediums

*Many business writers consider *data* a singular noun. They would write, "The data *is* new."

SINGULAR	PLURAL	ENGLISH PLURAL
memorandum	memoranda	memorandums
minimum	minima	minimums
neurosis	neuroses	
oasis	oases	
parenthesis	parentheses	
phenomenon	phenomena	
radius	radii	radiuses
stimulus	stimuli	
synopsis	synopses	
synthesis	syntheses	
thesis	theses	

 ## RULE 10

Many nouns are made up of two or more words linked to form one word. Such words are called *compound* nouns. When a compound noun is written as one *solid* word, without hyphens, form the plural by making the *last* part plural.

blackboard	blackboards	grandchild	grandchildren
businesswoman	businesswomen	handful	handfuls
bookcase	bookcases	letterhead	letterheads
bylaw	bylaws	spoonful	spoonfuls
classmate	classmates	stepchild	stepchildren
courthouse	courthouses	stockholder	stockholders
cupful	cupfuls	weekday	weekdays

 ## RULE 11

When forming the plural of a compound noun that is written as two or more separate words or with one or more hyphens, make the most important part plural.

attorney general	attorneys general	father-in-law	fathers-in-law
board of education	boards of education	mother-in-law	mothers-in-law
brother-in-law	brothers-in-law	notary public	notaries public
court-martial	courts-martial	sister-in-law	sisters-in-law
editor in chief	editors in chief		

 ## RULE 12

The plurals of letters, figures, signs, symbols, abbreviations, and individual words are formed by adding s, es, or 's. At one time the 's was generally used in all these situations. Although it is not wrong to form these plurals by using 's, current practice is to use the 's only when necessary to prevent confusion. Capital letters and abbreviations of capital letters without periods form the plural by adding s alone. Uncapitalized letters and abbreviations with internal periods (e.g., M.B.A.) form the plural by adding 's. Look at these examples:

SINGULAR	PLURAL	SINGULAR	PLURAL
9	9s	nine	nines
56	56s	fifty-six	fifty-sixes
1980	1980s	1040	1040s
B	Bs	YWCA	YWCAs
PTA	PTAs	IOU	IOUs
wk.	wks.	hr.	hrs.

yes	yeses	no	noes
mgr.	mgrs.	dept.	depts.
c.o.d.	c.o.d.'s	R.S.V.P.	R.S.V.P.'s
M.B.A.	M.B.A.'s	Ph.D.	Ph.D.'s
*	*'s	x	x's
#	#'s	a	a's
I	I's	A	A's
M	M's	U	U's

Remember: The circumstances described above are the *only* ones in which the *'s* is used to form the plural. Otherwise the plural is formed by adding *s* or *es* to the singular noun.

 ## RULE 13

What is the plural of *Mr.?* of *Mrs.?* of *Miss?* Often a business letter will be addressed to more than one person, and the plurals of these titles can become a problem. Here's how you solve that problem easily.

The plural of *Mr.* (Mister) is *Messrs.*, an abbreviation derived from the French word *Messieurs.* Accordingly, you may write: *Dear Messrs. Smith and Nathan.* Modern business usage, however, is tending away from this old-fashioned form, and many employers today prefer that you repeat the title of each person: *Dear Mr. Smith and Mr. Nathan.*

The plural of *Mrs.* is *Mmes.*, an abbreviation derived from the French word *Mesdames.* Accordingly, you may write: *Dear Mmes. Jones and Spencer.* You may also follow the preferred usage and repeat the title: *Dear Mrs. Jones and Mrs. Spencer.*

The plural of *Miss* is *Misses.* Again, it is preferable to repeat the title rather than use the plural term: *Dear Miss Hale and Miss Holsey* rather than *Dear Misses Hale and Holsey.*

Unless a woman specifically states that she wants to be addressed as *Mrs.* or *Miss,* it is preferable to use *Ms.* Like *Mr.* for men, *Ms.* makes no reference to marital status. You would write *Dear Ms. Jones and Ms. Spencer* or *Dear Ms. Hale and Ms. Holsey.* The plural for *Ms.* is *Mses.*, although it is seldom used.

Why should you bother to learn these plural forms if they are no longer considered preferable? First, because your particular employer may prefer these forms. Second, because you should be able to recognize them when they appear on letters received by your company or firm. Third, because they are still used widely in social correspondence. Fourth, because if you are writing to a firm in which three brothers are partners, you would not write *Dear Mr. Kern, Mr. Kern, and Mr. Kern.* In this instance it is proper to write: *Dear Messrs. Kern.* In this instance you may also write *Gentlemen.* When writing to a company made up of both men and women, you may write *Ladies and Gentlemen.* It is also permissible simply to omit the salutation on letters that are not addressed to a specific person or persons.

 ## RULE 14

A few nouns are written the same in both the singular and the plural forms. When one of these nouns is the subject of a sentence, you must look to the meaning of the sentence to determine whether to use a singular or a plural predicate.

corps*	fish	Japanese	sheep
deer	gross	means (method)	species
	head (of cattle)	series	

---

*Corps is pronounced *core* in the singular; it is pronounced *cores* in the plural.

Some nouns look plural but are really singular in meaning. Always use a singular predicate when one of the following words is the subject of a sentence:

economics	measles	mumps	physics
ethics	molasses	news	politics

For example: Politics *is* a vital field.

Some nouns are always plural, never singular. Always use a plural predicate when one of the following words is the subject of a sentence:

auspices	headquarters	proceeds (money)	thanks
goods (merchandise)	pants (clothing)	riches	trousers
	premises	scissors	

For example: The proceeds *were* turned over to charity.

PROGRAMMED REINFORCEMENT

S1   Circle the correct answer. Nouns are (name words, action words, joining words, describing words).

R1   name words

S2   As name words, nouns name persons, places, things, qualities, concepts, or actions. The nouns **letter** and **computer** are _____. The nouns **office** and **Fort Worth** are _____. The nouns **honesty** and **loyalty** are _____.

R2   things; places; qualities

S3   All nouns are either concrete or abstract. _____ nouns name specific things that can be experienced by one of the five senses; _____ nouns name qualities and concepts.

R3   concrete; abstract

S4   Which of the following nouns are concrete? Which are abstract? **typewriter, loyalty, Mary Jarvis, music, coffee, beauty**

R4   *Concrete:* typewriter, Mary Jarvis, music, coffee
Abstract: loyalty, beauty

S5   Nouns can also be divided into two classes—common nouns and proper nouns. A noun that names a general class of persons, places, or things is a _____.

R5   common noun

S6   The word **employee** is a common noun that names a _____.

R6   person

R7   thing—**package;**
place—**office**

S7   In the sentence *She sent a package to the office,* underline a noun naming a thing and circle one naming a place.

S8   A noun that names a specific person, a specific place, or a specific thing is called a _____. Proper nouns (always, sometimes, never) begin with capital letters. Underline the proper nouns in this sentence: **He was born in Boston near the Bunker Hill Memorial.**

R8   proper noun; always;
Boston; Bunker Hill Memorial

S9   In the following sentence pick out the proper nouns that name respectively (a) a specific person, (b) a specific place, and (c) a specific thing: **Frank Baker drove his Pontiac into Manhattan.**   Answers: a. _____
b. _____   c. _____

R9   a. **Frank Baker;**
b. **Manhattan;**
c. **Pontiac**

S10   Circle the proper nouns in this sentence: **The President addressed the Congress at the opening session on Thursday.**

R10   **President; Congress; Thursday**

S11   Most nouns change from singular to plural simply by adding the letter _____.

R11   *s*

S12   Most nouns that end in the sound of **sh, s, x, z,** or **ch** form their plurals by adding _____. Write the plurals of **glass, fox, watch, wish.** _____ _____ _____ _____

R12   es; **glasses; foxes; watches; wishes**

S13   If a noun ends in **y** preceded by a vowel **(a, e, i, o, u),** form the plural by adding _____. Write the plurals of **attorney, monkey, turkey, valley.** _____ _____ _____ _____

R13   s; **attorneys; monkeys; turkeys; valleys**

S14   If a noun ends in **y** preceded by a consonant (any letter other than **a, e, i, o, u**), form the plural by _____ _____. Write the plurals of **daisy, puppy, university, study.** _____ _____ _____ _____

R14   changing the *y* to *i* and adding *es;* **daisies; puppies; universities; studies**

S15   If a noun ends in **o** preceded by a vowel, form the plural by adding _____. Write the plurals of **folio, embryo, cameo, patio.** _____ _____ _____ _____

R15   s; **folios; embryos; cameos; patios**

S16   Many nouns ending in **o** preceded by a consonant form their plurals by adding _____. How would you write the plurals of **potato, hero, echo, veto?** _____ _____ _____ _____

R16   es; **potatoes; heroes; echoes; vetoes**

S17 Musical terms that end in **o** preceded by a consonant form plurals by simply adding _____. Write the plurals of **soprano, alto, banjo, solo.** _____ _____ _____

R17 *s;* **sopranos; altos; banjos; solos**

S18 Some nouns that end in **f** form their plurals by changing the **f** to **v: knife—knives.** Other such nouns just add **s.** Write the plurals of these correctly: **belief, wife, safe, calf.** _____ _____ _____

R18 **beliefs; wives; safes; calves**

S19 Some nouns have special foreign plural forms. How would you write these correctly? **phenomenon, alumnus, thesis, criterion.** _____

R19 **phenomena; alumni; theses; criteria**

S20 Nouns made up of two or more separate words are called _____. If they are written as one word without a hyphen, the plural is formed by making the last part plural. How would you form the plurals of these words? **handful, stepchild, courthouse, spoonful, businessman.**

_____ _____
_____ _____
_____

R20 **compound nouns; handfuls; stepchildren; courthouses; spoonfuls; businessmen**

S21 If the compound noun is written with a hyphen, make the principal or most important part plural: **brother-in-law—brothers-in-law.** Write the plurals of **sister-in-law, attorney general, editor in chief, father-in-law.**

_____ _____

R21 **sisters-in-law; attorneys general; editors in chief; fathers-in-law**

S22 Some nouns form their plurals either by some irregular change (**ox—oxen**) or by not changing the singular (**sheep—sheep**). How would you write the plurals of **deer, series, goose, gross?** _____
_____

R22 **deer; series; geese; gross**

S23 The plurals of letters, figures, signs, symbols, abbreviations, and individual words are formed by adding (a) *s*, (b) *es*, (c) *'s*, (d) all of the above, (e) none of the above.

R23 (d) all of the above

S24 Use the *'s* to form the plural (a) always, (b) never, (c) when necessary for clarity.

R24 (c) when necessary for clarity

S25 Write this sentence correctly: Dot the i s, cross the t s, and erase the 8 s.

R25 Dot the i's, cross the t's, and erase the 8s (or 8's).

Turn to Exercises 3.1 and 3.2.

POSSESSIVE NOUNS

Possessives are often used in business. A possessive noun is one that shows ownership, authorship, brand, kind, or origin:

The *company's* factory (ownership)   The *teachers'* convention (kind)
Shakespeare's play (authorship)   The *lamp's* glow (origin)
Campbell's soup (brand)

The rules for forming possessive nouns are simple and should cause you little trouble.

 ## SINGULAR NOUNS

1.   Form the possessive of a singular noun by adding *'s*.

boss	boss's	John	John's
box	box's	Knox	Knox's
company	company's	Mr. Ross	Mr. Ross's
hero	hero's		

2.   When the addition of *'s* to a singular noun would make pronunciation awkward, add only an **apostrophe.**

Moses	Moses' (Moses's: pronounced Moseses—too awkward)
Sophocles	Sophocles' (Sophocles's: pronounced Sophocleses—too awkward)
Achilles	Achilles' (Achilles' heel)
goodness	goodness' (for goodness' sake)

 ## PLURAL NOUNS

1.   Form the possessive of a regular plural noun (one ending in *s*) by adding only an apostrophe after the *s*.

bosses	bosses'	heroes	heroes'
boxes	boxes'	the Murpheys	the Murpheys'
companies	companies'	stockholders	stockholders'

2.   Form the possessive of an irregular plural noun (one not ending in *s*) by adding *'s*.

alumni	alumni's	men	men's
children	children's	people	people's
geese	geese's		

 ## A TEST FOR POSSESSIVE NOUNS

When you see the apostrophe in the possessive noun, it may be helpful for you to think that a prepositional phrase (see Chapter 1) has been left out of the sentence—generally, a phrase beginning with *of*. For example:

the company's factory = the factory of the company

Shakespeare's play = the play of Shakespeare
the lamp's glow = the glow of the lamp

This test will make it easy for you to decide on the correct use of the apostrophe in all possessive nouns. To decide whether a noun needs an apostrophe—and, if so, where to place it—simply test to see if an *of* phrase can be added in front of that noun.

If an *of* phrase can be added, then you put the apostrophe at the end of the word just as it would appear in the *of* phrase. For example:

1. This (companies, companies', company's) policy . . .

    Test: The policy of this company . . .   *Therefore:* This company's policy . . .
    (Apostrophe at end of *company*. Add *'s* because the noun does not end in *s*.)

2. These (companies, companies', company's) policies. . . .

    Test: The policies of these companies . . .   *Therefore:* These companies' policies
    (Apostrophe at end of *companies*. No *s* added because the noun ends in *s*.)

3. . . . in two (weeks, week's, weeks') time . . .

    Test: . . . in the time of two weeks . . .   *Therefore:* . . . in two weeks' time . . .

Be particularly alert to use an apostrophe in phrases that refer to a period of time:

a moment's hesitation	an hour's delay	a month's wait
a few moments' hesitation	four hours' delay	six months' wait
a minute's work	a week's salary	a year's interest
ten minutes' work	three weeks' salary	twenty years' interest

 POSSESSIVE WITH INANIMATE OBJECTS

Generally, avoid the use of the possessive with nouns naming inanimate (nonliving) objects. Some people object strongly to it. No one, however, will complain if you use the *of* phrase.

The building's architecture . . . or The architecture of the building . . .
The airplane's roar . . . or The roar of the airplane . . .

Don't change well-known phrases, however: *a stone's throw, a hair's breadth.*

 GUIDELINES FOR FORMING POSSESSIVE NOUNS
 JOINT OWNERSHIP

A problem arises when you want to show joint ownership. How would you write this phrase in possessive form?

The operetta by Gilbert and Sullivan . . .

Answer: Gilbert and Sullivan's operetta . . .
This means one operetta written by Gilbert and Sullivan.
To show *joint* ownership, write only the last name in possessive form.

Smith and Miller's firm . . .

This means one firm owned jointly by Smith and Miller. Other examples:

Johnson and Johnson's bandages . . .
Rodgers and Hammerstein's musical . . .

When you want to show *separate* ownership of distinct items, write the name of each owner in possessive form.

Smith's and Miller's firms are strong competitors.

This means two firms, one owned by Smith and the other by Miller.

New York's and Chicago's police forces are among the largest.

This refers to the police force of each city separately.

 ## ABBREVIATIONS

To write the possessive form of an abbreviation, place the *apostrophe s('s)* after the final period, or final letter if no periods are used. For a plural abbreviation, place an *apostrophe (')* after the *s* but not before it.

The U.S.A.'s tariff	The Wainright Co.'s staff	Three M.D.s' offices
John D. Rockefeller, Jr.'s, fortune	The YMCA's policy	The M.B.A.s' credentials

 ## COMPOUND NOUNS

To write the possessive form of an abbreviation, place the *apostrophe s ('s)* after the final word in the noun:

My brother-in-law's inheritance (One brother-in-law)
My brothers-in-law's inheritances (More than one brother-in-law)

 ## NOUN PHRASES

Sometimes the expression to be made possessive is made up of more than one word:

Catherine the Great's reign was long.
Someone else's hat is missing.
The *salesperson of the year's* record is outstanding.

In these cases, think of the whole phrase as one expression and put the possessive on the last word of it. Avoid this type of possessive if you can. In informal conversation, you might say:

The man wearing the red hat's brother owns the company.

Never use expressions of this sort in writing, however. Instead, say:

The brother of the man wearing the red hat owns the company.

 ## NAMES OF ORGANIZATIONS

Often an organization will choose to leave out the apostrophe from a plural noun that appears in its official title even though that noun is in the possessive. (Always follow the form that appears on the official letterhead or the official listing of the organization.)

National Sales Executives Club   Manufacturers Trust Company
Columbia University Teachers College

 NOUNS IN APPOSITION

Sometimes two nouns that refer to the same thing are used together, the second noun making the first clearer. For example:

Ms. Gomez, my secretary, is ill.

These two nouns are said to be in **apposition;** that is, the second identifies the first. The second noun is known as the **appositive.**

When these nouns are used in the possessive case, make only the appositive possessive.

Ms. Gomez, my secretary's, typewriter is broken.
That is Mr. DePietro, my supervisor's, car.

If such wording seems awkward to you, rephrase the sentence.

The typewriter of my secretary, Ms. Gomez, is broken.
That car belongs to Mr. DePietro, my supervisor.

 POSSESSIVE NOUNS MODIFYING
UNEXPRESSED NOUNS

Sometimes the possessive noun is not followed by the noun it modifies, either because that noun has been left out or because it appears elsewhere in the sentence. In either case, the possessive noun should still appear in the possessive form.

We went to Jim's [home] after work.
That briefcase is Sharon's.
Last year's sales were better than this year's.

 PROGRAMMED REINFORCEMENT

S26 When a noun shows ownership, authorship, brand, kind, or origin, a(n) _____ is added to it.

R26 apostrophe

S27 If a noun does not already end in **s**, possession is shown by simply adding **'s** to the noun. Write the possessive form of these phrases:
the books of the boy   _____
the hats of the men   _____
the offices of the company _____
the restroom of the women   _____

R27 **boy's books; men's hats;
company's offices; women's
restroom**

S28   If the noun that shows possession already ends with an *s*, you normally add only the apostrophe. If a singular noun of only one syllable ends in *s*, however, then add ___. Write these as possessives:

the sister of the boss   _____

the novels of Dickens   _____

the monument of the soldiers _____

the salary of two weeks   _____

R28   *'s*
the boss's sister; Dickens' novels; the soldiers' monument; two weeks' salary

S29   To show joint ownership by two or more people, write (only the first name, only the last name, both names) as a possessive. Place the apostrophe to show joint ownership: **Rodgers and Hammersteins music.**

R29   only the last name; **Rodgers and Hammerstein's music**

S30   Is this a correct possessive? **The U.S.A.'s laws.** Answer: _____.

R30   Yes

S31   The apostrophe is placed after the last word in an explanatory phrase. Place a possessive in this sentence: **The president ___ of the company ___ health is failing.**

R31   **The president of the company's health is failing.**

S32   When two nouns in apposition are used in the possessive case, (a) only the first noun is made possessive, (b) only the second noun is made possessive, (c) both nouns are made possessive.

R32   (b) only the second noun is made possessive.

S33   Place apostrophes or *'s* where needed: (a) **Ms. Furness, our secretary, desk is being replaced.** (b) **That is Dr. Alter, my professor, office.**

R33   (a) **secretary's**
       (b) **professor's**

S34   Some authorities think it is awkward to write a possessive for an inanimate object. Change these examples from the possessive form: **the table's strength** _____ _____ **the night's darkness** _____ _____

R34   **the strength of the table; the darkness of the night**

S35   Place apostrophes in any words that should show possession in this sentence: **The union agreement covers mens stores and ladies stores under Smiths presidency.**

R35   **men's; ladies'; Smith's**

S36   Rewrite the following sentence, using possessives. **The novels of Dickens, the operettas of Gilbert and Sullivan, and the poetry of G.B.S. are all products of Britain.**

R36   **Dickens' novels, Gilbert and Sullivan's operettas, and G.B.S.'s poetry are all Britain's products.**

Turn to Exercises 3.3 to 3.6.

EXERCISE 3·1A   PLURAL NOUNS

Write the plural form of each of these nouns in the space provided.

1.	book _____	**33.**	twenty-six _____
2.	invoice _____	**34.**	x _____
3.	office _____	**35.**	series _____
4.	business _____	**36.**	crisis _____
5.	tax _____	**37.**	veto _____
6.	match _____	**38.**	bus _____
7.	facility _____	**39.**	box _____
8.	colony _____	**40.**	roof _____
9.	body _____	**41.**	laboratory _____
10.	journey _____	**42.**	handkerchief _____
11.	attorney _____	**43.**	basis _____
12.	studio _____	**44.**	shelf _____
13.	hero _____	**45.**	thesis _____
14.	embargo _____	**46.**	watch _____
15.	auto _____	**47.**	receipt _____
16.	wife _____	**48.**	company _____
17.	half _____	**49.**	self _____
18.	chief _____	**50.**	datum _____
19.	plaintiff _____	**51.**	radio _____
20.	proof _____	**52.**	stimulus _____
21.	memorandum _____	**53.**	valley _____
22.	businesswoman _____	**54.**	alumnus _____
23.	bookkeeper _____	**55.**	criterion _____
24.	cupful _____	**56.**	Mrs. _____
25.	grandchild _____	**57.**	zero _____
26.	handful _____	**58.**	letterhead _____
27.	copyright _____	**59.**	census _____
28.	stepchild _____	**60.**	deletion _____
29.	father-in-law _____	**61.**	analysis _____
30.	commander-in-chief _____	**62.**	court-martial _____
31.	Mr. Hatch _____	**63.**	piano _____
32.	26 _____	**64.**	medium _____

65. bureau _____ **71.** agency _____

66. Miss _____ **72.** C.P.A. _____

67. A _____ **73.** Jones _____

68. five _____ **74.** spoonful _____

69. Mr. _____ **75.** gas _____

70. scissors _____

EXERCISE 3·1B   SINGULAR AND PLURAL NOUNS

Some of the words listed below are singular; others are plural. Put a checkmark in the appropriate column to show whether the word is singular or plural, and write the opposite form in the other column.

		SINGULAR	PLURAL
1.	test	_____	_____
2.	column	_____	_____
3.	lighters	_____	_____
4.	children	_____	_____
5.	ladies	_____	_____
6.	attorney	_____	_____
7.	knife	_____	_____
8.	shelves	_____	_____
9.	phenomenon	_____	_____
10.	alumnus	_____	_____
11.	datum	_____	_____
12.	alloys	_____	_____
13.	volcanoes	_____	_____
14.	cupful	_____	_____
15.	mother-in-law	_____	_____
16.	species	_____	_____
17.	sheep	_____	_____
18.	politics	_____	_____
19.	zero	_____	_____
20.	company	_____	_____

EXERCISE 3·2A   **PLURAL NOUNS**

This paragraph contains many plural nouns that are incorrectly spelled. Cross out each incorrectly spelled noun and write the correct form above it.

Industrys of all sorts have flourished in the central vallies of the Acme Mountains. Each year, huge quantities of tomatos and potatoes are shipped from the valleys to marketes across the country. The area is also famous for its fine tobaccoes, which are bought by all the large cigar companys. In addition to these agricultural products, the region has fine facilitys for steel foundrys and for the manufacture of computer componentses and accessorys. Analysises of the datas from the latest reports and surveyes confirm that the industries of this region should continue to flourish for year's to come.

EXERCISE 3·2B   SINGULAR AND PLURAL NOUNS

This exercise tests your ability to recognize singular and plural nouns. Choose the proper predicate in each of the following sentences. Remember, if the subject is singular, use a singular predicate. If the subject is plural, use a plural predicate. Each pair lists the singular predicate first.

1. The data (has, have) been stored on a floppy disk.   1. _____

2. Our most influential media (is, are) radio and television.   2. _____

3. Our curriculum (includes, include) courses in administrative
    sciences.   3. _____

4. The bases for my contention (is, are) twofold.   4. _____

5. (Was, Were) the memoranda left on my desk?   5. _____

6. The alumni (is, are) fully behind the dean.   6. _____

7. The stimulus (has, have) been measured in electrical units.   7. _____

8. The fathers-in-law (has, have) met for the first time.   8. _____

9. The crisis in her illness (is, are) finally past.   9. _____

10. The series of revisions (is, are) complete, at last.   10. _____

11. Riches (is, are) something to be thankful for.   11. _____

12. Proper ethics (was, were) the subject of his monthly magazine
    column.   12. _____

13. What (is, are) the major criterion in evaluating a résumé?   13. _____

14. The theses the philosopher expounded (was, were) stimulating.   14. _____

15. How many international crises (has, have) there been lately?   15. _____

16. The latest phenomenon in the electronics industry (seems, seem) to
    involve fiber optics.   16. _____

17. Three handfuls of rice (was, were) thrown at the couple.   17. _____

18. What new formulae (was, were) presented by her?   18. _____

19. Parentheses (presents, present) occasional punctuation problems.   19. _____

20. An editor realizes that plot synopses (is, are) important.   20. _____

EXERCISE 3·3A   **POSSESSIVE NOUNS**

This exercise asks you to form the possessive of nouns. Below are 25 possessive phrases. Rewrite them in the correct possessive form by eliminating the *of* phrase.

1. the clothes of the babies
2. the ties of the men
3. the books of the student
4. the wool of the sheep
5. the report of the boss
6. the meeting of the directors
7. the statement of the vice presidents
8. the poetry of Burns
9. the finances of the firm
10. the letters of the secretaries
11. the store of John
12. the association of the teachers
13. the children of my sister-in-law
14. the policy of R. H. Macy
15. the home of Dickens
16. the editorials of *The New York Times*
17. the engine of the old bus
18. the response of Eduardo, my assistant
19. the home of the Kelleys, my in-laws
20. the motor of the video cassette recorder
21. the answer given by John Ross
22. the work done by the volunteers
23. the closing remarks made by the speaker
24. the mistakes made by our clerks
25. the decisions made by the partners

1. _____
2. _____
3. _____
4. _____
5. _____
6. _____
7. _____
8. _____
9. _____
10. _____
11. _____
12. _____
13. _____
14. _____
15. _____
16. _____
17. _____
18. _____
19. _____
20. _____
21. _____
22. _____
23. _____
24. _____
25. _____

EXERCISE 3·3B   POSSESSIVE NOUNS

Rewrite the following phrases to avoid the use of the apostrophe.

1. the tariffs' effects   1. _____
2. landlords' and tenants' rights   2. _____
3. three weeks' vacation   3. _____
4. my father-in-law's beliefs   4. _____
5. my manager's secretary's desk   5. _____
6. my professor, Dr. Allerton's, office   6. _____
7. our company's policy   7. _____
8. six months' interest   8. _____
9. competitors' prices   9. _____
10. a month's delay   10. _____
11. clerks' salaries   11. _____
12. the pencil's point   12. _____
13. Ms. Benbrook, my attorney's, opinion   13. _____
14. Mr. Levine's secretary's replacement   14. _____
15. the editors in chief's meeting   15. _____
16. the companies' policies   16. _____
17. the U.N.'s policy   17. _____
18. the computer's memory capacity   18. _____
19. the children's books   19. _____
20. the video cassettes' contents   20. _____

EXERCISE 3·3C   POSSESSIVE NOUNS

Each of the following sentences contains one or more possessive nouns from which the apostrophe or 's has been omitted. In the space provided, rewrite these possessive nouns correctly.

1. Mr. Paul, the chairpersons, report included details on the proposed employees cafeteria.

   1. _____

2. The camp directors view was that drastic changes had to be made in Johns outlook.

   2. _____

3. At the meeting it was agreed that new couches should be installed in the womens lounge.

   3. _____

4. Yesterdays techniques cannot succeed in todays market.

   4. _____

5. You have one weeks time to accept or reject this companys offer.

   5. _____

6. The managers, at last Wednesdays meeting, agreed to rebuild the executives recreation hall.

   6. _____

7. The new sales managers plan was discussed at the boards last meeting.

   7. _____

8. Robertas trouble is that she takes nobodys advice.

   8. _____

9. We agree with Antonellis plan for improving our office forces morale.

   9. _____

10. We asked Charles opinion, but he refused to discuss Smiths plan.

    10. _____

11. Chan and Yeh is one of the citys finest firms.

    11. _____

12. Miller and Jones policies are in complete agreement with the District Attorneys suggested code of conduct.

    12. _____

13. Browns and Whites stores compete in the babies wear line.

    13. _____

14. Sanchez and Ruizs store handles a complete line of mens items.

    14. _____

15. A committee to support the U.S. s policy in Europe sent a flood of telegrams to Senator Aristophanes office.

    15. _____

16. The A.A.A.s vehicle policy is under the I.C.C.s direction.

    16. _____

17. My sister-in-laws child left college after two years work.

    17. _____

18. Frederick the Wises policies are comparable to the fiscal policies of the Farmers National Alliance.

    18. _____

19. The sales managers convention dealt with the new organizations policies.

    19. _____

20. Gomezs and Warners temporary agencies have been rivals for years.

    20. _____

EXERCISE 3·4 PLURAL AND POSSESSIVE NOUNS

This exercise tests what you have learned about the spelling of possessive nouns and plural nouns. Fill in the form of the noun called for in each column—singular possessive, plural, and plural possessive.

	SINGULAR	SINGULAR POSSESSIVE	PLURAL	PLURAL POSSESSIVE
1.	book	_____	_____	_____
2.	child	_____	_____	_____
3.	tax	_____	_____	_____
4.	Smith & Smith	_____	_____	_____
5.	life	_____	_____	_____
6.	ratio	_____	_____	_____
7.	body	_____	_____	_____
8.	criterion	_____	_____	_____
9.	attorney	_____	_____	_____
10.	businessman	_____	_____	_____
11.	radio	_____	_____	_____
12.	memorandum	_____	_____	_____
13.	sister-in-law	_____	_____	_____
14.	hero	_____	_____	_____
15.	stockholder	_____	_____	_____
16.	roof	_____	_____	_____
17.	journey	_____	_____	_____
18.	letterhead	_____	_____	_____
19.	committee	_____	_____	_____
20.	county	_____	_____	_____
21.	boss	_____	_____	_____
22.	medium	_____	_____	_____
23.	party	_____	_____	_____
24.	ox	_____	_____	_____
25.	attorney general	_____	_____	_____

EXERCISE 3·5   NOUNS

The following letter contains a number of errors in the use of noun plurals and possessives. Whenever you locate an error, cross out the incorrect form and write the correct form above it.

Dear Ms. Kurczeski:

Thank you for your letter of May 10 asking about the wayes in which we pay our representative's. We appreciate your interest in our operationes, and we are flattered that a businesswomen as successful as you would seek our advice.

We are sorry that we are unable to supply the information you requested. Each of our salespeoples works on an individual contract, so there are different basises on which each is paid. Our sales representatives' themselves have requested that we keep this information confidential. We would be violating our employee's confidence if we were to divulge the termes of these contractes. We feel that business ethics are involved. Accordingly, it is against our companies policy to give out this information. We are certain you understand our reason's for this position.

May we recommend instead Larry Moses's new pamphlet, "Establishing a Sale's Organization." Mr. Moses offers a variety of practical suggestion's to solve the particular problemes that arise when one is beginning a new business. We think you will find his analysises of the various problem's causes and effects most interesting. Mr. Moses has included the datas on which he bases his conclusions. His findings demonstrate, for example, that a businesses' net proceeds is not a meaningful criteria on which to base merit raises. We have found Mr. Mose's study very helpful and think that you will too.

Please accept our sincere best wish's on this latest venture and our hopes that our pleasant business relationship will continue.

Sincerely,

EXERCISE 3·6A COMPOSITION: PLURAL NOUNS

Compose complete sentences using the plural form of the nouns in parentheses.

1. (trade-in) _____

2. (up and down) _____

3. (beneficiary) _____

4. (half) _____

5. (datum) _____

EXERCISE 3·6B COMPOSITION: POSSESSIVE NOUNS

Compose complete sentences using the possessive form of the nouns in parentheses.

1. (business) _____

2. (keyboarder) _____

3. (politicians) _____

4. (Mr. Huan, my accountant) _____

5. (the O'Malleys) _____

PRONOUNS I
THE FORMS OF PRONOUNS

PERSONAL PRONOUNS, DEMONSTRATIVE
PRONOUNS, INTERROGATIVE PRONOUNS,
INDEFINITE PRONOUNS, RELATIVE PRONOUNS,
RECIPROCAL PRONOUNS

A **pronoun** is a word that is used in place of a noun. Compare the following pairs of sentences:

> **Without pronouns:** The Coca Cola Bottling Company announced that the Coca Cola Bottling Company intends to change the focus of the Coca Cola Bottling Company's advertising campaign to increase the sale of the Coca Cola Bottling Company's products.
> **With pronouns:** The Coca Cola Bottling Company announced that it intends to change the focus of its advertising campaign to increase the sale of its products.

> **Without pronouns:** John returned to John's home to change into John's evening clothes because John was to be the featured speaker at a banquet given by John's company to honor John.
> **With pronouns:** John returned to his home to change into his evening clothes because he was to be the featured speaker at a banquet given by his company to honor him.

These two sentences show how pronouns reduce sentence length, provide variety, and avoid awkwardness. In business you will need to know how to use pronouns correctly and effectively. This chapter will show you how.

 PERSONAL PRONOUNS

The most common pronouns are known as **personal pronouns.** These are used to refer to yourself and to other people. They indicate (1) the person speaking, (2) the person spoken to, (3) the person or object spoken about. Personal pronouns take different forms depending on how they are used in a sentence. In the sample sentence

> John returned to his home to change into his evening clothes because he was to be the featured speaker at a banquet given by his company to honor him.

three different pronouns are used as substitutes for John: *he, his,* and *him.*

The following chart summarizes the characteristics of personal pronouns and identifies correct forms. Refer to the chart as you read the definitions that follow it.

CASE:	SUBJECTIVE		OBJECTIVE		POSSESSIVE	
Number	Singular	Plural	Singular	Plural	Singular	Plural
First Person (the one speaking)	I	we	me	us	my mine	our ours
Second Person (the one spoken to)	you	you	you	you	your yours	your yours
Third Person (the one spoken about)						
Masculine Gender	he	they	him	them	his	their theirs
Feminine Gender	she	they	her	them	her hers	their theirs
Neuter Gender	it	they	it	them	its	their theirs

Case shows the relationship between a pronoun and the other words in the sentence. In English there are three cases or forms: the **subjective,** the **objective,** and the **possessive.**

The **subjective case** is used when the pronoun acts as the subject of a verb or as a subject complement.

The **objective case** is used when the pronoun serves as the object of a verb, a preposition, or an infinitive.

The **possessive case** is used when the pronoun shows possession or ownership.

The form of the pronoun in each case changes depending on **person, number,** and **gender.**

Person refers to who is speaking. **First** person personal pronouns refer to the speaker. **Second** person personal pronouns refer to the person spoken to. **Third** person personal pronouns refer to the person or thing spoken about.

Number refers to how many persons are speaking or being spoken about. Singular pronouns indicate one person or thing; plural pronouns indicate more than one.

Gender refers to the sex of the person or thing, which can be masculine, feminine, or neuter. Only pronouns in the third person show gender.

You have just studied how to form the possessive of nouns, so let's begin with the possessive case of pronouns.

 ## THE POSSESSIVE CASE

As you learned in Chapter 3, the possessive form of the noun shows ownership, authorship, brand, kind, or origin. The same is true of pronouns in the possessive case.

This is *John's* book
This is *his* book.
Joan and Jane's restaurant opened last week.
Their restaurant opened last week.
Maureen's secretarial skills are excellent.
Her secretarial skills are excellent.
The *corporation's* profits have reached an all-time high.
Its profits have reached an all-time high.

Notice, however, that unlike nouns, possessive pronouns are not written with an apostrophe.

Right: This book is yours.
Wrong: This book is your's.
Right: That desk is hers.
Wrong: That desk is her's.
Right: The victory was theirs.
Wrong: The victory was their's.
Right: The shipment reached its destination.
Wrong: The shipment reached it's destination.

Don't confuse the possessive pronoun *its* with the contraction *it is.* The word *its* is a pronoun. The word *it's* is a contraction for the words *it is.*

The company wanted to increase *its* sales.
   (The company wanted to increase the company's sales.)
It's not going to be easy to increase sales.
   (It is not going to be easy to increase sales.)

 # PROGRAMMED REINFORCEMENT

S1 A pronoun takes the place of a _____.

R1 noun

S2 Pronouns may be in the first person, the second person, or the third person. **I** is the _____ person; **you** is the _____ person; **they** is the _____ person.

R2 **I**—first person; **you**—second person; **they**—third person

S3 **I** is a pronoun that is in the first person singular. _____ is the first person plural pronoun.

R3 We

S4 The second person plural of the singular pronoun **you** is _____.

R4 you

S5 **Company's** is the _____ form of the noun **company.**

R5 possessive

S6 Pronouns also have possessive forms. The first person singular is **my, mine. You** and **yours** are in the _____ person; _____, _____, _____, and _____ are in the third person singular possessive.

R6 second; his; her; hers; its

S7 Possessives of nouns must have an apostrophe or 's. This (is, is not) true of pronouns. Circle the correct possessive form: (a) **yours, your's;** (b) **ours, our's;** (c) **theirs, their's.**

R7 is not; (a) **yours;** (b) **ours;** (c) **theirs**

S8 **It's** is a contraction that always means _____. The possessive pronoun is **its.** Circle the correct form:
a. **(It's, Its) time to punch the clock.**
b. **The company and (its, it's) affiliates are amalgamated.**

R8 it is; a. **It's;** b. **its**

Turn to Exercises 4.1 and 4.2.

THE SUBJECTIVE CASE

The **subjective case** is used when the pronoun acts as the subject of a verb.

> *I* want a raise.
> *We* want to leave early this evening.
> *You* don't seem to understand.
> *He* was fired.
> *She* was promoted.
> *They* transferred to another division.
> Bob and *I* share an office.
> *He* and *she* are getting married next month.

A pronoun and a noun may be used in apposition as the subject of the verb (see Chapter 3). The noun identifies the pronoun or makes it clearer, and the two are said to be *in apposition.*

> *We panelists* shared the platform.
> *We programmers* met for lunch.

Subjective case pronouns also are used as subject complements. When a pronoun follows a linking verb and renames the subject, it is called a **subject complement** because it adds to or *complements* the information about the subject. Subject complements must be in the subjective case. As you recall from Chapter 1, the most common linking verb is *to be*. It appears in these forms:

> *am   are   is   was   were*

as well as all verb phrases ending in

> *be   been   being*

> The *culprit was I.*
> The most helpful *person is he.*
> The *person* responsible for the delay *is she.*
> *Was it he* who raised this point?
> The *people* who are being evasive *are they.*
> The highest *scorer was thought to be she.*

Although it is grammatically correct to use the subjective case after a linking verb, what results may sometimes strike you as awkward or too formal. In this case rewrite the sentence by making the subject complement into the subject. Compare the following sentences with the ones above:

> *I was* the *culprit.*
> *He is* the most helpful *person.*
> *She is* the *person* responsible for the delay.
> *Did he raise* this *point?*
> *They are being* evasive *(people).*
> *She was thought to be* the highest *scorer.*

The subjective case also is used when the pronoun acts as an appositive after a subject or subject complement.

Appositive after subject: The *panelists,* Jean, Ralph, and *I,* shared the platform.
Appositive after subject complement: The people who met for lunch were the *programmers,* Lauren, Joanne, and *I.*

THE OBJECTIVE CASE

The **objective case** of the pronoun is used when the pronoun acts as the object of the verb or of a preposition. When the pronoun does the action, use the subjective form; when the pronoun is acted on, use the objective form.

> *He* hit the ball. (subjective)
> The ball hit *him*. (objective)
> *She* congratulated the two men. (subjective)
> The two men thanked *her*. (objective)
> The jury acquitted *him*. (objective)
> They questioned *me* about the new procedure. (objective)
> Mr. Davis asked Frank and *me* to help set up chairs for the conference. (objective)

In the above examples, the pronouns *him, her,* and *me* act as **direct objects** of their respective verbs. In the following sentences the pronouns are the objects of prepositions:

> Mr. Schwartz spoke with *her* about the bill. (*Her* is the object of the preposition *with.*)
> The desk was delivered by *him*. (*Him* is the object of the preposition *by.*)
> Ms. Gastner gave the order to *them*. (*Them* is the object of the preposition *to.*)

The last sentence could also be written this way:

> Ms. Gastner gave *them* the order.

In this sentence *them* is an *indirect object,* the indirect object of the verb *gave.* An **indirect object** comes before the direct object of the verb and tells to whom or for whom the action is done.
Look at these sentences:

> Mr. Jones sold *them* three cases of stationery.
> He sent *her* the bill.

In these sentences *them* and *her* are indirect objects. Like all indirect objects, they can be restated as prepositional phrases by using the preposition *to:*

> Mr. Jones sold three cases of stationery *to them*.
> He sent the bill *to her*.

Whether used as direct or indirect objects, these pronoun forms are used in the objective case.
The objective case is used when the pronoun acts as an appositive after a direct object, an indirect object, or an object of a preposition.

> I saw our *clients,* Joe and *her,* yesterday. (*Her* is in apposition with *clients,* the direct object of the verb *saw.*)
> I mailed the *representatives,* Luis and *him,* a check. (*Him* is in apposition with *representatives,* the indirect object of the verb *mailed.*)
> I met with the *auditors,* Bob Seidel and *her*. (*Her* is in apposition with *auditors,* the object of the preposition *with.*)

The objective case is also used for pronouns that serve as objects of infinitives. The **infinitive** is *to* plus the form of the verb listed in the dictionary. (We will discuss infinitives fully in Chapter 9.)

I want *to hire her.*
I intend *to help him* with the inventory.
Our superior wants *to transfer her* and *me* to corporate headquarters.

 ## COMPOUND PERSONAL PRONOUNS

Sometimes *self* or *selves* is added to some forms of the personal pronouns. The result is known as a **compound personal pronoun.** Here is a list of these pronouns:

myself	herself	yourselves
yourself	itself	themselves
himself	ourselves	

These pronouns have two uses.

1.   Reflexive pronouns

When used as reflexives, compound pronouns indicate that the action described by the verb comes back to or is received by the doer. In other words, the subject of the verb is also its object. For example:

I hurt *myself.*
Give *yourself* a pat on the back.
The boss gave *himself* a raise.
If we continue with our present policy, we will get *ourselves* into trouble.

2.   Emphatic or intensive use

Sometimes compound pronouns are used for added stress or emphasis.

I wrote this entire report *myself.*
President Stone *herself* attended the meeting.
You are going to have to do this *yourself.*

The above are the only two ways in which these compound personal pronouns can be used. Do not use them when the sentence calls for a pronoun in the subjective or objective case, that is, pronouns used as subjects or objects.

Right: Jack and I are staying late tonight.
Wrong: Jack and myself are staying late tonight.
Right: My spouse and I want to thank you.
Wrong: My spouse and myself want to thank you.
Right: He shipped the order to Teresa and me.
Wrong: He shipped the order to Teresa and myself.
Right: Thousands like you have been delighted with this fantastic device.
Wrong: Thousands like yourself have been delighted with this fantastic device.

 # PROGRAMMED REINFORCEMENT

S9   In addition to the possessive, there are two other cases of pronouns: the _____ and the _____.

R9   subjective; objective

S10   When the pronoun does the action, use the _____ case; when the pronoun is acted upon, use the _____ case.

R10   subjective; objective

S11   The pronouns **I, he, she, we,** and **they** are in the _____ case.

R11   subjective

S12   The pronouns **me, him, her, us,** and **them** are in the _____ case.

R12   objective

S13   **She** is in the _____ case. The objective case of **she** is _____.

R13   subjective; **her**

S14   Objective pronouns are used in two situations—as objects of _____ and as objects of _____.

R14   verbs; prepositions

S15   **Give the message to (he, him).** The correct pronoun is _____. It is in the _____ case because it is the object of the _____ **to.**

R15   **him;** objective; preposition

S16   **Give (she, her) the message.** The correct pronoun is _____. It is in the _____ case because it is the indirect object of the verb _____.

R16   **her;** objective; **give**

S17   The subjective pronoun is used in two situations—as _____ of a sentence or clause and after a _____ verb.

R17   subject; linking

S18   **(Me, I) want to apply for the job.** The correct pronoun is obviously _____. It is in the _____ case because it is the _____ of a sentence.

R18   **I;** subjective; subject

S19   **It was (they, them) who signed the petition.** The correct pronoun is _____. It is in the _____ case because it comes after the linking verb _____.

R19   **they;** subjective; **was**

S20   To be grammatically correct, you should not say **It is me** because **me** is in the _____ case. You should say **It is I** because the subjective case is needed after the _____ verb _____.

R20   objective; linking; **is**

S21   Circle the correct form in each sentence. In the space provided write the case.
       a. **I thought it was (she, her) who signed the petition.**
       _____
       b. **The invoice was signed by (I, me).** _____

R21   a. **she,** subjective
       b. **me,** objective

R22   Omit **Frank and;**
Correct pronoun: **me.**

R23   **her;** objective case; object
of preposition **by**

S24   **I;** subjective case; after
linking verb **are**

R25   subjective, objective

R26   1. **We;** subjective case; used
in apposition as subject
2. **I;** subjective case; used
in apposition to subject

R27   1. **him;** objective case; in
apposition to **supervisors**
as the object of the
preposition **with**
2. **her;** objective case; in
apposition to **supervisors**
as direct object of verb
see

R28   compound

S22   Underline the words that may be left out in this sentence to determine more easily which pronoun to use: **The telegrams were accepted by Frank and (me, I).** Circle the correct pronoun.

S23   Circle the correct pronoun. **The meeting was attended by John and (she, her).** Give the case and reason.
Case: _____
Reason: _____

S24   Circle the correct pronoun. **The newest employees are Helen and (me, I).** Give the case and reason.
Case: _____
Reason: _____

S25   Pronouns may be used in apposition to nouns in a sentence. When a pronoun is used in apposition as a subject, or is placed in apposition to a subject or subject complement, it should be in the (subjective, objective) case. When a pronoun is in apposition to a direct object, an indirect object, or an object of a preposition, it should be in the (subjective, objective) case.

S26   Circle the correct pronoun in each sentence. Give the case and reason.
1. **(We, Us) administrative assistants are underpaid.**
Case: _____
Reason: _____
2. **The three supervisors, Marva, Hank, and (I, me), discussed the problem yesterday.**
Case: _____
Reason: _____

S27   Circle the correct pronoun in each sentence. Give the case and reason.
1. **I disagree with the other supervisors, Marva and (he, him), about what to do.**
Case: _____
Reason: _____
2. **I will see the other supervisors, Hank and (she, her), again today.**
Case: _____
Reason: _____

S28   Sometimes **self** or **selves** is added to some forms of the personal pronoun to form _____ personal pronouns.

S29   Compound personal pronouns do two things. When they are used as _____ pronouns, they show that the subject of the verb is also its object.

R29   reflexive

S30   Fill in the correct reflexive pronouns:
   a. **She hurt** _____.
   b. **He gave** _____ **a bonus.**

R30   a. **herself;** b. **himself**

S31   Sometimes compound personal pronouns are used emphatically (to provide additional stress or emphasis). Which of the following sentences illustrates this use?
   a. **He himself will attend the meeting.**
   b. **He shipped the packages himself.**
   c. **He shipped the packages to himself.**

R31   a and b

S32   Compound personal pronouns should not be used when the sentence calls for a pronoun in the subjective or objective case. Which of the following sentences are correct?
   a. **I want to congratulate yourself on a job well done.**
   b. **Congratulate yourself on a job well done.**
   c. **My boss and myself attended the conference.**
   d. **I attended the conference myself.**

R32   b and d

Turn to Exercises 4.3 to 4.5.

DEMONSTRATIVE PRONOUNS

Pronouns that are used to point out definite persons, places, or things are known as **demonstrative pronouns.** There are two demonstrative pronouns: *this* and *that*. The plural of *this* is *these;* the plural of *that* is *those.*

> *This* is my desk.
> *That* is your desk.
> *These* are my books.
> *Those* are your books.

In Chapter 10 we'll discuss the use of these words as adjectives—demonstrative adjectives.

INTERROGATIVE PRONOUNS

Interrogative means questioning. **Interrogative pronouns** are pronouns that are used in asking questions. The interrogative pronouns are *who, whose, whom, which,* and *what*. Like other pronouns, they act as subjects and objects within their sentences.

> *Who* is the new manager of your department?
> *Whose* coat is this?
> For *whom* are you looking?
> *Which* of these coats is yours?
> *What* did you say?

We will discuss how to choose between *who* and *whom* in the next chapter.

What asks for general information concerning a person, thing, statement, and so forth. *Which* identifies the person or thing being referred to.

> *What* are your views?
> *What* are we going to do?
> *Which* car is yours?
> *Which* applicants do you wish to interview?

Whose and *who's* are sometimes confused. Like the apostrophe in *it's*, the apostrophe in *who's* indicates the contraction of two words, *who* + *is*.

> Who's going to the luncheon? (Who is going to the luncheon?)

Whose, without the apostrophe, is the *possessive pronoun*. Remember that possessive pronouns do not have apostrophes (*yours, his, hers, its, ours, theirs*).

> *Whose* book is lost?
> I don't know *whose* pen I have.

INDEFINITE PRONOUNS

A large number of pronouns do not refer to particular persons, places, or things. For this reason they are known as *indefinite pronouns*. Here are the most common ones:

all	everybody	one
another	everyone	one another
any	everything	ones
anybody	few	other
anyone	many	others
anything	neither	several
both	nobody	some
each	none	somebody
each one	no one	someone
each other	nothing	something
either		

Many of these pronouns are considered singular. They take a singular verb.

another	everybody	nothing
anybody	everyone	one
anyone	everything	somebody
anything	much	someone
each	neither	something
either	nobody	

A few of these pronouns are always plural and take a plural verb.

both	many	others
few	several	

Others are either singular or plural, depending on how they are used in the sentence.

all	more	none
any	most	some

We'll have more to say about these indefinite pronouns in the next chapter when we talk about antecedents.

RELATIVE PRONOUNS

In Chapter 2 you learned about a **clause**—a group of words that has both a subject and a predicate. As you recall, there are two types of clauses: independent clauses, which can stand by themselves, and dependent or subordinate clauses, which cannot stand by themselves as separate sentences.

As we saw in Chapter 1, many words (*e.g., since, although, when,* and *because*) can be used to subordinate one clause to another. The pronouns *who, whom, which,* and *that* also can relate one clause to another part of the sentence. These pronouns are called *relative pronouns* and the subordinate clauses they introduce are known as *relative clauses.* Look at these examples:

Here is the man *who will be our next president.*
The book, *which was one of my favorites,* was soon found.
Shorthand is the subject *that I like best.*
The man *to whom you were speaking* will be our next president.
She is not the type of manager *that our department needs.*

When should you use *who, whom, which,* or *that?*

1. *Who* or *whom* always refers to a person.
2. *Which* never refers to a person, only to an animal or inanimate object.
3. *That* is also used to refer to animals and inanimate objects. It may also be used to refer to people when they are spoken of as a class or type. Individual people are always referred to as *who* or *whom.*

RECIPROCAL PRONOUNS

There are two reciprocal pronouns: *each other* and *one another.* They indicate a mutual relationship between people or things.

One another always refers to three or more persons or things. **Each other** refers to only two persons or things.

The two women knew *each other.*
The three women knew *one another.*

PROGRAMMED REINFORCEMENT

S33   **This** and **that** are called **demonstrative pronouns.** The plural of **this** is _____; the plural of **that** is _____.

R33   these; those

S34   The pronouns **who, whose, whom, which,** and **what** form the group known as **interrogative pronouns.** They are used to _____.

R34   ask questions

R35   who is

S35   **Whose** and **who's** will never be confused if one remembers that **who's** is a contraction of the words _____.

S36   Circle the correct words: **Tell me (whose, who's) dictation this is, and I'll tell you (whose, who's) responsible for the confusion.**

R36   **whose; who's**

S37   Circle the correct words. **I wonder (whose, who's) pen this is and (whose, who's) going to claim it.**

R37   **whose; who's**

S38   A large number of pronouns do not refer to particular persons, places, or things. They are called **indefinite pronouns.** Circle the following indefinite pronouns that are singular; underline those that are plural.
both, each, either, few, nobody, one, several

R38   singular: **each, either, nobody, one**
       plural: **both, few, several**

S39   A **relative pronoun** generally relates to a previous word in the sentence. Circle the relative pronoun in this sentence. Underline the word it relates to. **Here is the machine that I want repaired.**

R39   **that; machine**

S40   Circle the relative pronoun and underline the word it relates to in this sentence: **I saw the worker who repaired the typewriter.**

R40   **who; worker**

S41   **Who** is a relative pronoun that refers to a person. _____ and _____ are relative pronouns that refer to things.

R41   which; that

S42   **Each other** and **one another** are known as reciprocal pronouns. **Each other** refers to _____ people or things; **one another** refers to _____ or more.

R42   two; three

Turn to Exercises 4.6 to 4.8.

EXERCISE 4·1   PERSONAL PRONOUNS

This exercise covers the various forms that pronouns take. Fill in the missing pronouns in the following table.

	SINGULAR	PLURAL	SINGULAR OBJECTIVE	PLURAL OBJECTIVE	SINGULAR POSSESSIVE	PLURAL POSSESSIVE
First Person	I	_____	_____	_____	my / _____	_____ / _____
Second Person	_____ / _____	_____	you	_____	your / _____	_____ / _____
Third Person	_____ / _____ / _____	they	_____ / _____	_____ / _____	_____ / _____ / _____	_____ / their / _____

EXERCISE 4·2A   POSSESSIVE PRONOUNS

This exercise concerns the possessive forms of pronouns. In the space provided, write the correct pronoun.

1. The book lay on (its) (it's) side.   1. _____
2. (Its) (It's) going to be a long day.   2. _____
3. The package on top is (ours) (our's).   3. _____
4. The agreement must stand or fall on (its) (it's) merits.   4. _____
5. (Yours) (Your's) truly,   5. _____

77

6. (There) (Their) (They're) certain the package is (theirs) (there's) (their's).

6. _____

7. This proposal of (ours) (our's) is similar to (yours) (your's) (yours').

7. _____

8. This report of (hers) (her's) is extremely clear in (its) (it's) analysis of (there) (their) accounting department.

8. _____

9. (Its, It's) not clear whether the package is (yours, your's) or (theirs, their's, theres, there's).

9. _____

10. Tell me (whose, who's) analysis is more accurate, mine or (hers, her's).

10. _____

EXERCISE 4·2B POSSESSIVE NOUNS AND PRONOUNS

This exercise covers the proper use of possessive nouns and pronouns. Wherever a possessive noun or pronoun is spelled wrong, cross it out and write the correct form above it.

Dear Mr. Byrnes:

Thank you for your order of a years supply of Rapture Perfumes and Soaps, which your buyer, Ms. Stoll, gave us yesterday.

Your's is an unusually large order and this, combined with Ms. Stolls enthusiasm about our line, is appreciated. Our's is a small company, so its very encouraging to receive an order the size of yours.

We know that our line of fragrances will meet the needs of several of your departments. You will find Rapture Perfume's are an especially good item for your Womens Fragrances Department. In addition, it's success has been proven in the Fine Gifts Department of many stores.

You'll find the attractive cases that accompany you're order will display all the products to there best advantage.

If we can be of any further service, please call upon us.

Very truly yours',

EXERCISE 4·3 SUBJECTIVE CASE PRONOUNS

This exercise gives you practice in using the subjective case pronoun as the subject of a sentence and after linking verbs. In the space provided, write the correct pronoun.

1. It is (I, me).

2. It was (he, him).

3. Contrary to our advice (them, they) bought the stock.

4. Initially (she, her) was uncertain of her duties.

5. I thought it was (they, them).

6. (Us, We) are certain (us, we) can reduce costs.

7. If it were my decision, (I, me) would tell them either (them, they) fulfill their contractual obligations or (us, we) sue for damages.

8. The last person to leave was (her, she).

9. If it was (he, him) who first noticed the discrepancy, (he, him) should be congratulated.

10. If I were (he, him) and she were (I, me), this would never have happened.

11. That's (he, him) entering the room now.

12. Could it have been (us, we) who were responsible?

13. The one to be promoted should have been (he, him).

14. The two people who were promoted, (he, him) and Miss Ortiz, were from our department.

15. The three accountants, Mr. Abrahms, Ms. Bedillo, and (she, her), examined the company's financial records.

1. _____

2. _____

3. _____

4. _____

5. _____

6. _____

7. _____

8. _____

9. _____

10. _____

11. _____

12. _____

13. _____

14. _____

15. _____

This exercise involves using the proper pronoun as the object of a verb or a preposition. In the space provided, write the correct pronoun.

1. She wanted to hire (he, him) for the job.   1. _____

2. The message was sent by (she, her).   2. _____

3. Permit (I, me) to raise an objection.   3. _____

4. Mr. Jurek walked right by (them, they) without even recognizing (they, them).   4. _____

5. They would not allow (she, her) to leave.   5. _____

6. Kate stared at (he, him) as he entered the room.   6. _____

7. The director told (us, we) that she had reached a decision.   7. _____

8. The idea came to (they, them) almost simultaneously.   8. _____

9. I have given Mr. Nash and (she, her) my answer.   9. _____

10. Jean stood between (I, me) and the door.   10. _____

11. Separate requests were submitted by Luis and (I, me).   11. _____

12. Mr. Marquand's recommendations upset Alfredo as much as they did (I, me).   12. _____

13. Ms. Bates promised to recommend (we, us) two management trainees for a bonus. 13. _____

14. Mr. McGuire spoke with their representatives, William Montanez and (she, her), earlier today.   14. _____

15. No one but Elaine and (I, me) were on duty when the fire broke out.   15. _____

EXERCISE 4·5 REFLEXIVE PRONOUNS

This exercise concerns the proper form and use of reflexive pronouns. In the space provided, write the correct pronoun.

1. Give (you, yourself) time to think.   1. _____

2. Mr. Robinson (himself, hisself) will be there.   2. _____

3. The committee members voted (themself, themselves) a twenty-
    percent pay increase.   3. _____

4. They assumed all the responsibility (theirselves, themselves).   4. _____

5. Ouch! I just hurt (me, myself).   5. _____

6. You will have to represent us (yourself, yourselve).   6. _____

7. He has no one to blame but (hisself, himself).   7. _____

8. The order (it's self, itself) was not shipped until Tuesday.   8. _____

9. We must cooperate to get (ourselfs, ourselves) out of financial
    difficulty.   9. _____

10. All of you should congratulate (yourself, yourselves) on a job well
    done.   10. _____

EXERCISE 4·6   NON-PERSONAL PRONOUNS

This exercise involves the proper use of non-personal pronouns. Write the correct pronoun in the space provided.

1.   (These, That, Those) stack of newspapers should be thrown away.   1. _____

2.   (Which, What) model have you selected?   2. _____

3.   (Who's, Whose) car is this?   3. _____

4.   (Who's, Whose) going to represent us?   4. _____

5.   She and I are acquainted with (each other, one another).   5. _____

6.   Where does (these, those, this) stack of boxes belong?   6. _____

7.   This is the girl (which, whom) I told you about.   7. _____

8.   You are the kind of salesperson (that, which) we need to attract.   8. _____

9.   Tell me (who's, whose) coming today.   9. _____

10.   (Whose, Who's) terminal needs to be repaired?   10. _____

11.   The committee members spoke with (one another, each other) until
      it was time to convene.   11. _____

12.   (What, Which) are your views on this matter?   12. _____

13.   A cat (who, that) does not go outside would be an excellent pet
      for him.   13. _____

14.   (Whose, What, Which) briefcase is this, his or hers?   14. _____

15.   Miss DeStephano spent the weekend comparing the four proposals
      with (one another, each other).   15. _____

EXERCISE 4·7   PRONOUNS

This exercise tests your ability to use the proper pronoun. If the sentence is correct, mark C in the space provided. If it is incorrect, use the space above the sentence to make the necessary changes.

1. Mr. Ali and myself are grateful for all your help.   1. _____

2. The store sent the bill to my wife and I.   2. _____

3. How do yourself and your committee intend to proceed?   3. _____

4. What company do you yourself think is more reliable, Alliance or Unity?   4. _____

5. What one of the trainees did Ms. Morales dismiss?   5. _____

6. Whose the recipient of this year's outstanding employee award, Cindy or him?   6. _____

7. The decision will be made by Alfredo and me.   7. _____

8. It was him who made the decision.   8. _____

9. It must have been her who left the message.   9. _____

10. The two keypunch operators, Elaine and her, worked overtime.   10. _____

11. The two candidates were my co-workers, Marge and her.   11. _____

12. Mr. Jamison expects everyone, including you and him, to be there.   12. _____

13. Will you proofread these series of reports for Frank and me?   13. _____

14. The candidate who was elected is her.   14. _____

15. She earns as much as him.   15. _____

16. Ms. Adelsohn gave the two programmers, Carol and she, a raise.   16. _____

17. I don't write as well as she.   17. _____

18. Mr. Cribbs asked Joe and myself to work overtime.   18. _____

19. Thomas and myself went to lunch.   19. _____

20. I, like yourself, prefer the older model.   20. _____

21. Divide the work evenly between yourself and I.   21. _____

22. The three of us, Irma, Carla, and I, were promoted.   22. _____

23. The company promoted three of us, Carla, Irma, and I.   23. _____

24. Us three, Irma, Carla, and I, were promoted.   24. _____

25. A busy person like yourself will profit greatly from such a program.   25. _____

COMPOSITION: PRONOUNS

Supply an appropriate pronoun where shown by the parentheses and write complete sentences to complete the following sentence starters.

1. My assistant and (   ) ————————————————————

2. The two trainees, Donna and (   ), ————————————————
——

3. Was it (   ) ——————————————————————————

4. George gave the clients, Ms. Cooper and (   ), ——————————
——

5. Leo sent (   ) ————————————————————————

6. Just between you and (   ), ————————————————————

7. Ask either (   ) or (   ) ————————————
——

8. Except for Laura and (   ), ————————————————————

9. It was (   ) ——————————————————————————

10. An experienced person like (   ) ——————————————
——

5

PRONOUNS II
PRONOUNS AND THEIR ANTECEDENTS, USING PRONOUNS

AGREEMENT OF PRONOUNS AND ANTECEDENTS,
PROPER USE OF PRONOUNS

PRONOUNS AND THEIR ANTECEDENTS

When a pronoun is used in place of a noun, the noun that it replaces is called the *antecedent* of that pronoun. (*Cede* means *to go* and *ante* means *before*. An antecedent *goes before* the pronoun.)

David says he is tired. (*David* is the antecedent of *he*.)
Mary knows she cannot succeed. (*Mary* is the antecedent of *she*.)
We have heard from our salespeople. They say they cannot fill the quota. (*Salespeople* is the antecedent of *they*.)

Because a pronoun renames, or stands in place of, its antecedent, the pronoun should be as similar to the antecedent as possible. If the antecedent is singular, the pronoun must be singular. If the antecedent is plural, the pronoun must be plural. This is called agreement in *number*. If the antecedent is masculine, the pronoun must be masculine. If the antecedent is feminine, the pronoun must be feminine. If the antecedent is neuter, the pronoun must be neuter. This is called agreement in *gender*.

Look at this sentence:

The instructor expects Tom to complete (his) (her) (their) assignment.

The antecedent is *Tom*, which is clearly masculine. Therefore, the feminine pronoun *her* is inappropriate. This solves the problem of gender. The next step is to determine whether the antecedent is singular or plural. Because the antecedent *Tom* is singular, the singular pronoun *his* is required. The sentence should read:

The instructor expects Tom to complete his assignment.

Once you learn to recognize antecedents, the selection of the correct pronoun should be easy. The following guidelines on the agreement of pronouns with their antecedents will help you.

GUIDELINES FOR AGREEMENT OF PRONOUNS WITH THEIR ANTECEDENTS

TWO ANTECEDENTS WITH *AND*

Try this easy sentence.

Jack and Jill are on (his, her, their) way.

Obviously, *their* is correct. The antecedent of *their* is *Jack and Jill*. Always use a plural pronoun to represent two or more antecedents connected by *and*.

Mr. Johnson and Ms. O'Leary are on their way here.
The Acme Company and the Ajax Company are merging their assets.

Now look at this sentence.

The secretary and treasurer rendered (his, her, their) report.

If the positions of secretary and treasurer are held by two different persons, *their* is obviously correct. If the two positions are held by only one person, *his* or *her* is correct. If, however, two people hold the two posts, the sentence would be better written:

The secretary and the treasurer rendered their report.

The inclusion of the second *the* clearly tells the reader that *two* officers are involved.

TWO ANTECEDENTS WITH *OR/NOR*

When two antecedents are connected by *or* or *nor*, the pronoun should agree in number with the nearer antecedent.

Neither Johnson nor Kahn knows *his* business. (*Kahn* is the nearer antecedent. *Kahn* is singular. Therefore, use *his*.)
Either Pulaski or Black will get *her* wish. (*Black* is the nearer antecedent. *Black* is singular. Therefore, use *her*.)
Neither the boys nor the girls are ready for *their* lessons. (*Girls* is the nearer antecedent. *Girls* is plural. Therefore, use *their*.)
Neither Mr. Demos nor his sons have done *their* best. (*Sons* is the nearer antecedent. *Sons* is plural. Therefore, use *their*.) *Note:* In a sentence like this, in which one antecedent is singular and the other is plural, it is better to place the plural antecedent *last*.

INDEFINITE PRONOUNS AS ANTECEDENTS

Remember that the following indefinite pronouns are always singular: *anybody, anyone, each, every, everybody, many a, nobody, no one, somebody, someone*. When used as a subject, each of these words calls for a singular predicate. Moreover, when used as an antecedent, each calls for a singular pronoun.

Nobody is eager to risk *his* life.
Many a woman has placed *her* confidence in our company.
Everyone should complete *his* assignment before noon.
We have selected each of the women on the basis of *her* merit.

Note: Prepositional phrases should be ignored in determining the antecedent of a sentence. The prepositional phrase *of the women* in the last sentence does not change the requirement that a singular pronoun be used. *Each* is the antecedent.

> Each of our competitors has reduced *its* sales.
> Each of the factories is operating at *its* peak capacity.

Remember also that *both, few, many, several,* and *others* are always plural. Each of these pronouns calls for not only a plural predicate but, when used as an antecedent, a plural pronoun as well.

> Few are eager to risk *their* lives.
> Many do *their* work efficiently.
> We have selected both of the representatives on the basis of *their* merit.

 ## THE GENDER PROBLEM

Most of the problems in choosing pronouns will involve number, but sometimes you may have difficulty determining which gender to use. For example, which pronoun should you use in the following sentence?

> Everyone in the class did (his) (her) homework.

Is *everyone* masculine or feminine? It could be either. In such cases, when the sex of the antecedent is indefinite, the rule is to use a masculine pronoun, which is considered the "common gender" pronoun.

> Not a person left *his* seat before the final curtain.
> One of the students left *his* books.

In practice, however, it is better if possible not to use *his* to refer to both men and women. You can avoid leaving out some of the people you are talking about and overemphasizing some others by using the plural or by changing your wording slightly:

> All the students in the class did their homework.
> Everyone in the class did Monday's homework.
> Not a person left the theater before the final curtain.
> The books were left by one of the students.

If the context of the sentence clearly indicates that the pronoun refers to a *feminine* antecedent, use a *feminine* pronoun:

> Each parolee from the Women's House of Detention must meet with her parole
> officer once a week.

In this sentence *Women's House of Detention* shows that the parolees are feminine. Thus, a feminine pronoun is needed.

> Neither of the waitresses does her job badly.

Now let's try this sentence.

> Each man and woman in the audience enthusiastically showed (his, her) approval.

Here you specifically refer to a masculine and a feminine antecedent, *man and woman.* In this instance, to avoid confusion, you must use both the masculine and the feminine pronoun.

Each man and woman in the audience enthusiastically showed his or her approval.

Because this is an awkward sentence, it would be better to rephrase the sentence into a less awkward construction.

Enthusiastic approval was shown by every man and woman in the audience.

or

All the men and women in the audience enthusiastically showed their approval.

Here is another example:

Awkward: The host or hostess should always personally greet his or her guests.
Better: Guests should be personally greeted by the host or hostess.

 ## EXPLANATORY PHRASES

When locating the antecedent, ignore explanatory phrases beginning with *as well as, in addition to, and not, together with, accompanied by, rather than,* and so forth.

John, as well as his brothers, is on his way.

The antecedent is *John*. Disregard *as well as his brothers*.

The boys, in addition to John, are on their way.

The antecedent is *boys*. Disregard *in addition to John*.

John, and not his brothers, is on his way.

The antecedent is *John*. Disregard *and not his brothers*.

John, rather than his brothers, is on his way.

The antecedent is *John*. Disregard *rather than his brothers*.

 ## COLLECTIVE ANTECEDENTS

Collective nouns such as *committee, jury, class, crowd,* and *army* may be either singular or plural depending upon their meaning in the sentence. Each of these words refers to a group of people. When you are referring to that group as a single unit, use a singular pronoun.

The committee held its meeting.
The class is in its room.

When you refer to the individuals that make up the group, however, use a plural pronoun.

The committee were called at their homes one at a time.
The jury brought in their split verdict.

Company names are generally thought of as collective nouns, and as such are usually considered singular.

Whitney's is having its biggest automotive department sale ever.
Price–Waterhouse offers summer seminars in writing to its staff accountants.

Because a company is made up of individuals, a writer could mean those individuals when he uses a company's name.

I called Sears to find out if they were accepting applications.

In this sentence a singular pronoun would sound awkward, so the plural *they* is preferable. Usually, however, company names are considered singular and call for singular verbs and pronouns for grammatical correctness.

 ## AMBIGUOUS REFERENCE

When using pronouns in your writing, be sure that the meaning of each pronoun is clearly understood. Look at this sentence:

The manager told Nicol that the meaning of his report was unclear.

Whose report is unclear—the manager's? or Nicol's? From this sentence you cannot tell because the reference of the pronoun is ambiguous. Either *Nicol* or *manager* could be the antecedent. Here's how this sentence could be improved:

The manager told Nicol that the meaning of Nicol's report was unclear.

This sentence, though better, is awkward. Let's rephrase it: *The meaning of Nicol's report was unclear, the manager told him.*

Ambiguous: Rico called Fred when he was in Seattle.
Clear: When Rico was in Seattle, he called Fred.
Ambiguous: I listened to Jan's plan and Frieda's argument against it and decided I agreed with her.
Clear: I listened to Jan's plan and Frieda's argument against it and decided I agreed with Jan.
Ambiguous: Rosalie and Anne were credited with coauthoring the report, but she wrote most of it.
Clear: Rosalie and Anne were credited with coauthoring the report, but Rosalie wrote most of it.
Ambiguous: We closed the sale and completed the shipment. It was a large one.
Clear: We closed the sale, which was a large one, and completed the shipment.

 # PROGRAMMED REINFORCEMENT

S1 The word that a pronoun refers to is called the _____ of that pronoun.

R1 antecedent

S2 If the antecedent that a pronoun relates to is singular, the pronoun must be _____. If the antecedent is plural, the pronoun must be _____.

R2 singular; plural

S3   **Our firm expects all employees to do (his, their) best work.** **Employees** is the antecedent of the pronoun. (a) **Employees** is (singular, plural). (b) The pronoun that agrees with **employees** is **(his, their).**

R3   a. plural; b. **their**

S4   **My manager expects every typist to do (his, their) best.** The antecedent to the pronoun is _____ which is (singular, plural). Therefore, the correct pronoun is _____.

R4   typist; singular; **his**

S5   A pronoun and its antecedent must agree not only in number (singular or plural), but also in gender (masculine or feminine). Circle the correct word. **The coach wants every girl to do (his, her, their) best.**

R5   **her**

S6   If the antecedent consists of two nouns connected by **and,** the pronoun must be _____ in number. Circle the correct word. **The Merit Company and the Vitality Company will make (his, its, their) decision known today.**

R6   plural; **their**

S7   When two antecedents are connected by **or** or **nor,** the pronoun will agree in number with the (nearer, farther) antecedent.

R7   nearer

S8   Underline the nearer antecedent and circle the correct pronoun in this sentence: **Neither the father nor the sons will do (his, their) share of the work.**

R8   **sons; their**

S9   **Either the parents or the girl will give her speech after the performance.** This sentence is awkward. Rewrite it to make it less awkward. _____

R9   Either the girl or her parents will give their speech after the performance.

S10   This is a partial list of indefinite pronouns: **anybody, anyone, each, everybody, everyone, nobody, no one, somebody, someone.** When used as an antecedent, each of these expressions calls for a (singular, plural) pronoun.

R10   singular

S11   Circle the correct pronoun.
a. **Nobody wants to give (his, their) support to unworthy causes.**
b. **Everybody did (his, their) practice typing at home.**

R11   a. **his**
b. **his**

S12   A phrase (a group of words) which comes between the singular antecedent and the pronoun does not alter the fact that the pronoun is singular. **Each of the women executives has (her, their) duties cut out for (her, them).**
a. Underline the group of words after the antecedent that you should ignore in determining the number of the pronoun.
b. Circle the correct pronouns.

R12   a. **of the women executives;**
b. **her, her**

S13 Where the sex of the antecedent is indefinite, the custom is to use the **(masculine, feminine)** pronoun.

R13 masculine

S14 **Everyone in the office gave (his, her, their) donation to United Charities.** Assuming both sexes are represented in the office, which pronoun does custom call for? _____

R14 **his**

S15 Revise the sentence in *S14* to avoid a common gender pronoun. _____

R15 **Everyone in the office gave a donation to United Charities.**
        or
Everyone in the office donated to United Charities.

S16 If the antecedent refers to females only, the pronoun should be _____. Circle the correct pronoun: **Each of the saleswomen at Neiman Marcus did (his, her, their) shopping at the home store.**

R16 feminine; **her**

S17 Phrases like **together with, accompanied by, in addition to,** and **as well as** do not make a singular word plural. Circle the correct pronoun: **John, accompanied by his brothers, did (his, their) best to stop the walkout.**

R17 his

S18 Words like **committee, jury, crowd,** and **army** are usually singular but may be plural if you are referring to the individuals in the group. Circle the correct pronouns: **The committee is holding (its, their) meeting. The committee received individual letters at (its, their) home(s).**

R18 **its; their**

S19 Because company names are thought of as collective nouns, normally they are considered (singular, plural). Circle the pronoun that correctly completes this sentence: **Levy Brothers lost half of (its, their) stock in a fire.**

R19 singular; **its**

S20 It is important to avoid the use of pronouns that are not clearly understood. In this sentence, which pronoun is not clear? **John told his brother that he was late.**

R20 **he**

Turn to Exercises 5.1 to 5.3.

 USING PRONOUNS

For many people the most difficult decision in using pronouns is determining whether a sentence calls for *who* or *whom*. If you are one of these people, this section should enable you to make the correct choice with confidence.

WHO/WHOM

Whom is the *objective* case of the pronoun *who*. You use *whom* as—

1. The *object* of a verb
2. The *object* of a preposition.

Who is the subjective case. You use *who*—

1. As the *subject* of a sentence or a clause
2. After a *linking* verb.

Here's a technique to help you find out which of these two pronouns to use. Whenever you choose between *who* and *whom*, simply substitute *he* or *him*, or *she* or *her*. If *he* or *she* fits, the subjective case, *who*, is correct. If *him* or *her* fits, then the objective case, *whom*, is correct.

Look at these examples:

1. (Who, Whom) is it?

   Substitute *he* or *him*.
   He is it. Not: *Him* is it. Therefore: *Who is it?*

2. It is (who, whom)?

   Substitute: It is *she*. Not: It is *her*. Therefore: *It is who?*

3. (Who, Whom) do you want?

   Substitute and place *he* or *him* at the end of the question: Do you want *him*?
   Not: Do you want *he*? Therefore: *Whom do you want?*

4. You were referring to (who, whom)?

   Substitute: You were referring to *her*. Not: You were referring to *she*. Therefore: *You were referring to whom?*

5. He is a person (who, whom) is loved by all.

   This sentence is slightly more difficult than the others. In this sentence *who* or *whom* is part of a relative clause, joining the second clause to the first. In sentences like this one, break the sentence into its separate clauses. Then test *who* or *whom* in its own clause. Whichever form is correct in its own clause is correct in the entire sentence.

   He is a person . . . (who, whom) is loved by all.

   Substitute: *he* is loved by all. Not: *him* is loved by all. Therefore: *He is a person who is loved by all.*

6. She is a person (who, whom) we all love.

   This sentence also divides into two clauses:

   She is a person . . . (who, whom) we all love.

Again we test *who* or *whom* in its own clause. Substitute: we all love *her*. Not: we all love *she*. Therefore: *She is a person whom we all love.*

7. There is an urgent need for people (who, whom) we can trust.

Substitute: . . . we can trust *him*. Not: *he*. Therefore: *There is a need for people whom we can trust.*

8. She is a person (who, whom) I am positive can be trusted.

Do not let *I am positive* fool you. This sentence can be rearranged to read: *I am positive she is a person (who, whom) can be trusted.* The rearranged sentence can be broken into:

I am positive she is a person . . . (who, whom) can be trusted.

Substitute: *She* can be trusted. Not: *Her* can be trusted. Therefore: *She is a person who I am positive can be trusted.*

9. (Who, Whom) did you say was at the door?

Rearrange this sentence to read: *Did you say (who, whom) was at the door?*
Substitute: *He* was at the door. Not: *Him* was at the door. Therefore: *Who did you say was at the door?*

10. The man (who, whom) I think will be our next President will be here soon.

Break this sentence down as follows:

The man will be here soon . . . (who, whom) I think will be our next President.

Substitute in its own clause: I think *he* will be our next President. Not: I think *him* will be . . . Therefore: *The man who I think will be our next President will be here soon.*

11. The person (who, whom) I believe we all love is standing next to me.

The person is standing next to me . . . (who, whom) I believe we all love.

Substitute in its own clause: I believe we all love *him*. Not: we all love *he*. Therefore: *The person whom I believe we all love is standing next to me.*
Remember, whenever you are unsure whether to use *who* or *whom*, test *who* or *whom* in its own clause by substituting *he* or *him* or *she* or *her*. You then should have little difficulty determining which is correct.

 # WHOEVER/WHOMEVER

Whoever is in the subjective case; *whomever* is in the objective. The problem whether to use *whoever* or *whomever* in a sentence can be solved much the same way as whether to choose *who* or *whom*. Ignore all words that come before *whoever* or *whomever*, then substitute *he* or *him* or *she* or *her*. Study the following examples.

1. (Whoever, Whomever) answers the phone should be pleasant.

Substitute: *He* answers the phone. Not: *Him* answers the phone. Therefore: *Whoever answers the phone should be pleasant.*

2.   Give the prize to (whoever, whomever) you please.

Ignore all words in the sentence before *whoever* or *whomever* (Give the prize to . . .). Substitute: You please *her*. Not: You please *she*. Therefore: *Give the prize to whomever you please.*

3.   Give the prize to (whoever, whomever) deserves it.

Ignore: Give the prize to. Substitute: *He* deserves it. Not: *Him* deserves it. Therefore: *Give the prize to whoever deserves it.*

4.   She always accepts help from (whoever, whomever) will give it.

Ignore: She always accepts help from. Substitute: *She* will give it. Not: *Her* will give it. Therefore: *She always accepts help from whoever will give it.*

 ## US/WE

Many people have trouble determining which of these two pronouns to use directly before a noun. For example, which is correct?

(We) (Us) designers have interesting work.

An easy way to determine the correct pronoun is to leave out the noun.

(We) (Us) have interesting work.   We have interesting work.

Therefore: *We* designers have interesting work. Here are some similar examples:

1.   The award was presented to (we) (us) men.

Leave out *men*. The award was presented to *us*. (Not: . . . to *we*.) Therefore: The award was presented to *us* men.

2.   Kyle asked (us) (we) boys to be present.

Kyle asked *us* . . . (Not: asked *we*.) Therefore: Kyle asked *us* boys to be present.

3.   (We) (Us) programmers deserve a raise.

We deserve . . . (Not: *Us* deserve.) Therefore: *We* programmers deserve a raise.
    Remember, if you aren't sure which pronoun to use in situations like these, simplify the sentence by leaving out the noun. The answer should then be obvious.

 ## THAN/AS

She is a better keyboarder than (I, me).
She was not so good as (he, him).

If you aren't sure which pronoun to use after *than* or *as*, mentally add a word to complete the meaning of the sentence. For example:

1.   She is a better keyboarder than (I, me).

This means: She is a better keyboarder than (I, me) *am.* Answer: . . . *I am.* Not: *me* am. Therefore: She is a better keyboarder than *I.*

2. She was not so good as (he, him).

    This means: She was not so good as (he, him) *was.* Answer: . . . *he was.* Not: *him was.* Therefore: She was not so good as *he.*

3. She does a better job than (I, me).

    This means: She does a better job than *I (do).*

4. He would rather eat with Janos than (me, I).

    This means: He would rather eat with Janos than *(with) me.*

 ## BETWEEN YOU AND ME

Sometimes in trying to be grammatically correct, people correct themselves when they are not in error. See what often happens when an introductory phrase places a pronoun near the beginning of a sentence.

Wrong: Between you and I, there's nothing to worry about.

Although the pronoun *I* comes near the beginning of the sentence, a position that normally calls for the subjective form of the pronoun, *me* is actually the correct pronoun here because it is the object of the preposition *between.* The proper phrase is always *between you and me,* never *between you and I.*

Between you and me, I think this will work.
Between you and me, who do you think will win?
The profits were divided between Ms. Smith and him.

 ## ANY ONE/ANYONE

No one is always written as two words.

There is sometimes confusion about whether to write *anyone, someone,* or *everyone* as one word or two. A simple rule to follow is to write it as two words when it is followed by an *of* phrase and to write it as one word at other times.

Everyone was present.
Every one *of* the salespeople was present.
Can anyone enter the contest?
Let any one *of* the members enter.

 ## REDUNDANT PRONOUNS

Mr. Kowalski will attend the banquet.
He will attend the banquet.

Obviously each of these sentences is grammatically correct. Look at this sentence:

Mr. Kowalski, he will attend the banquet.

The purpose of the pronoun *he* is to take the place of a noun. But the noun that *he* would replace, *Mr. Kowalski,* is already present. Therefore, *he* is unnecessary. In this sentence *he* is an example of a redundant pronoun. Here are other examples:

Right: Mr. Roberts and Mr. Stone will be here shortly.
Right: They will be here shortly.
Wrong: Mr. Roberts and Mr. Stone, they will be here shortly.
Right: Our firm is celebrating its tenth anniversary.
Right: It is celebrating its tenth anniversary.
Wrong: Our firm it is celebrating its tenth anniversary.

In each case the subject already has been stated; it should not be restated through the use of an unnecessary pronoun.

 # PROGRAMMED REINFORCEMENT

S21 The pronouns **who** and **whom** sometimes cause trouble. **Who** is in the _____ case whereas **whom** is in the _____ case.

R21   subjective; objective

S22 Because **who** is in the subjective case, it may be used in only two situations: as the _____ of a sentence or clause, or after a _____ verb.

R22   subject; linking

S23 Circle the correct pronoun. Give the case and reason. **(Who, Whom) in your opinion will win the game?**
Case: _____
Reason: _____

R23   **Who;** subjective; subject of the sentence

S24 **I wonder to (who, whom) we should give the prize.** Circle the correct pronoun. Give the case and reason.
Case: _____
Reason: _____

R24   **whom;** objective; object of the preposition **to**

S25 Circle the correct pronoun: **He is the man (who, whom) I believe erased the signature.**

R25   **who**

S26 Circle the correct pronoun: **Tell me (who, whom) you think is the mechanic to (who, whom) we should give the bonus.**

R26   **who**
whom

S27 Circle the correct pronouns in this sentence: **She is the writer (whom, who) I am positive is the one (whom, who) we should select as editor.**

R27   **who**
whom

S28 **Whoever** and **whomever** are used exactly like **who** and **whom.** That means that **whoever** is in the _____ case and **whomever** is in the _____ case.

R28   subjective
objective

S29 When choosing between **whoever** and **whomever,** disregard all words that come (before, after) it. In the following sentence, underline the words you should disregard and circle the correct pronoun. **I will choose (whoever, whomever I prefer.**

R29 before; Ignore **I will choose; whomever**

S30 Underline the words you should disregard and circle the correct pronoun. **I will choose (whoever, whomever) is better.**

R30 Ignore **I will choose; whoever**

S31 **(We, us) typists should study some kind of word processing.** You quickly know the correct form is _____ if you omit the word _____.

R31 **We; typists**

S32 Circle the correct pronoun. Underline the word you may omit to double check your choice. **Ms. Wong gave the merit award to (we, us) secretaries.**

R32 **us;** leave out **secretaries**

S33 To determine which case of pronoun should follow the conjunction **as** or **than,** it is wise to add a simple verb after the pronoun in question. What test verb would you use here? **He organizes as well as (me, I).** Answer: _____ Circle the correct pronoun.

R33 **do** or **organize; I**

S34 Circle the correct pronoun: **Frank is more ambitious than (her, she).** The _____ case is correct because the pronoun is the _____ of the understood verb _____.

R34 **she;** subjective; subject; **is (than she is)**

S35 Circle the correct pronoun: **He would rather work for Ms. Stein than (me, I).** The _____ case is correct because the pronoun is the _____ of the understood preposition _____.

R35 **me;** objective; object; **for (than for me)**

S36 **Between** is a preposition. Circle the correct pronouns: **The boss divided the work between (her, she) and (me, I).** The _____ case is correct because the pronouns are the _____ of the preposition _____.

R36 **her; me;** objective; objects; **between**

S37 Pronouns like **anyone, someone,** and **everyone** may be written as one word or two words. They are written as (one, two) word(s) when a phrase beginning with **of** follows: **(Everyone, Every one) of the crates was returned.**

R37 two; **Every one**

S38 Circle the correct words: **(Everyone, Every one) of the girls may go, but (noone, no one) has gone yet.**

R38 **Every one; no one**

S39 A **redundant pronoun** is an unnecessary pronoun because it repeats the subject of the sentence. Which pronouns should be omitted in the following sentences?
a. **Our company it makes gaskets.**
b. **My brother he owns his own business.**
c. **I will phone the manager myself.**

R39 a. **it**
b. **he**
c. **none**

S40 To review: A pronoun takes the place of a _____; each pronoun is singular or _____ and is in the first, second, or _____ person.

R40 noun; plural; third

S41 Circle the correct answers in this review sentence: **(It's, Its) clear that (ours, our's) is the machine (who, that) is superior.**

R41 **It's; ours; that**

S42 Circle the correct pronouns in this review sentence: **Our government expects each of its citizens to do (his, their) best because neither the President nor the members of Congress (is, are) able to do (his, their) work alone.**

R42 **his; are; their**

S43 Circle the correct pronouns: **It is (we, us) (who, whom) are more deserving than (he, him).**

R43 **we; who; he**

S44 Circle the correct pronouns: **Between you and (I, me) I don't care (who, whom) is promoted or (who, whom) they pick.**

R44 **me; who; whom**

S45 Circle the correct words: **(Anyone, Any one) of the managers but (she, her) works well under pressure.**

R45 **Any one; her**

Turn to Exercises 5.4 to 5.6.

EXERCISE 5·1 PRONOUNS—ANTECEDENTS AND NUMBER

In this exercise you are to identify pronouns and their antecedents. In the column marked *Pronoun* write the pronoun. In the column marked *Antecedent* write the antecedent. In the column marked *Number* write *S* if the antecedent is singular; write *P* if the antecedent is plural.

	PRONOUN	ANTECEDENT	NUMBER

1. The present equipment deserves all the praise given it.   1. _____ _____ _____

2. Mr. Perez is proud of his son.   2. _____ _____ _____

3. The Blairstown Ambulance Corps knows it can count on continued community support.   3. _____ _____ _____

4. The boys' bicycles lay on their sides.   4. _____ _____ _____

5. Ms. Deloria can protect the firm if she acts quickly.   5. _____ _____ _____

6. Our firm is proud of its record.   6. _____ _____ _____

7. Somebody forgot his briefcase.   7. _____ _____ _____

8. Each of the saleswomen has had her office refurnished.   8. _____ _____ _____

9. Mr. Kulczak and Ms. Berman are on their way to the meeting.   9. _____ _____ _____

10. Mr. Kulczak, as well as Ms. Berman, is on his way to the meeting.   10. _____ _____ _____

11. All members must do their share.   11. _____ _____ _____

12. The committee has been in its meeting room for hours.   12. _____ _____ _____

13. Neither the desk nor the table looks its age.   13. _____ _____ _____

14. Mr. Clemente, in addition to the entire staff, will offer his resignation.   14. _____ _____ _____

15. Neither Ms. Glenn nor the boys have invested their money wisely.   15. _____ _____ _____

EXERCISE 5·2A   COMMON GENDER PRONOUNS

Rewrite the following sentences to eliminate common gender pronouns.

1. Somebody forgot his briefcase. _____

2. Each member of our sales staff must do his share. _____

3. Each of the department heads has had his office refurnished. _____
    _____

4. If somebody does an outstanding job, he should be rewarded for his efforts. _____
    _____

5. Is a person still forced to retire when he reaches age sixty-five? _____
    _____

6. Many a person is promoted to a position he cannot perform properly. _____
    _____

7. A new car owner must have his car serviced regularly to keep his warranty in effect. _____
    _____

8. No one had his assignment finished. _____

9. Every applicant will have his résumé reviewed by each committee member. _____
    _____

10. If a person knows how to communicate effectively, he will go far in the business world. _____
    _____

EXERCISE 5·2B   AMBIGUOUS PRONOUN REFERENCES

Rewrite the following sentences to eliminate an ambiguous pronoun reference.

1. I read in the financial section that World Business Products intends to purchase a controlling interest in International Conglomerate and that the value of its stock has almost doubled.

2. Now that Mr. O'Rourke has assumed many of Mr. Park's responsibilities, he has been much happier.

3. The cleaners washed, waxed, and polished both the main floor and the second floor. They were very dirty. _____

4. Mr. Lee spoke sharply to Joe, telling him that unless his job performance quickly improved, he would be very unhappy. _____

5. The three supervisors told their staffs that they would receive the director's recommendations the following morning. _____

EXERCISE 5·3 AGREEMENT OF PRONOUN AND ANTECEDENT

This exercise involves the agreement of a pronoun with its antecedent. In the spaces provided, write the proper pronouns.

1. Smith and Desai Landscaping has grown till (it, they) is the largest business in (its, it's, their) field.

1. _____

2. If somebody does an outstanding job, (he, they) should be rewarded for (his, their) efforts.

2. _____

3. The memoranda have been filed in (its, their) proper place.

3. _____

4. Every girl in that class has become successful in (his, her, their) chosen field.

4. _____

5. The crisis will soon be over, but (its, their) effect will be permanent.

5. _____

6. Neither Ms. Chapman nor her associates had been in (her, their) office.

6. _____

7. No one in class raised (his, her, their) hand.

7. _____

8. Either Mr. Yoshimoto or one of his partners will be glad to offer (his, their) assistance.

8. _____

9. Somebody tried to force (his, their) way through the crowd.

9. _____

10. If Ms. Carter or Ms. Trantor orders at once, (she, they) will receive the merchandise before the holidays.

10. _____

11. Either Mr. Dunlap or Mr. Firestone left (his, their) lighter.

11. _____

12. Every man, woman, and child in the room owes (his, their) life to the quick thinking of Sally Keller.

12. _____

13. Acme Lumber, in addition to Zenith Lumber, is launching (its, their) annual campaign.

13. _____

14. Ms. Vicelli, but not her staff, is on (his, her, their) way here.

14. _____

15. All the members received (his, their) invitations.

15. _____

16. Each of the books had been autographed on (its, their) inside cover.

16. _____

17. This is one of those problems not easily solved on (its, their) bare facts.

17. _____

18. Neither Maria nor Madeline had been able to complete (his, her, their) assignment.

18. _____

19. None of the manufacturers will be prepared to make (his, their) views public.

19. _____

20. Mr. Lopez, accompanied by his sons, will be able to attend (his, their) friend's wedding.

20. _____

EXERCISE 5·4A **WHO, WHOM**

This exercise gives you practice in choosing between who or whom, whoever or whomever. In the space provided, write the correct word.

1. (Who, Whom) is next? 1. _____

2. (Who, Whom) do you want to meet? 2. _____

3. (Who, Whom) did you say phoned while I was out? 3. _____

4. We have chosen a woman (who, whom) you all know. 4. _____

5. We have chosen a woman (who, whom) is known by all. 5. _____

6. He likes (whoever, whomever) likes him. 6. _____

7. Elena is a person (who, whom) I think can be counted on to get the job done. 7. _____

8. (Who, Whom) were you speaking of? 8. _____

9. (Whoever, Whomever) gets there first should begin setting up. 9. _____

10. He likes (whoever, whomever) he meets. 10. _____

11. She is a person (who, whom) I feel confident we can rely on. 11. _____

12. One man (who, whom) was nominated refused to accept. 12. _____

13. Choose (whoever, whomever) you think is the best qualified. 13. _____

14. Have you decided (who, whom) you want for this position? 14. _____

15. (Who, Whom) do you think will win? 15. _____

16. The sales rep (who, whom) I expected was detained. 16. _____

17. Which is the boy (who, whom) you suspect of having stolen the money? 17. _____

18. I think (whoever, whomever) suggested this plan should be congratulated. 18. _____

19. (Who, Whom) will check the results in the files? 19. _____

20. The results will be divulged to (whoever, whomever) you choose. 20. _____

21. Their agent said that Mr. Smythe, (who, whom) is one of his friends, is the person we should hire. 21. _____

22. I know a person (who, whom) I think can do the job. 22. _____

23. Of all the people (who, whom) I know, he is the one (who, whom) can most be relied on. 23. _____

24. It was (she, her) to (who, whom) you spoke yesterday. 24. _____

25. The results will be made available to (whoever, whomever) requests them. 25. _____

EXERCISE 5·4B   PROPER USE OF PRONOUNS

This exercise concerns the proper use of certain pronouns. Cross out any incorrect words in the following sentences and write the correct word above it. There may be more than one error in a sentence.

1. Could it have been us trainees who were to blame?

2. Everyone of the officials except she has been assigned a post.

3. Us three, Jan, Jerrie, and me, were transferred.

4. There's would be a most difficult task for any one.

5. There roles would be exciting for any one with courage.

6. Every one wishes they could sing like he.

7. Between you and I, no one is sure of his part.

8. He is not so clever as me.

9. Our's is a perfect relationship, and every one knows it.

10. Julie and Anne, they are not so efficient as us.

11. Us salespeople must plan this campaign of our's carefully.

12. The order directed we secretaries to come to work fifteen minutes earlier.

13. Jane Zucker is more efficient than me.

14. She would rather work with Jan than he or me.

15. Between you and I these work is easy.

16. Mr. Zaroff from the main office, he will bring the copies of the contracts with him.

17. Mr. Torres is as good a manager as him.

18. Is Soonwon taller than she or yourself?

19. Them men would rather choose Robin than I.

20. It is up to us women to show her the correct way to do them jobs.

EXERCISE 5·5   PRONOUNS

The letter below includes many intentional errors. Cross out each incorrect word and write the correct word above it. Pay particular attention to the use of possessive pronouns and to the agreement of a pronoun with its antecedent.

Dear Ms. George:

We were very pleased to be invited by the National Organization of Professional Women to attend it's annual convention. I know that each of the members of our staff felt it their personal duty and pleasure to attend. Ms. Aziz, as well as Ms. Kupchak, they send their special thanks to you for the invitation.

Them two women and myself were especially interested in the talks given by Ms. Valdez and Mr. Brown. Their's is an unusual combination of talents. I noticed that during there talks every member of the audience were glued to their seats. I don't believe any one wanted to miss a word of what they said. Its a rarity those days to meet people who have such complete command of English and his subject matter.

I also wish to congratulate you on the fine job done by your banquet committee. Everyone of our representatives praised the excellent meal. Our compliments to whomever planned the menu. The banquet speakers, especially Ms. Schwartz, gave her presentations very well.

By the way, Ms. Schwartz is the woman which I told you about at lunch last week. I'm pleased that talent such as her's was recognized by your organization. She is one of those people which is exceptional in her accomplishments. Noone could have been a better speaker than her. Neither Ms. Aziz nor Ms. Kupchak were disappointed in their expectations. Each holds she in high esteem.

In closing, let me say that I believe wholeheartedly in the work of this organization of your's. Since ours' is a small firm, us representatives are especially proud to be members and show our support for your work. We look forward to attending next year's convention.

Sincerely,

COMPOSITION: PRONOUNS

Compose complete sentences that include the phrases in parentheses as antecedents of pronouns.

1. (either Anne or Louisa) _____

2. (neither Miss Zee nor her assistants) _____

3. (few) _____

4. (each of our clients) _____

5. (many a product) _____

6. (several people) _____

7. (Levy Brothers Department Store) _____

8. (every one) _____

9. (anyone) _____

10. (whomever) _____

6

VERBS I
VERB TYPES AND TENSES

THE TYPES OF VERBS, THE SIMPLE TENSES, THE
PERFECT TENSES, SUMMARY OF TENSES

In Chapter 2 we saw that a sentence must have both a subject and a predicate. In the last three chapters, we have studied two parts of speech, *nouns* and *pronouns*, either of which can serve as the subject of the sentence. Now we turn to the heart of the predicate, the *verb*. Because the verb is the part of speech that makes a direct statement about the subject, much of the interest and power in writing stem from the careful selection of verbs. Look at the following sentences, for example, and notice how our attitude toward Mr. Williams depends on the verb used to describe how he entered his office.

Mr. Williams went into his office.
Mr. Williams strode into his office.
Mr. Williams slunk into his office.
Mr. Williams retreated into his office.
Mr. Williams stomped into his office.
Mr. Williams scurried into his office.

Not only do skillful writers pay particular attention to the verbs they choose, they also make sure that they use these verbs correctly. The skillful selection of verbs is a matter of style; their proper use is a matter of grammar. This chapter will help you use verbs correctly.

 ## THE TYPES OF VERBS

Most of the verbs we use express *action*. *Hit, run, type, write, yell, sleep, instruct, direct, explode,* and thousands of others are **action verbs.** The other basic type of verb, to which we've referred briefly in earlier chapters, is the **linking verb,** a verb that joins or links one part of the sentence to another. For example:

Jan *is* the new department manager.
He *will be* very happy.
They *were* excited.
He *looks* sick.
She *appeared* nervous.

A linking verb does not express action. Instead, as the above sentences demonstrate, it expresses a condition or a state of being. For this reason linking verbs are also known as **state-of-being verbs.** The most important and most frequently used linking verb is *to be* in all of its forms. Other linking verbs include *feel, seem, appear, taste, sound,* and *look.*

If you aren't sure whether a verb is an action verb or a linking verb, try to picture in your mind the event described. Action verbs depict an event you can easily visualize; it is much more difficult to visualize the event referred to by linking verbs. Compare these two sentences:

The automobile swerved off the road.
It seems a good idea.

In your imagination you can probably picture the car *swerving,* but can you picture something *seeming?* Note that the linking verb *seems* can be replaced by the word *is.* This is true of all linking verbs. They do little more than stand in place of the word *is.*

It *seems* a good idea.
It *is* a good idea.

Some verbs may be either action verbs or linking verbs depending on how they are used in a sentence. Compare the use of the verb *taste* in the following sentences:

The cook *tasted* the soup to see if it was properly seasoned.
This soup *tastes* salty.

In the first sentence, *taste* is an action verb. It names the action of the cook in sampling the soup. In the second sentence, however, *taste* is a linking verb. It merely links the quality of saltiness to the subject *soup.* The word *is* could replace the word *tastes.*

This soup *tastes* salty.
This soup *is* salty.

Remember:

1. All forms of the verb *to be (am, are, is, was, were, be, being, been),* whether they appear alone or in combination with another verb, are linking verbs. A chart listing in full all these forms appears in Chapter 7.
2. Verbs such as *become, seem, appear, prove, grow, remain, feel, taste, sound, look,* and *smell* are linking verbs when they can be replaced by the word *is.* When they cannot be replaced by the word *is,* they are action verbs.

Linking Verbs:

Candy tastes (is) sweet.
Velvet feels (is) soft.
Buttermilk smells (is) sour.
The instructor appears (is) tired.

Action Verbs:

Taste the candy.
The dressmaker feels the cloth to determine its softness.
We smelled the flowers before we saw them.
Just as the class was preparing to leave, the instructor appeared in the doorway.

 # THE SIMPLE TENSES

Verbs change their form depending on the time of the event they depict. We call the different forms a verb may take the *tenses* of the verb.

You probably know and use correctly the three simple tenses: the *present* tense, the *past* tense, and the *future* tense. You would never say *I will go to the bank yesterday* because you know that when you refer to an action that occurred yesterday, you must use the past tense of the verb *to go*. You would correctly say *I went to the bank yesterday*.

Just as a review, however, here is an outline of the proper use of the three simple tenses:

1. The present tense is used to denote three types of action:

    a. It describes action going on at the present time.
        I am satisfied.   He is here.

    b. It describes action that is continued or habitual.
        I see him every day.   We sell hardware.

    c. It denotes a general truth.
        Cats are animals.   Candy is sweet.

    Remember: The third person singular *(he, she, it)* form of the verb always ends in *s* or *es*.

    He works.   She goes.   It is.

2. The past tense refers to a definite past event or action.

    I typed the letter this morning.
    I went to the movies yesterday.
    I sold the books last year.

Note: When you are asking a question in the simple present or past tense, the form is somewhat different. You do not say:

See you him every day?
Sells he hardware?

You say:

Do you see him every day?
Does he sell hardware?

You do not say:

Went you to the movies yesterday?
Sold he the books last year?

You say:

Did you go to the movies yesterday?
Did he sell the books last year?

The words *do, does,* and *did,* which you use in asking questions, are used only in the simple present and past tenses. Because they are used in these sentences to assist the main verb, they are known as **helping verbs** or **auxiliaries.**

These auxiliary verbs can also be used in making statements. For example:

You do see him every day.
He does sell hardware.
We did go to the movies yesterday.
I did sell the books last year.

These sentences illustrate the *emphatic* form of the verb, which is used to give greater emphasis to the action expressed by the verb.

Do, does, and *did* are also used to express negation.

> He does not sell hardware.
> We did not go to the movies yesterday.
> You do not see him every day.

You have undoubtedly been using these expressions correctly for years, so they should cause you little trouble.

3. The future tense applies to events that will take place at a future time. You form the future tense by placing *will* or *shall* before the verb.

At one time there were precise distinctions involving persons and kinds of expressions regarding when to use *shall* and when to use *will*. Most business writers no longer observe these distinctions. They use *will* for all persons and for all kinds of expressions. The use of *shall* is limited to the following situations:

1. Questions asking for permission are frequently begun with *shall*.

> Shall I call ahead for reservations?
> Shall I send in the next applicant?

2. In legal documents *shall* is used to express obligation.

> The undersigned shall pay to the lender the sum of Eight Hundred Dollars ($800).

The precise distinctions formerly applied to *should* (past tense of *shall*) and *would* (past tense of *will*) are also no longer observed. *Should* is used to express obligation, possibility, or probability. In all other situations use *would*.

> I should finish grading these exams before going to bed. (*obligation*)
> Unless something unexpected happens, I should have your exams for you by next class meeting. (*probability*)
> Should school be closed Wednesday due to snow, the examination will be rescheduled. (*possibility*)

 # PROGRAMMED REINFORCEMENT

S1   Circle one: A verb is a word that generally expresses (a) action, (b) the name of a place, (c) a description.

R1   (a) action

S2   There are two types of verbs, action verbs and _____ verbs.

R2   linking

S3   A linking verb like **seems** expresses state of being, not action. It may be replaced by the verb _____.

R3   is

S4   Verbs relating to the senses may often be either linking or action verbs depending on the way they're used. Circle the verb that expresses action:
a. **The boy tasted the cake.**
b. **The cake tasted good.**

R4   a. **tasted**

S5   In the sentence **The flower smells sweet,** the verb **smells** is a(n) (action, linking) verb.

R5   linking

S6   In the following groups of verbs, two are always action verbs; the others are usually linking verbs. Circle the two action verbs: **appear, become, seem, write, feel, speak.**

R6   **write; speak**

S7   Circle one: The tense of a verb is related to (a) person, (b) degree, (c) time.

R7   c. time

S8   There are three simple verb tenses: the _____, the _____, and the _____.

R8   present; past; future

S9   Consider the verb **to be.** In the first person singular the present tense would be **Now I _____ here.** The past tense would be **Yesterday I _____ here.** The simple future tense would be **Tomorrow I _____ here.**

R9   **am; was; will be**

S10   When we want to ask a question in the present or past tense, we need to use one of three helping verbs: _____, _____, and _____.

R10   do, does, did

S11   When **do, does,** and **did** are used as helping verbs in a statement, this is known as the _____ form of the verb.

R11   emphatic

S12   At one time there were a number of rules regarding the use of *shall* and *will* in forming the future tense. Most business writers today (do, do not) observe these rules. They form the future tense by placing _____ before the verb.

R12   do not; will

S13   Current practice is to use *shall* rather than *will* in which of the following situations? (a) In questions asking for permission, (b) in legal documents to express obligation, (c) in statements to express great emotion.

R13   (a) and (b)

S14 In choosing between *should* and *would,* you generally use _____ to express obligation, possibility, and probability; otherwise you use _____.

R14   should; would

S15 Use either *should* or *would* to complete each of the following sentences.
1. I _____ like to see your résumé.
2. I _____ have my résumé professionally typed.
3. I _____ have my résumé professionally typed if I could afford it.

R15   1. would, 2. should, 3. would

Turn to Exercises 6.1 and 6.2.

THE PERFECT TENSES

There are three other tenses in English—the *perfect* tenses. They are called the perfect tenses because they refer to an action that is completed or *perfected* at the time of the statement. The three perfect tenses are the *present perfect* tense, the *past perfect* tense, and the *future perfect* tense. Each perfect tense requires a form of the verb *to have* as a helping verb plus a special form of the main verb called the *past participle*. For example, *brought* is the past participle of the verb *to bring*.

> *Present perfect:* has or have brought
> *Past perfect:* had brought
> *Future perfect:* will have brought

We'll examine the formation of the past participle in the next chapter. First, let's examine each of these three perfect tenses.

 ## THE PRESENT PERFECT

The present perfect tense refers to an action that was completed in the past but is part of a series of actions that is continuing into the present. You form the present perfect tense by combining the verb *has* or *have* (depending on the subject) with the past participle of the main verb. For example:

Luis has filed only one report so far.

This means that Luis filed a report; the phrase *so far* indicates he will probably file more reports.
Here are some more sentences illustrating the use of the present perfect tense.

1. He has shopped in our store many times.

Has shopped indicates that you expect him to shop some more at your store. If you don't expect him back, you would say *He shopped in our store many times*. The simple past tense *shopped* shows that the action is completed once-and-for-all.

2.   Kareem and Jane's bickering has gone on for years.

Has gone indicates that it is still going on. If the bickering had finally stopped, then you would say *Kareem and Jane's bickering went on for years.*

3.   The O'Briens have traveled to this park year after year.

Do the O'Briens intend to come back again? Certainly. *Have traveled* indicates they expect to continue to do so. If they didn't expect to return any more you would say *The O'Briens traveled to this park year after year.*
  Thus the decision whether to use the simple past or the present perfect depends on the precise meaning you wish to convey.

1.   Ms. Pulaski (came) (has come) to see us on many occasions.

Which is right, *came* or *has come?* The answer depends on what we mean. If Ms. Pulaski still comes to see us, then use *has come. Ms. Pulaski has come to see us on many occasions.* But if Ms. Pulaski doesn't visit us any more, use *came. Ms. Pulaski came to see us on many occasions.*

2.   The boys (spoiled) (have spoiled) their little sister.

If she is still being spoiled: *The boys have spoiled their little sister.* If she is no longer being spoiled: *The boys spoiled their little sister.*

3.   Our offices (were) (have been) on the same corner for years.

If they still are on that corner, use *have been. Our offices have been on the same corner for years.* If they have been moved elsewhere: *Our offices were on the same corner for years.*
  Note 1: The present perfect tense may also be used to indicate that an action has just been completed.

I have just finished reading Simon's report.
Eureka! I have found it.
Her plane has just landed.
Kareem and Jane's bickering has finally stopped.

Note 2: A common error is to substitute the present tense for the present perfect tense. Note these examples—and avoid making the error.

Right: I have been in this office for three months.
Wrong: I am in this office for three months.
Right: I have been living in this house since September.
Wrong: I am living in this house since September.

THE PAST PERFECT

You form the past perfect tense by combining the auxiliary verb *had* with the past participle of the principal verb. This tense denotes an action that was completed before another event, which was also in the past. For example:

I had shipped the order by the time the message arrived.
She had left before I completed the assignment.

It also indicates an action that was completed before a past time. For example:

It had stopped raining by noon.
By nightfall the shipment had arrived.

You should have no difficulty determining whether to use the simple past or past perfect tense if you remember that the past perfect always refers to an action completed before another event in the past.

1. We (completed) (had completed) the assignment three days before last Friday's deadline.

    Ask: Did one event occur before another occurred?
    Answer: Yes. The assignment was completed before the deadline.
    Therefore: Use the past perfect. *We had completed the assignment three days before last Friday's deadline.*

2. We (suspected) (had suspected) his statements even before we received the police report.

    Ask: Did one event occur before another occurred?
    Answer: Yes. We had suspected before we received the report.
    Therefore: Use the past perfect. *We had suspected his statements even before we received the police report.*

3. Spring (arrived) (had arrived) early last year.

    Ask: Did one event occur before another occurred?
    Answer: No. There is only one event—the arrival of spring.
    Therefore: Use the simple past. *Spring arrived early last year.*

4. Did he know that you (heard) (had heard) from the home office?

    Ask: Did one event occur before another occurred?
    Answer: Yes. You had heard before he did know. Even though this sentence is in the form of a question, treat it as an affirmative statement, as you learned to do in determining the subject and predicate of a sentence in Chapter 2. Treat this sentence as though it reads: *You had heard from the home office before he did know that.*
    Therefore: Use the past perfect tense. *Did he know that you had heard from the home office?*

 ## THE FUTURE PERFECT

The future perfect tense is used to show action that will be completed by a definite time in the future or before another event in the future occurs. You form it by combining *will have* with the past participle of the principal verb.

By the time the message arrives, John will have left.
By June 30 our firm will have completed its expansion plans.
I will have finished my report by noon tomorrow.

The decision whether to use the simple future or the future perfect is similar to that of whether to use the simple past or the past perfect. The three examples above all involve action that will be completed before another event or before a specific time. Look at this sentence, however:

Wrong: They will have submitted their report on Thursday.

The submission of the report will not take place before another event or specified time. Accordingly, the tense called for is the simple future, not the future perfect.

Right: They will submit their report on Thursday.

Here are several more examples:

I will complete this project on schedule.
I will have completed this project by the end of March.
In a few years they will open a branch office in DesPlaines.
By the time their branch office is open, we will have completed construction of our new facilities.

 SUMMARY OF TENSES

In English, then, there are six tenses of the verb: three simple tenses and three perfect tenses. The following outline summarizes these tenses and the relationship between the simple and perfect form of each.

TENSE	REFERS TO	EXAMPLE
Simple Present	An action going on in the present	arrive
Present Perfect	A completed action that is part of a continuing series of such actions	has arrived have arrived
Simple Past	A completed past action	arrived
Past Perfect	A completed past action that came before another completed past action	had arrived
Simple Future	A future action	will arrive
Future Perfect	A future action that will be completed before another future action or by a definite time in the future.	will have arrived

 PROGRAMMED REINFORCEMENT

S16   The perfect tenses are used to refer to an action that is _____ at the time of the statement.

R16   perfected *or* completed

S17   The form of the principal verb used in all perfect tenses is called the _____.

R17   past participle

S18   The present perfect tense always uses the helping verb _____ or _____.

R18   have; has

S19 Each perfect tense requires a form of **to have** as a helping verb in conjunction with the past participle. The three forms of **to have** that are used are: _____, _____, and _____.

R19 has, have, had

S20 The present perfect tense describes a past action that is part of a series of actions that continues through the present. Circle the present perfect tense: **Frank has worked here since 1960 when he was discharged from the army.**

R20 **has worked**

S21 Circle the correct sentence:
a. **She has been a good secretary, and still is!**
b. **She was a good secretary, and still is!**

R21 a.

S22 Identify the tenses of the verb in each sentence. Is the verb correct or incorrect?
a. **I am in this office for a year already.**
  Answer: _____ tense
b. **I have been in this office for a year already.**
  Answer: _____ tense

R22 a. Present tense—incorrect;
b. Present perfect—correct

S23 The past perfect tense describes an action that was completed (**before, after**) another action in the past. Circle the past perfect verbs in these two sentences:
a. **He had just left the office when the storm broke.**
b. **The accountant had checked the books before the bookkeeper arrived.**

R23 before;
a. **had left**;
b. **had checked**

S24 Since the past perfect tense, consisting of **had** and the past participle, always precedes another action in the past, what tense is the other verb in the sentence: **Mr. Smith learned that Ann had reported the error.**
Answer: _____ tense.

R24 **learned** is past tense

S25 The future perfect tense is used to show action that will be completed by a definite time in the future. It contains **will have.** Circle the future perfect tense: **I will have completed the book by the time they arrive.**

R25 **will have completed**

S26 Circle the correct sentence:
a. **They will have submitted the report by Friday.**
b. **They will submit the report by Friday.**

R26 a.

S27 To review: Circle the verbs in this sentence and indicate the tense of each: **Joe had expected the promotion, but Lee arrived, and nothing has been the same since.**
Answer: _____ tense; _____ tense; _____ tense

R27 **had expected**—past perfect; **arrived**—past tense; **has been**—present perfect

Turn to Exercises 6.3 to 6.6.

EXERCISE 6·1A   ACTION AND LINKING VERBS

Below is a list of verbs. In the space next to each verb mark *A* if it is an action verb; mark *L* if it is a linking verb; mark *E* if it could be either.

1. edit _____
2. spend _____
3. had been _____
4. programmed _____
5. lie _____
6. were _____
7. seem _____
8. inherit _____
9. would have been _____
10. looks _____
11. was _____
12. recline _____
13. rested _____

14. mail _____
15. becoming _____
16. thinks _____
17. tastes _____
18. embezzle _____
19. receives _____
20. feels _____
21. taste _____
22. smell _____
23. touch _____
24. appear _____
25. desire _____

EXERCISE 6·1B   ACTION AND LINKING VERBS

Find the verb of each sentence listed below and write it in the space provided. In the other space provided, write *A* if the verb is an action verb; write *L* if the verb is a linking verb.

		VERB	ACTION OR LINKING
1.	This booklet will show you how to cut fuel costs.	1. _____	_____
2.	We feel certain of your success.	2. _____	_____
3.	Did you feel the texture of the fabric?	3. _____	_____
4.	The meat tasted spoiled.	4. _____	_____
5.	I tasted the soup.	5. _____	_____
6.	This job becomes tedious after a few weeks.	6. _____	_____
7.	The situation looks promising.	7. _____	_____
8.	He will be there.	8. _____	_____
9.	She looked over the list of applicants.	9. _____	_____
10.	Lie down before dinner.	10. _____	_____
11.	Ms. Levi looked for her files.	11. _____	_____
12.	The exam looked very easy to everyone.	12. _____	_____
13.	The dinner smells delicious.	13. _____	_____
14.	I can smell the fumes from here.	14. _____	_____
15.	Did you taste those pies?	15. _____	_____
16.	Don't they taste too sweet?	16. _____	_____
17.	The advertisement appeared in yesterday's paper.	17. _____	_____
18.	I don't feel well.	18. _____	_____
19.	He feels bad about losing his job.	19. _____	_____
20.	Pedro appears certain of a promotion.	20. _____	_____

EXERCISE 6·2A   THE SIMPLE TENSES

Fill in the blanks by changing the verb to the indicated tense.

WORK

1. a. Present: I _____
   b. Past: They _____
   c. Simple future: We _____
   d. Emphatic present: You _____

SAY

4. a. Present: You _____
   b. Past: He _____
   c. Simple future: They _____
   d. Emphatic present: She _____

SELL

2. a. Present: He _____
   b. Past: You _____
   c. Simple future: I _____
   d. Emphatic past: They _____

BE

5. a. Present: She _____
   b. Past: He _____
   c. Past: They _____
   d. Simple future: It _____

HEAR

3. a. Present: They _____
   b. Past: We _____
   c. Simple future: You _____
   d. Emphatic past: I _____

EXERCISE 6·2B   COMPOSITION: THE SIMPLE TENSES

Compose complete sentences containing the specified forms of the verbs in parentheses.

1. (first person simple future tense of *pay*)

_____

2. (third person simple past tense of *be*)

_____

3. (third person past emphatic tense of *buy*)

_____

4. (third person present tense of *sell*)

_____

5. (second person emphatic present tense of *work*)

_____

EXERCISE 6·3A   THE PERFECT TENSES

In the space provided, write the correct verb for each of the following sentences.

1.   Ever since I entered the room, the clerk (do) nothing.   1. _____
2.   The former governor (be) in office for one term.   2. _____
3.   We (be) here for the past hour.   3. _____
4.   We (go) shopping three times last week.   4. _____
5.   The present governor (be) in office for seven years.   5. _____
6.   Since you left the sales floor, there (be) very little activity.   6. _____
7.   I (be) in this office since 9 A.M.   7. _____
8.   He (hold) the position for nearly twenty years now.   8. _____
9.   She (fly) to Chicago last week.   9. _____
10. I (work) on this job since graduating.   10. _____
11. The computer (be) down for nearly an hour.   11. _____
12. The clerk (do) nothing the entire time I was in the room.   12. _____
13. Profits (drop) sharply since the remodeling of the mall began.   13. _____
14. The computer (be) down most of yesterday afternoon.   14. _____
15. Because he was unemployed, he (default) on his loan.   15. _____

EXERCISE 6·3B   THE PERFECT TENSES

In the space provided, write the correct verb for each of the following sentences.

1. The mail (arrive) before we opened the office.   1. _____

2. Our department (ship) the order before we received your wire.   2. _____

3. We (see) him distributing leaflets last week.   3. _____

4. Your officers (be) very courteous to us throughout yesterday's meeting.   4. _____

5. The inspector found that the crowd (be) dispersed before she arrived.   5. _____

6. We saw smoke just after we (hear) the explosion.   6. _____

7. As the bell rang, I (finish) answering the final question.   7. _____

8. By the time the bell rang, I (finish) answering the final question.   8. _____

9. My supervisor (dictate) five letters by noon.   9. _____

10. By 10 A.M. I (contact) every member of the committee.   10. _____

EXERCISE 6·3C   THE PERFECT TENSES

In the space provided, write the correct verb for each of the following sentences.

1. She (finish) her report by then.   1. _____

2. By the time this message reaches you, we (finalize) our plans.   2. _____

3. I (drive) you to the airport tomorrow.   3. _____

4. I (escort) you to lunch after the conference.   4. _____

5. By noon Wednesday we (withdraw) the offer.   5. _____

6. We (withdraw) the offer on Wednesday.   6. _____

7. We (implement) these changes by the time you return from your vacation.   7. _____

8. Ms. Hodge (reach) the motel by dark.   8. _____

9. When will she (reach) the motel?   9. _____

10. By the time you arrive we (sell) most of the special items.   10. _____

EXERCISE 6·4   VERB TENSES

Verbs in each of the following sentences have been italicized. In the spaces provided write the tense of each italicized verb.

1. She *does expect* to receive a reply soon.   1. _____

2. Ted *met* with his accountant yesterday.   2. _____

3. Sheila *has been employed* by Wareman's since 1975.   3. _____

4. The motion *had been made* and *seconded* before Fred could voice an objection.   4. _____

5. By the time Diana has edited the first portion of the manuscript, Keith *will have written* another section.   5. _____

6. In April we *will have been affiliated* with Xerxes Corporation for two years.   6. _____

7. You *do understand* my position, don't you?   7. _____

8. Unless we are able to reach an agreement by Friday, we *will be forced* to submit the dispute to binding arbitration.   8. _____

9. My car *depreciated* in value nearly 30 percent during the first twelve months.   9. _____

10. The department assistants *had collated* and *stapled* the class handouts by noon.   10. _____

EXERCISE 6·5   VERB TENSES

The following letter contains many intentional errors in verb tenses. Cross out all errors and make the necessary corrections in the space above them.

Dear Ms. Akeo:

During the last four years we have come to think of you as one of our best customers. You had sent us an order regularly every other week. That was why we are puzzled now. You always express your complete satisfaction with our products and service. Our records indicated that we have not received an order from you in nearly two months. Had something happened? Possibly something has developed of which we are unaware.

If we have made a mistake in filling an order, if a letter has been answered improperly, or if you are disappointed in one of our products, please let us know. We at Clarkson Company valued our good customers and will try to keep our good customers satisfied. A satisfied customer was the foundation of our company. We did not feel satisfied until you were.

If there will be a problem, please let us know so that we can correct it. If not, won't you please review the list of our latest merchandise, which I have enclosed. You noticed that we instituted a new type of billing procedure that I think you would have liked. It is more convenient for you than our previous one. I also wanted to bring to your attention the current wholesale price reductions: there is a 15 percent reduction in the deluxe line and a 20 percent reduction in the standard and budget lines. These reductions were explained more fully on the enclosed list.

These new prices and procedures will have illustrated our continuing efforts to satisfy our customers. Why not take advantage of them by placing an order today? We have hoped to hear from you soon.

                       Very truly yours,

EXERCISE 6·6   COMPOSITION: VERB TENSES

There is an error in the use of verbs in each of the following sentences. Correct the error. Then, in one or more complete sentences, explain as specifically as you can the reasons for any changes you made.

1. We had solved our cash flow problem last year.

   _____

2. The board members agreed on this plan of action before they adjourned for lunch.

   _____

3. Lois's chronic absenteeism will have caused her to be fired.

   _____

4. Irene will complete her analysis by the end of the week.

   _____

5. Right now Edgar planned to major in business education.

   _____

7

VERBS II
PROGRESSIVE FORM, PRINCIPAL PARTS, TRANSITIVE/INTRANSITIVE VERBS

THE PROGRESSIVE FORM, PRINCIPAL PARTS OF THE VERB, TRANSITIVE AND INTRANSITIVE VERBS

THE PROGRESSIVE FORM

In Chapter 6 we discussed the six tenses of the verb and the forms used to show them. Now we are going to look at a special form of the verb called the **progressive form.** The progressive form is used to show that the action described is continuing or unfinished at the time indicated by one of the six tenses. Look at these sentences:

I am working on the books right now.

This means that you are at work on the books at present and have not finished them yet. Your work is unfinished.

I was studying when Jean came in.

This means that your studying was interrupted by Jean. You were not finished studying. Your studying was unfinished.

Notice that each of the principal verbs—*working* and *studying*—ends in *ing.* The form of the verb to which *ing* is added is called the *present participle.* Also notice that each is preceded by a form of the verb *to be.* In other words, to indicate that an action is, was, or will be unfinished, use the progressive form of the verb, which is formed by using the appropriate form of the verb *to be* with the *ing* form of the principal verb (the present participle).

Here are the progressive forms of the verb *to phone* for the six tenses, using the third person singular.

Present progressive: She is phoning all our clients.
Past progressive: She was phoning all our clients.
Future progressive: She will be phoning all our clients.
Present perfect progressive: She has been phoning all our clients.
Past perfect progressive: She had been phoning all our clients.
Future perfect progressive: She will have been phoning all our clients.

Occasionally you will have to decide whether to use a simple tense or the progressive form. Just ask yourself if the action is or was finished. If finished, use the simple tense. If unfinished, use the progressive.

1. I (walked, was walking) down the street yesterday when the wind blew my hat off.

    Ask: Was the action finished?
    Answer: No. It was interrupted by the hat incident.
    Therefore: Use the progressive form. *I was walking down the street when the wind blew my hat off.* (Past Progressive)

2. He (writes) (is writing) the report at this very moment.

    Ask: Is the action finished?
    Answer: No. He is still working on the report.
    Therefore: Use the progressive form. *He is writing the report at this very moment.* (Present Progressive)

3. We (stuffed) (were stuffing) envelopes every day last week.

    Ask: Was the action finished?
    Answer: Yes. It was completed by the end of the week.
    Therefore: Use the simple tense. *We stuffed envelopes every day last week.*

4. They (worked) (were working) feverishly until dawn.

    Ask: Was the action finished?
    Answer: Yes. This is tricky. Dawn did not interrupt their work. It merely marked the moment when they stopped work.
    Therefore: Use the simple tense. *They worked feverishly until dawn.* (Simple Past)
    But: They were working feverishly when time ran out.

5. I (listened) (was listening) to the radio when the accident happened.

    Ask: Was the action completed?
    Answer: No. It was interrupted by the accident.
    Therefore: Use the progressive form. *I was listening to the radio when the accident happened.* (Past Progressive)

6. They will be working on the final copy by the time you arrive. (Future Progressive)

    By now you should know exactly why *will be working* is required, and not *will work.*

 # THE PRINCIPAL PARTS OF THE VERB

In the outline of the six tenses, the verb *to arrive* was used. Did you notice that all six tenses were formed by using either *arrive* or *arrived* plus a helping verb (the simple present and past, of course, require no helping verb)?

REGULAR VERBS

This is true of most verbs. Most verbs are what we call **regular verbs.** By this we mean that they form the past tense merely by adding *d* or *ed* to the present tense, and they form the present perfect tense by placing the word *has* or *have* before the present tense, which is identical in form to the past participle. For example, the following are some regular verbs:

PRESENT	PAST	PRESENT PERFECT
receive	received	has or have received
like	liked	has or have liked
allow	allowed	has or have allowed
call	called	has or have called

Note: Regular verbs ending in a consonant plus *y* change the *y* to *i* and add *ed.*

cry	cried	has or have cried
comply	complied	has or have complied

These three forms—present, past, and perfect; or present, past, and past participle—are known as the **principal parts** of the verb. By knowing these principal parts you can form all simple and perfect tenses. Because so many verbs are regular verbs—that is, verbs that form the past tense and past participle by simply adding *d* or *ed*—you automatically know the principal parts of these verbs. Therefore, you can form all six tenses without any difficulty. Here, for example, are the six tenses of the verb *to receive* for all persons:

PRESENT TENSE	SINGULAR	PLURAL
First person:	I receive	we receive
Second person:	you receive	you receive
Third person:	he, she, it receives	they receive

PAST TENSE		
First person:	I received	we received
Second person:	you received	you received
Third person:	he, she, it received	they received

FUTURE TENSE		
First person:	I will receive	we will receive
Second person:	you will receive	you will receive
Third person:	he, she, it will receive	they will receive

PRESENT PERFECT TENSE		
First person:	I have received	we have received
Second person:	you have received	you have received
Third person:	he, she, it has received	they have received

PAST PERFECT TENSE	SINGULAR	PLURAL
First person:	I had received	we had received
Second person:	you had received	you had received
Third person:	he, she, it had received	they had received

FUTURE PERFECT TENSE	SINGULAR	PLURAL
First person:	I will have received	we will have received
Second person:	you will have received	you will have received
Third person:	he, she, it will have received	they will have received

 # IRREGULAR VERBS

Many verbs, however, do not form their past and perfect tenses in this regular manner. For this reason they are called **irregular verbs.** The two most common irregular verbs are used to form the perfect and the progressive tenses—*to be* and *to have.* The principal parts of *to have* are *have* (or *has*), *had,* and *had.* The verb *to be*—the most important verb in the language—is also the most irregular. The following chart details this important verb in all its forms.

PRESENT TENSE	SINGULAR	PLURAL
First person:	I am	we are
Second person:	you are	you are
Third person:	he, she, it is	they are

PAST TENSE	SINGULAR	PLURAL
First person:	I was	we were
Second person:	you were	you were
Third person:	he, she, it was	they were

FUTURE TENSE	SINGULAR	PLURAL
First person:	I will be	we will be
Second person:	you will be	you will be
Third person:	he, she, it will be	they will be

PRESENT PERFECT TENSE	SINGULAR	PLURAL
First person:	I have been	we have been
Second person:	you have been	you have been
Third person:	he, she, it has been	they have been

PAST PERFECT TENSE	SINGULAR	PLURAL
First person:	I had been	we had been
Second person:	you had been	you had been
Third person:	he, she, it had been	they had been

FUTURE PERFECT TENSE	SINGULAR	PLURAL
First person:	I will have been	we will have been
Second person:	you will have been	you will have been
Third person:	he, she, it will have been	they will have been

Fortunately the other irregular verbs are not this irregular. In fact, most follow one of several basic patterns and thus can be grouped into "families." For instance, there is obvious similarity among these forms:

drink	drank	drunk
sink	sank	sunk
shrink	shrank	shrunk

The following list groups words according to these patterns. When studying these word families, be sure to read them *aloud* so that you can *hear* the similarities. *Hearing* these sound patterns is the quickest and surest way to master the principal parts of these verbs. No helping verb has been provided with the past participle because the helping verb will change with the tense and speaker. In the case of the past participle *drunk*, for example, the perfect tense would be *has drunk* (third person singular) or *have drunk* (all other persons); the past perfect would be *had drunk;* the future perfect would be *will have drunk.*

1. *Present*	*Past*	*Past Participle*
think	thought	thought
bring	brought	brought
buy	bought	bought
fight	fought	fought
seek	sought	sought
teach	taught	taught

2. *Present*	*Past*	*Past Participle*
begin	began	begun
swim	swam	swum
ring	rang	rung
sing	sang	sung
spring	sprang	sprung
sink	sank	sunk
shrink	shrank	shrunk
drink	drank	drunk
run	ran	run

3. *Present*	*Past*	*Past Participle*
blow	blew	blown
grow	grew	grown
know	knew	known
throw	threw	thrown
fly	flew	flown
draw	drew	drawn
withdraw	withdrew	withdrawn
wear	wore	worn
swear	swore	sworn
tear	tore	torn
show	showed	shown

4.

Present	Past	Past Participle
bend	bent	bent
lend	lent	lent
spend	spent	spent
deal	dealt	dealt
feel	felt	felt
keep	kept	kept
sleep	slept	slept
sweep	swept	swept
weep	wept	wept
mean	meant	meant
leave	left	left
lose	lost	lost

5.

Present	Past	Past Participle
break	broke	broken
choose	chose	chosen
freeze	froze	frozen
speak	spoke	spoken
steal	stole	stolen
forget	forgot	forgotten

6.

Present	Past	Past Participle
strive	strove	striven
arise	arose	arisen
take	took	taken
mistake	mistook	mistaken
shake	shook	shaken
write	wrote	written
typewrite	typewrote	typewritten
underwrite	underwrote	underwritten
eat	ate	eaten
fall	fell	fallen
forbid	forbade	forbidden
give	gave	given
hide	hid	hidden

7. The verbs in this group are irregular because they don't change at all. They are the same in the present, past, and perfect tenses.

Present	Past	Past Participle
bid	bid	bid
burst	burst	burst
cost	cost	cost
cut	cut	cut
forecast	forecast	forecast
hurt	hurt	hurt
let	let	let
put	put	put
quit	quit	quit
read	read	read
spread	spread	spread
thrust	thrust	thrust

8. The verbs in this final group don't belong to any of the above families and illustrate a variety of patterns. Say the words aloud until they sound familiar.

Present	Past	Past Participle
come	came	come
become	became	become
bleed	bled	bled
lead	led	led
flee	fled	fled
get	got	got
meet	met	met
bind	bound	bound
stand	stood	stood
win	won	won
hold	held	held
stick	stuck	stuck
strike	struck	struck
string	strung	strung
have	had	had
say	said	said
make	made	made
do	did	done
go	went	gone

 PROGRAMMED REINFORCEMENT

S1 The **progressive form** of the verb ends in _____. It is known as the _____ _____.

R1 ing; present participle

S2 In the sentence **I am reading now,** the progressive form of the verb means that the action is (finished, unfinished).

R2 unfinished

S3 The simple tense and the progressive form often seem interchangeable. The progressive form, however, should be used when the action is (finished, unfinished). Circle the correct sentence: (a) **I was typing when the ribbon broke.** (b) **I typed when the ribbon broke.**

R3 unfinished
(a)

S4 1. **Maria (enter) the room right now.** The correct form of the verb **enter** is _____.
2. **We (shelve) merchandise all day.** The correct form of the verb **shelve** is _____.
3. **We (watch) television when the power went out.** The correct form of the verb **watch** is _____.

R4 1. **is entering** (present perfect)
2. **shelved** (simple past)
3. **were watching** (past perfect)

S5 The **present tense,** the **past tense,** and the **perfect tense (past participle)** of the verb are known as the _____ _____ _____ of the verb.

R5 principal parts

S6 Verbs may form their past and perfect tenses in a regular or an _____ manner.

R6 irregular

S7 The verb **walk** is an example of a _____ verb. Its principal parts are: present: _____; past: _____; past participle: _____.

R7 regular; walk, walked, walked

S8 In a regular verb, the past tense and the _____ _____ are identical.

R8 past participle

S9 Which of the following are regular verbs? **call, try, bring, teach, talk**

R9 **call, try, talk**

S10 The verb **drink** is a(n) _____ verb. Write the principal parts of the verb **drink**: Present: _____; Past: _____; Past Participle: _____

R10 irregular; drink, drank, drunk

S11 **I brought the list to the manager who had begun the inventory.** The tense of **brought** is _____; the tense of **had begun** is _____.

R11 past; past perfect

S12 Fill in the appropriate verbs:

Present tense	Past tense	Past participle
	drew	
tear		
		flown

R12 draw, drew, drawn; tear, tore, torn; fly, flew, flown

S13

Present tense	Past tense	Past participle
		grown
spring		
	shrank	

R13 grow, grew, grown; spring, sprang, sprung; shrink, shrank, shrunk

S14 Write the correct verbs in these sentences:
a. **I went along because I (think) you knew the answer.** _____
b. **He (quit) the team last week.** _____
c. **Our pipes have (freeze).** _____

R14 a. **thought;** b. **quit;** c. **frozen**

S15 Write the correct verbs in these sentences:
a. **I (swim) early in the morning yesterday.** _____
b. **The fire has (blow) out.** _____
c. **He had (see) things on his trip.** _____

R15 a. **swam;** b. **blown;** c. **seen**

> S16   Write the correct verbs in these sentences:
>   a. **He has (choose) a few samples.**   _____
>   b. **The pipe (burst) in the factory.**   _____
>   c. **The dinner has (cost) me more in
>   the past.**   _____

R16   a. **chosen;** b. **burst;**
        c. **cost**

Turn to Exercises 7.1 to 7.3.

 # TRANSITIVE AND INTRANSITIVE VERBS

You know that a sentence must have a noun or pronoun as its subject and a verb as its predicate, but you can combine a noun and a verb and still not have a meaningful sentence.

The student mailed . . .

Although this expression contains a subject/noun *student* and a predicate/verb *mailed*, it is incomplete by itself. It lacks an explanation of what was mailed. What is needed is an object of the verb *mailed*—a word that will tell us what was mailed. For example: *The student mailed the package. Package* is the object of the verb *mailed* because it tells us what was mailed.

To find the object of a verb, you merely ask yourself Whom? or What? after the verb. *The student mailed . . .* What? The *package. Package* is the object of the verb *mailed. The President gave . . .* What? A speech. *Speech* is the object of the verb *gave. John loves . . .* Whom? Naomi. *Naomi* is the object of John's affections.

Of course, many verbs do not require objects to complete the meaning of a sentence. For example:

The President spoke.

Here the verb *spoke* is complete without an object.

The plaster shook.
The group met.

A verb that needs an object to make sense is called a **transitive verb** because the action *transfers* to the object. *Milos put the letter on the table. Put* is transitive; *letter* is its object. A verb that does not take an object is called an **intransitive verb.** Its action is complete in itself. *Milos sleeps on the couch every afternoon. Sleeps* is intransitive. It does not take an object.

The verbs *lie* and *lay, sit* and *set,* and *rise* and *raise* are frequently confused. Once you are familiar with the difference between transitive and intransitive verbs, however, deciding which is the proper verb should be simple.

 ## LIE/LAY

Look at the pair *lie* and *lay.* These two words are probably confused more often than any other pair of words in the language. Yet they have very different meanings:

To lie means *to recline. To lie* is *intransitive.*
To lay means *to place. To place* is *transitive.*

Memorize the principal parts of these two verbs:

Present	Past	Past Participle
lie	lay	lain
lay	laid	laid

Here are some sentences using *lie*.

Present tense: I lie on the grass.
Past tense: I lay on the grass yesterday.
Perfect tense: I have lain on the grass every afternoon this week.

Here are some sentences using *lay*.

Present tense: I lay the book on the table.
Past tense: I laid the book on the table yesterday.
Perfect tense: I have laid the book on the table as you requested.

Because *lie* is intransitive, it never needs an object to complete its meaning. Because *lay* is transitive, it always needs an object to complete its meaning. Look at these examples:

1. I lay the book on the table.
    Lay what? The book.

2. *I lie on the grass.*
    Lie what? No answer. Lie does not take an object.

3. I laid the carpeting yesterday.
    Laid what? The carpeting.

4. I lay in bed all day yesterday.
    Lay what? No answer. Lay, the past tense of lie, does not take an object.

5. They have laid their cards on the table.
    Have laid what? Their cards.

6. He has lain in a hospital bed for over a month.
    Has lain what? No answer. Lain does not take an object.

Let's try some problems using this method.

7. The workers have (laid, lain) the vinyl flooring in the kitchen.
    Have (laid, lain) what? *The vinyl flooring.* Therefore, *laid* is correct because *laid* always takes an object. *The workers have laid the vinyl flooring in the kitchen.*

8. The books have (laid, lain) on the shelves for years.
    Have (laid, lain) what? No answer. Therefore, use *lain* because *lain* never takes an object. *The books have lain on the shelves for years.*

If you understand the difference between *lie* and *lay*, you will easily master the distinction between *sit* and *set* and between *rise* and *raise*.

 # SIT/SET

To sit means *to be seated. To sit* is *intransitive*.
To set means *to place. To set* is *transitive*.

Memorize their principal parts:

Present	Past	Past Participle
sit	sat	sat
set	set	set

For example:

The director sits at the head of the table.
The director sat at the head of the table yesterday.
The director has sat at the head of the table at every meeting.
He sets the diskette on top of the monitor.
He set the diskette on top of the monitor yesterday.
He has set the diskette on top of the monitor as you requested.

Again *sit* never takes an object to complete its meaning. It is intransitive. *Set* is transitive and always needs an object to complete its meaning. It requires a word to tell us what was set.

Michael can (sit, set) in front of the computer for hours.

(Sit, set) what? No answer. Therefore, use *sit* since *sit* never takes an object.

Michael can sit in front of the computer for hours.

 # RISE/RAISE

To rise means *to get up. To rise* is *intransitive.*
To raise means *to lift. To raise* is *transitive.*

These two verbs have the following principal parts. Memorize them.

Present	Past	Past Participle
rise	rose	risen
raise	raised	raised

For example:

I rise early every morning.
I rose early yesterday.
I have risen early every morning this week.
We raise the flag each morning.
We raised the flag at dawn this morning.
We have raised the flag every morning this summer.

Once more, *rise* never takes an object to complete its meaning. It is intransitive. *Raise* is transitive and always needs an object to complete its meaning. It requires a word to tell us what was raised.

1. After she fell, she (rose, raised) herself from the floor.
    (Rose, raised) what? Herself. Therefore, use *raised* because *raised* always takes an object.
    She raised herself.

2. The balloon (rose, raised) from the ground.
    (Rose, raised) what? No answer. Therefore, use *rose* because *rose* never takes an object.
    The balloon rose from the ground.

How can you remember all these distinctions? Here's a trick. The word *intransitive* begins with the letter *i* and the three verbs which contains i's—*lie, sit, rise*— are intransitive; they do not require an object. The other three verbs—*lay, set, raise*— are transitive and thus require objects to complete their meaning.

Whenever there is no answer to the question *What?* after the verb, you know that the verb is intransitive and that it must be a form of the verbs *lie, sit,* or rise.

 # PROGRAMMED REINFORCEMENT

		S17	A sentence may be incomplete if the receiver of the action is not stated. **The officer approved the loan. Loan** is the "receiver" of the action. It is the _____ of the verb _____.
R17	object; **approved**	S18	To find the object of a verb, ask yourself **what** or _____ after the verb.
R18	**whom**	S19	Circle two objects of verbs in this sentence: **He complimented his assistant and gave a bonus to her.**
R19	**assistant; bonus**	S20	A verb that takes an object is called a **transitive** verb. A verb that does not need an object is called an _____ _____ verb.
R20	intransitive	S21	Circle the transitive verbs in these sentences: **He put the mail on the desk.** **The sun shines on the window.** **Lay the envelope on the desk.**
R21	**put; lay**	S22	**To lie** means to **recline; to lay** means **to place.** What are the three parts of the verb **to lie?** Present _____ Past _____ Past Participle _____. What are the three parts of the verb **to lay?** Present _____ Past _____ Past Participle _____.
R22	present, **lie;** past, **lay;** past participle, **lain;** present, **lay;** past, **laid;** past participle, **laid**	S23	Circle the verb that is intransitive: **to lie** or **to lay.**
R23	**to lie**	S24	Circle the correct forms: a. I wish **(to lie, to lay)** down on the couch. b. He has **(laid, lain)** on the grass for an hour.
R24	a. **to lie;** b. **lain**		

S25 Circle the correct forms:
a. She (**lay, laid**) the carpet on the floor.
b. I'm going to (**lie, lay**) down the law.

R25   a. **laid;** b. **lay**

S26   **Set** is a transitive verb; that means it needs an object to complete its meaning. Circle the object of **to set: I want you to set the table for two.**

R26   **table**

S27   **Sit** is intransitive, requiring no object. Which is correct? **Michelle likes to (sit, set) in front of the computer screen.**

R27   **sit**

S28   **Rise** is intransitive; it never takes an object. Which is correct? **The salesperson's speech will (raise, rise) the consumer's spirits.**

R28   **raise**

Turn to Exercises 7.4 to 7.6.

EXERCISE 7·1   **THE PROGRESSIVE FORM**

In the space provided, write the proper verb for each of the following sentences.

1. They (work) when the supervisor arrived.   1. _____
2. Ms. Chan (see) Mr. Pulaski in his office at this very minute.   2. _____
3. Last Christmas we (sell) hundreds of home video games.   3. _____
4. While we (talk) the phone rang.   4. _____
5. Lee Johnson (complete) the application right now.   5. _____
6. We (send) all our customers the new price list last month.   6. _____
7. Weren't you (visit) the home office when the fire broke out?   7. _____
8. They (leave) when the order was delivered.   8. _____
9. Yesterday we (file) the invoices that were received last week.   9. _____
10. She (try) to complete the assignment before she leaves today.   10. _____
11. I (send) you additional materials throughout the summer.   11. _____
12. We (receive) further information about this dramatic story as it
    develops.   12. _____
13. Now we (experience) the effects of last month's cutbacks.   13. _____
14. The pictures (develop) now.   14. _____
15. I (speak) with Ms. Chiaia when we were disconnected.   15. _____

EXERCISE 7·2A   **REGULAR VERBS**

Fill in the missing verbs in this table.

	PRESENT TENSE	PAST TENSE	PRESENT PERFECT TENSE
1.	work		has
2.		signed	has
3.	order		have
4.		replied	has
5.	notify		has
6.			have complained
7.		expected	has
8.	interfere		have
9.		convened	has
10.	adjourn		have

EXERCISE 7·2B   REGULAR VERBS

In the space provided, fill in the correct form of the verb for each of the following sentences.

1. Our agency (distribute) advertising leaflets for twelve years so far.

1. _____

2. By this time next week we (close) on the house.

2. _____

3. We hereby (acknowledge) receipt of your order.

3. _____

4. The board (submit) the dispute to binding arbitration last week.

4. _____

5. We (expect) your reply by next Monday.

5. _____

6. Ms. Perez (leave) for the airport when she was called to the phone.

6. _____

7. We (describe) this process in detail in the next issue.

7. _____

8. We (accumulate) too large an inventory last year.

8. _____

9. By this time last year we (accumulate) too large an inventory.

9. _____

10. The committee members (bicker) among themselves at yesterday's meeting.

10. _____

11. This morning we (invite) the mayor to attend our banquet.

11. _____

12. So far, 12 people (respond) to our questionnaire.

12. _____

13. Ms. Wu (work) here since 1965.

13. _____

14. Petra (study) for the accounting exam until midnight.

14. _____

15. Was he (allow) to examine your records?

15. _____

16. She always (attend) every meeting.

16. _____

17. Mr. Mintz (dictate) the letter right this minute.

17. _____

18. The message on the television screen read: "We (experience) technical difficulties. Please stand by."

18. _____

19. Elsa Swenson (grant) a leave of absence without pay.

19. _____

20. Mark (collate) all twelve copies of the proposal later today.

20. _____

EXERCISE 7·3A **IRREGULAR VERBS**

In the space provided, write the correct form of the verb shown in each of the following sentences.

1. I (awake) before dawn this morning.   1. _____
2. By the time he arrived, she had (become) very tired.   2. _____
3. He had (arise) by the time I called.   3. _____
4. I (bid) $50 for the vase at yesterday's auction.   4. _____
5. The dog had (bite) the pet store owner.   5. _____
6. The tire had (blow) out.   6. _____
7. All sales records have been (break).   7. _____
8. They have (build) a factory on the river.   8. _____
9. Yesterday the pipe (burst).   9. _____
10. Enrico was (choose) to accompany you.   10. _____
11. I have (come) to offer my condolences.   11. _____
12. By noon it had already (cost) me two weeks' salary.   12. _____
13. It was (cut) across the top.   13. _____
14. The problems were (deal) with as they (arise).   14. _____
15. Isaac had (do) no wrong.   15. _____
16. This convention has (draw) a huge crowd.   16. _____
17. He had (drink) too much.   17. _____
18. We discovered that prices had (fall).   18. _____
19. Father (forbid) their leaving the house.   19. _____
20. Bjorn has (fly) millions of miles.   20. _____
21. The weather bureau has (forecast) a storm.   21. _____
22. By morning the water had (freeze).   22. _____
23. The situation has (get) out of control.   23. _____
24. Ms. Moralez was (give) a raise.   24. _____
25. Most of the staff had already (go) home.   25. _____
26. Our company has (grow) rapidly in recent years.   26. _____
27. She has not (hear) of your product.   27. _____
28. The invoice was (hide) under a pile of paper.   28. _____
29. He had (hurt) himself.   29. _____
30. Have you (keep) all your receipts?   30. _____
31. Had I (know) of the detour, I would have (choose) a different road.   31. _____

32. She has (lose) her opportunity.

32. _____

33. Estelle has (lend) me the balance.

33. _____

34. David (mean) what he said.

34. _____

35. Chris had (meet) most of them before.

35. _____

36. I had (mistake) you for him.

36. _____

37. Your account is (overdraw).

37. _____

38. He has (prepay) the postage.

38. _____

39. Have you (read) the contract?

39. _____

40. We had (put) the matter before the board.

40. _____

41. Has she (quit) the gubernatorial race?

41. _____

42. The copies had been (run) off before noon.

42. _____

43. Colleen had (see) many examples of mismanagement.

43. _____

44. They have (seek) the answer in vain.

44. _____

45. The building (shake) under the force of the earthquake.

45. _____

46. Has Jonathan (show) you how to operate it?

46. _____

47. The profits (shrink) drastically last week.

47. _____

48. Beverly Sills has (sing) this opera many times.

48. _____

49. The ship had (sink) to the bottom.

49. _____

50. I (sleep) until noon yesterday.

50. _____

51. Had she (speak) to you about it?

51. _____

52. We (spend) several hours last night discussing the problem.

52. _____

53. The coil (spring) from its covering.

53. _____

54. Our company has always (stand) for the finest quality.

54. _____

55. The two pieces had (stick) together.

55. _____

56. Catastrophe (strike) the city.

56. _____

57. All year long Sarah (strive) for the top.

57. _____

58. The jury was (swear) to secrecy.

58. _____

59. The storm (sweep) all in its path.

59. _____

60. I (swim) at the lake last week.

60. _____

61. You have (take) too much.

61. _____

62. Had I (teach) the course, I would have (teach) it differently.

62. _____

63. Has she (tear) up those papers?

63. _____

64. I had (think) he was much taller.

64. _____

65. Mr. Wallace has (throw) his support to Mr. Magome.

65. _____

66. I have (tell) you how I feel about this.

66. _____

67. Sol's aunt (undertake) his obligations last week.

67. _____

68. The company had (underwrite) all his debts.

68. _____

69. Yesterday I (wear) my blue suit.

69. _____

70. He has (wear) a hole through his sleeve.

70. _____

EXERCISE 7·3B   **IRREGULAR VERBS**

On each line is printed the present tense of an irregular verb. Write the past tense and the present perfect tense of each of these verbs.

	PRESENT	PAST	PRESENT PERFECT
1.	I am	I _____	I _____
2.	You show	You _____	You _____
3.	It breaks	It _____	It _____
4.	It bursts	It _____	It _____
5.	They cost	They _____	They _____
6.	You deal	You _____	You _____
7.	We drive	We _____	We _____
8.	I forbid	I _____	I _____
9.	We fly	We _____	We _____
10.	They go	They _____	They _____
11.	I hide	I _____	I _____
12.	She knows	She _____	She _____
13.	I lead	I _____	I _____
14.	You mistake	You _____	You _____
15.	We pay	We _____	We _____
16.	He reads	He _____	He _____
17.	You seek	You _____	You _____
18.	I shrink	I _____	I _____
19.	We sing	We _____	We _____
20.	You speak	You _____	You _____
21.	I spend	I _____	I _____
22.	They stand	They _____	They _____
23.	We take	We _____	We _____
24.	She teaches	She _____	She _____
25.	We tear	We _____	We _____
26.	You throw	You _____	You _____
27.	I write	I _____	I _____
28.	He wears	He _____	He _____
29.	I withdraw	I _____	I _____
30.	You eat	You _____	You _____

EXERCISE 7·4A   VERBS AND THEIR OBJECTS

In the space provided, write the verb and the object of that verb for each of the following sentences.

		VERB	OBJECT OF VERB
1.	Mrs. Morris read the report.	1. _____	_____
2.	O'Brien sent me to the factory.	2. _____	_____
3.	Our firm makes the finest clothing.	3. _____	_____
4.	We appreciate your letter of September 20.	4. _____	_____
5.	We hear the important events of the day on the evening news.	5. _____	_____
6.	We will send our representatives next week.	6. _____	_____
7.	Will you mail your remittance tomorrow?	7. _____	_____
8.	We are enclosing a copy of the contract form.	8. _____	_____
9.	We discussed the entire matter with him.	9. _____	_____
10.	They advised her against the contract.	10. _____	_____

EXERCISE 7·4B   VERBS: TRANSITIVE AND INTRANSITIVE

This exercise involves the proper use of lie or lay; sit or set; and raise or rise. From the words in parentheses, choose the correct verb and write the correct form in the space provided.

1. Have you been (sit, set) here all afternoon?

2. Prices had (raise, rise) faster than expected.

3. The journal has (lie, lay) on the shelf for years.

4. They were so tired they just (sit, set) right down on the ground.

5. The plane will (rise, raise) beyond the clouds shortly.

6. (Rise, Raise) the curtains.

7. The auditor (lay, lie) the ledger on the desk.

8. Please (lie, lay) down.

9. He has (set, sit) in the same spot for hours.

10. The blame was (lie, lay) at her doorstep.

11. (Sit, Set) down at the table before the guests arrive.

12. Regulations have been (lie, lay) down by the board.

13. Have they (sit, set) long enough to be rested?

14. The value of this stock has (rise, raise) almost thirty points.

15. Do you intend to (raise, rise) an objection?

16. He will (lie, lay) the carpet tomorrow.

17. She (lay, lie) the foundations for a solid business.

18. (Sit, Set) down in that chair.

19. Can you (raise, rise) to the situation?

20. (Set, Sit) the table down carefully.

21. They had (lie, lay) the goods on top of the table.

22. Please (raise, rise) your hand if you agree.

23. We must try to (raise, rise) above such petty bickering.

24. (Sit, Set) the desk in the corner.

25. The reports have (lie, lay) on the table for weeks.

1. _____

2. _____

3. _____

4. _____

5. _____

6. _____

7. _____

8. _____

9. _____

10. _____

11. _____

12. _____

13. _____

14. _____

15. _____

16. _____

17. _____

18. _____

19. _____

20. _____

21. _____

22. _____

23. _____

24. _____

25. _____

146

EXERCISE 7·5 THE PROGRESSIVE FORM AND IRREGULAR VERBS

The following excerpt is from the manuscript of an article offering advice on interviewing for a job. It has many errors in the use of verbs. Cross out all errors and make the necessary changes in the space above them.

The interviewer will be evaluating you from the moment you step through the door until sometime after you leave. Thus it will be very important to have made a good first impression. Be sure to dress appropriately. If you are a man, you should have been wearing a coat and tie. If you were a woman, you should have worn a dress or suit. By all means be on time. Strove to arrive early if you could have. If for some reason you are delayed, call to have notified the interviewer and explain why. Arriving late will be making you feel nervous. It will also be giving the interviewer the impression that you are unreliable.

After you have came in, meeted the interviewer, and shaked hands, set down in the chair the interviewer will be indicating. While you were talking, don't be playing with objects like a pen or pencil you may have brung with you. An interviewer will be interpreting such obvious nervousness as an inability to perform well under pressure on the job itself. Above all, don't be fiddling with objects on the interviewer's desk. Let them lay there.

The interviewer will ask you about your past and present work experience. Don't evaluate your jobs. Just be describing them as accurately and as fully as you could. Don't say, "My last job isn't much. I was just waiting on tables. And the duties that I perform now aren't very demanding either." No matter how insignificant you thinked a job was, the interviewer will be seeing it as demonstrating your initiative, ability to work with others, and sense of responsibility.

EXERCISE 7·6   COMPOSITION: VERB TENSES

Compose complete sentences using the following verbs in the tenses called for in parentheses.

1. apply (future progressive) _____

2. speak (simple past) _____

3. lie (future perfect progressive) _____

4. begin (past perfect) _____

5. grow (present perfect) _____

6. give (future perfect) _____

7. invest (simple present) _____

8. mean (simple future) _____

9. set (past progressive) _____

10. raise (past perfect progressive) _____

8

VERBS III
AGREEMENT OF SUBJECT AND PREDICATE

AGREEMENT GUIDELINES

In the last two chapters you learned how to write all six tenses and the progressive form of both regular and irregular verbs. In this chapter we are going to look at the proper grammatical relationship between these verb forms and the subject of the sentence. We call this proper relationship the **agreement** of subject and predicate.

For a sentence to be grammatically correct, its predicate must agree with its subject in number. This means that if the subject is singular, you use a singular predicate. If the subject is plural, you use a plural predicate. Look at this sentence:

One person in this firm of hundreds (is, are) to be honored.

To solve this problem merely ask yourself: What is the subject of this sentence? Who is to be honored? *One person* is to be honored, not *this firm of hundreds.* Since the predicate must agree with the subject in number, use the singular predicate *is.* The sentence now reads: *One person in this firm of hundreds is to be honored.*

The following guidelines will help you determine whether to use a singular or a plural predicate.

 AGREEMENT GUIDELINES

 COMPOUND SUBJECT

Jack and Jill (is, are) going up the hill.

This problem sentence is easy. It contains two subjects (Jack, Jill) connected by *and.* The sentence means that both of them are going up the hill, so it calls for the plural predicate *are. Jack and Jill are going up the hill.*

This illustrates the general rule: Whenever a sentence contains two or more subjects connected by *and,* use a plural predicate. Usually this is obvious and natural:

The Acme Company and the Omega Company are merging.
Good keypunch operators and good programmers are in great demand.

There is one exception to this rule. When both subjects really refer to one person or one thing, use a singular predicate. For example:

The treasurer and secretary is here.

One person holds both positions. That person is here. If the positions are held by two different people, however, then the general rule applies:

The president and the secretary are here.
But: Bread and butter is my favorite snack.

Bread and *butter* are so closely identified in this sentence that they are considered one unit; therefore, use the singular predicate *is*.

But: Bread and butter are on my shopping list.

 ## EITHER–OR/NEITHER–NOR

1. Jack or Jill (is, are) going up the hill.

In this problem, notice first that the two subjects are connected by *or—Jack or Jill*. Whenever two or more subjects are connected by *or* or *nor*, make the predicate agree with the subject closest to it.
 Jill is closer to the predicate. *Jill* is singular. Therefore, use the singular predicate *is going*. *Jack or Jill is going up the hill.*
 Here are other examples:

2. Either Dr. Kim or Mr. Shapiro *has* the application.
3. Neither the chair nor the table *has* arrived.
4. The desks or the cabinets *are* going to be replaced.
5. Neither the chairs nor the tables *have* arrived.
6. Either the managers or their assistants *are* to blame.

Now look at this sentence:

7. Either Mr. Sawyer or his sons (has, have) studied your problem.

This sentence is a little more complicated. One of the subjects is singular, *Mr. Sawyer*. The other subject is plural, *sons*. Because *sons* is closer to the predicate, we use the plural word *have: Either Mr. Sawyer or his sons have studied your problem.*

8. Either the boys or Mr. Sawyer has studied your problem.

Here *Mr. Sawyer* is closer to the predicate. Therefore, use *has*. Although this sentence is grammatically correct, it sounds awkward. Hence, as a general rule of business usage, it is better to place the plural subject closer to the predicate. Thus, although both sentences are correct, Sentence 7 is better than Sentence 8 because it sounds better.
 Similarly, although both of the following sentences are grammatically correct, the second is preferable because it sounds better.

9. Neither the chairs nor the table has arrived.
10. Neither the table nor the chairs have arrived.

11. Mr. Stevens, Ms. Lopez, or their aides have completed the report.

In this sentence there are three subjects connected by *or*. This is no problem for our general rule. *Aides* is closest to the predicate; therefore, we use the plural word *have*.

SINGULAR PRONOUNS

The following pronouns are singular. When any one of them is the subject of a sentence, use a *singular* predicate.

anyone	someone	each
anybody	somebody	either
everyone	one	neither
everybody	nobody	

Anyone *is* qualified for the position.
Anybody *is* capable of filling this position.
Everyone in town *was* angry when the plant closed.
Everybody here *wants* to go to the meeting.
Someone *is going* to suffer for this.
Somebody *has missed* the point.
One of our aircraft *is* missing.
Nobody *does* it better.
Either of his sons *is* able to help you.
Neither of her mistakes *was* significant.
Each of the officers in the firm *holds* a graduate degree.

When *each*, *every*, or *many a* is used to modify a subject, that subject should be considered *singular* even though it may have more than one part.

Each person here is expected to contribute.
Every employee is eligible for a raise.
Every man and woman who purchases a ticket has an equal chance of winning.
Many a satisfied customer has passed through these doors.

 ## PREPOSITIONAL PHRASES

When determining the subject of a sentence, ignore prepositional phrases. Some of the most common prepositions are *of, in, with, for, at, by, from,* and *to.* The following sentences illustrate this principle:

Either (of his sons) is able to help you.
Neither (of her mistakes) was significant.
Each (of the officers in the firm) holds a graduate degree.

Here are a few more examples:

No one at headquarters is capable of doing a better job.
Chief among my objections is the cost.
The invoice for the last three shipments has been lost.
The range of applications is extensive.

 ## EXPLANATORY AND ADDITIONAL PHRASES

Always ignore expressions beginning with *as well as, together with, in addition to, accompanied by,* and the like. These expressions give supplementary, incidental information that could be omitted. They do not change the subject.

1. The printer, as well as the paper, has been received.

    The subject is *printer*. Ignore *as well as the paper.*

2. My employer, in addition to her associates, was pleased.

   The subject is *employer*. Ignore *in addition to her associates.*

3. Mr. Smith, together with his assistant, is scheduled to arrive at noon.

   The subject is *Mr. Smith*. Ignore *together with his assistant.*

4. The salesman, accompanied by his family, takes the plane tonight.

   The subject is *salesman*. Ignore *accompanied by his family.*

MEANING

In determining whether a subject is singular or plural, always look to the meaning of the word rather than to its form. For example, although the word *news* ends in *s*, it is singular in meaning. Therefore, it calls for a singular predicate:

No news is good news. The news is encouraging.

Similarly, although the word *series* ends in *s*, it too is singular:

The series of revisions is completed.
A series of changes has been made.

Finally, the names of some school subjects and some diseases end in *s* but are singular in meaning: *economics, politics, civics, physics, linguistics, mathematics, measles,* and *mumps.*

Economics is a required subject, but linguistics is not.
Measles is a mild disease.
Physics is a basic tool of modern industry.
Mumps is a dangerous illness if not treated properly.

QUANTITY

When a quantity is measured in one lump sum, it should be treated as though it were one item. For example:

1. Five tons is a great deal of coal.

   We are really referring to one large amount of coal.

2. Eighty miles per hour is too fast.

   Eighty miles per hour is one speed.

3. Two hundred dollars is a fair amount.

   We are referring to one sum of money.

   On the other hand, when a quantity is measured in piece-by-piece units, use a plural predicate.

4. There are five persons waiting.

5. In this box are 80 shirts.
6. Two hundred units have been produced.

You may have trouble when the word *number* is the subject of a sentence. Remember this rule-of-thumb: When *number* is preceded by *the,* use a singular predicate. When any other word, including *a,* precedes *number,* use a plural predicate.

> The number of failures is low.
> A number of people have failed.

 ## TITLES OF BOOKS AND ARTICLES

Beware of titles of books, magazines, and articles that sound plural. For example:

1. **Right:** *Business Letters* is a fine book.

You are referring to one book, though its title sounds plural.

Right: "The Three Little Pigs" is a favorite children's story.

2. **Right:** "Notes on Fashions" is in this issue of *Jones Magazine.*

This is one article; therefore, use the singular predicate.

Right: *Better Homes and Gardens* offers helpful redecorating ideas.

 ## COLLECTIVE NOUNS

Certain words refer to a number of people or things that make up one group—words such as *committee, jury, class, faculty, crowd,* and *mob.* These words, known as **collective nouns,** may be either singular or plural depending upon their meaning in a sentence. When the entire group to which they refer acts as a single unit, use a singular predicate.

> The committee is scheduled to meet at one o'clock.
> The class was led in the procession by the principal.
> The jury has rendered its verdict.

When, however, you refer to the individuals that make the group, use a plural predicate.

> The committee are violently debating the merits of the proposed system.
> The class were arguing with one another.
> The jury have been embroiled in major disagreement for three hours.

Although these three sentences are grammatically correct, there is no denying that they sound extremely awkward. For this reason, it would be better to rewrite these sentences as follows:

> The committee members are violently debating the merits of the proposed system.
> The students in the class were arguing with one another.
> The men and women of the jury have been embroiled in major disagreement for three hours.

 ## A COMPANY AS SUBJECT

The name of a firm frequently includes the names of more than one person, and it often includes the word *company.* Again, you must decide whether the company name is being used in a particular sentence in a singular or in a plural sense.

Merrill Lynch, Pierce, Fenner & Smith is America's largest brokerage house.
The American Steel Company has its main offices in Pittsburgh.

In both sentences we have treated the firm as a single unit and have therefore used a singular predicate. In actual business practice, however, the representatives of a firm usually refer to their company as *we* rather than *it*. Compare these two sentences:

American Steel is pleased to announce that it has developed a new type of alloy especially designed to solve your problem.
American Steel is pleased to announce that we have developed a new type of alloy especially designed to solve your problem.

The use of *it* in the first sentence is cold and impersonal. The use of *we* in the second sentence adds a touch of warmth to the statement; it gives an image of the many hard-working men and women who have toiled to create this new alloy. This human company image may be just the subtle touch that creates a sale for one company rather than for another. For this reason, the use of a company name in the plural sense has become a common practice in American business today.

 ## SOME/NONE

The word *none* can be either singular or plural depending upon its reference in a sentence. Most often it is considered plural and requires a plural predicate:

None of the orders have been processed yet.

Also correct, however, is *None of the orders has been processed yet*, because *none* can mean *not one: Not one . . . has been processed yet*. However:

We needed a conference room, but none was available.

Here the meaning of *none* is clearly singular, and *was* is the only appropriate choice.
The word *some* may be singular or plural depending upon its meaning in a particular sentence. When *some* refers to a quantity taken as a whole, it is generally singular in meaning. When it refers to a number, it is plural in meaning. Here is an easy way to tell the difference in most sentences containing this word. Generally, *some* is followed by a phrase beginning with *of*. If the noun or pronoun in such a phrase is plural, treat *some* as plural:

Some of the employees have returned to work.

If the noun or pronoun in the phrase is singular, treat *some* as singular:

Some of the work is considered unsatisfactory.
Some of the firm's capital is being earmarked for expansion.

The words *any, all,* and *most* can also be either singular or plural depending on their reference in a sentence.

Is any of the property in a flood zone?
Are any of the workers still here?
All the members are in favor of a strike.
All this area is zoned for commercial use.
Most of the road is paved.
Most of the employees are union members.

FRACTIONS AND PERCENTAGES

Frequently a fraction or percentage is used as the subject of a sentence.

Three-fifths of the people have arrived.
Sixty percent of our quota has been met.

The same rule-of-thumb that we used with *some* applies to these fractions and percentages:

Half of the farms in this area are for sale.
Fifty percent of this farm is lying fallow.
One quarter of the order has been shipped.
Twenty-five percent of the orders have been shipped.

 # INVERSION OF SUBJECT AND VERB

You have already been introduced to the type of sentence in which the predicate appears before the subject. You learned that you can easily recognize the parts of this type of sentence if you mentally rearrange it into the usual subject-before-predicate order. For example, try this sentence:

Inverted: Listed among those suggested for promotion (was, were) Rita Perez.

By reversing the order for the sentence, you easily find the solution:

Reversed: Rita Perez was listed among those suggested for promotion.

Many predicate-before-subject sentences begin with the adverbs *there* or *here.*

Inverted: There (is, are) three new designs that have been selected.

This problem can be solved the same way—by mentally reversing the elements.

Reversed: Three new designs that have been selected are there.

See how this procedure works with the following sentence:

Inverted: There (is, are) a large area of disagreement between the factions.
Reversed: A large area of disagreement between the factions is there.

How about these sentences?

Here (is, are) the brochures you requested.
Here (is, are) the stack of applications.

Just reverse the order of the sentences, and the answers become obvious.

Reversed: The brochures you requested are here.
Reversed: The stack of applications is here.

 # LINKING VERBS

A linking verb should agree with its subject (which comes before the verb), not with its complement (which comes after the verb).

Right: Repeated absences were the reason for his being fired.
Right: The reason he was fired was his repeated absences.

CLAUSES WITH RELATIVE PRONOUNS

So far we have looked at the agreement of the verb with the subject of the sentence. Verbs must also agree with the subject of their clauses. A relative pronoun—*who, which, that*—is often followed by a verb that must agree in number with the antecedent of the relative pronoun. Recognizing the real antecedent, however, is not always easy. For example, try this sentence:

She is one of those people who (is, are) conscientious in following directions.

In this sentence what word does *who* relate to, *one* or *people?* Look at the sentence carefully and you will see that a statement is being made about a broad characteristic of *those people. Who,* therefore, relates to the plural word *people* and requires the plural verb *are: She is one of those people who are conscientious in following directions.*
Now examine this sentence:

She is the one person among all the applicants who (is, are) able to do the job.

Who shows the ability to do the job in this sentence—*all the applicants* or *the one person?* Clearly *who* relates to *one person;* it is therefore a singular subject and takes the singular predicate *is.* When faced with such sentences, then, be careful to think through the meaning of the relative clauses carefully to determine which is the real antecedent.

 # PROGRAMMED REINFORCEMENT

	S1 If the subject of a sentence is singular, the predicate must be _____.
R1 singular	**S2** If the subject of a sentence is plural, the predicate must be _____.
R2 plural	**S3** Circle your answer: **The chief and her assistant (is, are) ready to leave the office.**
R3 **are**	**S4** Two subjects connected by **and** make the subject plural. If the two subjects are always identified as one, however, the subject is singular. **Peanut butter and jelly (is, are) my favorite sandwich. The horse and buggy (was, were) once a popular mode of transportation.**
R4 **is; was**	**S5** When the word **or** or **nor** is used to connect two subjects, the predicate will agree with the subject that is _____ to it.
R5 closer	**S6** **The sales representatives or their manager (is, are) able to do the job.** The correct predicate is _____ because the subject that is closer to it is the word _____, which is (singular, plural).
R6 **is; manager;** singular	

S7 **Neither the desk nor the chairs (seem, seems) in good condition.** The subject closer to the verb is **chairs;** therefore, the correct predicate is the word _____, which is (singular, plural).

R7 **seem;** plural

S8 **Either the chairs or the desk (has, have) to be replaced.** Since the subject nearer the verb is **desk,** which is singular, the predicate must be the word _____, which is also _____.

R8 **has;** singular

S9 The words **each, everyone, anybody,** and **nobody** are all (singular, plural). When they are used as subjects, the predicate must also be _____.

R9 singular; singular

S10 Circle your answer: **Anybody (is, are) able to succeed with hard work.**

R10 **is**

S11 **Each of the posters (has, have) to be redone.** The subject is _____. The correct predicate is _____.

R11 **Each; has**

S12 **Each of the bank tellers (is, are) capable.** The subject is _____. The correct predicate is _____.

R12 **Each; is**

S13 Complete these sentences correctly.
a. **Nobody (knows, know) the trouble I've seen.**
b. **Many a successful executive (has, have) spoken to our organization.**
c. **Every boy and girl in the class (is, are) going to receive a present.**

R13 a. **knows,** b. **has,** c. **is**

S14 There are certain expressions like **as well as, accompanied by, together with, in addition to** that do not change a singular subject into a plural subject. **The father, accompanied by his children, (is, are) coming by plane.** The subject is _____. The correct predicate is _____.

R14 **father; is** (coming)

S15 **Ms. Jones, together with her assistants, (is, are) expected at two o'clock.** The subject is _____. The correct predicate is _____.

R15 **Ms. Jones; is** (expected)

S16 **The news (is, are) good.** The subject is _____, which is (singular, plural). The correct predicate is _____.

R16 **news;** singular; **is**

S17 **Politics (make, makes) strange bedfellows.** The subject is _____, which is (singular, plural). The correct predicate is _____.

R17 **Politics;** singular; **makes**

S18 A quantity that is the subject may look plural, but if it represents one lump sum, it is singular. Example: **Five dollars (was, were) a lot for a tip.**

R18 **was**

S19 Circle your answer: **Ten print wheels (was, were) missing.**

R19 **were**

S20 When the word **number** is the subject of a sentence and is preceded by **the,** use a singular predicate. **The number of bankruptcies (is, are) decreasing. The number** is considered a (singular, plural) subject.

R20 **is;** singular

S21 When the word **number** is preceded by **a,** use a plural predicate. **A number of checks (seem, seems) to have been mislaid. A number** is considered a (singular, plural) subject.

R21 **seem;** plural

S22 Circle your answer: **"Hints to an Executive" (appear, appears) in a magazine this week.**

R22 **appears**

S23 Words that refer to a group **(committee, jury, class, crowd, mob)** may be either singular or plural depending upon their meaning in the sentence. When the entire group acts as a single unit, the predicate is _____ _____. When the group is thought of in terms of its individual members, the predicate is _____.

R23 singular; plural

S24 Circle your answer: **The committee (is, are) ready to give its report.**

R24 **is**

S25 Which verb correctly completes this sentence? **The faculty (is, are) arguing among themselves.** How would you rewrite it to make it sound less awkward? _____ _____

R25 **is; The faculty members are arguing among themselves.**

S26 Circle your answer: **Abrams, Kerr, and Philips (is, are) a well-known moving firm.**

R26 **is**

S27 The word **none** may be either singular or plural. Most often it is considered _____ and therefore requires a plural predicate.

R27 plural

S28 **Some** may be singular or plural. If the noun in the **of** phrase that follows **some** is singular, then **some** is singular. **Some of the work (is, are) too hard.** The noun in the **of** phrase is _____, which is (singular, plural). The correct predicate, therefore, is _____.

R28 **work;** singular; **is**

S29 **Some of the workers (is, are) unsatisfactory.** The noun in the **of** phrase is _____, which is (singular, plural). The correct predicate, therefore, is _____.

R29 **workers;** plural; **are**

S30 The words *any, all,* and *most* (may, may not) be singular or plural depending on their reference in a sentence. Circle the words that correctly complete the following sentences:
1. **Most of the offices (is, are) unoccupied.**
2. **Most of the office space (is, are) still available.**
3. **All the road (is, are) under repair.**
4. **All the workers (has, have) gone home.**

R30 **may;** 1. **are,** 2. **is,** 3. **is,** 4. **have**

S31 Fractions used as subjects follow the same rule as **some;** that is, if the phrase following the fraction has a singular noun, the predicate is _____; if the phrase has a plural noun, the predicate is _____.

R31 singular; plural

S32 Choose the correct predicates:
One-third of the mechanics (have, has) arrived.
Fifty percent of the stock (is, are) worthless.

R32 **have; is**

S33 Sometimes the subject will appear after the predicate. **There were three speeches given.** Rewrite this sentence in subject-before-predicate order. _____

R33 **Three speeches were given there.**

S34 Circle the subject and the correct predicate in this sentence: **Picked among the candidates (was, were) the new vice president.**

R34 subject—**vice president;** predicate—**was (picked)**

S35 A linking verb should agree with its (subject, complement).

R35 subject

S36 Which sentence is correct?
a. **The cause of his dismissal was his frequent absences.**
b. **The cause of his dismissal were his frequent absences.**

R36 a.

S37 Sometimes the true antecedent of a relative pronoun is found in the phrase following the subject. **She is one of those people who (do, does) (her, their) best work under pressure.** Underline the true antecedent. Circle the correct answers.

R37 **people; do, their**

S38 To review, a singular subject calls for a _____ predicate; a plural subject calls for a _____ predicate.

R38 singular; plural

Turn to Exercises 8.1 to 8.7.

EXERCISE 8·1A   SUBJECTS

In the column headed Subject, write the subject of each sentence. In the column headed Number, write *S* if the subject is singular and *P* if the subject is plural.

	SUBJECT	NUMBER

1. Ms. Ortega called at your office today.

2. Ms. Ortega, accompanied by her assistant, called at your office.

3. The number of bankruptcies this year was higher than last year.

4. Macy's and Gimbel's are friendly competitors.

5. Efficient supervisors and executives have always been at a premium.

6. Both the designer and the engineer seem competent workers.

7. Peaches and cream is my favorite breakfast dish.

8. A supervisor for all keyboarders must be picked today.

9. Bread and butter is a staple in the American diet.

10. Office machinery must be covered and carefully protected.

1. _____ _____

2. _____ _____

3. _____ _____

4. _____ _____

5. _____ _____

6. _____ _____

7. _____ _____

8. _____ _____

9. _____ _____

10. _____ _____

EXERCISE 8·1B   PREDICATES

In the column headed Predicate, write the predicate of the sentence. In the column headed Number, write S if the subject is singular and P if the subject is plural.

	PREDICATE	NUMBER

1. Mr. Isuzu and his partner will speak at the meeting today.

2. Either Mikki or her friends will be the best models for the new uniform.

3. Neither time nor effort should be spared in developing an effective résumé.

4. Neither the computer nor the diskettes have arrived at the office.

5. Each of the applicants must complete a questionnaire.

6. Any one of the export firms is able to handle the shipment.

7. Everybody in the sales force is asked to use the suggestion box.

8. Somebody in the executive office is responsible for time studies.

9. The news of the sales losses is coming over the wire.

10. Each cartridge and each cassette must be carefully stored.

1. _____ _____
2. _____ _____
3. _____ _____
4. _____ _____
5. _____ _____
6. _____ _____
7. _____ _____
8. _____ _____
9. _____ _____
10. _____ _____

EXERCISE 8·1C   SUBJECTS AND PREDICATES

This exercise asks you to pick out the subjects and predicates in this business letter. Underline each subject once and each predicate twice.

Dear Mr. Silberman:

In your recent letter you ordered several items for immediate delivery. Our production manager and our consulting engineer have informed me of some delays in retooling machines for your order. We will expedite this adjustment and put your order into work quickly. The shipping department will, of course, inform you of the shipping date, and Ms. Cifelli will visit you personally if necessary. Please understand our problems in retooling and accept our assurance of careful attention. Both Ms. Cifelli and I look forward to serving you.

Sincerely,

EXERCISE 8·2   AGREEMENT OF SUBJECT AND PREDICATE

In the space provided, write the predicate that agrees with the subject.

1. Each order (has, have) been received.   1. _____

2. Each of the orders (has, have) been received.   2. _____

3. Nobody among the trainees (seem, seems) capable of supervising such an important project. 3. _____

4. My boss, together with his assistant, (was, were) able to attend the convention.   4. _____

5. Ms. Chen, together with her spouse, (is, are) conducting an advanced accounting seminar.   5. _____

6. A series of changes in recordkeeping procedures (is, are) expected soon.   6. _____

7. News of the price decreases (was, were) announced to the buyers.   7. _____

8. Six tons of steel (was, were) delivered last month.   8. _____

9. The number of marriages in the firm (is, are) increasing.   9. _____

10. A number of programmers and designers (has, have) applied.   10. _____

11. Many an employee (has, have) invested in company stock.   11. _____

12. Neither of the setbacks (was, were) very costly.   12. _____

13. Every boy and girl who toured the plant (was, were) given a souvenir.   13. _____

14. Each employee who completed the course successfully (was, were) acknowledged in the staff newsletter. 14. _____

15. All the people who participated (was, were) given commendations.   15. _____

AGREEMENT OF SUBJECT AND PREDICATE

Choose the correct predicate. Indicate whether the predicate is singular or plural—writing S if it is singular, P if it is plural.

	PREDICATE	NUMBER

1. *Writing Better Letters* (is, are) a good book for business students.

   1. _____ _____

2. "Ideas on Office Improvement" (was, were) put aside for Ms. O'Hare to examine.

   2. _____ _____

3. The committee (has, have) decided to issue their report next week.

   3. _____ _____

4. The jury (was, were) asked by the judge to render its decision.

   4. _____ _____

5. The faculty of the school (seem, seems) to be against new proposals.

   5. _____ _____

6. Pearson, French, Hein, and Jackson (is, are) a leading publishing house.

   6. _____ _____

7. The Providence Producing Company (appear, appears) on the top of the list.

   7. _____ _____

8. The members of the ANTA Playhouse Company (is, are) planning a road trip.

   8. _____ _____

9. A number of checks (was, were) returned marked "No funds."

   9. _____ _____

10. The number of area apartments available for rent (is, are) very small.

   10. _____ _____

11. Most of the damage to the store and its contents (was, were) minor.

   11. _____ _____

12. (Is, Are) all this area zoned residential?

   12. _____ _____

13. Here (is, are) the series of articles you requested on improving productivity.

   13. _____ _____

14. The worst part of the evening (was, were) the after-dinner speeches.

   14. _____ _____

15. The after-dinner speeches (was, were) the worst part of the evening.

   15. _____ _____

EXERCISE 8·4 AGREEMENT OF SUBJECT AND PREDICATE

In the first space write the subject; in the second, write the predicate.

	SUBJECT	PREDICATE

1. Among those with the highest sales totals (was, were) Jim Deloria.

2. There (is, are) several ways of making stencil corrections.

3. There (was, were) three comments in the suggestion box.

4. The closing slides (was, were) the most effective part of the presentation.

5. None of the methods of transcription (is, are) beyond criticism.

6. Some of the company's investments (seem, seems) to have been affected by the market changes.

7. Some of the diskettes (have, has) been ruined by careless handling.

8. Three-fifths of the crop (has, have) to be stored in silos.

9. Forty percent of the letters (have, has) to be corrected.

10. Half of the order (appear, appears) to be damaged.

11. Each order (has, have) been processed.

12. Each of the orders (has, have) been processed.

13. There (is, are) a table and a lamp still unshipped.

14. One million dollars (is, are) a great deal of money.

15. Anybody with a sound mind (are, is) eligible to enter.

16. The number of books available for sale (are, is) low.

17. Thirty-six percent of our total production (has, have) been sold.

18. None of the suppliers (has, have) called since our orders were sent.

19. Hundreds of teachers, together with their students, (hail, hails) our product.

20. Measles (is, are) a contagious disease.

21. This series of figures (is, are) much too confusing.

22. Any number of consequences (is, are) possible.

#	SUBJECT	PREDICATE
1.	_____	_____
2.	_____	_____
3.	_____	_____
4.	_____	_____
5.	_____	_____
6.	_____	_____
7.	_____	_____
8.	_____	_____
9.	_____	_____
10.	_____	_____
11.	_____	_____
12.	_____	_____
13.	_____	_____
14.	_____	_____
15.	_____	_____
16.	_____	_____
17.	_____	_____
18.	_____	_____
19.	_____	_____
20.	_____	_____
21.	_____	_____
22.	_____	_____

23. Mathematics as well as economics (is, are) required. 23. _____ _____

24. The members of the jury (is, are) in complete disagree-ment. 24. _____ _____

25. The jury and the judge, as well as the general public, (is, are) convinced of the defendant's innocence. 25. _____ _____

EXERCISE 8·5   CLAUSES WITH RELATIVE PRONOUNS

In the space provided, write the correct verb or pronoun.

1. James Randall is one person who (realize, realizes) the value of this investment. 1. _____

2. James Randall is one of the people who (realize, realizes) the value of this investment. 2. _____

3. She is one of those people who (is, are) always complaining about (his, her, their) heavy responsibilities. 3. _____

4. She is different from any of those executives who (remain, remains) calm when (she, they) (is, are) harassed. 4. _____

5. Ethan is the only member of our department who still (smoke, smokes). 5. _____

6. Jill is one of those people who always (make, makes) (his, her, their) opinions known. 6. _____

7. Ms. Rosenfield is one of those executives who (is, are) unable to delegate responsibility. 7. _____

8. Anne Brady is the only member of the department who (know, knows) how to operate this machine properly. 8. _____

9. We are looking for one of those people who (is, are) not afraid to be aggressive. 9. _____

10. Miss Garcia is the one person among our entire staff who (is, are) capable of making the project a success. 10. _____

EXERCISE 8·6   AGREEMENT OF SUBJECT AND PREDICATE

The letter below contains a number of intentional errors in subject and verb agreement. Cross out all incorrect words and correct the statement in the space above the line.

Dear Ms. Diaz:

Our records indicates that each of your offices have failed to renew its subscription to <u>Modern Times</u>. We assure you we regret this very much. Each of our previous letters express our appreciation of having you as a subscriber and explain our desire to have all your offices remain as regular subscribers.

Everyone on our staff are concerned over your failure to renew. Was this failure due to something that somebody in my office have said or done? We would appreciate hearing from you. Either a suggestion on how to improve our service or your general comments on <u>Modern Times</u> is always welcome. We assure you that we will take all possible steps to remedy any problems.

You know <u>Modern Times</u> are the finest magazine in its field. Whether drama, science, current events, or politics are your area of interest, <u>Modern Times</u> have articles of interest to you. Our new series of articles on the impact of architecture promise to be especially fascinating.

Articles like these are written for a discriminating, intelligent reader like you. Surveys indicate that more than half of our subscribers is doctors, lawyers, and engineers. Many a reader have written to express unqualified praise for <u>Modern Times</u>. Professor Ramon Garcia, one of the several hundred thousand people who is a charter subscriber, says all his issues of <u>Modern Times</u> is an invaluable record of contemporary culture.

The number of satisfied readers of <u>Modern Times</u> keep growing. We do hope that you will continue to be part of that number. Please forward your renewal so that we may retain your name on our list of subscribers and friends. After all, are there anything more important than loyal friends?

Sincerely yours,

EXERCISE 8·7 COMPOSITION: AGREEMENT OF SUBJECT AND PREDICATE

Complete the following sentence starters in a meaningful way.

1. The committee (has, have) _____.

2. None of the people who (has, have) _____.

3. Not one of the proposals (was, were) _____.

4. Many a business student (feel, feels) _____.

5. Half of the audience (was, were) _____.

9

VERBS IV
VOICE, MOOD, VERBALS

VOICE, MOOD, AVOIDING SHIFTS IN VERBS, VERBALS

 VOICE

So far we have been looking at the chief property of verbs—their ability to indicate time through tense. In this chapter we are going to look at some of the other properties of verbs. One of these is called *voice.*

Voice is the term we use to indicate whether the subject of the sentence is *performing* or *receiving* the action described by the verb.

If the subject *does* the action, we say that the sentence is in the **active voice.**

> Maria mailed the package.
> Larry is keying the letter.
> The manager should have fired the checker.
> Jan will make the necessary arrangements.

If the subject is *acted upon,* we say that the sentence is in the **passive voice.**

> The package was mailed by Maria.
> The letter is being keyed by Larry.
> The checker should have been fired by the manager.
> The necessary arrangements will be made by Jan.

It is not necessary to include the doer of the action in the sentence.

> The package was mailed yesterday.
> The letter is being keyed now.
> The checker should have been fired.
> The necessary arrangements will be made.

Whether the doer of the action is mentioned, the passive voice always consists of a form of the verb *to be* followed by a past participle.

You may have heard that you should never use the passive voice. This is not true. Sometimes the passive voice is the natural choice. For example:

> Our firm was established in 1877.

Here it is the establishment of the firm itself that is important, not the names of the people who established it.

Similarly, when the performer of the action is less important than the receiver, the passive voice is appropriate.

Al Jackson was presented with an award by the president.

In the above sentence Al Jackson is seen as the important person in the ceremony and receives the greater emphasis by being made the subject of the sentence. If you want to emphasize the giver of the award rather than the recipient, then use the active voice.

The president presented Al Jackson with an award.

The passive voice also is used for reasons of *tact*.

Active: The assistant made two errors in the report.
Passive: Two errors were made in the report.
Active: We checked your credit references.
Passive: Your credit references were checked.
Active: You failed to send your payment.
Passive: Your payment has not been received.

In each of these pairs of examples, the passive voice construction would ordinarily be preferred.

In addition to being used for tact and emphasis, the passive voice also may be employed occasionally for the sake of sentence variety. You should not, however, use both active and passive voice in the same sentence.

As you can see, the passive voice does have its particular uses. In general, however, most business writers prefer the active to the passive voice because the active voice is more direct and less wordy. The careful business writer thus makes sure that the doer of the action is the subject of the sentence.

 # MOOD

The other property that verbs have is called **mood,** which refers to the manner in which the action or state of being of the verb is expressed. There are three moods in English. The first of these, used to make statements and to ask questions, is the **indicative mood.** This is the mood most often used and is the mood we have been discussing up to now in this chapter.

I would like to apply for a position in your marketing division.
We have no positions open right now.
Do you expect any openings soon?

The second mood, the **imperative,** is used to give a command, make a request, or give directions. It appears only in the present tense, second person.

Close the door.
Please pass the salt.
Turn right at the next intersection.

Neither the indicative nor imperative moods should give you any problems, but the third, the **subjunctive,** is troublesome to many people. This is because the subjunctive requires you to change the form of the verb (nearly always the verb *to be*). In the subjunctive the correct forms are not *I was* and *he was* but *I were* and *he were.* The following chart shows the differences between the indicative mood and the subjunctive mood.

SUBJUNCTIVE FORMS OF VERB "TO BE"

Present Tense	INDICATIVE MOOD		SUBJUNCTIVE MOOD	
	Singular	Plural	Singular	Plural
First person:	I am	we are	I *be*	we *be*
Second person:	you are	you are	you *be*	you *be*
Third person:	he is	they are	he *be*	they *be*
	she is		she *be*	
	it is		it *be*	

Past Tense				
	Singular	Plural	Singular	Plural
First person:	I was	we were	I *were*	we *were*
Second person:	you were	you were	you *were*	you *were*
Third person:	he was	they were	he *were*	they *were*
	she was		she *were*	
	it was		it *were*	

The subjunctive is most frequently used in two situations: to express a situation or condition that is contrary to fact and to express a wish. The following sentences are subjunctive because they express a situation that is known to be contrary to fact.

> If I were king, I would free all people from servitude.
> If I were you, I would be more discrete.
> If Mrs. Edwards were here, your demands would be quickly met.

Remember, use this form only if the situation is known to be false. Look at this sentence:

> If he was at the party, I didn't see him.

You don't know for sure that he was not there, so you use the regular past tense, *if he was.* If you know that he is not at the party, however, you might say: *If he were at this party, it would be really lively.*

These sentences require the subjunctive because they express a wish:

> I wish I were king.
> I wish she were here now.
> We wish we were able to answer your question more fully.
> Would that I were younger.

The subjunctive mood is also used in *that* clauses following certain verb constructions.

The subjunctive verb form *be* is used in *that* clauses following verbs expressing a desire, recommendation, demand, suggestion, resolution, or formal motion.

> Sue recommended that all employees who resigned be given an exit interview.
> Our instructor requires that all papers be typed with two-inch left margins.
> I move that the meeting be adjourned.
> Be it resolved that Robert Brunson be awarded the honorary degree of Doctor of Humane Letters.

AVOIDING SHIFTS IN VERBS

What's wrong with this sentence?

George came into the office yesterday and explains to the manager about the delay.

The sentence is inconsistent in its use of tenses. It combines both the past tense and the present tense. Because this incident occurred yesterday, all of the verbs should be in the past tense: *George came into the office yesterday and explained to the manager about the delay.*
Here are several more examples of inconsistent shifts in verb tense:

Wrong: I have edited the letters and Ms. Paterson reviewed them.
Wrong: I will be in New York on Thursday, and she is going to be in Washington.

These sentences should be changed to eliminate these shifts:

Right: I have edited the letters, and Ms. Paterson has reviewed them.
Right: I will be in New York on Thursday, and she will be in Washington.

A sentence may combine several tenses, but this combination must be logical. For example:

I have edited the letters, and Ms. Paterson is reviewing them right now.
I was in New York on Thursday, and she will be in Washington next Tuesday.
I *saw* her yesterday, *am seeing* her today, and *will see* her tomorrow.
I *thought* so then, *think* so now, and *will* always *think* so.
What did Ms. Worth say her first name is?
She told me her name is Helen. (Not: *was* Helen. Unless Ms. Worth has changed her first name, it remains Helen—it *is* Helen.)

You should also be careful that the mood and voice of the verbs in a sentence are consistent. For example:

If my partner was still alive and I were richer, this business would be a success.

This sentence improperly combines the indicative and the subjunctive moods. It should read: *If I were richer and my partner were still alive, this business would be a success.*
Similarly, avoid awkward shifts from active to passive voice in the same sentence:

Judy changed from the afternoon to the night shift, but the new shift was not liked by her.

This sentence should be revised to read: *Judy changed from the afternoon to the night shift, but she did not like the new shift.*
As a general rule, try to be consistent and logical in your use of verbs, and avoid awkward and inconsistent shifts in tense, mood, and voice.

PROGRAMMED REINFORCEMENT

S1 **Voice** indicates whether the subject is the **doer** or **receiver** of the action described by the verb. If the subject **does** the action, the sentence is in the _____ voice. If the subject is acted upon, the sentence is in the _____ voice.

R1 active; passive

S2 As a general principle, in business writing it is preferable to use the _____ voice.

R2 active

S3 Which of the following sentences are in the active voice?
  a. **Jack is phoning his wife now.**
  b. **Jack's wallet was stolen.**
  c. **Someone stole Jack's wallet.**
  d. **Jack said that his wallet had been stolen.**

R3 a, c, d

S4 Sometimes, for purposes of tact or emphasis, the passive voice is preferable. Which of the sentences in each of the following pairs is more tactful?
  1. (a) You failed to sign the check.
     (b) The check was not signed.
  2. (a) The proposal contains several factual errors.
     (b) You made several factual errors in your proposal.

R4 1. b; 2. a

S5 Which of the following sentences places greater emphasis on Knox College?
  1. Knox College was founded in 1837 in Galesburg, Illinois.
  2. Galesburg, Illinois, is the home of Knox College, which was founded in 1837.

R5 Sentence 1

S6 There are three moods in English: the **indicative,** the **imperative,** and the **subjunctive.** Which mood is used in giving commands? _____

R6 the **imperative**

S7 Which mood is used to express a wish or a situation contrary to fact? _____

R7 the **subjunctive**

S8 Circle the correct verb:
  a. **I wish I (was, were) younger.**
  b. **If he (was, were) still alive, things would be different.**
  c. **If she (was, were) here, I didn't see her.**
  d. **If I (was, were) you, I'd consider quitting.**

R8 a. **were;** b. **were;** c. **was;** d. **were**

S9 What verb will correctly complete each of the following sentences?
  a. **I demand that everyone present _____ questioned.**
  b. **Karla moved that the proposal _____ approved as amended.**

R9 a. be; b. be

S10 Because verb tenses reflect logical relationships in time, they should not be used inconsistently. Rewrite the following sentences to make the verb tenses consistent.
   a. **Yesterday he comes into the office and resigned.**

   _____

   b. **I ordered the computer terminals last week, but the company had failed to send them.**

   _____

   c. **I will be leaving next month, but she stays.**

   _____

R10 a. Yesterday he came into the office and resigned.
   b. I ordered the computer terminals last week, but the company failed to send them.
   c. I will be leaving next month, but she will be staying.

S11 The **mood** and **voice** of the verb in a sentence should also be consistent. Rephrase the following sentences:
   a. **Our problems would be more easily solved if I were richer or if he was still in charge.**

   _____

   b. **Judy operated the postage meter while the letters were addressed by Larry.**

   _____

R11 a. **Our problems would be more easily solved if I were richer or if he were still in charge.**
   b. **Judy operated the postage meter while Larry addressed the letters.**

Turn to Exercises 9.1 to 9.3.

 VERBALS

Up to now, we have been examining the various forms a verb can take when it is performing its most important function: serving as the predicate of the sentence. Verbs can also take other forms and serve other functions, however. For example:

George decided to run in the park on weekends.
Because running is an excellent form of exercise, he felt that running would keep him physically fit.
Running through the park last weekend, George tripped and sprained his ankle.

Here the verb _to run_ is used in several different forms, but never as the predicate of the sentence. Rather it tells us what George decided; tells us what is an excellent form of exercise and what would help keep George physically fit; and helps to modify George, who tripped and sprained his ankle.

Each of the various forms of _run_ illustrated in these sentences is a **verbal,** which is a verb form used as a noun, an adjective, or an adverb. The three kinds of verbals are _infinitives, gerunds,_ and _participles._ Although verbals are taken from verbs and are like verbs in many ways, they cannot act as the predicate of a sentence. Let's look at each of these verbals more closely.

INFINITIVES

The **infinitive** almost always is preceded by the word *to*. In fact, we often use the infinitive form when speaking of a verb: we usually say *to be, to have, to read, to bring* rather than *be, have, read, bring*.

The infinitive is used most often as a *noun*, both as a subject and as an object.

> *To succeed* was his sole desire. (subject)
> She wanted desperately *to succeed*. (object)

It can also be used to modify or describe other words in the sentence, in which case it acts as an *adjective* or *adverb*.

> Clothes *to suit* the occasion should be worn. (suitable clothes)
> He needed a permit *to build*. (building permit)
> I'd be glad *to help*. (adverb modifying the adjective *glad*)
> She stayed late *to help*. (adverb modifying the verb *stayed* to explain purpose)

There will be more information about adjectives and adverbs in the next two chapters.

The infinitive can be expressed in both the present and the perfect tenses. Take the infinitive *to see*, for instance:

> *To see* Paris is exciting. (present tense, active voice)
> *To have seen* Paris is to have fulfilled a dream. (present perfect tense, active voice)
> *To be seen* in Paris is chic. (present tense, passive voice)
> *To have been seen* in Paris is something to talk about. (present perfect tense, passive voice)

Note 1: The pronoun used after an infinitive is exactly the same as the pronoun used after any other verb. For example:

> The director plans to visit him and me. (*Him* and *me* are objects of the infinitive *to visit*.)
> The boss says he wants to see me in the office. (*Me* is the object of the infinitive *to see*.)

Note 2: Many people mistakenly use *and* in sentences like these:

> You must try and do it.
> Try and stop me.

As you know, *and* is a coordinating conjunction. These sentences do not call for a word to join two equal components; rather, they require objects of the verb *try*: the infinitives *to do* and *to stop*. These sentences should say:

> You must try to do it.
> Try to stop me.

Similarly, *and* is mistakenly used in these two sentences:

> Before signing a contract, a person should be sure and read all the fine print.
> Please be sure and call when you arrive.

The adjective *sure* requires a modifying adverb: the infinitives *to read* and *to call.*

Please be sure *to* call when you arrive.
Before signing a contract, a person should be sure *to* read all the fine print.

Note 3: You probably have heard of a *split infinitive.* A split infinitive simply means that a word or words have been placed between *to* and the verb. You have probably also heard that you should not split an infinitive. This is generally true, especially when the expression is awkward. For example:

Awkward: I wish to frequently visit you.
Right: I wish to visit you frequently.
Awkward: I have to sadly leave you.
Right: Sadly, I have to leave you.
Awkward: I want to next fall go to England.
Right: I want to go to England next fall.

Other expressions seem less awkward. Some writers would find the following split infinitive acceptable style:

To never be late for a meeting is a remarkable record.

Others would prefer that the sentence be revised to leave out the split infinitive:

Never to be late for a meeting is a remarkable record.

GERUNDS

The infinitive, as you have seen, can serve as several parts of speech. The **gerund,** however, is more limited. This verb form, which ends in *ing,* can act only as a *noun.* Look at these sentences:

Running is excellent exercise.

Here the gerund *running* is the subject of the sentence. In this next sentence, *running* is the subject complement.

One excellent form of exercise is running.

In the following sentence *running* acts as the object of the verb *enjoyed.*

George enjoyed running in the park.

With few exceptions, the use of gerunds should pose no problems for you. The first and most important of these exceptions, the placement of gerunds within the sentence, will be discussed shortly.
The other problem involves the case of the noun and pronoun used to modify a gerund. Which is correct?

We did not learn of (his, him) leaving the company until yesterday.
(Jacob, Jacob's) resigning from the committee came as a complete surprise.

The rule is a simple one: a noun or pronoun used to modify a gerund must be in the possessive case. Therefore, these two sentences are correct:

We did not learn of his leaving the company until yesterday.
Jacob's resigning from the committee came as a complete surprise.

 # PARTICIPLES

The third verbal, the **participle,** functions as an *adjective,* describing or modifying a noun. Unlike the gerunds and the infinitives, which involve only one basic change—the addition of *ing* or *to,* respectively—the participle can take several different forms.

 ## THE PRESENT PARTICIPLE

The most common form adds *ing* to make the *present participle.*

Running through the park, George tripped.

Here *running* modifies George by describing George when he tripped.

The person standing by the door wishes to speak with you.

Which person? The one near the door.

 ## THE PAST PARTICIPLE

The second form, the *past participle,* usually is formed by adding *ed,* which, as you know, is the way to form the past participle of regular verbs.

Angered by the lack of progress in contract negotiations, the union members threatened to strike.
The arbiter, called into the negotiations, attempted to help the two sides reach a settlement.

In the first sentence, *angered by the lack of progress in contract negotiations* describes the union members; in the second, *called into the negotiations* describes the arbiter.
Irregular verbs, as you know, form their past participles in various other ways. These, too, can serve as adjectives in sentences.

The painting, *bought* for only a few hundred dollars, was later discovered to be a valuable masterpiece.
"Manuscript *Found* in a Bottle" is the title of a short story by Edgar Allan Poe.
The roadside was littered with garbage and debris *thrown* from passing cars.

 ## THE PERFECT PARTICIPLE

The third form of participle used as an adjective is the *perfect participle.* It is formed by adding *having* to the past participle, whether it is a regular or irregular verb: *having called, having drunk, having seen, having completed.*

Having said what he wanted to say, Fred left the room.
The secretary, having finished the report, sat down.
The missing child having been found, the search was ended.

USES OF PARTICIPLES

The present participle is used to show action occurring at the same time as the action expressed by the main verb of the sentence. This main verb may be in the present, past, or future tense.

Running through the park, George tripped.
(While George was running, he tripped.)
The person standing by the door wishes to speak with you.
(The person is standing by the door and wishes to speak with you.)

The past participle and the perfect participle are used to express an action that took place *before* the action expressed by the main verb.

The painting, bought for only a few hundred dollars, was later discovered to be a valuable masterpiece. (After the painting had been purchased for a few hundred dollars, it was discovered to be a valuable masterpiece.)
Having said what he wanted to say, Fred left the room. (Fred said what he wanted to say; then he left.)
The secretary, having finished the report, sat down. (The secretary sat down after finishing the report.)

 # DANGLING VERBAL MODIFIERS

As we have seen, verbals frequently are used in phrases that describe other words in the sentence. It is important that each of these phrases be used correctly and placed properly in the sentence so that its relationship to other words in the sentence is absolutely clear. If it isn't, the result often is what is known as a *dangling modifier*. For example:

Walking down the street, the building came in sight.

Obviously the building was not doing the walking, a person was. The sentence should be rewritten to make this clear.

Walking down the street, the building was seen by Carmen.

Although this sentence indicates who saw the building, it still isn't correct because it still sounds as though the building is walking. This sentence also must be rewritten if the relationship between *walking down the street* and the word it modifies is to be absolutely clear.

Walking down the street, Carmen saw the building.

Now we know for certain who was walking down the street.
The rule is, when a verbal phrase (in this instance a participle) begins the sentence and modifies the subject of that sentence, the subject should follow it immediately.

Washing the walls and repainting the woodwork, the visitor noticed the maintenance crew.

Obviously the washing and repainting were done by the maintenance crew, not the visitor. The sentence should read:

Washing the walls and repainting the woodwork, the maintenance crew was noticed by the visitor.

We could also rewrite the sentence this way:

The visitor noticed the maintenance crew washing the walls and repainting the wood-work.

Other statements that are not so clearly humorous demand the same kind of logical relationship. For example:

Dangling Participle: Skilled in achieving compromise, a strike was averted by the arbiter.
Correct: Skilled in achieving compromise, the arbiter averted a strike.
Dangling Gerund: By using this new technique, time can be saved.
Correct: By using this new technique, you can save time.
Dangling Gerund: On hearing the weather forecast, the class trip should be postponed, the teacher decided.
Correct: On hearing the weather forecast, the teacher decided to postpone the class trip.
Dangling Infinitive: Unable to swim, a lifeguard rescued me.
Correct: Unable to swim, I was rescued by a lifeguard.
Dangling Infinitive: To determine its value, the book will be appraised.
Correct: To determine its value, we will have the book appraised.

It is also possible for a verbal modifier to dangle at the end of the sentence. Here again you must rephrase the sentence logically so that the relationship between the verbal phrase and the word it describes is clear.

Dangling Participle: The student was unable to answer the teacher, not having read the assignment.
Correct: The student, not having read the assignment, was unable to answer the teacher.
Correct: Not having read the assignment, the student was unable to answer the teacher.

 # PARALLEL CONSTRUCTION

Parallelism or **parallel construction** means to give the same structure to two or more parts of a sentence. This compound sentence, for example, demonstrates parallel construction:

Carlos wanted to leave, but Greta wanted to stay.

When we spoke earlier about avoiding shifts in verb tenses, in a sense we were talking about maintaining parallelism.

Ms. Pulaski *picked* up the receiver, *dialed* her broker, and *places* an order for one hundred shares.

As you know, this sentence contains an inconsistent shift in tense. It should read:

Ms. Pulaski picked up the receiver, dialed her broker, and placed an order for one hundred shares.

Now all three verbs are in the same tense (simple past).
Similarly, when verbals are used in a series, they should be in the same form throughout. For instance:

Wrong: I like swimming, boating, and to hike.

In this sentence you are using as the objects of the verb *like* two gerunds (*swimming* and *boating*) and one infinitive (*to hike*). You should use the same form throughout. Either use all gerunds (*I like swimming, boating, and hiking*) or use all infinitives (*I like to swim, to boat, and to hike*). In other words, don't mix the types of verbals used in a series, but rather keep them the same—keep them parallel. Let's look at another example:

Wrong: I like to read, to paint, and playing the piano.

This sentence could also be revised in several ways: Either *I like to read, to paint, and to play the piano;* or *I like reading, painting, and playing the piano.*

 # PROGRAMMED REINFORCEMENT

	S12 A verb form that is used as a noun, adjective, or adverb is called a _____.
R12 verbal	**S13** A verb preceded by the word **to** is an _____.
R13 infinitive	**S14** An infinitive may be used as a noun, adjective, or adverb. **To listen is important. To listen** is used as the _____ _____ of the verb **is.**
R14 subject	**S15** **I like to listen to good music.** The infinitive **to listen** in this sentence is used as the _____ of the verb **like.**
R15 object	**S16** An infinitive may also be followed by objects. Circle the objects of the infinitive in this sentence: **I plan to visit my friends and my relatives in the country.**
R16 **friends; relatives**	**S17** What word splits the infinitive here: **I want to clearly state my intentions.** Rewrite the sentence to eliminate the split infinitive. _____
R17 **clearly;** I want to state clearly my intentions.	**S18** Sometimes people say *try and* when *try to* would be correct. Circle the correct word in the following sentences: a. **We must try (and, to) get her back.** b. **Please try (and, to) see my side of things.** c. **We may be forced to try (and, to) try again several times before we are successful.**
R18 a. **to;** b. **to;** c. **and**	**S19** An **ing** form of a verb, if it is used as part of the progressive form, is called a **present** _____. Circle the present participle in this sentence: **I am waiting for the operator.**
R19 participle; **waiting**	

S20 A verb form ending in **ing** and used as a noun, as in the sentence **Hiking is healthful,** is called a _____.

R20 gerund

S21 Because a gerund is really a noun that is formed from a verb, it may be used as a subject or object in a sentence. **He enjoyed writing to his friends.** In this sentence the gerund is _____ and it is a(n) _____.

R21 **writing;** object

S22 **Listening is an underdeveloped activity.** In this sentence the gerund is _____ and it is a(n) _____.

R22 **listening;** subject

S23 A noun or pronoun used to modify a gerund takes the _____ case.

R23 possessive

S24 Circle the correct answer:
a. **We were surprised at (him, his) leaving so soon.**
b. **(Jean, Jean's) quitting came as a complete shock.**

R24 a. **his;** b. **Jean's**

S25 **Filing is tedious work.**
In this sentence **filing** is a _____.
She was filing the letters. In this sentence **filing** is a _____ _____.

R25 gerund; present participle

S26 Circle the noun that **walking** modifies in this sentence:
Walking down the street, the man saw the store.

R26 **man**

S27 Participles can also take other forms. Circle the participle in these sentences:
a. **Annoyed by the waiter's attitude, the customer called the restaurant manager.**
b. **Having completed her assignment early, Rita decided to go to the movies.**

R27 a. **Annoyed;** b. **Having completed**

S28 The present participle is used to show an action occurring (before, at the same time as, after) the action expressed by the main verb in the sentence. The past participle and the perfect participle are used to express an action occurring (before, at the same time as, after) the action expressed by the main verb in the sentence.

R28 at the same time as; before

S29 Supply the proper form of the participle to complete the following sentences correctly:
1. **(Peel) an onion, Marcia cut her finger.**
2. **(Cut) her finger, Marcia put a bandage on it.**

R29 1. Peeling, 2. Having cut

S30 If the participle does not clearly relate to the noun that it modifies, it is called a **dangling participle.** Circle the dangling participle here: **Walking along the street, the store came in sight.** Circle the word that **walking** seems to modify.

R30 **walking; store**

S31 Is this a dangling participle construction? **Speaking softly because of a sore throat, the audience listened to the lecturer.** Answer: _____.

R31 Yes

S32 Is this a dangling participle construction? **Knowing the result, he quickly phoned his broker.** Answer: _____.

R32 No

S33 Rewrite the following sentences to eliminate dangling modifiers.
1. Walking through the hall, the floor was slipped on by Rhonda.
2. To access the computer, your identification number should be entered first.
3. While correcting the mistake, further errors were discovered.

R33 1. Walking through the hall, Rhonda slipped on the floor.
2. To access the computer, first enter your identification number.
3. While correcting the mistake, we discovered further errors.

S34 Good writers maintain parallel structure in their sentences. Circle the word that destroys the parallelism of this sentence: **To swim, to hike, to play, and boating are enjoyable summer activities.** What word(s) would maintain parallelism in this sentence? _____

R34 **boating;** to boat

S35 Show two different ways you could change this sentence to correct the lack of parallel structure. **Speaking, listening, and to take notes are standard student activities.**
1. _____
2. _____

R35 **Speaking, listening, and taking notes . . .**
To speak, to listen, and to take notes . . .

Turn to Exercises 9.4 to 9.7.

EXERCISE 9·1A   ACTIVE AND PASSIVE VOICE

For each of the following sentences, write the subject and the predicate in the spaces provided. In the voice column, place an *A* if the sentence is in active voice; place a *P* if the sentence is in passive voice.

	SUBJECT	PREDICATE	VOICE
1. Your check has not been received.			
2. We received your letter yesterday.			
3. Your letter arrived yesterday.			
4. Our company began operations 20 years ago.			
5. Our firm was founded by three brothers 20 years ago.			
6. Every employee was given a bonus.			
7. The project will be completed ahead of schedule.			
8. A review of the proposed contract by the full committee was requested by the union representative.			
9. Information regarding a client's financial status should be kept confidential.			
10. The proposed contract was presented to the rank and file for ratification.			

EXERCISE 9·1B   PASSIVE VOICE

The following sentences are all written in the passive voice. In the space provided, rewrite each of these sentences in the active voice. Supply an appropriate subject where one is necessary.

1. The annual conference was attended by Carlos and Angela. _____

_____

2. The documents were photocopied by Mrs. Montoya's assistant. _____

_____

3. Each employee was given a Christmas bonus. _____

_____

4. Protective eyeglasses should be worn at all times. _____

_____

5. A refund will be sent to you within the next two weeks. _____

_____

6. The correct use of the subjunctive is discussed in this chapter. _____

_____

7. Our suggestions were considered by the board, but no specific recommendations were announced. _____

8. Your order was shipped yesterday. _____

9. Chester Martin's report should be studied carefully. _____

_____

10. All stock should be rotated regularly. _____

EXERCISE 9·2   THE SUBJUNCTIVE

This exercise concerns the proper use of *was*, *were*, and *be*. In the space provided, fill in the proper word.

1. If I (was, were) you, I would accept the invitation.   1. _____

2. I wish I (was, were) President.   2. _____

3. She (was, were) not here Tuesday.   3. _____

4. If he (was, were) to disappear into thin air, I would be pleased.   4. _____

5. I don't know if she (was, were) at the meeting.   5. _____

6. (Was, Were) I you, I would do the same.   6. _____

7. If I (was, were) the manager of this firm, I would change things.   7. _____

8. Since the report proved unfounded, I (was, were) relieved.   8. _____

9. Here is how I would act if I (was, were) in your place.   9. _____

10. I certainly wish it (was, were) cooler.   10. _____

11. If he (was, were) promoted, he kept it a secret.   11. _____

12. I wish it (was, were) possible to start the day over again.   12. _____

13. The dean recommended that only three of the eight professors (was, were, be) granted tenure.   13. _____

14. I propose that Frank Hanson (was, were, be) granted the title Professor Emeritus.   14. _____

15. In line with the dean's recommendation, only three of the eight professors (was, were, be) granted tenure.   15. _____

EXERCISE 9·3   **SHIFTING VERBS**

If the sentence is correct, mark C in the space provided. If it is incorrect, use the space above the sentence to indicate the necessary changes.

1. Yesterday he comes into the office and complained about his reassignment.

1. _____

2. Niels had written the original draft and Janet revised it.

2. _____

3. I will supply the materials for next week's workshop if you furnish the labor.

3. _____

4. I have seen the report but will read it again before the meeting.

4. _____

5. If Bob was here, or if his father were still alive, we would not have to face these difficulties.

5. _____

6. At 10 A.M. tomorrow, after she talks to Mr. Ramirez, she will meet the supervisor.

6. _____

7. I wish you were younger or I was older.

7. _____

8. At tomorrow's teleconference I will answer your questions and further data will be supplied.

8. _____

9. What did she say her name was?

9. _____

10. The document was not signed by Miss Mason, nor did she even read it.

10. _____

EXERCISE 9·4 DANGLING VERBAL MODIFIERS

Each of the following sentences contains a dangling verbal modifier. In the spaces provided, rewrite each sentence to correct these errors and to show clearly the logical relationship between sentence parts.

1. By using teleconferencing, meetings can be held by business people who work in different cities.
   _____

2. To achieve success, your best should always be done. _____

3. When shopping for a computer, available software must always be considered by the buyer.
   _____

4. Having displayed strong management potential, the personnel director offered Kathleen a position in the management trainee program. _____
   _____

5. After determining the noun that is being modified, the sentence should be rewritten. _____

6. Running through the park, George's ankle was sprained. _____
   _____

7. While entering the room, Mr. McCartney was seen leaving. _____
   _____

8. Skilled in five computer languages, the program was quickly revised by Miss Yen. _____
   _____

9. In locating the error, much time was lost. _____
   _____

10. In a hurry to catch a plane, an important telephone call stopped Mr. Perez as he was leaving for the airport. _____
    _____

EXERCISE 9·5   INFINITIVES, GERUNDS, AND PARTICIPLES

If the sentence is correct as it is, mark C in the space provided. If it is incorrect, use the space above the sentence to indicate the changes that have to be made. Be sure to correct any verbals that lack parallel structure.

1. I intend to strongly complain about the errors in my bill. 1. _____

2. I was supposed to have gone to the conference last week. 2. _____

3. The boss says he wants to see you and I after work. 3. _____

4. Please try and correct the error. 4. _____

5. The manager, studying the problem, found no solution. 5. _____

6. The manager studying of the problem brought no solution. 6. _____

7. She wants to see Rafael and me and to carefully explain how the new office arrangement will improve productivity. 7. _____

8. Knowing the answer, he raised his hand. 8. _____

9. Us working together has resulted in substantial savings. 9. _____

10. To determine its feasibility, the program will be studied by a team of experts. 10. _____

11. How accurate is Ms. Conlan keyboarding? 11. _____

12. Reading the paper at lunch, the news of the stock market upset us. 12. _____

13. On a vacation we should plan to rest, to dream, and puttering in the garden. 13. _____

14. We want to carefully proofread the manuscript. 14. _____

15. Mrs. Cagnon would like to know whether you and he will be at the meeting. 15. _____

16. Ms. Jurek asked her to try and locate the lost files. 16. _____

17. What's your reaction to him winning the bonus? 17. _____

18. Working at top speed, the audit was finished on time by the accountant. 18. _____

19. You must be sure and fully reply to this letter. 19. _____

20. The ability to think logically, organizing clearly, and to communicate effectively is characteristic of the successful executive. 20. _____

21. Harper decided to admit his mistake and to ask for another chance to redeem himself. 21. _____

22. Listening to popular music no longer appeals to me as much as classical music. 22. _____

23. I intend to closely study all reports before making any recommendations. 23. _____

24. To err is human; forgiving, divine. 24. _____

25. Mr. O'Leary asked Marion and I to join him for lunch. 25. _____

187

EXERCISE 9·6A COMPOSITION: VOICE AND MOOD

Below are five sentence starters. Complete them according to the directions in parentheses.

1. (Complete the sentence using the subjunctive mood.)

   If Ms. Collins _____.

2. (Complete the sentence using the subjunctive mood.)

   Mr. Chen recommended_____.

3. (Complete the sentence using the passive voice.)

   The report _____.

4. (Complete the sentence using the active voice.)

   The report _____.

5. (Complete the sentence using the passive voice.)

   Mr. Chen _____.

EXERCISE 9·6B COMPOSITION: VERBALS

Below are five sentence starters. Complete them according to the directions in parentheses.

1. (Use this phrase as the subject of the sentence.)

   To be successful _____.

2. (Use this phrase to modify the subject of the sentence.)

   To be successful, _____.

3. (Use this phrase to modify the subject of the sentence.)

   While waiting for a cab, _____.

4. (Use this phrase to modify the subject of the sentence.)

   Having read the report, _____.

5. (Use this phrase as the subject of the sentence.)

   Reading the report _____.

EXERCISE 9·7   VERBS AND VERBALS

The following letter contains a number of errors in the use of verbs and verbals. Whenever you locate an error, cross it out and write the correct form above it.

Dear Mr. Robinson:

I was very disappointed that you do not send your representative to watch the test of our new Starfire 498 last week. I, together with my staff, were certain that he would be impressed by the way the Starfire performed, as was the hundreds of others who was there. I know he is one of those people who wants to be aware of the latest technological advances. Perhaps he forgot the date of this demonstration.

If he were to have attended, he would be seeing a new concept in automotive design and engineering. The Starfire 498 was an all-new car. It had a new engine, new streamlining, new controls.

Until the new line of Starfires were unveiled last week, the automotive industry has been lagging behind other industries in the use of plastics. The Starfire 498 has changed this. Because of the special design features made possible by high-strength plastics, at last week's demonstration the Starfire 498 accelerated from 0 to 60 miles per hour in under five seconds. I need not have told you how impressed the representatives of other companies were when they seen this spectacular performance. I am sure many of them will already tell you about it themselves.

Having demonstrated the car's excellent acceleration, the Starfire 498 was then put through a series of maneuvers by the testdriver. In these tests the Starfire had demonstrated its ability to corner, veer sharply, climb, brake, and generally handling with ease.

Until you have seen the Starfire and drove in it, you will have missed the thrill of your life. If I was you, I would try and make arrangements to be attending the next demonstration, which will be holded next Thursday at four o'clock at the Grand Plaza Arena. We know that by six o'clock next Thursday you are convinced that you going to the demonstration is one of the wisest moves of your life.

You knew our company for many years, Mr. Robinson. You have seed us become the leader in our field. You know that during the past three years we have spended many millions of dollars to built the Starfire 498 and that we will spend many millions more improving it. We have stroved to shaken off the shackles of conservative thinking that has hold the automotive industry back for years. We undertook a difficult task these past three years. While others were resting on their laurels, our research people were stroving for perfection.

The Starfire 498 has been brung into being by this devotion to a concept. It has sprang into being out of the minds and energy of America's top automotive engineers. In the same way that the jet plane shrunk the highways of the air, so will the Starfire 498 shrink the highways of the earth.

We felt that with the Starfire 498 we have lain the groundwork for all new automobiles. We have setted new standards in the field of transportation. Won't you find out for yourself all about the all-new Starfire? I look forward to see you on Thursday at the next demonstration.

Sincerely,

10

ADJECTIVES

FORMS OF THE ADJECTIVE, ADJECTIVES AFTER LINKING VERBS, USING ADJECTIVES, ARTICLES

An **adjective** is a word that describes or limits a noun or pronoun.

DESCRIPTIVE ADJECTIVES	LIMITING ADJECTIVES
a *stimulating* speech	*one* problem
new policy	*three* machines
helpful advice	*several* checks
incredible experience	*many* employees
lucky you	*much* excitement

Each of these adjectives *modifies* the noun or pronoun that follows it. Adjectives give life and color to language. The ability to use them skillfully is essential to good business writing. In this chapter we will look at the forms of adjectives and how to use adjectives skillfully and correctly.

Salespeople use adjectives in describing their products. A salesperson might tell a customer about the *new, improved* model that is *safe, nonpolluting, durable,* nearly *maintenance free,* and clearly *superior* to its competitors while remaining quite *inexpensive.* Managers use adjectives in writing letters of recommendation. Was the employee *dependable, industrious, personable, articulate, intelligent?* Or was the person *irresponsible, lazy, dull, inarticulate, stupid?*

People who write advertising copy are often noted for their extravagant use of adjectives: The dust jacket that proclaims a book *Stunning! Remarkable! Extraordinary! A runaway bestseller!* is one example.

Compare these two classified advertisements. Which woman will win the job?

WOMAN, college education, looking for job as secretary in theatrical field.

DIPLOMATIC, energetic young woman, with college education and experience, desires challenging position as secretary to overburdened theatrical executive.

Compare these two advertisements placed by rival employment agencies. Which position sounds more appealing? Which advertisement will draw the larger response?

EXECUTIVE SECRETARY
Work for President of Midtown firm. 3—5 years secretarial background preferred. Good benefits.

EXECUTIVE SECRETARY
SUPER POSH
This elegant Park Avenue firm is looking for a polished, refined, elegant executive secretary to fit into a team. Excellent benefits. Everything about this one is super.

The writers of the second advertisements have sought a positive reaction from the reader through the forceful use of adjectives.

FORMS OF THE ADJECTIVE

POSITIVE, COMPARATIVE, AND SUPERLATIVE DEGREES

There are three **forms** or **degrees** of the adjective: the simple or positive, the comparative, and the superlative. The **simple** form of an adjective describes a single item or a single group of items.

> *fine* book, *smart* assistants, *fast* cars, *long* letters

The other two forms of the adjective not only describe an item or group of items, they also give you the ability to compare one item with others. The **comparative** form of an adjective is used when you are comparing two things. To form the comparative of most simple adjectives, add *er*.

> This is a *finer* book than that one.
> Jane is *smarter* than Kurt.
> Sports cars are *faster* than stock cars.
> These letters are *longer* than those.

The **superlative** form of an adjective is used when you are comparing *three or more* things. To form the superlative of most simple adjectives, add *est*.

> This is the *finest* book I ever read.
> Jane is the *smartest* of the three assistants.
> This is the *fastest* sports car in the world.
> This is the *longest* letter we have received.

Remember, use the comparative form only when comparing two items. Use the superlative when comparing three or more.

> **Right:** John is the taller of the two.
> **Wrong:** John is the tallest of the two.
> **Right:** Of the five men at the table, John is the tallest.
> **Wrong:** Of the five men at the table, John is the taller.

Not all adjectives, however, form their comparatives and superlatives by adding *er* and *est*. Long adjectives such as *comfortable* would become tongue-twisters if we were to add *er* or *est*. So, instead of adding *er* or *est* to the end of such an adjective, we place the word *more* or *most* in front of it.

To form the *comparative* of long adjectives we say:

more comfortable   more difficult   more grateful   more durable

To form the *superlative* we say:

most comfortable   most difficult   most grateful   most durable

Note, however, that the rule about comparatives and superlatives still applies.

> More comfortable compares only *two*.
> Most comfortable compares *three or more*.

These are the general rules for when to add *er* or *est* and when to put *more* or *most* before the adjective.

1. If the positive form of the adjective is one syllable, add *er* or *est*.

short	shorter	shortest
long	longer	longest
sad	sadder	saddest

2. If the positive form is one or two syllables and ends in *y*, change the *y* to *i* and add *er* or *est*.

dry	drier	driest
lazy	lazier	laziest
lovely	lovelier	loveliest
happy	happier	happiest

3. For all other adjectives of two or more syllables, add *more* or *most*.

helpful	more helpful	most helpful
attractive	more attractive	most attractive
beautiful	more beautiful	most beautiful
intelligent	more intelligent	most intelligent

A few adjectives are irregular and form their comparatives and superlatives in a different way. You are already familiar with most of them.

Simple	*Comparative*	*Superlative*
bad	worse	worst
good	better	best
little	less	least
many \ much /	more	most
late	later latter	latest last
far	farther further	farthest furthest

ABSOLUTE ADJECTIVES

Some adjectives should not be compared because the simple form of the adjective expresses the quality to the highest degree. For example, because *unique* means *one of a kind*, nothing can be *more unique* or *most unique*. *Unique* is already superlative; it cannot be compared. Similarly, if a tank is *empty*, another tank cannot be *more empty*.

Here is a list of some of these *absolute adjectives*.

alone	perfect	straight
complete	perpendicular	supreme
empty	right	unanimous
final	round	unique
full	single	vertical
horizontal	square	wrong
instantaneous		

In casual conversation we might say that one line is straighter than another, or the straightest of all, that one bowl is rounder than another or the roundest of all the bowls present. When we do, we are being imprecise and, technically, incorrect. When we use these absolute adjectives in a comparison, we should compare degrees to which items approach these absolute qualities by using *nearly.*

This line is more nearly straight than that one.
Of all these bowls, this one is most nearly round.

AVOIDING DOUBLE COMPARATIVES AND SUPERLATIVES

In using the comparative and the superlative forms of adjectives, be careful to avoid the following constructions:

Wrong: I am more happier than Bob about our new assignment.
Wrong: This is the most best job I've ever had.
Wrong: This is the bestest job I've ever had.

Each of these three sentences is incorrect because each has a double comparison. In the first sentence, *happier* is already in the comparative degree; *more happier* is redundant and grammatically wrong. *Best* is itself a superlative; you can't be better than best. Therefore, both *most best* and *bestest* are incorrect. These double superlatives should also be avoided.

Right: I am happier than Bob about our new assignment.
Right: This is the best job I've ever had.

ADJECTIVES AFTER LINKING VERBS

In Chapter 6 we discussed linking verbs—verbs that express a state of being rather than an action. Linking verbs include all forms of the verb *to be* (for example: *am, was, will be, should have been*) and also verbs like *feel, seem,* and *appear* when they are used in such a manner that they could be replaced by the verb *is.*

We have a heavy schedule.
Our schedule is heavy.
Our schedule looks heavy.

Normally an adjective directly precedes the noun it modifies. In the first sentence above, *heavy* is an adjective. But *heavy* is also an adjective in the second sentence. In both, *heavy* modifies *schedule.* In the second sentence *heavy* is serving as a *predicate adjective.* A **predicate adjective** follows a linking verb and modifies the subject of the sentence.

This day is long.
This day seems long.
His argument is forceful.
His argument appears forceful.

Both *long* and *forceful* are predicate adjectives; *long* modifies *day* and *forceful* modifies *argument.* Remember that an adjective is still an adjective even if it is separated from its subject by a linking verb. We'll discuss the significance of this fact in the next chapter when we see how to determine whether a sentence calls for an adjective or an adverb.

PROGRAMMED REINFORCEMENT

S1 An adjective is a word that describes a _____ or _____.

R1 noun; pronoun

S2 Circle one: Adjectives as a rule make sentences more
a. colorful; b. brief; c. grammatical.

R2 a. colorful

S3 Circle three adjectives in this sentence: **A red tie and green socks do not go with conservative clothing.**

R3 **red; green; conservative**

S4 Circle three adjectives in this sentence: **The young applicant gave five answers to the revised questionnaire.**

R4 **young; five; revised**

S5 **He coughed loudly, then resumed speaking. Loudly** is not an adjective because the word it modifies (**coughed**) is not a _____; it is a _____.

R5 noun; verb

S6 Adjectives may be used to compare one item with others. When we compare two things, we use the _____ _____ form.

R6 comparative

S7 The comparative form of an adjective generally adds the letters _____ to the simple form.

R7 er

S8 Circle the simple adjective and underline the comparative adjective: **The modernized factory is busier than it has been in years.**

R8 simple adjective— **modernized;** comparative— **busier**

S9 The superlative form of the adjective generally ends with the letters _____.

R9 est

S10 Circle two superlative form adjectives in this sentence: **John is the strongest and fastest worker in the warehouse crew.**

R10 **strongest; fastest**

S11 Some adjectives of more than one syllable would sound awkward with the addition of **er** for the comparative or **est** for the superlative form. The word **beautiful** is compared by having the word _____ precede it in the comparative form and _____ in the superlative form.

R11 more; most

S12 Circle any comparative forms; underline any superlatives:
The longest runway today is too short for the larger, more powerful jets planned for the future.

R12 comparatives—**larger; more powerful;** superlative—**longest**

S13 Write the comparative and superlative of the following simple adjectives:
lovely _____ _____
attractive _____ _____
bad _____ _____

R13 lovely, lovelier, loveliest; attractive, more attractive, most attractive; bad, worse, worst

S14 **This is the most unique plan.** Because *unique* means *one and only,* circle the incorrect word in the sentence.

R14 **most**

S15 In using adjectives you must be careful not to make the mistake of using double comparatives or superlatives. Circle the incorrect words in these sentences:
My word processor is more better than hers.
This is the most prettiest arrangement of flowers I've ever seen.

R15 **more; most**

S16 Circle the adjectives in these two sentences: **Here is a solid desk. This desk is solid.** In the second example, **solid** is still an adjective even though it is separated from its noun by a _____ verb.

R16 **solid; solid;** linking.

Turn to Exercise 10.1.

USING ADJECTIVES

THIS/THAT, THESE/THOSE

These four words are called **demonstrative pronouns.** They often act in sentences as adjectives. The plural of *this* is *these.* The plural of *that* is *those.* Be sure that the adjective corresponds in number to the noun it modifies.

This summary is excellent.
These summaries are excellent.
That office is ten minutes from here.
Those offices are ten minutes from here.

Be careful with words such as *kind, sort,* and *type,* nouns that may sound plural but are actually singular. Write *this kind* or *that kind,* not *these kind* or *those kind.* The correct plural forms would be *these kinds* and *those kinds.*

THEM

The word *them* is a pronoun, not an adjective. Never use *them* to modify a noun or another pronoun.

Right: Those ledgers are mine. (Not: Them ledgers are mine.)
Right: That kind is no good. (Not: Them kind is no good.)

 LESS/FEWER

Most supermarkets have at least one checkout lane marked *Ten items or less*. This widely used sign is grammatically incorrect. *Less* should be used to refer to abstract nouns and to items measured in bulk.

This assignment took less time than I had anticipated.
We are using less electricity than last year.
Less copper was mined this year than last.

Fewer should be used to refer to items that can be counted separately.

I spent fewer hours on this project than I had expected.
We used far fewer kilowatts this month than last.
Fewer tons of copper are available this year.

The supermarket signs should read *Ten items or fewer* or *Ten or fewer items*.

 FARTHER/FURTHER; FARTHEST/FURTHEST

Sometimes these forms of the adjective *far* are used incorrectly. The words *farther* and *farthest* should be used in reference to an actual physical distance.
An easy way to remember is to think of the *a* in *space* and the *a* in *farther* and *farthest*.

Our car will travel farther on less gas.
Our offices are in the building farthest from the main entrance.

Use *further* and *furthest* in all other situations.

Study this chapter further.
If we delve further, we will find the solution.

 LATER/LATTER

Later is the comparative form of the adjective *late* and refers to time.

I shall be there later.
The speech was given later than I had expected.

Latter means the second of two; it is usually used as the opposite of *former*, which means the first of two.

The latter part of the book is the more interesting.

Stern and Hines were both successful—the former through luck; the latter through hard work.

If you are referring to more than two items, use *first* or *last* rather than *former* or *latter*.

 ## FIRST/LAST

When using the word *first* or the word *last* to modify a number, always place it *directly before* the number.

The first eight pages have been typed.
Not: The eight first pages.

The last six people arrived late.
Not: The six last people arrived late.

 # PROGRAMMED REINFORCEMENT

	S17 The word **kind** or **type** when preceded by **this** or **that** is perfectly correct. When we use the plural **kinds** or **types**, we must change **this** to _____ and **that** to _____.
R17 these; those	**S18** Circle the incorrect adjective in this sentence. **I like these kind of scissors.**
R18 these	**S19** Circle the incorrect adjective in this sentence. **Let us stock those type of ribbons.**
R19 those	**S20** This sentence contains a flagrant error in which a pronoun is used instead of an adjective. Circle the improper word. **Them notes were taken at the last conference.** The proper word is _____.
R20 **Them;** These or Those	**S21** Rewrite this sentence correctly: **Them kind is not any good.** _____
R21 **That** kind (or **This** kind) . . .	**S22** **Less** and **fewer** are adjectives that are sometimes confused. We say **less money** but **fewer checks.** We use **less** when items (are, are not) counted separately; we use **fewer** when items (are, are not) counted separately.
R22 are not; are	**S23** Circle the correct sentence: **a. Fewer receptionists are available now than before.** **b. Less engineers are unemployed today.**
R23 a.	

S24 **Farther** and **further** are adjectives that are sometimes confused. The word that refers to an actual physical distance is _____.

R24 **farther**

S25 Circle the correct answer: **He threw the ball the (farthest, furthest).**

R25 **farthest**

S26 Circle the correct answer: **I will tolerate no (farther, further) delays.**

R26 **further**

S27 **Later** and **latter** are adjectives sometimes confused. The word that refers to time is _____. The word that refers to position is _____.

R27 later; latter

S28 Circle the correct answer: **I will see you (later, latter).**

R28 **later**

S29 **Latter** is the second of two as opposed to _____, which is the first of two. Circle the correct answer: **The former answer is wrong; the (latter, later) is correct.**

R29 former; **latter**

S30 Circle the misplaced adjective: **The three last days have been trying.** Rewrite the sentence correctly. _____

R30 **last; The last three days have been trying.**

S31 Circle the misplaced adjective: **The six first people at the concert were relatives.** What word should this adjective precede? _____

R31 **first** should precede **six.**

Turn to Exercise 10.2.

 # COMPARISON WITH A GROUP

What is wrong with this sentence?

Wrong: I am smarter than any person in my class.

I am in my class. I cannot be smarter than myself. I must therefore exclude myself from the rest of the group by the use of the word *other* or the word *else* as follows:

Right: I am smarter than any other person in my class.
Right: I am smarter than anyone else in my class.
Right: I am the smartest person in my class.

Here is another example:

Wrong: Newark is larger than any city in New Jersey.
Right: Newark is larger than any other city in New Jersey.
Right: Newark is the largest city in New Jersey.

Thus the advertisement for a sporting goods manufacturer that says *We make more tennis balls than any company in America* is grammatically incorrect. It should state *We make more tennis balls than any other company in America.*

 ## CAPITALIZING PROPER ADJECTIVES

Proper adjectives are adjectives that are derived from proper nouns—the names of specific people, places, or things. Words like *American, Asiatic,* and *Victorian* are capitalized just like the proper nouns from which they come.

Some proper adjectives, however, are no longer thought of in connection with the original proper noun. Here are a few such adjectives that are not capitalized: *morocco binding, oriental rug, jersey wool.*

Many trademarks have become so common in everyday use that they have passed into the public domain and have lost their status as trademarks—and thereby their capital letters. Here are just a few examples: *aspirin, escalator, cellophane, shredded wheat, thermos bottle.* There are hundreds of others.

We will discuss the capitalization of proper nouns at length in Chapter 20.

 ## COMPOUND ADJECTIVES

The word *compound* means the uniting of two or more elements. We have already studied compound subjects, compound predicates, compound sentences, and compound nouns. Now let's examine the **compound adjective;** for example: *bluish green, up to date, out of work, high grade.* The question is: When are compound adjectives hyphenated and when aren't they? Do you write *up-to-date* or *up to date?* The answer is simple. Compound adjectives are generally hyphenated when they immediately come *before* the noun they describe; they are usually not hyphenated when they come *after* the noun. Look at these examples:

> Our up-to-date styles can't be surpassed.
> Our styles are known to be up to date.
> We sell first-class products.
> The products we sell are first class.
> A high-grade copier is hard to find.
> We are looking for a copier that is high grade.

Compound adjectives are often formed by joining a numeral with words of measure like *inch, foot, mile, pound, month, quart.* The basic rule still pertains:

a three-foot ruler	a ruler three feet long
a five-mile walk	a walk of five miles
a four-year period	a period of four years

Note that in the hyphenated adjectives that precede the noun, the unit of measure is always singular: *a five-pound cake, not a five-pounds cake.*

There are a few compound adjectives that are always hyphenated regardless of their position in a sentence.

Right-handed and *left-handed* are always hyphenated.

> Mr. Golen is right-handed.
> Propane tank valves are fitted with left-handed threads.

A hyphen is used in all compound adjectives formed with *self.*

He is a self-made man.
This truth is self-evident.

(Note: *selfhood, selfish, selfless,* and *selfsame* are not hyphenated.)
A hyphen should be used in numerical adjectives from twenty-one through ninety-nine.

We celebrated our twenty-fifth anniversary.
She was elected on the thirty-second count.
This attempt was their one hundred and twenty-ninth.

Although *well* is technically an adverb in most situations, compounds such as *well-known, well-handled, well-bred,* and *well-read* are considered adjectives. As such, they too follow the basic rule.

Our well-known label is easily recognized.
Our label is well known.

Be careful not to extend the principle of hyphenating compound adjectives to other types of compound modifiers. For example, when a compound modifier contains an adverb ending in *ly,* it should *not* be hyphenated in any position.

A frequently misspelled word is *maintenance.*
The word *maintenance* is frequently misspelled.

In a series of compound adjectives, be sure to retain the hyphen even though all of the adjectives are not fully expressed.

The biology class included two-, three-, and four-hour laboratories.
One-, three-, and six-acre parcels of land were available through the developer.

Remember: If you are unsure whether a hyphen is required, consult your dictionary.

MISPLACED MODIFIERS

As we saw in Chapter 9, a participial phrase may be used to modify a noun. If it is not used properly, however, the problem of the dangling participle may result.

Wrong: Serving lunch, a banana peel tripped the waitress.
Right: Serving lunch, the waitress tripped on a banana peel.

Similarly an *adjective phrase* may be used to modify a noun. For example, in the sentence *The desk with the steel legs is sturdy,* the adjective phrase *with the steel legs* describes the noun *desk.*
You should always place an adjective phrase as close as possible to the word it modifies. Failure to do so can result in strange sentences like these:

Wrong: They delivered the piano to the woman with mahogany legs.
Right: They delivered the piano with mahogany legs to the woman.
Wrong: I bought a fan for my friend that was reconditioned.
Right: I bought a fan that was reconditioned for my friend.
Right: I bought a reconditioned fan for my friend.

Although the problem of a misplaced adjective phrase can often be corrected simply by shifting it closer to the noun it modifies, sometimes you may have to revise the sentence.

Original: I bought a camera in Chicago last year at a discount store that cost less than $100.

Revision: Last year at a discount store in Chicago I bought a camera that cost less than $100.

ARTICLES

DEFINITE AND INDEFINITE ARTICLES

In grammar the three adjectives *a, an,* and *the* have a special name—**articles.** The word *the* is called the *definite article.* The words *a* and *an* are called the *indefinite articles.*

When we say *The book is on the desk,* we are pointing out a particular book on a particular desk. When we say *A book is on the desk,* we are not referring to any specific book, we are simply indicating that some book is on the desk.

Although you should never have any trouble using the definite article, you may wonder sometimes *which* of the indefinite articles to use. It's all determined by ease of pronunciation.

Whether to use *a* or *an* depends upon the sound of the next word. When the next word begins with a *consonant* sound—the sound of any letter in the alphabet except *a, e, i, o, u*—you use the article *a.*

a boy   a woman   a happy boy   a young woman

Note that you say: *a* happy boy. On the other hand you say: *an* honest man. Why? Because in the word *honest,* the *h* is silent. Because the word *honest* does not begin with a consonant *sound,* use *an.*

an hour   an honor   a house   a hotel

You use *an* wherever a word begins with a *vowel* sound. The vowels are *a, e, i, o, u.*

an apple   an event   an incident   an orange
                     an umbrella   a university

Note that while you should say *an umbrella,* you also say *a university.* Why? Because the *u* in *university* sounds like the *y* in *you.* Remember, it is the *sound* that counts, not the spelling.

a union   a usurer   an ulcer   an undertaking

 ## REPEATING THE ARTICLE

Occasionally, you will be faced with a problem of whether to repeat the article when you are listing a series of things. For example:

The red and (the) white coats are on sale.

Should you use the extra *the?* This depends upon what you mean. If each coat is part white and part red, then omit the extra *the: The red and white coats are on sale.* (For the sake of clarity, you might better use hyphens here to express your meaning: *The red-and-white coats are on sale.*) If, however, there are two types of coats—one all white and the other all red—then add the extra *the: The red and the white coats are on sale.*

The president and the chairman arrived. (Two people.)
The president and chairman arrived. (One person holding both positions.)
The steel and the plastic cabinets are in place. (Some cabinets are all steel; some, all plastic.)
The steel and plastic cabinets are in place. (Cabinets of part steel and part plastic.)

 PROGRAMMED REINFORCEMENT

	S32 In the sentence **He is more personable than any executive,** what word has been incorrectly omitted before the word **executive?** Answer: _____.
R32 other	**S33** Proper adjectives are derived from proper names. When they are thought of in connection with the original proper name they are (capitalized, not capitalized).
R33 capitalized	**S34** Change the capitalization of proper adjectives where necessary: **The american soccer team wore Jersey wool sweaters.**
R34 American; jersey	**S35** Do the same with this sentence: **The Victorian age was marked by ornateness like Oriental designs tooled on Moroccan leather.**
R35 Victorian; oriental; moroccan	**S36** A compound adjective like **well made** or **high grade** is usually hyphenated when it comes (before, after) the noun modified.
R36 before	**S37** Circle the compound adjective in this sentence. **This account is up to date.** It (is, is not) hyphenated because it comes (before, after) its noun.
R37 up to date; is not; after	**S38** Circle the compound adjective in this sentence. **She has an up-to-date showroom.** It is hyphenated because it comes _____ its noun.
R38 up-to-date; before	**S39** A numerical compound adjective from **twenty-first** to **ninety-ninth** is (always, sometimes, never) hyphenated when spelled out. Circle the correct answer: **This anniversary is the (twenty fifth, twenty-fifth).**
R39 always; **twenty-fifth**	**S40** Compound adjectives involving the word **self**—for example, **self-evident**—are (always, sometimes, never) hyphenated.
R40 always	

S41 Here are compound adjectives combining a numeral with words like **inch, mile, foot.** Insert hyphens where necessary: **half inch ruler; three mile run; box of four pounds; four pound box.**

R41 **half-inch ruler; three-mile run; four-pound box**

S42 In a series of compound adjectives preceding a noun, hyphens should be retained even though all the adjectives are not completely expressed. Indicate where hyphens should be placed in the following sentence: **In graduate school Roger had two, three, and four hour classes.**

R42 **two-, three-, and four-hour classes.**

S43 A group of words describing a noun is called an adjective phrase. Such a phrase should be placed next to the noun it describes. Circle the group of words that is misplaced. **The filing cabinet belongs to the purchasing department with the scratched top.** Underline the word this circled phrase should follow.

R43 **with the scratched top** should follow **filing cabinet**

S44 Do the same in this sentence: **I gave the pen to the typist with the erasable ink.**

R44 **with the erasable ink** should follow **pen**

S45 The article **an** rather than **a** is used in **an antique** because **antique** begins with a _____ sound.

R45 vowel

S46 You should write **an understatement** because the **u** has a _____ sound. You write a **union** because here the **u** has a _____ sound.

R46 vowel; consonant

S47 Insert **a** or **an:** _____ unique problem; _____ usual offer; _____ unusual offer; _____ error; _____ honest mistake.

R47 **a** unique; **a** usual; **an** unusual; **an** error; **an** honest

S48 The article **the** repeated in the sentence **The president and the treasurer spoke,** means that (one, two) people are involved.

R48 two

S49 As a review, an adjective modifies a _____. It may be compared by changing the simple form to the _____ when comparing two; to the _____ when comparing more than _____.

R49 noun; comparative; superlative; two

Turn to Exercises 10.3 to 10.7.

EXERCISE 10·1A   ADJECTIVES

Underline with one line the adjective in each of the following sentences. Then underline with two lines the word each adjective modifies.

1. She picked up the brown case.
2. He prepared a light supper.
3. The colored lights were dimmed.
4. It was a very efficient system.
5. We have complete records.
6. Our latest records show a deficit.
7. We sent an order for farm machinery.
8. He slowly walked to his first class.
9. These are first-class goods.
10. Here is our new catalog.
11. Send me your final approval.
12. Where is my wool hat?
13. Forgive my late reply.
14. The table has a smooth finish.
15. We went horseback riding.
16. It's a very smooth-riding car.
17. This is an easy problem.
18. This problem is easy.
19. I am hungry.
20. He looks tired.

EXERCISE 10·1B   DEGREES OF ADJECTIVES

In the space provided, write the proper form of the adjective in parentheses.

1. Although Mr. Pulaski and Ms. Jones are intelligent, Mr. Roberto is the (wise). 1. _____
2. Which of this pair has the (bright) colors? 2. _____
3. Though our Raleigh plant is large, the Durham plant is (large). 3. _____
4. New York is the (exciting) of the two cities. 4. _____
5. New York is the (exciting) city in the world. 5. _____
6. She is the (tall) person in the whole office. 6. _____
7. The left sleeve is (long) than the right. 7. _____
8. Of all our forty-three offices, the (large) is in Los Angeles. 8. _____
9. Test this one, then that one, and choose the (good). 9. _____
10. Which of the designs is the (pretty)? 10. _____
11. Which of these two posts is (vertical)? 11. _____
12. Of all these boxes, which one is (square)? 12. _____
13. Peter is the (irresponsible) person I've ever met. 13. _____
14. I know of no one (irresponsible) than he. 14. _____
15. Which city has the (dry) climate, Phoenix or Dallas? 15. _____

EXERCISE 10·1C DEGREES OF ADJECTIVES

On each line of the following table is written one of the three adjective forms. Fill in the other two forms. For an absolute adjective, write the comparative and superlative forms of how something approaches this quality.

	SIMPLE	COMPARATIVE	SUPERLATIVE
1.	efficient		
2.		busier	
3.	familiar		
4.			most
5.		less	
6.			last
7.		hotter	
8.	good		
9.			farthest
10.		sadder	
11.	difficult		
12.		worse	
13.	unusual		
14.			loveliest
15.	friendly		
16.	important		
17.	afraid		
18.	wealthy		
19.		happier	
20.	dry		
21.	funny		
22.		further	
23.			smartest
24.	empty		
25.	horizontal		

EXERCISE 10·2A   THIS, THAT, THESE, THOSE

In the space provided next to each sentence, write the proper adjective.

1. (This) (These) forms of investment are government insured.   1. _____
2. (That) (Those) make of cars sells very well.   2. _____
3. Mr. Battista always wears (this) (these) style of trousers.   3. _____
4. (That) (Those) kind of investment can be very risky.   4. _____
5. Where do you buy (this) (these) type of shoes?   5. _____
6. I don't associate with (that) (those) kind of people.   6. _____
7. I don't associate with (that) (those) people.   7. _____
8. (This) (These) type of fabric is very durable.   8. _____
9. Do you like (that) (those) kind of pants?   9. _____
10. Would you call (this) (these) models the best for our purposes?   10. _____

EXERCISE 10·2B   LESS AND FEWER

In the space provided, write the correct word.

1. They delivered (less) (fewer) coal than we had ordered.   1. _____
2. They delivered (less) (fewer) tons of coal than we had ordered.   2. _____
3. There were (less) (fewer) than ten customers today.   3. _____
4. We can do the same amount of work with (less) (fewer) assistants.   4. _____
5. Their firm has sent (less) (fewer) orders than anticipated.   5. _____
6. There is (less) (fewer) unemployment than anticipated.   6. _____
7. This air conditioner uses (less) (fewer) electricity than any other model.   7. _____
8. This air conditioner uses (less) (fewer) kilowatts of electricity than any other model.   8. _____
9. This personal computer weighs (less) (fewer) than twenty pounds.   9. _____
10. (Less) (Fewer) than ten people applied for the position.   10. _____

EXERCISE 10·2C FARTHER-FURTHER AND LATER-LATTER

In the space provided, fill in the proper word.

1. Our hotel suite is (farther, further) from the elevator than yours is.   1. _____
2. Lee sat in the chair (farthest, furthest) from the interviewer.   2. _____
3. I will go to the (farthest, furthest) place in the world for you.   3. _____
4. (Further, Farther) than that, I cannot go in compromising with you.   4. _____
5. The (later, latter) we meet tonight, the less time we will have.   5. _____
6. The (later, latter) part of the address contained some important points.   6. _____
7. The former speaker introduced the guest; the (later, latter) spoke at length.   7. _____
8. The two senators spoke. The former said: "It is (later, latter) than you think."   8. _____
9. The (later, latter) portion of the report recommended specific changes.   9. _____
10. Resigning is the (farthest, furthest) thing from my mind.   10. _____

EXERCISE 10·2D FIRST AND LAST

In only one of the following five sentences is the word first or last properly placed. Write C in front of that sentence. Make the changes necessary to correct the other sentences.

1. We enjoyed the two last weeks.
2. I don't understand the eight first pages.
3. We haven't heard from him for the last three days.
4. We have read all but the eight last pages.
5. Only the six first people were admitted.

EXERCISE 10·3A   COMPARISON WITH A GROUP

Write C in front of the sentence if it is correct. If the sentence is incorrect, make the necessary corrections.

1.   My current job is more satisfying than any job I've ever had.

2.   John is bigger, smarter, and more handsome than any of his classmates.

3.   Mr. Czerny is shrewder than anyone in his department.

4.   Who is quicker than any girl in her group?

5.   Our PCII is the most portable home computer on the market today.

6.   The new Volvo is safer than any car on the road.

7.   Of all the tenants, Ms. Kelly is least objectionable.

8.   Professor Martinez is more qualified than any person in her department.

9.   More level-headed than any man in his company, Kareem was promoted.

10. This is the best and most efficient of any other system used today.

EXERCISE 10·3B   CAPITALIZING AND HYPHENATING

In the space provided, fill in the proper word.

1. The (American, american) Indian created (well-made, well made) tools.

   1. _____

2. The (Victorian, victorian) age began in the 1830's.

   2. _____

3. A (Persian, persian) rug may be very valuable.

   3. _____

4. She heard (Martial, martial) music on the radio.

   4. _____

5. He was a (well-intentioned, well intentioned) worker who made mistakes.

   5. _____

6. The fact that she cannot perform the work is (self-evident, self evident).

   6. _____

7. A (first-rate, first rate) mechanic is difficult to find.

   7. _____

8. The owners put up a (last-ditch, last ditch) effort to avoid bankruptcy.

   8. _____

9. This latest branch opening was our (twenty-first, twenty first).

   9. _____

10. In this office we need workers who are (well-disciplined, well disciplined).

    10. _____

11. She wore a (hand-knitted, hand knitted) sweater made from real (Jersey, jersey) wool.

    11. _____

12. Do you know when the (Alaskan, alaskan) pipeline was completed?

    12. _____

13. The (Japanese, japanese) imports have captured a large share of the automobile market.

    13. _____

14. Listen to WKSH for (up to the minute, up-to-the-minute) news.

    14. _____

15. The housing development contained both (three and four bedroom, three- and four-bedroom) homes.

    15. _____

16. Leon's prophecy of failure was largely (self fulfilling, self-fulfilling).

    16. _____

17. This is our (forty second, forty-second) year in business.

    17. _____

18. Diskettes are available in (3½ inch, 5¼ inch, and 8 inch; 3½-inch, 5¼-inch, and 8-inch) formats.

    18. _____

19. She has the (selfsame, self-same) attitude toward achieving success as he does.

    19. _____

20. I admire Alfredo's (never say die, never-say-die) attitude.

    20. _____

EXERCISE 10·4   PLACEMENT OF MODIFIERS

Each of the sentences below is incorrect because of a misplaced modifier. Rewrite these sentences correctly in the space provided.

1. People cannot fail to notice vast changes in office procedures who are in touch with business offices.

    _____

    _____

    _____

2. We saw the new building walking down East Shore Drive.

    _____

    _____

3. He told a joke at the convention that was ribald.

    _____

    _____

4. Take the book to the manager with the beautiful leather binding.

    _____

    _____

5. She listened to the complaining customer with utter disbelief.

    _____

    _____

6. He went to the interview with a great deal of anxiety.

    _____

    _____

7. They watched the parade pass by standing at the corner.

    _____

    _____

8. The woman boarded a plane at the airport that was going to Boston.

    _____

    _____

    _____

9. I met a young man while vacationing in Japan who would like to invest in our company.

    _____

    _____

211

10. Several employees met for lunch recently promoted.

_____

_____

11. The delivery truck was towed to the garage after it broke down on the highway.

_____

_____

12. A seminar will be offered Saturday in the county library on preparing effective résumés.

_____

_____

13. My supervisor always checks my reports after I submit them for mechanical errors.

_____

_____

14. She was advised not to submit a report to her supervisor that was incomplete.

_____

_____

15. The buildings are for rent on the next block.

_____

_____

EXERCISE 10·5A   USING THE ARTICLES A, AN

In the spaces provided, write either _a_ or _an_, whichever is correct.

1. _____ man wearing _____ unusual jacket left _____ package.

2. _____ humorist is _____ human being with _____ peculiar sense of humor.

3. _____ understanding of all operations in our plant is _____ necessity for _____ supervisor.

4. _____ hour before dawn is _____ inhuman hour for _____ human being to be awakened.

5. _____ union leader should be _____ honest person, for to lead _____ union is _____ undertaking of great responsibility.

EXERCISE 10·5B   REPEATING THE ARTICLE

In some of the following sentences, the article has been incorrectly repeated or left out. Make any necessary corrections. Write the letter C in front of any sentence that is correct.

1. The secretary and vice president met at noon.
2. Carlos was elected to be both the vice president and the secretary.
3. The car has a blue and a white finish.
4. We have in stock two models, a chromium and aluminum one.
5. She wore a red and a green sweater.

EXERCISE 10·6   ADJECTIVES

The letter below has many errors. Cross out all errors and make the necessary changes in the space above them.

Dear Miss Arnez:

Video Mart's metropolitan area sale on video discs and cassettes has proved to be our bestest ever. The sale is excitinger and spectacularer than any sale in our history.

During the two first weeks we sold no less than 10,000 cassettes in each of our local two stores. In fact, the South Street store has sold the greatest number of cassettes even though the store is furthest from the heart of town. This is a extremely unusual situation, most unique in the history of them two stores.

While we couldn't be more happy with the success of the South Street store, we are puzzled about the relative drop in sales experienced by our central store, which annually receives our first, second, or third place award in the eastern region for most sales. Because you are a well known and highly-respected marketing analyst, we are seeking your expert advice.

We would like you to visit our Sixth Avenue store on Monday. You can't miss it, walking down Sixth Avenue toward Elm. Ms. Johnson, our manager, and her assistant, Mr. Kahn, know you are coming. The first will provide you with any information you require regarding the operation of the store.

Please determine the reasons why this store has least sales than the South Street store. Also, please give us a honest opinion of Ms. Johnson's effectiveness as manager. With your assistance we hope the central store will regain its status as the top store in the area and one of the more better Video Mart outlets in the East.

Sincerely,

EXERCISE 10·7 COMPOSITION: ADJECTIVES

Compose complete sentences containing the form of the adjective called for in parentheses.

1. (the comparative form of *good*) _____

_____

2. (the superlative form of *intelligent*) _____

_____

3. (the comparative form of *busy*) _____

_____

4. (the superlative form of *full*) _____

_____

5. (both *less* and *fewer*) _____

_____

6. (both *later* and *latter*) _____

_____

7. (*out of date*) _____

_____

8. (*once in a lifetime*) _____

_____

9. (*hard to find*) _____

_____

10. (two or more compound adjectives in series) _____

_____

11

ADVERBS

FORMING ADVERBS, CHOOSING BETWEEN ADJECTIVES AND ADVERBS, USING ADVERBS

As we saw in the last chapter, adjectives modify nouns and pronouns. *Adverbs* are more versatile modifiers. Not only do adverbs modify verbs, they can also modify adjectives and other adverbs.

> The production team worked swiftly. (The adverb *swiftly* modifies the verb *worked.*)
> Broadway is an extremely wide street. (The adverb *extremely* modifies the adjective *wide.*)
> The accountant spoke very rapidly. (The adverb *very* modifies the adverb *rapidly.*)

An **adverb** is a word that tells *how, when, where,* or *to what degree* (*how much, how often, how large, how small, how long,* and so on).

> The book was printed carefully. Printed *how?* Carefully.
> The order was shipped promptly. Shipped *when?* Promptly.
> The officials came here. Came *where?* Here.
> They were very pleased. Pleased *how much?* Very.
> They are seldom satisfied. Satisfied *how often?* Seldom.

In this chapter we will study how to form and use adverbs correctly, and how to choose between an adjective and an adverb.

 FORMING ADVERBS

Many adverbs are formed from adjectives merely adding *ly* to the adjective:

ADJECTIVE	ADVERB	ADJECTIVE	ADVERB
swift	swiftly	familiar	familiarly
careful	carefully	sole	solely

In spelling, remember that the *ly* adverb ending is simply attached to the existing word in most cases. Adjectives that end with e or *al* fall into the same category—just attach the *ly.*

> separate + ly = separately   accidental + ly = accidentally
> scarce + ly = scarcely   cordial + ly = cordially
> authoritative + ly = authoritatively   official + ly = officially

When the adjective ends in *y*, to form the adverb change the *y* to *i* and add *ly*.

ADJECTIVE	ADVERB	ADJECTIVE	ADVERB
busy	busily	satisfactory	satisfactorily
happy	happily	temporary	temporarily

When the adjective ends in *able* or in *ible*, to form the adverb drop the final e and add y.

ADJECTIVE	ADVERB	ADJECTIVE	ADVERB
noticeable	noticeably	forcible	forcibly
considerable	considerably	horrible	horribly

Notice that some adjectives change spelling when we change them into adverbs.

ADJECTIVE	ADVERB	ADJECTIVE	ADVERB
due	duly	whole	wholly
true	truly		

Thus a great many adverbs may be formed by adding the *ly* suffix to adjectives. In addition, there are many other adverbs that do not end in *ly*. Here is a partial list:

again	here	often	so	twice
almost	how	quite	soon	very
far	much	rather	then	well
fast	near	seldom	there	when
hard	now	since	too	where

 # PROGRAMMED REINFORCEMENT

S1   Adjectives modify (describe) nouns; adverbs modify _____, _____, and _____.

R1   verbs; adjectives; adverbs

S2   **The girl typed slowly.** The adverb **slowly** modifies the word _____ which is a _____.

R2   **typed;** verb

S3   **This is a very efficient operation.** The adverb **very** modifies the word _____ which is an _____.

R3   **efficient;** adjective

S4   **He filed the paper quite carelessly. Quite** is an adverb that modifies the word _____ which is a(n) _____.

R4   **carelessly;** adverb

S5   An adverb usually answers which of the following questions? (a) **how,** (b) **when,** (c) **where,** (d) **to what degree,** (e) **all of the above.**

R5   e

S6 Most adverbs are formed by adding _____ to the adjective.

R6 ly

S7 **Swiftly** is an _____ derived from the _____ _____ **swift.**

R7 adverb; adjective

S8 Circle the two misspelled adverbs: **separately, accidentally, minutly, purposly.** Write them correctly: _____ _____ .

R8 minutely; purposely

S9 When an adjective ends in **y**, to form the adverb you change the y to _____ and add _____ as in **busy-busily. happy–happily.**

R9 i; ly

S10 Change the following adjectives into adverbs: **easy, satisfactory, lazy.** _____ _____ _____ .

R10 **easily; satisfactorily; lazily**

S11 To form the adverb from an adjective ending in **able** or **ible,** as in **noticeable,** drop the _____ and add _____ .

R11 **e; y**

S12 Change the following adjectives into adverbs: **forcible, peaceable, changeable.** _____ _____ _____ .

R12 forcibly; peaceably; changeably

S13 Some adjectives become adverbs by other spelling changes. Write the adverbs for **true, whole, due.** _____ _____ _____ .

R13 **truly; wholly; duly**

Turn to Exercise 11.1.

CHOOSING BETWEEN ADJECTIVES AND ADVERBS

LINKING VERBS AND ACTION VERBS

Frequently in your writing you will have to determine whether to use an adjective or an adverb. For example, which is correct?

The situation looks (bad, badly).

The answer hinges on the distinction between action verbs and linking verbs. If you aren't certain of the difference, review Chapter 6.

In the previous chapter we looked at this sentence:

His argument is forceful.

We saw that *forceful* is a predicate adjective modifying the noun *argument*. Remember, a predicate adjective follows a linking verb and modifies the subject of the sentence.

Now look at this sentence:

He argued forcefully.

Here the word *forcefully* is an adverb and modifies the action verb *argued*.

Hence the rule governing whether to use an adjective or an adverb is very simple: Use an *adverb* to modify an *action* verb. Use an *adjective* after a *linking* verb.

> The fire burned fiercely. *Burned* is an *action* verb; therefore, we use the adverb *fiercely*.
>
> The material was sent promptly. *Sent* is an *action* verb; therefore, we use the adverb *promptly*.
>
> The manager shouted excitedly. *Shouted* is an action verb; therefore, we use the adverb *excitedly*.
>
> The excited manager shouted. Here *excited* describes the noun *manager;* it is an adjective.

What about this sentence:

The manager is excited.

Here *excited* is a predicate adjective. *The manager is excited* is the same as saying *the excited manager.*

The same is true in this sentence: *The manager looks excited.* You know that *looks* in this sentence is a linking verb. *Looks* could be replaced by *is: The manager looks (is) excited.* Again we use the adjective *excited* because it follows a linking verb and really describes the subject-noun *manager* and not the verb *looks.*

What about this sentence: *He looked (excited, excitedly) for the missing wallet.* Is *looked,* as used here, an action or a linking verb? Could it be replaced by *was?* No. Therefore, *looked* is an action verb (meaning *searched*) and requires the adverb *excitedly: He looked excitedly for the missing wallet.*

Earlier in this lesson, we gave as an example the problem sentence: *The situation looks (bad) (badly).* You should be able to solve this easily now. *Looks,* as used here, is a *linking* verb; therefore, we use the adjective *bad: The situation looks bad.*

Here is a similar sentence:

The child feels (bad) (badly).

It is conceivable that either word may be used if you stretch your imagination. How? If the child has burned her fingers and they have become insensitive, you could say *The child feels badly (with her fingers).* The adverb *badly* is then used to describe the action verb *feels.* Hardly likely, but possible!

For our purposes, however, *feels* in this sentence is a linking verb that really means *is. The child feels (is) bad (unhappy).* Remember, therefore, to say *I feel bad* if you want to describe your emotional or physical condition—not *I feel badly.*

Now look at this sentence:

Dinner tasted (good) (well).

Good is an adjective. *Well* is usually an adverb. Because *tasted* is a linking verb, we use the adjective *good. Dinner tasted good.* Note again that *tasted* really means *was: Dinner was good* or *a good dinner.* Simple, isn't it?

He performed (good) (well).

Performed is an *action* verb; therefore, we use the adverb *well*. *He performed well*. The only exception to this rule occurs when *well* is used as an adjective meaning *healthy*. In such a case, because *well* is an *adjective,* it can be used after a linking verb. *He is well (healthy). He feels well (healthy). He looks well (healthy).* But remember:

The bread smells good.   She spoke good English.
He works well.   She spoke English well.

 ## CONFUSED PAIRS

In addition to *good/well* and *bad/badly,* there are a few other pairs of words that are often misused. Usually the adjective is used incorrectly instead of the necessary adverb.

 ## MOST/ALMOST

Most can be an adjective, noun, or adverb. As an adjective or noun it means *the majority.*

Most students take a course in composition during their first semester in college.

As an adverb it means *to the greatest degree.*

Of all the proposals, I like Jack's most.

The word *almost* is an adverb meaning *nearly.*

The tickets are almost sold out.

Be careful not to use *most* when you mean *almost.*

Right: Almost all the T-shirts were sent.
Wrong: Most all the T-shirts were sent.

If you aren't sure whether to use *most* or *almost,* substitute the word *nearly.* If *nearly* fits, use *almost;* if it doesn't, use *most.*

 ## REAL/REALLY/VERY

I am (real) (very) pleased.

Real is an adjective that means *genuine. Very* is an adverb that means *extremely.* When faced with a choice of *real* or *very,* substitute *genuine* or *extremely.* If *genuine* fits, *real* is correct. If *extremely* fits, *very* is correct.
Our problem sentence reads properly if we insert *extremely: I am extremely pleased.* Therefore, use *very: I am very pleased,* not: *I am real pleased.*
Let's substitute *genuine* or *extremely* to check a few other sentences:

Right: It gives me real (genuine) pleasure to introduce the next speaker.
Right: We are very (extremely) well pleased with the outcome.
Right: It was a real (genuine) diamond.
Right: It was a very (extremely) wonderful movie.

Really is also an adverb. Although its meaning is different from that of *very* (*really* means *truly* or *genuinely*), the two words are often used interchangeably.

I am very (extremely) interested in this position.
I am really (truly) interested in this position.

If you know when to use *real* or *very*, you know when to use *real* or *really*.

 SURE/SURELY

Don't use the adjective *sure*, which means *confident* or *certain*, when you want to say *certainly* or *undoubtedly*. In that case you must use the adverb *surely*.

> He (sure, surely) did an unusually effective job! We must use *surely* because we mean *certainly*.

> (Sure, Surely) I'll go with you. (*Surely*, meaning *certainly*.)
> *But:* He is quite sure of himself. (Confident)

 PROGRAMMED REINFORCEMENT

	S14 In deciding whether to use an adjective or an adverb after a verb, you should remember that an adverb modifies an _____ verb while an adjective comes after a _____ verb.
R14 **action; linking**	**S15** A linking verb shows a state of being, not an action. It may be substituted by the verb _____.
R15 **is** (or **to be**)	**S16** **She writes (good, well).** We use the adverb _____ because **writes** is a(n) (action, linking) verb.
R16 **well;** action	**S17** **They feel (bad, badly).** We use the adjective _____ because **feel** is a(n) (action, linking) verb.
R17 bad; linking	**S18** **This machine is slow.** We use the _____ **slow** because **is** is a(n) _____ verb. **This machine runs slowly.** We use the _____ **slowly** because **runs** is a(n) _____ verb.
R18 adjective; linking; adverb; action	**S19** Choose the correct form: a. **The flowers smell (sweet, sweetly).** b. **The cake tastes (bitter, bitterly).** c. **He feels (healthy, healthily).**
R19 a. **sweet;** b. **bitter;** c. **healthy**	**S20** **Well** is usually an adverb, as in **She runs well.** In the sentence **She feels well,** the word **well** is an _____ that means _____.
R20 adjective; healthy	**S21** **(Almost, Most) everyone was present.** The correct word is _____, meaning **nearly.**
R21 **Almost**	

S22 Which is correct? **(Almost, Most) all the order was returned. (Almost, Most) of the order was returned.**

R22 **Almost; Most**

S23 **Real** and **very** are sometimes confused. _____ is an adjective meaning **genuine;** _____ is an adverb meaning **extremely.**

R23 **Real; very**

S24 **I am (real, very) happy to work here.** The correct word, _____, is an _____ modifying **happy,** which is a(n) _____.

R24 **very;** adverb; adjective

S25 **Really** is an _____ meaning *truly* or *genuinely.* **We are (real, really) sorry we cannot comply.** The correct word _____ is an _____ modifying **sorry,** which is a(n) _____.

R25 adverb; **really;** adverb; adjective

S26 **Sure** means **certain; surely** means **certainly. I am (sure, surely) happy that prices have leveled off.** The correct word is _____, which is an _____ that modifies **happy,** which is an _____.

R26 **surely;** adverb; adjective

S27 **(Sure, Surely) I'll lend you the money.**

R27 **Surely**

Turn to Exercises 11.2 and 11.3.

USING ADVERBS
COMPARISON OF ADVERBS

Adverbs may be compared, just like adjectives. One- or two-syllable words add *er* and *est: soon, sooner, soonest; early, earlier, earliest* (Exception: *often, more often, most often*). Adverbs that are longer usually are formed by using the words *more* and *most: happily, more happily, most happily; sincerely, more sincerely, most sincerely.* Remember to use the comparative form when comparing two; use the superlative when comparing three or more. *I will arrive earlier than he. Of them all, I arrived earliest.* How about this sentence: *I arrived earlier than any of them.* Why do we use the comparative when *them* tells us that there are at least two others? We use *earlier* because it compares you with *any of them,* and you know from Chapter 5 that *any* is singular—it means any one.

A few adverbs are compared irregularly. Some of these words appeared in the last chapter under the list of irregular adjectives. Such words are used both as adjectives and as adverbs.

POSITIVE	COMPARATIVE	SUPERLATIVE
far	farther	farthest
far	further	furthest
badly	worse	worst
well	better	best
little	less	least
much	more	most

Like absolute adjectives, some adverbs cannot be compared. The following adverbs do not have a comparative or superlative degree.

back	no	there
before	not	thus
by	now	too
ever	past	very
here	so	whenever
never	then	yes

As with adjectives, when comparing adverbs be careful to avoid double comparatives and double superlatives.

 DOUBLE NEGATIVES

Another double construction that is grammatically incorrect is the *double negative*. Here is a common example:

Wrong: They don't know nothing.

This sentence contains two negative words, *don't* and *nothing*. Each of these negatives cancels the other. By eliminating either one of them we get a correct sentence:

Right: They know nothing.
Right: They don't know anything.
Right: She didn't say anything.
Right: She said nothing.
Wrong: She didn't say nothing.
Right: It was nothing.
Right: It wasn't anything.
Wrong: It wasn't nothing.

Some words that don't look negative really are—words such as *scarcely, hardly, never, neither, but.* These words are *negative* in themselves. Never add the word *not* to them.

1. We can scarcely see you in this fog. Not: We *can't* scarcely see you. . . .
2. We could hardly have decided otherwise. Not: We *couldn't* hardly. . . .
3. It could never happen here. Not: It *couldn't* never happen here.
4. It was neither of them. Not: It *wasn't* neither of them.
5. I understand all but one of them. Not: I *don't* understand all but one. . . .

In the last example, if you really mean what is said in the latter sentence, your sentence would be clearer if you said: *I understand only one of them.*

 PLACEMENT OF ONLY

The four sentences below show how we can completely change our meaning by merely moving the word *only.*

1. *Only* Bob was accused of embezzlement. (No one else was accused.)
2. Bob was *only* accused of embezzlement. (He was accused but not convicted.)

3. Bob was accused of *only* embezzlement. (Embezzlement is not a very serious offense.)
4. Bob was accused of embezzlement *only*. (He was not accused of anything else.)

From these sentences learn this rule of good English. Always place the word *only* as close as possible to the word it modifies so that its meaning is absolutely clear.

Right: I paid only $8.50.
Wrong: I only paid $8.50.
Right: I filed my application only a day late.
Wrong: I only filed my application a day late.

 ## COMPOUND MODIFIERS WITH ADVERBS

In Chapter 10 we discussed the compound adjective. You learned that compound adjectives are generally hyphenated when they come immediately before the noun they describe; they are usually not hyphenated when they come after the noun.

When a compound modifier contains an adverb in the *ly* form, it does not need to be hyphenated in any position.

Word processing is a rapidly expanding field.
The field of word processing is rapidly expanding.
The overly eager trainee upset the tray.
The trainee, who was overly eager, upset the tray.

For purposes of clarity, however, compound modifiers with adverbs lacking the *ly* are governed by the same rule as compound adjectives.

The fast-talking salesperson pressured him into buying the more expensive model.
The medicine provides long-lasting relief.
This medicine provides relief that is long lasting.

 ## UNNECESSARY ADVERBS

Sometimes the adverbial meaning of *how, when, where,* or *how much* is expressed in other words in the sentence. In that case do not use the adverb unnecessarily. In the following sentences, each word in parentheses is redundant and therefore unnecessary.

Recopy this page (*over*).
I shall repeat the question (*again*).
He has returned (*back*) from Europe.
They must cooperate (*together*) to be a perfect pair.
Erase this (*out*).
We must seek (*out*) a solution.

 ## COMPOUND WORDS CONFUSED WITH ADVERBS

Sometimes you can be confused between compound expressions, usually beginning with *all*, that resemble adverbs, and the adverbs themselves. If you examine these expressions, however, you will see that the meanings are quite different.

all together (meaning *many combined*)
altogether (meaning *completely*)
They worked *all together* until they were *altogether* satisfied with the results.

all ways (meaning *every manner*)
always (meaning *forever*)
Always remember that there are *all ways* of reaching happiness.

all ready (meaning *completely prepared*)
already (meaning *previously*)
The employees were *all ready* at 5 P.M., though some had *already* punched out.

some time (meaning a *period of time*)
sometime (meaning *at some unspecified time*)
Sometime next week I must spend *some time* straightening my office.

 # HOPEFULLY

Hopefully is an adverb meaning *with hope*.

He opened the letter from the college admissions office hopefully.

The careful business writer does not use it to mean *I hope* or *it is to be hoped,* which is what people usually mean when they begin a sentence with *hopefully.*
Hopefully, I'll complete the assignment in time really means *I will complete with hope the assignment in time,* not *I hope I'll complete the assignment in time.*
The careful business writer avoids this common error.

 # PROGRAMMED REINFORCEMENT

S28 Adverbs may be compared just like adjectives. Write the comparative and superlative for these adverbs:
soon _____ _____
quietly _____ _____
well _____ _____

R28 soon; sooner; soonest; quietly; more quietly; most quietly; well, better; best

S29 Write the correct form: **This copier performs the** (superlative of **badly**) **of all three.** Answer: _____.

R29 **worst**

S30 Circle the two negative words in the sentence **She didn't file nothing correctly in the file cabinet.** This sentence illustrates the error called the _____.

R30 **didn't; nothing;** double negative

S31 Rewrite this double-negative sentence correctly: **The salesperson wasn't able to see none of the buyers.**

R31 **The salesperson wasn't able (or was unable) to see any of the buyers. Or, The salesperson was able to see none of the buyers.**

S32 **We aren't never going to go.** The double negative in this sentence can be corrected by changing the word _____ to _____, or the contraction _____ to _____.

R32 **never** to **ever** or **aren't** to **are**

S33 **I can't hardly wait until vacation.** To correct this sentence change the contraction _____ to _____.

R33 **can't** to **can**

S34 **It wasn't neither of them who made the error.** To correct this sentence, change the word _____ to _____ or change the word _____ to _____.

R34 **wasn't** to **was; neither** to **either**

S35 Misplaced modifiers can change the meaning of a sentence. In the sentence **Only Luis worked on Saturday,** the word **only** refers to the noun _____.

R35 **Luis**

S36 In the sentence **Luis only worked on Saturday,** the word **only** refers to the verb _____.

R36 **worked**

S37 In the sentence **Luis worked only on Saturday,** circle the word that **only** refers to.

R37 **Saturday**

S38 When a compound modifier contains an adverb in the *ly* form, the modifier is (a) **always,** (b) **sometimes,** (c) **never** hyphenated.

R38 a. **never**

S39 Compound modifiers with adverbs lacking the *ly* are usually hyphenated when they come **(before, after)** the word they modify.

R39 **before**

S40 Which of the following compound modifiers should be hyphenated?
a. **She was very well prepared for the interview.**
b. **A truly inspiring speech highlighted the conference.**
c. **I need a fast acting medication for my headache.**
d. **Who is the most successful?**

R40 c. **fast-acting**

S41 Unnecessary adverbs should be eliminated. Circle the words that should be omitted: (a) **He returned the bills back to me.** (b) **Please repeat the dictation again.**

R41 a. **back**
b. **again**

S42 Circle the words that should be omitted:
(a) **Recopy the page over.** (b) **Erase this mistake out.**

R42 a. **over**
b. **out**

S43   **Altogether** and **all together** are sometimes confused.
_____ means **many combined;**
_____ means **completely.**

R43   all together; altogether

S44   **The members of the staff worked (altogether, all together) until they were (altogether, all together) satisfied.**

R44   all together; altogether

S45   **(All ways, Always) try to excel in (all ways, always).**

R45   Always; all ways

S46   **The workers were (all ready, already) finished by noon, and they were (all ready, already) for lunch.**

R46   already; all ready

S47   **Some time** and **sometime** occasionally are confused.
_____ means _a period of time._ _____
means _at some unspecified time._

R47   some time; sometime

S48   **Please set aside (some time, sometime) for a meeting (some time, sometime) tomorrow.**

R48   some time; sometime

S49   The careful business writer does not use _hopefully,_ meaning _with hope,_ to mean _I hope_ or _it is to be hoped._ In which of these sentences is _hopefully_ used correctly?
a. **Hopefully, we'll be able to have lunch together.**
b. **Hopefully, your order will reach you by Friday.**
c. **Hopefully, he read the list of those who had passed the examination.**

R49   c.

S50   To review: (a) An adverb modifies a _____ , an _____, or another _____. (b) It usually answers the question _____, _____, _____, and to _____ _____. (c) It often ends in the letters ____.

R50   a. verb, adjective, adverb
b. where, when, how, to what degree
c. ly

Turn to Exercises 11.4 to 11.6.

EXERCISE 11·1A   **RECOGNIZING ADVERBS**

With one line underline the adverb in each of the following sentences. Then, with two lines, underline the word it modifies.

1. The space shuttle lifted swiftly from the launch pad.

2. We are very pleased to hear from you.

3. We walked quietly to the hospital.

4. Quickly he leaped into his car.

5. The matter is entirely finished.

6. No two people are completely alike.

7. This occurrence is most unfortunate.

8. We strongly urge you to accept this offer.

9. Proofread carefully all statistical entries.

10. They came here much later than expected.

11. She was primarily interested in securing a patent.

12. We were extremely impressed by the quality of his work.

13. Watch this maneuver intently.

14. Mr. Heinz arrived at the meeting exactly at the appointed hour.

15. Your money will be cheerfully refunded if you are not satisfied with your purchase.

16. Our new terminal is not functioning properly.

17. She travels to Memphis on business often.

18. I feel rather tired.

19. Mr. Drake responded angrily to the charges against him.

20. Yours is an exceptionally generous offer.

EXERCISE 11·1B CHANGING ADJECTIVES INTO ADVERBS

Below is a list of adjectives. In the space next to each adjective, write the equivalent adverb.

1. careful _____
2. sole _____
3. busy _____
4. primary _____
5. noticeable _____
6. principal _____
7. whole _____
8. true _____
9. considerable _____
10. substantial _____

11. real _____
12. extraordinary _____
13. extreme _____
14. accidental _____
15. willful _____
16. crafty _____
17. credible _____
18. annual _____
19. bad _____
20. good _____

EXERCISE 11·2A REVIEW OF ACTION AND LINKING VERBS

Underline the verb in each of the following sentences. Then, in the space provided, mark *A* if it is used as an action verb; mark *L* if it is used as a linking verb.

1. He looked at me with a piercing stare.   1. _____
2. The two systems seem quite compatible.   2. _____
3. This bread smells very fresh.   3. _____
4. Iwao lay down on his bed after dinner.   4. _____
5. This proposition is a once-in-a-lifetime opportunity.   5. _____
6. Mr. Maki looks taller than his brother.   6. _____
7. This analysis seems highly improbable.   7. _____
8. Joan rests.   8. _____
9. By tomorrow I will have been there and back.   9. _____
10. She knows the answer to our problems.   10. _____

EXERCISE 11·2B CHOOSING BETWEEN ADVERBS AND ADJECTIVES

In the space provided, write the proper form of the word in parentheses in each sentence.

1. Fudge tastes (sweet).   1. _____
2. He tasted the mixture (careful).   2. _____
3. Return the merchandise as (quick) as possible.   3. _____
4. She is very (content).   4. _____
5. The situation seems (bad).   5. _____
6. I am (extreme) tired from my long journey.   6. _____
7. The plant grew more and more (quick).   7. _____
8. The whole garden smells (sweet).   8. _____
9. We (certain) hope you are comfortable.   9. _____
10. We feel he has been (extraordinary) competent at his task.   10. _____
11. Ordinarily the bell tolls (soft), but today it sounds (loud).   11. _____
     _____

12.	Our situation has grown (bad).	12. _____
13.	The display looks (beautiful).	13. _____
14.	We can accomplish our goals (easy).	14. _____
15.	Kristen has done (good, well) in her new post.	15. _____
16.	Our stock is becoming more and more (desirable) to investors.	16. _____
17.	Mr. Dumont became (angry) and threatened his employee (loud).	17. _____
		_____
18.	He feels (indignant) because he cannot attend.	18. _____
19.	The whole story sounds (strange).	19. _____
20.	You are paying an (extreme) large amount.	20. _____
21.	We will (glad) repay your losses.	21. _____
22.	This is a very (poor) designed work station.	22. _____
23.	The river flowed (rapid).	23. _____
24.	Do business conditions look (bad) to you?	24. _____
25.	Rewrite the entire page (correct).	25. _____
26.	Please analyze these sales figures (quick).	26. _____
27.	Mr. Roberts certainly is a (quick) thinker.	27. _____
28.	When faced with an emergency, Mr. Schumann thought (quick).	28. _____
29.	There is no doubt about Mr. Schumann's being (quick).	29. _____
30.	Ms. Hamada tasted her soup (hungry).	30. _____
31.	To Ms. Hamada, the soup tasted (delicious) and (inviting).	31. _____
		_____
32.	The table was set (inviting).	32. _____
33.	I feel (bad) about your leaving.	33. _____

EXERCISE 11·3A   GOOD AND WELL

In the space provided, write the proper word—either *good* or *well*.

1. You did the job very (good, well).   1. _____
2. You did a very (good, well) job.   2. _____
3. It sounds (good, well) to me.   3. _____
4. You look (good, well) in your new suit.   4. _____
5. She performs (good, well) under pressure.   5. _____
6. The job was done quite (good, well).   6. _____
7. The proposition sounds (good, well).   7. _____
8. We feel confident you will do (good, well) in your new position.   8. _____
9. Though he was sick, he is now completely (good, well).   9. _____
10. He was very (good, well) in the part of Hamlet.   10. _____

EXERCISE 11·3B   MOST AND ALMOST, REAL AND REALLY, SURE AND SURELY

In the space provided, write the proper word.

1. Dana was (real, really) pleased to meet them.   1. _____

2. We are (sure, surely) grateful for your continued support.   2. _____

3. These are (most, almost) all of the supplies that are left.   3. _____

4. It gives us (real, really) satisfaction.   4. _____

5. (Sure, Surely) you will want to consult your attorney.   5. _____

6. We found that (most, almost) people did not know.   6. _____

7. Were the (real, really) situation known, there might be a scandal.   7. _____

8. That is the only (sure, surely) way to deal with this problem.   8. _____

9. (Most, Almost) every department was finished with the inventory by
    noon.   9. _____

10. We have (real, really) valid reasons for our stand.   10. _____

11. We (sure, surely) hope you feel better soon.   11. _____

12. (Most, Almost) of the time we work quite hard.   12. _____

13. Are you (real, really) sure of your facts?   13. _____

14. She is (sure, surely) of her skills.   14. _____

15. (Most, Almost) anyone who dresses (well, good) can look (well, good).   15. _____

_____

_____

EXERCISE 11·4A COMPARISON OF ADVERBS AND DOUBLE NEGATIVES

Rewrite the following hastily written memo, correcting all double-negative expressions and incorrect adverbs.

TO: *Joe*
FROM: *Alison*
DATE: *March 8, 198_*
SUBJECT: *Update on Temple Laboratories*

Jim Marshall hasn't scarcely visited us more than a few times (two or three at the mostest) in the past few months. I hope we haven't done nothing to offend him. After all, we haven't hardly started in our association with Temple Laboratories, and we certainly don't want to do nothing that would jeopardize our relationship.

Look into this situation more further and report back to me.

EXERCISE 11·4B ONLY

Only is correctly placed in one of the following sentences. Place a C in front of this sentence. In each of the remaining sentences, *only* is improperly placed. Indicate the proper placement of the word *only* in these sentences.

1. The director only read the first letter.

2. He only saw three familiar faces.

3. I only met her twice.

4. We only filed our applications one day late.

5. Bill and Ralph were allowed to leave; only Bob was forced to stay.

6. Lauren only leaves early on Fridays.

7. She was only convicted of a misdemeanor.

8. He only promotes the most aggressive employees.

9. We have only seen her once.

10. It only is eleven o'clock.

EXERCISE 11·4C   COMPOUND MODIFIERS

In the space provided, write the correct form of the compound modifier.

1. I think you'll be (pleasantly surprised, pleasantly-surprised).
1. _____

2. These are (increasingly difficult, increasingly-difficult) problems that must be solved.
2. _____

3. This promotion campaign was (well designed, well-designed).
3. _____

4. (Strategically located, Strategically-located) display cases should be placed in each store.
4. _____

5. The consequences of this decision will be (far reaching, far-reaching).
5. _____

6. Lorraine is an (exceedingly capable, exceedingly-capable) young person.
6. _____

7. The three children were (well behaved, well-behaved).
7. _____

8. No one disputes your (exceptionally high, exceptionally-high) standards.
8. _____

9. This is the (best tasting, best-tasting) coffee I've ever had.
9. _____

10. This decision will have (far reaching, far-reaching) consequences.
10. _____

EXERCISE 11·4D   UNNECESSARY ADVERBS

If an adverb is used unnecessarily, write it in the space; if there is no unnecessary adverb, write the letter C for correct.

1. Please repaint this wall again.
1. _____

2. Exit out this way.
2. _____

3. Return those papers back to me.
3. _____

4. Cooperate together with your associates.
4. _____

5. Please repeat the letter again.
5. _____

6. Let us reconvene again on Monday morning.
6. _____

7. In reexamining the ledger, they discovered the error.
7. _____

8. We want nations to coexist together in harmony.
8. _____

9. The new fan has conquered over all competition.
9. _____

10. Try to cooperate as fully as you can.
10. _____

11. The plane circled around the airport for several hours before landing.
11. _____

12. The bus shuttled back and forth between the hotel and the convention center.
12. _____

234

EXERCISE 11·4E   COMPOUND EXPRESSIONS

This exercise contains compound expressions and single adverbs that are often confused. In the space provided, write the correct word or words.

1. He is (all together, altogether) biased in his views.   1. _____

2. In (all ways, always) this edition seems superior.   2. _____

3. Many students have (all ready, already) taken some college courses.   3. _____

4. (All together, Altogether) I counted thirty-three people.   4. _____

5. The new business failed (all together, altogether).   5. _____

6. Jean is in (all ways, always) a model employee.   6. _____

7. I think the truck drivers are (all ready, already) to end their wildcat strike.   7. _____

8. You may go when you are (all ready, already).   8. _____

9. I will meet with you (some time, sometime) tomorrow afternoon.   9. _____

10. I have (some time, sometime) free tomorrow afternoon.   10. _____

EXERCISE 11·5   ADVERBS

The following letter contains many errors. Cross out all errors and make the necessary changes in the space above them.

Dear Mr. Mazzoni:

It was a pleasure to see you at the Acme Convention in Pittsburgh. I thought you looked real good, especially considering your hectic travel schedule. Hopefully you enjoyed your visit to Pittsburgh and found it all together relaxing.

The Acme Company is growing very quick. Last year's sales are a tiny fraction of our anticipated sales this year. We surpassed last-year's totals only in the first month. Our situation is growing more better every day. I am all together certain that, if we cooperate together, the goals we set for ourselves in Pittsburgh can be easily-accomplished.

One situation I feel badly about is the growth of competition in the South. If one looks close at sales figures in the South, one will see that the rate of increase isn't hardly a third of what we had originally projected. I am real concerned with this problem. We can sure do better.

On the other hand, our office in the West has done extremely good. They are real quick rising up to number one in the nation. I wish that our other offices followed our advice as complete and thoroughly as they do.

By the way, Terry Cortazzo feels indignantly because she was not asked to speak in Pittsburgh. Even though her association with the company is real shortly, she has good ideas. Although I am not positive that there will be time for her at the next convention, hopefully we can squeeze her in.

Please write and let us know your assessment of the sales situation in the South.

Sincerely,

EXERCISE 11·6   COMPOSITION: ADVERBS

Compose complete sentences using the adverbs called for in parentheses.

1. (the adverb form of *confident*) _____
2. (the adverb form of *official*) _____
3. (the adverb form of *busy*) _____
4. (the adverb form of *true*) _____
5. (the superlative form of *badly)* _____
6. (the superlative form of *little*) _____
7. (the comparative form of *well*) _____
8. (*fast*) _____
9. (*hopefully*) _____
10. (*very* modifying a predicate adjective) _____

12

PREPOSITIONS

USING PREPOSITIONS, CHOOSING THE RIGHT PREPOSITION

Words like *of, at, in, on,* and *between* are prepositions. A **preposition** is a word that connects a noun or pronoun with the body of the sentence. It shows the relationship between that noun or pronoun and another word in the sentence. The noun or pronoun that the preposition connects to the body of the sentence is called the *object* of that preposition.

of Ohio—*Ohio* is the *object* of the preposition *of.*
at the time—*time* is the *object* of the preposition *at.*
in the room—*room* is the *object* of the preposition *in.*
on the way—*way* is the *object* of the preposition *on.*
between you and me—*you* and *me* are the *objects* of the preposition *between.*

The phrase introduced by a preposition is called simply a **prepositional phrase.**

I arrived on time.

In this sentence *on time* is a prepositional phrase. *On* is the preposition; *time* is the object of the preposition. *On* shows the relationship between *arrived* and *time.*

I went to the office.

The prepositional phrase is *to the office. To* is the preposition; *office* is its object. *To* shows the relationship between *office* and *went.*

I went to the newly decorated office.

The prepositional phrase is *to the newly decorated office.* The preposition is *to;* its object is still *office* despite the introduction of the descriptive words *newly decorated.*

The letters are on the desk.

In this sentence the preposition *on* shows the relationship between *desk,* the object of the preposition, and *letters.* We could use a number of prepositions to show the relationship between letters and desk. Each preposition would express a different relationship.

The letters are in the desk.
The letters are behind the desk.
The letters are under the desk.
The letters are near the desk.
The letters are across from the desk.

Thus, even though prepositions are very familiar words, you must be careful to select the correct preposition to convey the precise meaning you want to express. This chapter will help you in choosing the right preposition and using it correctly.

Here is a list of the most common prepositions. Don't memorize this list, but learn to recognize these words as prepositions:

> about, above, across, after, against, along, around, at, before, behind,
> below, beneath, beside, besides, between, beyond, but, by, concerning,
> down, during, except, for, from, in, inside, into, like, near, of, off, on,
> over, regarding, respecting, since, through, throughout, till, to, toward,
> under, underneath, until, up, upon, with, within, without

In addition, there are a number of familiar word groups that are used as though the whole group were a preposition. Learn to recognize these word groups (known as *compound prepositions*) as prepositions:

> as to, as for, as regards, apart from, by way of, contrary to, devoid of,
> from out, from beyond, instead of, in place of, in regard to, in reference
> to, on account of, to the extent of, with respect to

 # USING PREPOSITIONS

 ## CONFUSED PAIRS

 ### AMONG/BETWEEN

There is a difference of opinion (among) (between) you and me.

Between is correct only when there are *two* people or things involved. *Among* is correct when there are *three* or *more*. Our sentence should read *between you and me* because there are only *two* people involved—*you* and *me*.

Right: Between you and me, we have nothing to fear.
Right: We will place your display among the many others.
Right: We will place your display between the other two.

 ### IN/INTO

What is the difference between these two sentences?

1. The director is in the room.
2. The director went into the room.

In means *within*. *Into* means *from the outside to within*. In other words, *into* expresses an action of moving from one place (outside) to another place (inside). *In* expresses no action.

The carbon is in the drawer.
She reached into the drawer to get the dictating machine.

The words *in* or *into* in the same sentence may change the meaning completely.

He ran in the ring. (Was he afraid?)
He ran into the ring. (Was he eager?)

BESIDE/BESIDES

To avoid confusing these two prepositions, remember that *beside* means *by the side of.*

I sat down beside her *(at her side).*

Besides with the *s* has a completely different meaning: *in addition to. (Memory Aid: In addition to* calls for the addition of an *s* = besides.)

> **Right:** The office will send a supervisor besides the typist and me.
> **Right:** No one will be there besides us two.
> **Wrong:** He sat down besides her.

 ## LIKE/AS

The two words *like* and *as* cause many people a great deal of trouble. The usual error is to use *like*, a preposition, as a conjunction instead of the correct word, *as.* For example, *My new job is not working out like I had hoped it would* is grammatically incorrect. The statement should be *My new job is not working out as I had hoped it would.* Sometimes people are so worried about using *like* improperly that they use *as* where *like* is really the correct word.

> **Wrong:** *He performed his duties just as a professional.*

Good business writing demands that you distinguish between *like* and *as* and use each one correctly. Fortunately, knowing whether to use *like* or *as* isn't difficult.
Like is a *preposition* meaning *similar to* or *in a similar manner to.*

> **Right:** Milos looks like his father.
> **Right:** Like his father, Milos always arrived early.
> **Right:** She handled the equipment like an expert.
> **Right:** Your typewriter looks just like mine.

Use the preposition *like* with a noun or pronoun in the objective case (see Chapter 4) that is not followed by a verb. In general, when you use *like* you are comparing nouns.
Like is never a conjunction. When you need a conjunction to express similarity, the correct word is *as* (or *as if* or *as though*).

> **Right:** "As Maine goes, so goes the nation" is an old political proverb.
> **Right:** He doesn't perform as he once did.
> **Right:** I will do as you advised me.
> **Right:** She worked as if there were no tomorrow.
> **Right:** They talked as though they had a chance of winning.

Thus *as* is usually used with an adverbial clause. When you want to compare verbs, use *as.*
Note: In elliptical constructions that leave out the verb, you may use *like.*

> **Right:** Estelle took to drafting like a duck to water.

If the verb is present, however, use *as.*

> **Right:** Estelle took to drafting as a duck takes to water.

Although *as* is most often a *conjunction*, it is occasionally used as a *preposition.* In these cases it means *in the role or capacity of.*

Right: Rico works as a bartender on weekends.

If Rico works very hard, he works *like a horse.* If he is paid to dress up in a horse costume, he works *as a horse.*

 ## AROUND/ABOUT

Do not use *around* (meaning *circular*) for *about* (meaning *approximately*).

Right: I'll be at the bank about an hour from now.
Wrong: I'll be at the bank around an hour from now.

Conversely, don't use *about* when you mean *around.*

Right: Lena paced around the room.
Wrong: Lena paced about the room.

 # INCORRECT PREPOSITIONS
 ## FROM/THAN

When one thing is unlike another, that something is *different from* something else. It is *never* different *than* something else. (It may help you to remember that the *f* of *different* must be followed by the *f* of *from*.)

Right: This may differ from what you had thought.
Right: My theory is different from the one held by my boss.
Right: Approach this problem differently from the way you did the previous one.

When *differ* is used as a verb meaning *disagree*, it calls for the preposition *with.*

Right: We differ with your conclusion.

 ## OVER/TO/AT/DURING/FOR

Do not use *over* when you mean *to, at, during,* or *for. Over* means *above* or *in excess of.*

Right: Come to my house tonight. Not: *over my house.*
Right: Let's have the meeting at my home. Not: *over my home.*
Right: We held the meeting during the weekend. Not: *over the weekend.*

 ## TO/TOO/TWO/AT

In the lesson on verbs, you studied the word *to* as part of the infinitive: *to walk, to study,* and so on. Now let's consider *to* as a preposition: *to the office, to next week.* Do not use *to* for *at. At* indicates location whereas *to* indicates motion.

Right: I was at a meeting last night. Not: *to a meeting.*
Right: I was at her graduation. Not: *I was to her graduation.* But: I went *to* her graduation.

Do not use the adverb *too* (meaning *also* or *excessively*) or the numeral *two* (meaning *2*) for the preposition *to.*

Right: There are too many people to give out only two prizes.
Right: Too much has been said to the public about the two world powers.

OFF/OFF OF/FROM/HAVE

Do not use the word *of* after the word *off*.

Right: The radio fell off the table. Not: The radio fell *off of* the table.
Right: He is coming off the gangplank. Not: He is coming *off of* the gangplank.

Do not use *off of* when you mean *from*.

Right: They borrowed the money from me. Not: They borrowed the money *off of* me.
Right: She bought my old car from me. Not: She bought my old car *off of* me.

Do not use *of* when you mean *have*. Although it is true that when you speak quickly, the helping verb *have* sounds like the preposition *of*, that should not mislead you. The word *of* never directly follows the word *might, must, could, should,* or *would*.

Right: I might have gone. Not: I might *of* gone.
Right: I would have been there by now.
Right: I should have known this would happen.

 # COLLOQUIAL EXPRESSIONS

Many expressions that we use in casual conversation and informal writing are not considered appropriate for more formal situations. Such informal conversational expressions are called *colloquial*. These expressions are not substandard, but the careful business writer avoids using them in business correspondence. Here are three such colloquial expressions.

 ## OUTSIDE OF/EXCEPT

Do not use the colloquial expression *outside of* when you mean *except*.

Colloquial: Everyone was present outside of Peter.
Preferred: Everyone was present except Peter.

 ## INSIDE OF/WITHIN

Inside of properly refers to place. Its colloquial use in reference to time should be avoided in favor of the more proper *within*.

Colloquial: She will leave inside of a week.
Preferred: She will leave within a week.

 ## IN BACK OF/BEHIND

Use *behind* instead of the more colloquial *in back of*.

Colloquial: They sat in back of us at the concert.
Preferred: They sat behind us at the concert.

 # UNNECESSARY PREPOSITIONS

Avoid unnecessary prepositions that merely clutter your sentence without adding content.

1. **Right:** Where are you going? Not: Where are you going *to*?

2. **Right:** Where is your home? Not: Where is your home *at?*
3. **Right:** I cannot help expressing my gratitude. Not: I cannot help *from* expressing my gratitude.
4. **Right:** I want you to see this. Not: I want *for* you to see this.
5. **Right:** Until yesterday, I would have agreed. Not: *Up* until yesterday, I would have agreed.
6. **Right:** In two weeks it will be over. Not: In two weeks it will be over *with.*

 # FORGETTING NECESSARY PREPOSITIONS

Although you should avoid unnecessary prepositions, you should be careful not to omit prepositions that are necessary. The word *of* should not be forgotten in combinations such as *type of* and *style of.*

> **Right:** What type of work do you do? Not: What type work do you do?
> **Right:** Tell him what style of cabinet we want. Not: Tell him what style cabinet we want.

The word *of* must also be used in *all of* and *both of* constructions when *all* or *both* is followed by a pronoun. It is not used when *all* or *both* is followed by a noun, however.

> **Right:** All the furniture has been damaged.
> **Wrong:** All of the furniture has been damaged.
> **Right:** All the letters must be retyped.
> **Right:** All of them must be retyped.
> **Right:** Both letters must be retyped.
> **Right:** Both of them must be retyped.

Do not omit the preposition *from* after the verb *to graduate.*

> **Right:** I graduated from high school two years ago. Not: I graduated high school.

 # ENDING A SENTENCE WITH A PREPOSITION

At one time language authorities were opposed to ending any sentence with a preposition, and many conservative writers still follow this practice, especially in formal writing. Look at these examples:

> **Awkward:** George is the person whom I went to the meeting with.
> **Better:** George is the person with whom I went to the meeting. (Or, I went to the meeting with George.)
> **Awkward:** Whom are you giving the check to?
> **Better:** To whom are you giving that check?

Other writers, however, no longer follow this practice so rigidly. Although they would revise sentences to eliminate an awkward final preposition, they would not revise sentences that end naturally with a preposition. For example, these writers would find this sentence natural and acceptable: *I don't know which organization he's a member of.*

Others would prefer *I don't know of which organization he is a member,* or *I don't know to which organization he belongs.*

What should you do? Whenever possible, construct sentences that do not end with a preposition, but if a sentence ends naturally with a preposition, leave it there. Do not construct an awkward sentence to eliminate a perceived breach of the rules. Remember what

Sir Winston Churchill is reported to have said when told that he should not end a sentence with a preposition: "That is the sort of English up with which I will not put."

PROGRAMMED REINFORCEMENT

S1 A preposition (connects, does not connect) a noun or pronoun with the body of the sentence. It (shows, does not show) the relationship that exists between that noun or pronoun and another word in the sentence.

R1 connects
shows

S2 The word that the preposition connects to the body of the sentence is called the _____ of that preposition.

R2 object

S3 . . . **to the office.** . . . In this phrase **to** is a _____ and **office** is the _____ of **to**.

R3 preposition; object

S4 Here is a list of prepositions with one adverb and one adjective inserted: **To, with, for, ever, until, certainly, besides, during, smart, against.** The adverb is _____ and the adjective is _____.

R4 adverb—**certainly**;
adjective—**smart**

S5 Groups of two or three words sometimes act as a preposition. Circle two such phrases: **In regard to the order, the duplicate was used in place of the original.**

R5 **In regard to; in place of**

S6 **Between** is a preposition that is used when (two, three or more) people are involved.

R6 two

S7 Circle the correct word: **This year's profits were divided (between, among) the ten supervisors.**

R7 **among**

S8 **He walked (in, into) the room.** (a) **In** is correct, (b) **Into** is correct, (c) Both may be correct.

R8 c. Both may be correct

S9 **She got out of her car and went (in, into) the office.**

R9 **into**

S10 **Besides** and **beside** can be easily differentiated if you remember that _____ means **by the side of.**

R10 **beside**

S11 **(Besides, Beside) all other considerations, the treasurer should sit (besides, beside) the president.**

R11 **Besides; beside**

S12   Which of these two words is never a conjunction? **Like; As**

R12   Like.

S13   Circle the correct word in the following sentences.
a. **Mary looks just (like, as) her mother.**
b. **Mary works (like, as) a retail clerk after school.**
c. **Although she is only a trainee, Mary handles herself (like, as) a professional.**
d. **You performed (like, as) I knew you would.**
e. **(As, Like) I was saying, you should buy this stock immediately.**

R13   a. like; b. as; c. like; d. as; e. As

S14   The prepositions *around* and *about* should not be used interchangeably. The word that means *approximately* is (around, about); the word that means *circular* is (around, about).

R14   about; around

S15   Circle the word that correctly completes this sentence: **I'll be back in (about, around) fifteen minutes.**

R15   about

S16   The preposition that should follow the word **different** is **(from, than).**

R16   from

S17   Which preposition is correct? **Come (over, to) my house this evening.**

R17   to

S18   Circle the correct answer: **I worked on the accounts (over, during) the weekend.**

R18   during

S19   **I was (to, at) a meeting this afternoon.**

R19   at

S20   **Too** means **excessively** or **also,** as distinguished from **two** (one plus one) and **to** (direction). Circle the correct forms. **I am (to, two, too) busy (to, two, too) send the advertising copy to the (to, two, too) agencies.**

R20   too; to; two

S21   Circle the preposition that should be eliminated. **Please take that calendar off of the desk and put it into the basket.**

R21   of

S22   In the sentence **He borrowed money off of the cashier,** the prepositions incorrectly used are _____ _____; the correct preposition is _____.

R22   off of; from

S23   **I should of gone to the meeting.** The preposition **of** is incorrectly substituted for the verb _____.

R23   have

S24 Circle the prepositions the careful business writer would prefer in the following sentences.
  a. **Everyone (outside of, except) Marjorie and Phil was able to attend.**
  b. **I expect to complete this project (inside of, within) a week.**
  c. **The company holds season tickets (in back of, behind) home plate.**

R24 a. **except;** b. **within;** c. **behind**

S25 Unnecessary prepositions should be eliminated. Circle two you should eliminate in this sentence: **I want for you to tell me where you will be at this afternoon.**

R25 **for; at**

S26 Circle prepositions that are unnecessary in this sentence: **Where are you going to, and up until when will you stay?**

R26 **to; up**

S27 What necessary preposition is omitted in this sentence? **What type _____ addressing machine do you use?**

R27 **of**

S28 Which of the following sentences are grammatically *incorrect?*
  a. **Both of the computers need repair.**
  b. **Both of them need repair.**
  c. **Both computers need repair.**
  d. **All of the employees are present.**
  e. **All of them are present.**

R28 **a, d**

S29 Sentences should not end awkwardly with a preposition. Revise the following sentences to eliminate such awkwardness.
  a. **Whom did you wish to speak to?**
  b. **Mr. Cupo is the person I had the interview with.**
  c. **A preposition is something you shouldn't end a sentence with.**

R29 a. **To whom did you wish to speak?**
  b. **Mr. Cupo is the person with whom I had the interview.**
    or,
    I had the interview with Mr. Cupo.
  c. **You should not end a sentence with a preposition.**
    or,
    Do not end a sentence with a preposition.

Turn to Exercises 12.1 to 12.5.

CHOOSING THE RIGHT PREPOSITION

Certain words call for one preposition and not another to express their intended meanings clearly. In other cases it is possible to use several prepositions with the same word to convey different but acceptable meanings. You will be constantly using many such words in your work. Below is a list of words and their proper prepositions. Study this list carefully. Repeat each expression over and over until it becomes familiar to you.

abide by (a decision)   We will *abide by* your decision.

accompanied by (a person)   The manager was *accompanied by* her executive secretary.

accompanied with (an object)   The payment was not *accompanied with* the original statement.

acquainted with (familiar with)   Are you *acquainted with* the new regulations?

adapted from (taken and modified from)   These new plans were *adapted from* an earlier set.

adapted to (adjusted to)   These plans can be *adapted to* fit your needs.

agree with (an opinion)   I *agree with* what you're saying.

agree to (terms)   They *agreed to* the terms of the sale.

agree upon (a plan)   They *agreed upon* a plan of action.

allude to (refer indirectly to)   She *alluded to* several personnel problems in the main plant.

angry at (an occurrence or object)   The attorney was *angry at* the judge's ruling.

angry with (a person)   Mr. Lawson was *angry with* his partner.

annoyed by (something)   She was *annoyed by* the sticking desk drawer.

annoyed with (a person)   Ms. Engle was *annoyed with* her assistant.

argue for (something)   They *argued for* a radical change in the billing system.

argue with (a person)   The two men *argued with* each other.

compare to (suggest a similarity)   The Fletcher Plant may be *compared to* a small community.

compare with (examine for specific similarities)   *Compare* this machine *with* any of its competitors.

compensate for (make up for)   We must work harder to *compensate for* the time we wasted.

comply with (not *to*)   We must *comply with* a new set of regulations.

concur in (an opinion)   I *concur in* the opinion expressed by the majority.

concur with (a person or thing)   In this matter I *concur with* Ms. Carter.

consistent with (compatible)   Is this decision *consistent with* established policy?

convenient for (a purpose)   This is a *convenient* location *for* a variety of reasons.

convenient to (a location)   The new site is *convenient to* public transportation.

correspond by (by means of)   They *corresponded by* telegram.

correspond to (equivalent)   This machine *corresponds to* our current model.

correspond with (writing letters)   She *corresponds with* friends in Europe.

deal in (kind of business)   My broker *deals in* municipal bonds and securities.

deal with (people)   My broker does not know how to *deal with* troublesome clients.

deal with (subjects)   At the press conference the President declined to *deal with* the topic of acid rain.

differ from (a thing)   Prices will *differ from* one store to another.

differ with (an opinion)   Bob *differs with* my view regarding this investment.

disappointed at (or *in* a thing)   I'm *disappointed at* the poor quality of this dictaphone.

disappointed with (a person)   Janet Wilson is an outstanding employee; you will never be *disappointed with* her.

encroach on (or *upon*; to intrude gradually)   Be careful not to *encroach on* another salesperson's territory.

equivalent to (equal)   Her gross pay is roughly *equivalent to* mine.

identical with (uniform with, equal to)   This year's model is *identical with* last year's.

independent of (not *from*)   I reached my decision *independent of* yours.

indicative of (not *to*)   This report is *indicative of* the high quality of her work.

indifferent to (uncaring)   A poor sales representative is *indifferent to* the needs of customers.

inquire of (to ask a person)   Feel free to *inquire of* our representative if the need arises.

inquire about (interrogate or question)   Mr. Jacobs is going to *inquire about* office space in that building.

inquire after (one's health)   They *inquired after* the supervisor's health.

interfere in (something)   Don't *interfere in* my affairs.

interfere with (a person)   Don't *interfere with* me.

liable for (responsible)   When you rent this truck, you will be *liable for* any damages.

liable to (susceptible)   During the winter months we are more *liable to* colds and flu.

live in (a town)   He *lives in* Hopewell.

live on (a street)   He *lives on* Maple Avenue in Hopewell.

live at (a certain address)   He *lives at* 125 Maple Avenue in Hopewell.

live by (means of livelihood)   He was forced to *live by* his wits.

necessity for (urgent need)   There is an absolute *necessity for* immediate action on this matter.

necessity of (unavoidable obligation)   Due to an error, we are faced with the *necessity of* absorbing a sizeable loss.

need for (urgent occasion for)   There is a true *need for* a quick solution to this problem.

need of (lack or want)   We are in *need of* new equipment.

object to (to oppose)   I *object to* this proposed price increase.

payment for (an article)   Enclosed is a check in *payment for* last week's shipment.

payment of (a fee or bill)   Enclosed is a check in *payment of* the bill for last week's shipment.

proceed from (to come forth)   *Proceed from* the meeting room to the reception area.

proceed with (to continue)   You may *proceed with* your filing afterwards.

rely on (someone or something)   You can *rely on* me.

reminiscent of (not *from*)   Today's conference is *reminiscent of* last year's.

responsible for (liable)   Elaine was directly *responsible for* the care and maintenance of her machine.

responsible to (accountable)   You are *responsible to* your immediate superiors.

specialize in (not *at*)   Annette decided to *specialize in* tax law.

take exception to (usual combination)   I *take exception to* your last remark.

talk to (to speak to a person)   He *talked to* the audience for nearly one hour.

talk with (converse)   She *talked* at length *with* several people following her address.

wait for (to delay until)   Having missed the bus, Jesse had to *wait for* the next one.

wait on (to serve)   The store manager *waited on* customers all morning.

 # PROGRAMMED REINFORCEMENT

S30   Certain words call for one preposition and not another. Circle the correct ones:
   a. **Abide (by, with) a decision**
   b. **Accompanied (by, with) a person**
   c. **Accompanied (by, with) a remittance**

R30   a. **by;** b. **by;** c. **with**

S31 a. **Agree (with, to) an opinion**
b. **Agree (with, to) terms**
c. **Angry (with, at) a person**
d. **Angry (with, at) an occurrence or object**

R31 a. **with**; b. **to**; c. **with**; d. **at**

S32 a. **Please comply (with, to) this request.**
b. **This store is convenient (with, to) all transportation.**

R32 a. **with**; b. **to**

S33 a. **Correspond to** means **(equivalent, writing letters)**;
b. **correspond with** means **(equivalent, writing letters)**.

R33 a. **equivalent**; b. **writing letters**

S34 a. **Joe and I differ (from, with) each other on this.**
b. **I am disappointed (at, with) the poor level of service.**
c. **Ms. Jacoby is going to inquire (about, after, of) obtaining more current data.**

R34 a. **with**; b. **at**; c. **about**

S35 a. **The enclosed check is in payment (of, for) last month's statement.**
b. **I talked (to, with) several of their representatives during lunch.**
c. **I have been waiting (on, for) the express bus for more than half an hour.**

R35 a. **of**; b. **with**; c. **for**

S36 As a review, circle the correct words in the following sentence: **He should (have, of) divided the bonuses (between, among) the two supervisors whose ideas were different (than, from) the others.**

R36 have; between; from

S37 Circle the correct words: **She cleaned the debris (off of, off) the table and threw it (in, into) the basket (beside, besides) the window.**

R37 off; into; beside

S38 **Come (over, to) the factory accompanied (with, by) an engineer (over, during) the weekend.**

R38 to; by; during

S39 A phrase that is introduced by a preposition is called a _____ phrase. The noun or pronoun at the end of the phrase is called the _____ of the preposition.

R39 prepositional; object

Turn to Exercises 12.6 to 12.8.

EXERCISE 12·1 RECOGNIZING PREPOSITIONS

In each of the following sentences, underline all prepositions with one line. Then circle the objects of those prepositions.

1. The reputation of Empire Fans has been built on high standards and fair dealings at all times.

2. Between you and me, I feel certain that one of the representatives will call at your office within a week.

3. In regard to any orders from your firm, we feel sure of our ability to fill them in time for your fall shipment.

4. With respect to your claim for damages, we are certain of a recovery to the extent of $3,000.

5. Contrary to our expectations, you will be refused a passport for the duration of the present emergency.

6. They have agreed among themselves to honor, without any question, all the demands made by our client.

7. Against all odds, we have succeeded beyond expectation in our endeavor to enlist support for our cause.

8. Instead of being discouraged by his failure, he seemed to gain the strength of a lion in all his subsequent attempts.

9. Walking into the hall, the President of the United States and the members of his cabinet were greeted by the complete silence of the assembled guests.

10. In spite of her aversion to the tactics of high-pressure salespeople, Ms. Zola was so impressed by this young sales representative that she agreed to buy the full line of goods.

EXERCISE 12·2A AMONG OR BETWEEN

In the space provided, write either among or between, whichever is correct.

1. There is a difference of opinion _____ the two administrators.

2. There is a difference of opinion _____ the jury.

3. The Big Three often differ _____ themselves.

4. Chicago is _____ New York and Seattle.

5. _____ the people present were the President, the Vice President, and the Secretary of State.

6. The jewelry was found _____ her belongings.

7. _____ you and me, this plan is certain to fail.

8. _____ the reasons for his success were his wisdom, honesty, and fairness.

9. What is the main difference _____ the Apple and the IBM?

10. There is little difference _____ these five VCRs.

EXERCISE 12·2B   IN OR INTO

In the space provided, write either in or into, whichever is correct.

1. She walked _____ the room from the hall.

2. Behind a closed door, he paced back and forth _____ his office all day.

3. There are some interesting articles _____ today's newspaper.

4. It doesn't take much to get _____ an argument with her.

5. What sort of work would you like to get _____?

6. Promotion is rapid, once you have established a name _____ this field.

7. He opened the door and rushed _____ his office.

8. I would tear this contract _____ a thousand little pieces if I could.

9. Do you think you can get _____ the public relations field?

10. Continue _____ the confidence of your superior by remaining discreet about office business.

EXERCISE 12·2C   LIKE OR AS

In the space provided, write either like or as, whichever is correct.

1. I shall write the memo (like, as) you suggested.   1. _____

2. It looks (like, as if) it might rain.   2. _____

3. He repaired the machine (like, as) a professional.   3. _____

4. She is (like, as) her mother in everything she does.   4. _____

5. Your copier is (like, as) the one we purchased last year.   5. _____

6. (Like, As) I told you, the Copely Copier makes the sharpest copies.   6. _____

7. You look (like, as though) you had seen a ghost.   7. _____

8. (Like, As) father, (like, as) son.   8. _____

9. On weekends he moonlights (like, as) a guard.   9. _____

10. The situation is exactly (like, as) I described it on the phone.   10. _____

EXERCISE 12·3   MISUSE OF PREPOSITIONS

In the space provided, write the proper word or words.

1. Money was stolen (off of, from) the safe.   1. _____

2. The child fell (off of, off) the chair.   2. _____

3. All the drivers (except, outside of) Lionell have returned.   3. _____

4. They took the receipts (off of, from) me.   4. _____

5. We all got (off of, off) the elevator at the same floor.   5. _____

6. He borrowed money (off of, from) the secretary.   6. _____

7. They should (have, of) known he was lying.   7. _____

8. Tomas sat down (beside, besides) his friend.   8. _____

9. Our course may differ (from, with) what you had expected.   9. _____

10. The shirt was almost ripped (off of, off) the singer's back.   10. _____

11. With luck she might (have, of) pulled through.   11. _____

12. Her assistant stood (behind, in back of) her throughout the meeting.   12. _____

13. I stepped (off of, from) the car.   13. _____

14. They could (have, of) made many changes (among, between) the
    three of them.   14. _____

15. He would (have, of) had very different opinions (from, than) mine.   15. _____

16. What can we do (beside, besides) writing a letter of complaint?   16. _____

17. I had a fine time (over, at) my friend's house.   17. _____

18. I'll be home in (about, around) an hour.   18. _____

19. Approach the topic differently (from, than) the way you did last time.   19. _____

20. I'll be there (during, over) the holidays.   20. _____

21. (Around, About) thirty people attended the conference.   21. _____

22. She wants the revised report (inside of, within) a week.   22. _____

23. She was (to, at) the celebration last week.   23. _____

24. Come (over, to) my house for dinner next week.   24. _____

25. During the operation the medical students stood (behind, in back
    of) the doctor.   25. _____

26. (Two, To, Too) many times I hear the same complaints.   26. _____

27. What we differ (from, with) is your desire for haste.   27. _____

28. I (too, to, two) feel that (too, to, two) hours will be enough.   28. _____

29. The board differed (with, from) the advice of the director.   29. _____

30. Pedro bought Al's old chain saw (off, off of, from) him.   30. _____

31. All the committee members were present (outside of, except) Juanita.

31. _____

32. The construction should be completed (inside of, within) two months.

32. _____

33. The course that they chose was different (from, than, with) that outlined in the manual.

33. _____

34. When you went (in, into) this field, you should (have, of) been prepared for a life very different (from, than) college life.

34. _____

35. Standing (between, among) his brothers, John and Bob, he would (have, of) looked very different (from, than) either of them.

35. _____

EXERCISE 12·4   NECESSARY AND UNNECESSARY PREPOSITIONS

Cross out each incorrect preposition and write it in the space provided at the end of the sentence. If a necessary preposition is missing, insert it in the sentence and write it in the space provided at the end of the sentence. If the sentence is correct, write C in the space.

1. This is the place where I am going to.   1. _____

2. Do you know where Mr. Chang is at?   2. _____

3. Did the packages fall off of the shelves?   3. _____

4. Here is a copy of the plans you ordered.   4. _____

5. We wanted for you to receive the prize.   5. _____

6. Up until last week we had not received any report.   6. _____

7. What type software do you intend to use?   7. _____

8. It's a relief that summer is over with.   8. _____

9. By the end of the summer your shipment will be ready.   9. _____

10. Open up all the windows.   10. _____

11. I didn't remember of having received the bill.   11. _____

12. If I'd of known the answer, I would have won the contest.   12. _____

13. In another few minutes it will be done with.   13. _____

14. Where do you live at?   14. _____

15. Get the books off of the desk.   15. _____

16. Miss Chavez ordered a new style message pads.   16. _____

17. What type of fabric is this?   17. _____

18. This style of office furniture is too uncomfortable.   18. _____

19. When did you graduate high school?   19. _____

20. Both of the applicants are in the reception room.   20. _____

21. Both of them appear nervous.   21. _____

22. All of the procedure was spoiled.   22. _____

23. All of the forms must be completed in triplicate.   23. _____

24. Crystal graduated from college in 1971.   24. _____

25. I can't help from feeling envious at her good fortune.   25. _____

EXERCISE 12·5   SENTENCES ENDING WITH A PREPOSITION

Rewrite the following sentences so that they no longer end awkwardly with a preposition.

1. Whom are you offering the position to? _____

    _____

2. Which advertising agency was this campaign developed by? _____

    _____

3. Who is the person you were at the symposium with? _____

    _____

4. Whom was the typewriter invented by? _____

    _____

5. Sheena is the person the flowers were intended for. _____

    _____

EXERCISE 12·6 THE PROPER PREPOSITION

In the space provided, write the preposition that best completes the thought.

1. Compare one computer _____ another.

2. Accompanied _____ the boss.

3. In payment _____ our recent order.

4. Accompanied _____ a full payment.

5. Live _____ Elm Street.

6. Agree _____ the terms of the contract.

7. Indicative _____ a level of performance.

8. Agree _____ his views on politics.

9. Wait _____ bedridden patients.

10. Angry _____ the superintendent.

11. Buy _____ a sales representative.

12. Borrow _____ a friend.

13. Comply _____ your request.

14. Live _____ 123 Elm Street.

15. Convenient _____ all trains.

16. Allude _____ several hidden motives.

17. Convenient _____ all business needs.

18. Correspond _____ my understanding.

19. Differ _____ her outlook on life.

20. Agreement _____ the three of us.

21. Disappointed _____ the outcome.

22. Deal _____ a problem.

23. Inquire _____ stock options.

24. Deal _____ stocks and bonds.

25. Agreement _____ the two of us.

26. Argue _____ a change in marketing strategy.

27. Equivalent _____ a full gallon.

28. A necessity _____ promptness.

29. Specialize _____ pediatrics.

30. Inquire _____ one's neighbor.

31. Angry _____ the drop in sales.

32. Agree _____ a course of treatment.

33. Adapted _____ your needs.

34. Talk _____ her audience.

35. Distinguish _____ the two methods.

36. Different _____ other methods.

37. Correspond _____ air mail.

38. Wait _____ a cab.

39. Correspond _____ a friend overseas.

40. Identical _____ the original.

41. Concur _____ an opinion.

42. Abide _____ the court's ruling.

43. Proceed _____ the current plan.

44. Annoyed _____ her broker.

45. Interfere _____ the negotiations.

46. Need _____ adequate funding.

47. Liable _____ damages.

48. Independent _____ other factors.

49. Choose _____ the three.

50. Responsible _____ her actions.

EXERCISE 12·7   REVIEW OF PREPOSITIONS

In the following letter, many prepositions are used incorrectly. Cross out each incorrect preposition and write the correct preposition above it.

Dear Mr. Jurek:

I received your letter last week. I am willing to comply to most of your provisions when I buy the business off you, but I object with your interpretation of a portion of our contract. At this point your interpretation is entirely different than mine. Unfortunately, my attorney, accompanied with her family, will be vacationing up until next week so that I have been unable to talk to her about this. I am trying to correspond to her by mail. I should of heard from her by now, but I am still waiting on her to contact me.

I feel there is an immediate need of settling this difference of opinion among you and me. Please realize that I am not angry at you. I am angry at the conditions that brought about this situation.

I am quite willing to comply to all the provisions in Paragraph X, but I cannot agree to your present interpretation of Paragraph XI, which is not consistent to what it was when I agreed to sign this contract.

Was it merely convenient to you to change your mind once I was bound to the contract? You cannot be indifferent to standard business practice, and my understanding to the contract is completely in keeping with standard business usage. Paragraph XI is identical to Paragraph VII of the Standard Business Contract No. 109, which you are certainly familiar with.

I am forwarding a copy of this letter, accompanied by a copy of Paragraph XI, up to the National Business Board. I expect a reply in around a week.

I will abide with their decision if you will agree to abide with it too.

Respectfully,

EXERCISE 12·8　　COMPOSITION: PREPOSITIONS

Compose complete sentences using the words in parentheses.

1.　(different) _____

2.　(like) _____

3.　(besides) _____

4.　(among) _____

5.　(into) _____

6.　(agree with) _____

7.　(comply with) _____

8.　(independent of) _____

9.　(responsible for) _____

10.　(talk with) _____

13

CONJUNCTIONS AND INTERJECTIONS

CONJUNCTIONS AND SENTENCE STRUCTURE, USING CONJUNCTIONS, CONJUNCTIVE ADVERBS, INTERJECTIONS

In Chapter 1, you learned that a **conjunction** is used to join a word or thought to another related word or thought.

A conjunction does more than connect two or more ideas; it also shows the relationship between ideas. In your writing you must therefore use conjunctions carefully so that they express the precise relationship that you intend.

For example, in each of the following sentences, which conjunction better shows the relationship between the ideas it connects?

1. I applied for a loan, (and, but) my application was turned down.
2. I applied for a loan, (and, but) my application was approved.

Obviously, to convey the exact meaning intended in Sentence 1, *but* is correct. In Sentence 2 *and* is correct. The hundreds of conjunctions in our language offer you a rich choice of words to show precise shades of relationship. Here are just a few that you use constantly:

> accordingly, and, as soon as, because, besides, but, consequently, hence, inasmuch as, in order that, moreover, notwithstanding, or, otherwise, therefore, though, thus, unless, until

In this chapter we'll study the correct use of these and other conjunctions, and we'll also look at another kind of connective, the conjunctive adverb.

CONJUNCTIONS AND SENTENCE STRUCTURE

Let's review what we already know about how sentences are composed, and then let's add some new concepts involving the proper use of conjunctions.

The fundamental type of sentence is the simple sentence. A *simple sentence* must have two essential parts—a subject and a predicate—and it must express a complete thought. In its simplest form we might have something like this: *Snow fell*. To add greater meaning to our simple sentence, we can add words and phrases that describe the subject or the predicate or both. For example: *Freezing snow fell on the highway*. This is still a simple sentence, but it provides added description. We have built up our simple thought by the addition of modifiers

259

that describe our subject and predicate—an adjective, *freezing*, and a prepositional phrase, *on the highway*. We still have only a simple sentence consisting of a subject plus a predicate.

A simple sentence can have more than one subject or more than one predicate. For example:

Snow and sleet fell.

This is a simple sentence with a compound subject. We might also have written:

Snow fell and froze.

This is a simple sentence with a compound predicate. Now look at this example:

Snow fell and sleet froze.

Is this still a simple sentence? No. In effect, we have two complete sentences that are connected by the conjunction *and*: *Snow fell.* (and) *Sleet froze.* The sentence *Snow fell and sleet froze* is called a compound sentence. A **compound sentence** is a sentence that is composed of two or more simple sentences that are joined together by a conjunction or a semicolon. We call each simple sentence that is part of a compound sentence an **independent clause**. In our example sentence, *Snow fell* is an independent clause. *Sleet froze* is another independent clause. They are independent because they can stand by themselves as complete sentences. This sentence also could be written using a semicolon to take the place of the conjunction *and*:

Snow fell; sleet froze.

In a compound sentence, the conjunction that connects one clause with another is called a **coordinate conjunction**. *And, but, or, nor, for, so, yet*—these are coordinate conjunctions. They are called *coordinate* because they connect two coequal parts. In a compound sentence they connect two coequal independent clauses.

Coordinate conjunctions can be used as part of a compound subject—for example, *snow and sleet*—in which case they connect two equal subjects. Coordinate conjunctions also can be used as part of a compound predicate—for example, *fell and froze*—in which case they connect two equal predicates.

Now, let's turn to another type of sentence—the complex sentence.

In Chapter 2 you learned about the **dependent clause**, a clause that contains a subject and predicate but does not express a complete thought by itself. For example, *since the snow fell* is a dependent clause; it does not express a complete thought. It depends upon another thought to complete its meaning. Thus we might complete it like this: *We have received no shipments since the snow fell*. Now we have a complete sentence composed of an independent clause—*we have received no shipments*—and a dependent clause—*since the snow fell*. This type of sentence composed of an independent clause plus a dependent clause is called a **complex sentence**. Observe in the following examples of complex sentences how two thoughts—an independent clause and a dependent clause—have been combined to show the relationship of one to the other.

We selected their computer *because* it is compatible with our present system.
We will ship the order *unless* we hear from you by Thursday.
They will be on time *if* the weather is good.

In each of the above examples, notice the conjunction that introduces the dependent clause—*because, unless, if*. Each of these conjunctions is called a **subordinate conjunction** because when it is added to an independent clause, it makes that clause incomplete by itself and dependent upon another clause for completion. In other words, it *subordinates* that clause to an independent clause.

Let's look at a few examples to see how this works. If we start with the independent clause *Snow falls* and add to it a subordinate conjunction like *if, when, although,* or *in case,* we end with a dependent clause:

If snow falls . . .
When snow falls . . .
Although snow falls . . .
In case snow falls . . .

There are hundreds of subordinate conjunctions. Here are just a few of the commonly used ones:

after	if	though
although	notwithstanding	unless
as	on condition that	until
as if	otherwise	when
as soon as	provided	whenever
because	since	where
before	so that	whereas
even if	supposing	wherever
even though	than	while
except	that	why

Note that in a complex sentence, the so-called natural sequence is for the independent clause to come first. For example:
Natural sequence:

Independent Clause   Dependent Clause
We will pay the bill unless we hear from you.

You can reverse this sentence if you like.
Reverse sequence:

Dependent Clause   Independent Clause
Unless we hear from you, we will pay the bill.

The most important point to notice is that you use a comma to separate the clauses only when you follow the reverse sequence. Look at these paired examples:

This plant will close when the patents expire.
When the patents expire, this plant will close.

The luncheon will be held even if it rains.
Even if it rains, the luncheon will be held.

Remember: the natural sequence does not require a comma; the reverse sequence does.
There is one more basic sentence type, the **compound-complex sentence**. As its name indicates, this is the result when you combine a compound and a complex sentence.

Although his broker advised against it, Mr. Parker invested heavily in steel, and recent events have proved the wisdom of his decision.
I am willing to remain until the package arrives, but then I must leave.
When she got there, the cupboard was bare, and so her poor dog had none.

As you see, each of these examples contains two independent clauses plus one subordinate clause. A compound-complex sentence always contains at least two main clauses plus at least one subordinate clause.

To review: There are four types of sentences: (1) the simple sentence, (2) the compound sentence, (3) the complex sentence, and (4) the compound-complex sentence.

We will have more to say about these four types of sentences and how to use them effectively in the next chapter.

PROGRAMMED REINFORCEMENT

S1 A conjunction is a part of speech that (describes, joins, modifies) thoughts.

R1 joins

S2 A simple sentence contains a _____ and a _____ and expresses a complete thought.

R2 subject; predicate

S3 A clause is a group of words containing a subject and a predicate that (must, may or may not) express a complete thought.

R3 may or may not

S4 A clause that expresses a complete thought is called an _____ clause.

R4 independent

S5 A clause that does not express a complete thought is called a _____ clause.

R5 dependent

S6 A sentence that is composed of one independent clause is called a _____ sentence.

R6 simple

S7 **We purchased stock** is a simple sentence because it is composed of one _____ clause.

R7 independent

S8 **We purchased stock   then we sold it.** Each of these clauses contains (one, two) clause(s).

R8 two

S9 **We purchased stock   then we sold it.** Each of these clauses is a(n) _____ clause.

R9 independent

S10 **We purchased stock and then we sold it.** This is a _____ sentence because it consists of two independent clauses connected by a conjunction.

R10 compound

S11 **We purchased stock; then we sold it.** This is a _____ _____ sentence because it is composed of two _____ clauses connected by the mark of punctuation known as a _____ .

R11 compound; independent; semicolon

S12 **We purchased stock and then we sold it.** The word **and** is a conjunction. It is called a _____ conjunction because it connects equal parts. In a compound sentence it connects two _____ clauses.

R12 coordinate; independent

S13 A coordinate conjunction connects equal parts. It can connect two subjects, like **Jack and Jill,** in which case we have a _____ subject.

R13 compound

S14 A coordinate conjunction can connect two predicates, like **sink or swim,** in which case we have a _____ predicate.

R14 compound

S15 A coordinate conjunction can connect two independent clauses, in which case we have a _____ sentence.

R15 compound

S16 A compound sentence is a sentence containing two or more _____ clauses connected by a _____ conjunction or a semicolon.

R16 independent; coordinate

S17 A _____ sentence is a sentence containing two or more independent _____ connected by a _____ conjunction or a _____ .

R17 compound; clauses; coordinate; semicolon

S18 **We regret the delay.** This is a _____ sentence containing one _____ clause.

R18 simple; independent

S19 **We regret the delay, but it was unavoidable.** This is a _____ sentence containing two _____ clauses connected by a _____ .

R19 compound; independent; coordinate conjunction.

S20 **We regret the delay; it was unavoidable.** This is a _____ sentence consisting of two _____ clauses connected by a _____ .

R20 compound; independent; semicolon

S21 **We regret the delay, it was unavoidable.** This is an example of the error we call a run-on sentence. Here we have two _____ clauses connected by a comma. To create a correct compound sentence, you need either a _____ conjunction (with a comma) or a _____ .

R21 independent; coordinate; semicolon

S22 **Although we regret the delay**. . . . This is a clause because it contains a _____ and a _____ _____. It is a dependent clause because it does not express a _____ _____.

R22 subject; predicate; complete thought

S23 **If it was unavoidable**. . . . This is a(n) _____ ____ clause because, although it contains a subject and predicate, it does _____ express a complete thought.

R23 dependent; not

S24 In S22 and S23, the words **although** and **if** are _____ _____ conjunctions because they render a clause incomplete and therefore dependent.

R24 subordinate

S25 **Although we regret the delay, it was unavoidable.** This sentence contains (one, two) clause(s). The first is a _____ _____ clause because it is not complete by itself. The second is an _____ clause because it expresses a complete thought.

R25 two; dependent; independent

S26 **Although we regret the delay, it was unavoidable.** This sentence contains a dependent clause and an independent clause. It is an example of a _____ sentence.

R26 complex

S27 A complex sentence contains an _____ clause and a _____ clause.

R27 independent; dependent

S28 **There will be a delay if it is unavoidable.** This is an example of a _____ sentence because it contains an _____ clause and a _____ clause. The word **if** is a _____ conjunction.

R28 complex; independent; dependent; subordinate

S29 **There will be a delay if it is unavoidable.** This sentence follows the natural sequence for a complex sentence; that is, the _____ clause comes first, followed by the _____ clause.

R29 independent; dependent

S30 **If it is unavoidable, there will be a delay.** In this sentence the _____ clause comes first. This (is, is not) the natural sequence. We insert the comma after the _____ clause to indicate that this sentence is not in natural sequence.

R30 dependent; is not; dependent

S31 A fourth type of sentence, a combination of a compound sentence and a complex sentence, is called a _____ _____ sentence.

R31 compound-complex

S32 A compound-complex sentence contains at least _____ main clause(s) plus at least _____ subordinate clause(s).

R32 two; one

S33 Identify the subordinate clause(s) in each of these compound-complex sentences:
  a. **When the lights went down, the curtain rose and the play began.**
  b. **Although we regret the delay, it was unavoidable, so we do hope you understand.**
  c. **There will be a delay if it is unavoidable; therefore you should take this into account when you estimate the final cost.**

R33
  a. **When the lights went down**
  b. **Although we regret the delay**
  c. **if it is unavoidable; when you estimate the final cost**

Turn to Exercises 13.1 and 13.2.

USING CONJUNCTIONS

AND AND *BUT* AS SENTENCE OPENERS

You have probably learned that you should not begin a sentence with *and* or *but*. There is a logical reason for this view. Because these two words are coordinating conjunctions, they must have something to coordinate or connect.

Hence a sentence that begins with *and* or *but* is actually part of the preceding sentence. For example, *I saw Frank. But he didn't see me* should really be written as one sentence because *But he didn't see me* is technically a sentence fragment:

I saw Frank, but he didn't see me.

However, many people—including a number of professional writers—sometimes begin sentences with *and* or *but* to avoid a long compound sentence or to achieve a particular effect. Look at this excerpt from Lincoln's Second Inaugural Address:

Both parties deprecated war; but one of them would *make* war rather than let the nation survive; and the other would *accept* war rather than let it perish. And the war came.

Some sentences in this book begin with the word *but*. Accordingly, for the sake of variety and emphasis, you may occasionally decide to begin a sentence with *and* or *but*. But don't overdo it.

 ## LIKE/AS

In the previous chapter you learned that *like* can be used as a preposition but never as a conjunction. You learned why this statement is incorrect: *My new job is not working out like I had hoped it would.* Properly, it should read *My new job is not working out as I had hoped it*

would. In other words, a conjunction (*as*) is required to join the clauses, not a preposition (*like*). Don't make the error of confusing *like* with *as*.

Right: He looks like me.
Right: It was done as you wanted.
Right: As I said, this is an outstanding machine.
Wrong: Like I said, this is an outstanding product.

CONJUNCTIONS AND PREPOSITIONS

You may sometimes wonder whether to use the objective case (*me, him, her*) or the subjective case (*I, he, she*) after words like *before, after, but*. These words may be used either as conjunctions (followed by the subjective case) or prepositions (followed by the objective case), depending upon how you want to use them.

Right: I got to the office after him. (Preposition)
Right: I got to the office after he did. (Conjunction)
Right: She filed the letters before me. (Preposition)
Right: She filed the letters before I did. (Conjunction)
Right: No one will go but her. (Preposition meaning *except*)
Right: No one will go, but he may come later. (Conjunction)

PAIRS OF CONJUNCTIONS

Certain conjunctions act together to connect ideas. They are called *correlative conjunctions* because they *correlate*, or relate, one thought with another.

1. Either . . . or: *Either* you work harder, *or* you leave.
2. Neither . . . nor: We want *neither* sympathy *nor* charity.
3. Both . . . and: The true leader is *both* self-confident *and* humble.
4. Not only . . . but also: We want you *not only* to visit our office *but also* to inspect our plant.
5. Whether . . . or: *Whether* you act now *or* wait is a matter of great concern.
6. As . . . as: He is *as* tall *as* his father.
7. So . . . as: She is not *so* tall *as* I had thought.

The major points to remember about these paired conjunctions are these:

1. With *neither* always use *nor* (not *or*).

   We want *neither* sympathy *nor* charity.

   Remember that *neither* and *nor* go together; the positive equivalents are *either* and *or*. We want *either* cash *or* a money order.

2. With *not only* always use *but also* (not *but* alone).

   We want you *not only* to visit our office *but also* to inspect our plant.

3. When two affirmative statements are joined by paired conjunctions, use *as . . . as*; when a negative statement is involved, use *so . . . as.*

He is *as* tall *as* his father.
She is not *so* tall *as* I had thought.

4. Paired conjunctions should stand as near as possible to the words they connect.

    Right: My job has given me both pleasure and satisfaction.
    Wrong: My job has both given me pleasure and satisfaction.
    Right: The announcer has reported neither the time nor the place of the event.
    Wrong: The announcer has neither reported the time nor the place of the event.

5. When you use correlative conjunctions, be sure that they connect sentence elements that are parallel in form. Look at these examples:

    Awkward: We judge people not only by what they say but also their actions.
    Parallel: We judge people *not only* by what they say *but also* by what they do. *Or:* . . . but also by how they act.
    Awkward: You can reach the airport either by cab or a special limousine may be taken.
    Parallel: You can reach the airport *either* by cab *or* by special limousine.
    Awkward: I will either place the order with you or the Miller Corporation.
    Parallel: I will place the order *either* with you *or* with the Miller Corporation.
    Awkward: Ms. Felson should either ship us the machines immediately or she should refund our deposit.
    Parallel: Ms. Felson should *either* ship us the machines immediately *or* refund our deposit.

Notice that in each revision the wording of the sentence element following the second conjunction is similar to—parallel to—that following the first.

    by what they say is parallel to *by what they do or by how they act*
    by cab is parallel to *by limousine*
    with us is parallel to *with the Miller Corporation*
    ship us the machines is parallel to *refund our deposit*

In the final example sentence, for example, *either* was originally followed by a phrase beginning with the verb *ship,* whereas *or* was followed by an independent clause. In the revision, both are followed by verbs which begin verb phrases. Thus, to maintain parallelism, be sure that correlative conjunctions introduce elements of similar structure.

 # PROVIDED/PROVIDING

Provided is a subordinate conjunction meaning *on condition, if.*

We will arrive on time *provided* we have a tailwind.
Provided there is time, you can give your speech.

Many people mistakenly use *providing* in these situations instead of *provided. Providing* is a form of the verb *provide.* It is never a conjunction and should never be used to join two parts of a sentence.

    Right: I will come provided my expenses are paid.
    Wrong: I will come providing my expenses are paid.

TRY AND AND *BE SURE AND*

Remember, do not use such expressions as *try and* or *be sure and*. These expressions require the infinitive form of the verb, not a conjunction.

> **Right:** Try to arrive before noon.
> **Wrong:** Try and arrive before noon.
> **Right:** Be sure to mail your packages early.
> **Wrong:** Be sure and mail your packages early.

See the discussion of infinitives in Chapter 9.

 ## THE REASON IS BECAUSE

The reason is because is a widely used phrase. It is also an incorrect one. The proper phrase is *The reason is that.*

> **Right:** The reason was that I overslept.
> **Wrong:** The reason was because I overslept.
> **Right:** The reason I was unable to complete the assignment was that I was tired.
> **Better:** I was unable to complete the assignment because I was tired.
> **Wrong:** The reason I was unable to complete the assignment was because I was tired.

 ## *WHERE* FOR *THAT*

Similarly, don't use the conjunction *where*, which refers to location, instead of *that*.

> **Right:** I read in the magazine that the price had been lowered.
> **Wrong:** I read in the magazine where the price had been lowered.

That should also be used instead of *but what*, which is too informal.

> **Right:** I have no doubt that my proposal, when adopted, will solve our problem.
> **Wrong:** I have no doubt but what my proposal, when adopted, will solve our problem.

 # PROGRAMMED REINFORCEMENT

S34 It is (sometimes, never) acceptable to begin a sentence with *and* or *but*.

R34   sometimes

S35 **Like** is never used as a conjunction. Correct this sentence. **He dictates like I do.**
Answer: _____

R35 **He dictates as I do;** or **He dictates the way I do;** or **He dictates like me.**

S36 Correlative conjunctions are found in pairs. Complete each of the following pairs: neither, _____; either, _____; not only, _____ _____.

R36   neither-**nor;** either-**or;** not only-**but also**

S37 Paired conjunctions should stand as close as possible to the words they connect. Which sentence is preferable: (a) **My employer has studied neither in high school nor in college.** (b) **My employer has neither studied in high school nor in college.**

R37   a.

S38 Correlative conjunctions should relate sentence elements of similar structure. Revise each of these awkward sentences to maintain parallel structure between the conjunctions.
1. **You should either buy the book or it should be returned to us.**
2. **She is both accurate and she is efficient.**

R38 1. **You should either buy the book or return it to us.**
         or
      Either you should buy the book or you should return it to us.
   2. **She is both accurate and efficient.**

S39 When an affirmative comparison is made, we say, for example: **She is as rich as Midas.** When a negative comparison is made, we say: **He is not _____ strong as Hercules.**

R39   so

S40 **Provided** and **providing** are sometimes confused. _____ _____ is a conjunction; _____ is a verb.

R40   **Provided; providing**

S41 **I will report early (provided, providing) that the boss is (provided, providing) for a longer lunch hour.**

R41   **provided; providing**

S42 **Try and** is incorrect. Instead of the conjunction **and** you should use the word _____. For example: **Please try _____ finish by five o'clock.**

R42   **to; to**

S43 **Try (and, to) rectify the shortage in receipts.**

R43   **to**

S44 Which word is better? **I read in the Wall Street Journal (that, where) stock prices are advancing.**

R44   **that**

Turn to Exercise 13.3.

 # CONJUNCTIVE ADVERBS

So far we have been studying the two types of conjunctions—coordinate and subordinate. There is another basic type of sentence connector. Look at these examples.

There were many unexpected delays in construction; *however,* the work was completed only one month behind schedule.

LaMar did not go on to graduate school; *instead,* he began work as a management trainee.

You have failed to meet your last two payments; *accordingly,* we must ask you to vacate.

Eloise was ill the last weeks of the semester; *thus* she was unable to take the final exam and received an incomplete for the course.

Each of the italicized words is called a *conjunctive adverb.* It acts as an adverb because it modifies the clause that it introduces. It acts as a conjunction because it joins two independent clauses.

Here is a list of the most common conjunctive adverbs:

accordingly	however	nevertheless
also	incidentally	next
anyway	indeed	otherwise
besides	instead	still
consequently	likewise	then
finally	meanwhile	therefore
furthermore	moreover	thus
hence		

Pay particular attention to how the sample sentences are punctuated. In each sentence a semicolon is placed before the conjunctive adverb; this semicolon joins the two independent clauses. In addition, a comma is placed after conjunctive adverbs of more than one syllable. A comma after conjunctive adverbs of one syllable (for example, *hence, then, thus*) is considered optional. When a comma is included, it tends to emphasize the connective.

A number of words act as connectors in much the same way as conjunctive adverbs. These words are known as *transitional phrases.* Here are some common ones:

after all	by the way	in other words
as a result	for example	in the second place
at any rate	in addition	on the contrary
at the same time	in fact	on the other hand

Like conjunctive adverbs, when these phrases are used to join two independent clauses, they are always preceded by a semicolon; in addition, they are always followed by a comma. For example:

I don't think that Mr. Rooney is disagreeable; on the contrary, I find him very helpful and friendly.

Thus conjunctive adverbs and transitional phrases, along with a semicolon, can link two independent clauses. Unlike conjunctions, however, conjunctive adverbs and transitional phrases do not have fixed positions within the sentence. They begin or take other positions in the second main clause. When this happens, the clauses continue to be linked by semicolons; the conjunctive adverbs or transitional phrases themselves are then set off by commas. For example:

We had many unexpected delays in construction; the work, however, was completed only one month behind schedule.

Our sales are increasing everywhere; Denver sales figures, for example, are up 35%.

We had many unexpected delays in construction; the scheduled completion date, as a result, was revised several times.

Whatever the placement of these words within the second main clause, remember that the clauses themselves are joined by a semicolon. If they are joined only by a comma, you have a comma-fault and a run-on sentence.

INTERJECTIONS

An *interjection* is a word or group of words that expresses strong feeling or sudden emotion. An interjection has no grammatical relationship to any other word in the sentence. It stands by itself. Usually we punctuate interjections—exclamations—with an exclamation point.

> Good! Surprise! Well done! Oh! Magnificent!
> Wow! Look at the cost of this proposed addition.
> Ouch! I stubbed my toe.

Sometimes, when the exclamation is mild, or when it is used to begin a sentence, the exclamation is followed instead by a comma. *Well, I for one am not satisfied.* With the exception of advertising copy, in business writing the interjection is almost always inappropriate. Save interjections and exclamation points for your personal diary.

PROGRAMMED REINFORCEMENT

S45 A connecting word that functions as both a conjunction and an adverb is called a ＿＿＿＿＿ ＿＿＿＿＿.

R45 conjunctive adverb

S46 Circle the conjunctive adverbs in the following words: **accordingly, because, but, consequently, however, thus, until**

R46 **accordingly, consequently, however, thus**

S47 When a conjunctive adverb is used to join two independent clauses, the mark of punctuation which always precedes the conjunctive adverb is a ＿＿＿＿＿.

R47 semicolon

S48 Punctuate these sentences correctly:
1. **She argued persuasively however the executives were not convinced.**
2. **The Swanson Corporation is located only five miles away moreover their rates are lower than those we are presently paying.**

R48 1. **She argued persuasively; however, the executives were not convinced.**
2. **The Swanson Corporation is located only five miles away; moreover, their rates are lower than those we are presently paying.**

S49 Words that act as connectors in a way similar to conjunctive adverbs are known collectively as ＿＿＿＿＿ ＿＿＿＿＿.

R49 transitional phrases

S50   Conjunctive adverbs and transitional phrases do not always begin the second main clause. When either appears in other positions within the second clause, a comma appears **(before, after, both before and after)** it. (Circle the correct answer.)

R50   **both before and after**

S51   Punctuate the following sentences:
   1. **Juan can come tomorrow in addition he will give us a discount.**
   2. **Her rates are very reasonable she will repair this machine for example for half of what Leo charges.**
   3. **Joe works very rapidly his work however is often slipshod.**

R51   1. **Juan can come tomorrow; in addition, he will give us a discount.**
   2. **Her rates are very reasonable; she will repair this machine, for example, for half of what Leo charges.**
   3. **Joe works very rapidly; his work, however, is often slipshod.**

S52   A word or a group of words that expresses strong feeling, like **Ouch,** is called an _____. It is usually followed by an _____ _____.
   When the exclamation is mild, it may be followed by a _____.

R52   interjection; exclamation point; comma

S53   As a review, choose the correct answers: The conjunctions **and, but, or** and **yet** are called (coordinate, subordinate) conjunctions because they connect (equal, unequal) parts.

R53   coordinate; equal

S54   Choose the correct forms: **Neither Maria (nor, or) Jane types like (I, me), so be sure (to, and) request a raise for me.**

R54   nor; me; to

S55   Choose the proper words: **The tax penalty will not be (as, so) high as before (providing, provided) that forms are filed on time.**

R55   so; provided

Turn to Exercises 13.4 to 13.7.

EXERCISE 13·1A   INDEPENDENT CLAUSES

Underline each independent clause. Be sure to underline all words in the clause.

1. Since we conferred last week, the situation has grown worse.
2. Forgetting her manners, she failed to introduce herself.
3. We won't forget this if we live to be a hundred.
4. They came; they saw; they conquered.
5. I feel satisfied.
6. Mail a check for the balance as soon as possible.
7. They tried to sell their holdings, but they could not find a buyer.
8. Either they will pay for damages, or we will seek legal action.
9. Although she is inexperienced, she learns quickly.
10. Won't you settle your account without further delay?

EXERCISE 13·1B   DEPENDENT CLAUSES

Underline each dependent clause, if any. If there is no dependent clause in a sentence, leave it blank.

1. Since we conferred last week, the situation has grown worse.
2. Forgetting her manners, she failed to introduce herself.
3. We won't forget this if we live to be a hundred.
4. They came; they saw; they conquered.
5. Although I am tired, I feel satisfied.
6. Mail a check for the balance as soon as possible.
7. They tried to sell their holdings, but they could not find a buyer.
8. We will seek legal action if we must.
9. Although she is inexperienced, she learns quickly.
10. We will settle our account when you fulfill the terms of the contract.

EXERCISE 13·2A   TYPES OF SENTENCES

In the space to the right of each sentence, show what type of sentence it is—simple, compound, complex, or compound-complex.

1. Since we conferred last week, the situation has grown worse.   1. _____

2. Forgetting her manners, she failed to introduce herself.   2. _____

3. We won't forget this if we live to be a hundred.   3. _____

4. They came; they saw; they conquered.   4. _____

5. I feel satisfied.   5. _____

6. Mail a check for the balance as soon as possible.   6. _____

7. They tried to sell their holdings, but they could not find a buyer.   7. _____

8. Either they will pay for damages or we will seek legal action.   8. _____

9. Although she is inexperienced, she learns quickly.   9. _____

10. Won't you settle your account without further delay?   10. _____

11. You may remain in the room; however, if you interrupt the discussion, you will be asked to leave.   11. _____

12. If you want my advice, sell that stock before it's too late.   12. _____

13. When Ruth left for lunch, Joan went with her, but Cheryl remained in the office.   13. _____

14. Get out and stay out!   14. _____

15. Although my supervisor gave me a superior rating, she did not recommend me for promotion.   15. _____

16. My supervisor gave me a superior rating, but she did not recommend me for promotion.   16. _____

17. If you are married, you and your spouse may be able to file a joint return, or you may file separate returns.   17. _____

18. Both you and your spouse must include all your income, exemptions, and deductions on your joint return.   18. _____

19. When preparing your résumé, list all your jobs in reverse chronological order.   19. _____

20. When you prepare your résumé, list all your jobs in reverse chronological order, and specify your duties in each.   20. _____

EXERCISE 13·2B   COMPLEX SENTENCES

In the space to the right of each of these complex sentences, mark *N* if the sentence follows the natural sequence; mark *R* if the sequence is in reverse order. Place a comma in any sentence from which it is left out.

1. As soon as we arrived the conference began.   1. _____
2. Even if she was right she should not have proceeded without further instructions.   2. _____
3. We will order now although we are overstocked.   3. _____
4. Until I hear from you I will take no further action.   4. _____
5. Although he is still a minor he is old enough to be responsible.   5. _____
6. Because she was modest she refused adulation.   6. _____
7. Before I leave let me congratulate you.   7. _____
8. You cannot enter the room while filming is in progress.   8. _____
9. We will continue to press our case until we receive adequate compensation.   9. _____
10. Don't feel discouraged if you fail to find a job immediately after graduation.   10. _____
11. Even though the auditorium was large it could not accommodate the huge crowd that had gathered.   11. _____
12. List all your jobs in reverse chronological order when you prepare your résumé.   12. _____
13. The attorney read the will as soon as all the parties were present.   13. _____
14. Bertha keeps a separate record of her business expenses whenever she travels.   14. _____
15. Unless business improves soon we will be forced to close.   15. _____

EXERCISE 13·3A   CORRELATIVE CONJUNCTIONS

In the space provided, write the word from the following list that will correctly complete the sentence.

and   as   but also   nor   or   so

1. Either you honor the agreement _____ I will sue.   1. _____
2. Neither the chair _____ the desk is in perfect condition.   2. _____
3. Both the fuel pump _____ the carburetor were defective.   3. _____
4. He not only refused to accept the current shipment _____ refused to pay for the previous one.   4. _____
5. Neither the dictionary _____ the glossary included the term.   5. _____
6. They not only gave us dinner _____ invited us to stay for the evening.   6. _____
7. During this special promotion you will receive not only a discount _____ a bonus gift.   7. _____
8. They offered her either a straight salary _____ a commission.   8. _____
9. Our latest model is not only functional _____ decorative.   9. _____
10. Either the ledger _____ the receipt is incorrect.   10. _____
11. I am as sure _____ I can be.   11. _____
12. I am not _____ sure as I once was.   12. _____

EXERCISE 13·3B   PROPER CONJUNCTIONS

In the space provided, write the proper word.

1. I acted (as, like) she advised.   1. _____
2. Would you try (and, to) correct the error.   2. _____
3. We will accept (provided, providing) you lower your price.   3. _____
4. We would appreciate it if you would try (and, to) locate the lost files.   4. _____
5. The old computer was fully (as, so) large as a room.   5. _____
6. We will go not only to Paris (but, but also) to London.   6. _____
7. This contract is valid (provided, providing) the shipment arrives on schedule.   7. _____
8. (Like, As) I said yesterday, this problem must be solved.   8. _____
9. Neither time (or, nor) effort is to be spared (provided, providing) they cooperate.   9. _____
10. It looks very much (like, as) your company car.   10. _____

276

EXERCISE 13·3C   **CORRECTING CONJUNCTIONS**

Wherever necessary, cross out incorrect words or insert correct words. If a sentence is correct, write C in front of it.

1. He is not as smart as I thought he was.

2. I have no doubt but what censorship is on the increase.

3. The reason I resigned was because I was offered a better position with another firm.

4. The reason she was discharged was because she had been late too often.

5. Acme Products is not as large as General Electric.

6. The gain is not so great as I had anticipated.

7. I notice in the newspapers where employment figures are increasing.

8. I read where China and Russia are in a dispute regarding their border.

9. I heard where Judith was promoted to assistant buyer.

10. These projections look excellent like I had expected.

11. Tell Ellie to be sure and call us when she arrives.

12. You may double your contribution to an IRA providing both you and your spouse work.

EXERCISE 13·4   CONJUNCTIVE ADVERBS AND TRANSITIONAL PHRASES

Punctuate the following sentences correctly.

1. The defense attorney's arguments were very convincing therefore the jury voted to acquit the accused.

2. The defense attorney's arguments were very convincing the jury voted therefore to acquit the accused.

3. She explained her position to me however I remained unconvinced.

4. The sale will last the entire month moreover it will involve all departments.

5. All items have been drastically reduced this coat for example is now half price.

6. The two sides bargained for over a month but were unable to reach an agreement finally an arbiter was called in.

7. He explained his position to me I remained unconvinced however of its validity.

8. We should not expect too much of Leonard he is after all still a trainee.

9. We are not satisfied with the service that you have given us accordingly we are closing our account and transferring our business to another store.

10. I am sorry you disagree with this position nevertheless we will proceed as scheduled.

11. I don't think Ms. Fazio is difficult to work with on the contrary I find her most cooperative.

12. We are facing a severe shortage of parts due to the strike thus we have been forced to lay off some of our employees.

13. Federal laws prohibit employers from discriminating on the basis of race sex and age hence it is inappropriate to include a picture as part of your résumé.

14. Many companies used to administer psychological tests to job applicants nowadays however most companies no longer use these tests.

15. I am convinced that sales will be going up soon on the other hand costs will be going up as well.

EXERCISE 13·5   INTERJECTIONS

Punctuate the following statements correctly.

1. Well I never

2. Well I never expected to win anyway

3. Wow Did you see the latest sales figures

4. Hurrah

5. Oh I'm just a little tired I guess

6. Watch out Don't touch that

7. What a remarkable performance

8. Unbelievable She actually used to work for Howard Hughes

9. Gee I never considered organizing the report that way

10. No she never returned your call

EXERCISE 13·6   CONJUNCTIONS

In the following copy, cross out all errors and write your corrections in the space above each. Insert any punctuation that has been left out.

TO: Paula Erlich, Regional Sales Director

FROM: Anthony Santos, Manager, Longview Office

DATE: April 10, 1985

SUBJECT: Quarterly Sales Figures

Like I said in my last memo, we are not only losing sales but we are losing some salespersons too. This is not as bad as you might think because we were going to try and hire some new salespersons anyway. You probably have read in the papers where the reason sales are down is because demand has fallen, consequently we were unable to meet last quarter's sales quota. Providing this downward trend in demand is reversed I have no doubt but what our sales will soon be back to record levels. And our branch back to its normal position of number one.

EXERCISE 13·7   COMPOSITION: CONJUNCTIONS

Compose complete sentences according to the directions in parentheses.

1. (a sentence in natural sequence with *since*) _____

_____

2. (a sentence in reverse sequence with *unless*) _____

_____

3. (a sentence beginning *Even though*) _____

_____

4. (a sentence beginning *Because*) _____

_____

5. (a sentence containing *either . . . or*) _____

_____

6. (a sentence containing *not only . . . but also*) _____

_____

7. (a sentence containing *in fact*) _____

_____

8. (a sentence containing *as a result*) _____

_____

9. (a sentence containing *furthermore*) _____

_____

10. (a sentence containing *however* set off by commas) _____

_____

14

THE SENTENCE REVISITED

CRITERIA FOR A SENTENCE, SIX BASIC SENTENCE
PATTERNS, FOUR BASIC SENTENCE TYPES, THE
WRITER'S TOOLS, THE PARAGRAPH,
CHARACTERISTICS OF EFFECTIVE BUSINESS WRITING

You have now completed your study of all eight parts of speech. Let's review some of the things you have learned.

You know how to form the plurals and possessives of both regular and irregular *nouns*, and you know how to form the various types of *pronouns* and how to use them. You can correctly form all six tenses, plus the progressive, of both regular and irregular *verbs*. You are familiar with the voice and mood of the verb, and you know how to create and use *verbals*. You know how to form and when to use the positive, comparative, and superlative forms of *adjectives* and *adverbs*. You are familiar with a variety of *prepositions* and when to use them, and you know how to use *conjunctions* to connect ideas. And you know a great deal more.

As you are aware, what is most important is not how you use these parts of speech separately, but how you put them together in a sentence. That is why throughout the course of our study we have looked first at the role of each part of speech within the sentence and then at how one part relates to another. For example, we studied nouns and verbs separately and then we studied them together when we discussed the agreement of subject and predicate. We talked about adjectives and adverbs and their roles as modifiers, and then we looked at the problems caused by misplaced modifiers.

The parts of speech are exactly that—parts. These parts must be put together to form a whole—the sentence. As we said in Chapter 2, the sentence, and not the word, is the basic unit of communication in the language because it is the sentence that expresses a complete thought. Let's briefly review what we learned about the criteria for a sentence in Chapter 2 and then go on to look at the ways in which the parts of speech serve as tools to create effective sentences. (Because of the nature of the discussion, there will be no Programmed Reinforcement material in this chapter.)

REVIEW: CRITERIA FOR A SENTENCE

As you know, for a statement to be a sentence, it must meet three requirements: 1) it must contain a subject; 2) it must contain a predicate; and 3) it must express a complete thought. None of the following statements is a sentence because none of them meets all three criteria.

Your order of May 10.
Processed by the shipping department yesterday.
Your order of May 10. Was processed by the shipping department yesterday.
Your order of May 10, processed by the shipping department yesterday.
When your order of May 10 was processed by the shipping department yesterday.

In contrast, these statements are sentences; they meet all three criteria.

> Your order of May 10 was processed by the shipping department yesterday.
> When your order of May 10 was processed by the shipping department yesterday, the supervisor noted an apparent error on the invoice.

There is actually one further requirement a statement must meet for it to be a sentence: The words must be in a particular sequence. Look at these two statements.

1. To walks work morning Sue every.
2. Walks to work every morning Sue.

The first statement is nonsense. It is just a series of words strung together. The second statement seems to make sense, but not in this sequence. As speakers of English we automatically want to rearrange the words, moving *Sue* to the front.

> Sue walks to work every morning.

This is a sentence. It has a subject and a verb, and it expresses a complete thought. Moreover, it *sounds* like a sentence.

In other words, English sentences must do more than contain a subject and a verb and express a complete thought. The words they contain must be in a particular sequence. In the next section, we will examine the six basic sequences that we recognize as sentences.

 # SIX BASIC SENTENCE PATTERNS

There are six basic *patterns*, or sequences, in English sentences.

 ## 1. SUBJECT–VERB

subject	verb		subject	verb		subject	verb
The package	arrived.		We	are working.		Dr. O'Brien	is being paged.

 ## 2. SUBJECT–VERB–DIRECT OBJECT

subject	verb	direct object		subject	verb	direct object		subject	verb	direct object
We	shipped	the package.		The receptionist	paged	Dr. O'Brien.		I	ordered	supplies.

 ## 3. SUBJECT–VERB–INDIRECT OBJECT–DIRECT OBJECT

subject	verb	indirect object	direct object		subject	verb	indirect object	direct object
We	shipped	them	the package.		Joe	handed	Mrs. Swenson	his résumé.

subject	verb	indirect object	direct object
The personnel manager	offered	Luanne	a position.

4. SUBJECT–LINKING VERB– SUBJECT COMPLEMENT

             linking predicate
     subject verb adjective
The shipment was lost.

           linking predicate
    subject verb adjective
The supplies seem expensive.

           linking   predicate
    subject verb nominative
Ms. Rutcosky is the sole beneficiary.

Notice that all four of these patterns follow the same basic sequence: the subject comes before the verb. The subject–verb–object or subject–verb–complement pattern is known as *normal sequence.* The vast majority of English sentences follow this pattern.

The preceding examples have all been simple sentences arranged in normal sequence. That is, they consist of one independent clause with the subject appearing before the verb. Moreover, they have all been short, uncomplicated sentences. The principle of normal sequence applies equally to longer, more complicated sentences. In these sentences the subject may be a compound noun or noun equivalent. There may be a number of modifiers for both the subject and the predicate. The predicate may be compound. The sentence may be compound, complex, or compound–complex. Whatever the case, the basic pattern in each clause is still that of normal sequence: subject–verb–object or subject–verb–complement.

Look at these examples, each showing the normal sequence:

SIMPLE SENTENCES

         subject verb   direct object
Working late during the week plus weekends, we finished production of the order and

        direct
  verb object
shipped it by overnight air express.

                           direct
   subject   verb   object
Last month Mr. Sawyer, accompanied by his two assistants, visited every branch office in the region.

    subject   verb direct object
Running away from your problems will not solve them.

   subject   indirect
       verb object direct object
Being made a full partner gave her immense satisfaction.

COMPOUND SENTENCES

     verb   predicate
subject   direct object   subject verb adjective
You have completed all your payments ahead of schedule, so you are eligible for our special bonus.

              subject   verb

This morning Mrs. Abdul, together with her son, called to see you,

   subject verb indirect   direct object

            object

but I told them you would be out of the office for the remainder of the day.

◼ COMPLEX SENTENCES

  subject   verb   indirect   direct

                  object   object

We will automatically mail you this month's selection

  subject   verb   direct

                         object

if we do not receive the enclosed card by May 1.

   subject   verb

Because you have faithfully met your financial obligations by making your monthly   direct object

                                 predicate

                       subject verb adjective

payments on time for the last year, you are eligible for our preferred customer status.

◼ COMPOUND–COMPLEX SENTENCES

                                subject

         subject   verb   verb

Although her broker advised against it, Ms. Maletsky invested heavily in steel, and

       subject   verb   direct object

recent events have proved the wisdom of her decision.

                          verb

       subject

When your order of June 10 was processed by the shipping department yesterday,

                 direct object

      subject   verb

the supervisor noted an apparent error on the invoice,

          direct object   verb

subject verb   subject   direct object

so we need to reconfirm several figures before we can complete the shipment.

The last two basic sentence patterns reverse the normal sequence of subject before verb.

◼ 5. EXPLETIVE–VERB–SUBJECT

expletive verb   subject   expletive verb   subject

There were several packages on the loading dock.   There is not enough time left.

expletive verb   subject

There will be a meeting this afternoon.

expletive verb   predicate adjective   subject

It is very difficult to hold down two full-time jobs.

expletive verb   predicate adjective   subject

It is important that I speak with you before the end of the day.

expletive   verb   subject

It will take us less than two hours to reach Topeka.

In the preceding sentences *there* and *it* are not the subjects. They simply serve to introduce each sentence, to get it started. When *there* and *it* act this way, they are called *expletives*. The word *expletive* comes from a Latin word meaning "to fill up." That's exactly what expletives do. They fill up the sentences, but they are not essential to the meaning of the sentences. In fact, when these sentences are rearranged, *it* and *there* can be dropped without altering the meaning.

subject   verb

Several packages were on the loading dock.

subject   verb

A meeting will be this afternoon.

subject   verb

Not enough time is left.

subject   verb   predicate adjective

To hold down two full-time jobs is very difficult.

subject   verb   predicate adjective

That I speak with you before the end of the day is important.

subject   verb

To reach Topeka will take us less than two hours.

Note:

Here comes Miss Tong now.
Here is the information you requested.
Here are the latest sales figures.

In these sentences *here* serves essentially the same purpose as *there* and *it*, and some people refer to *here* as an expletive. Technically, however, *here* is still an adverb in these sentences. When the sentences are rearranged, the adverbial nature of *here* is clear.

Miss Tong comes here now.
The information you requested is here.
The latest sales figures are here.

6. QUESTIONS

Several different patterns are used in forming questions.

HELPING VERB–SUBJECT–VERB

helping verb   subject   verb

Have all the applicants been screened?

helping verb   subject   verb   direct object

Do you know what time it is?

ADVERB–VERB–SUBJECT

adverb *verb* *subject* *verb*
When are you leaving?

adverb *verb* *subject* *verb* direct object
Where should I put this package?

INTERROGATIVE PRONOUN–VERB–SUBJECT

interrogative pronoun   verb subject verb
Which job offer have you decided upon?

interrogative pronoun   verb subject verb
What did you say?

Whether a question begins with a helping verb, an adverb, or an interrogative pronoun, the normal subject–verb pattern is reversed. The verb comes before the subject. Hence questions are said to be in *inverted sequence*.

Note: Occasionally writers invert patterns 1 through 4. For example:

predicate adjective
verb subject
Last but not least is Rosalie.

verb subject
At the top of the form is the space for the candidate's name.

These are not new patterns. They are simply a reversal of the basic patterns. Don't let them confuse you.

FOUR BASIC SENTENCE TYPES

The six basic sentence patterns that you just studied offer you a wide range of ways to express your ideas. In addition, each pattern can be used in forming the four basic types of sentences found in English—simple, compound, complex, and compound–complex. The *simple sentence* is composed of a subject and predicate that express a complete thought. The *compound sentence* is composed of two or more independent clauses connected by a coordinate conjunction such as *and, or, but*, or by a semicolon. The *complex sentence* is composed of an independent clause connected to a dependent clause that contains a subordinate conjunction such as *since, if, because*. The *compound–complex sentence* is composed of at least two independent clauses and at least one dependent clause.

The following series of sentences illustrates the richness and variety of all four types.

SIMPLE SENTENCE

I bought a computer.
Kathleen and I bought a computer.
Kathleen and I shopped for and bought a computer.

COMPOUND SENTENCE

I bought a computer, but I don't know how to use it.
I bought a computer and I'm glad I did.
I bought a computer, but I don't know how to use it, so I'm taking a course in computer programming.
I bought a computer, and I'm glad I did, for it has been invaluable in my work.

COMPLEX SENTENCE

Although I bought a computer, I don't know how to use it.
I bought a computer even though I don't know how to use it.

 ## COMPOUND–COMPLEX SENTENCE

Although I bought a computer, I don't know how to use it, so I'm taking a course in
  computer programming.
As soon as I bought a computer, I was glad I did, for it has been invaluable in my work.

These four types of sentences, together with the six sentence patterns and the parts of speech, are the tools the business writer uses to communicate effectively. Effective communication is, of course, very important in the business world. The typical business letter, for example, is only about 150 words long. That's less than one page. The business writer must therefore convey the message fully, accurately, and successfully in a short space. Poorly written messages waste time and money. Mistakes in grammar, for instance, create a poor image of the writer and distract the reader. The reader looks at the mistakes rather than the message. If a message is unclear or incomplete, then a sale is lost, an order is not completed, a meeting is missed, an interview is denied, a payment is delayed. Often, an ineffective message requires a follow-up message to clarify it.

In the remainder of the chapter we will look at ways you can use these tools of the language to build effective messages. We will also talk about the common characteristics of effective business writing.

Turn to Exercises 14.1 to 14.3.

 ## THE WRITER'S TOOLS

We have said that, like the parts of speech, the various sentence patterns and sentence types serve as tools to help you construct effective messages. Why have people developed so many types and patterns of sentences? Would not just a few be enough? Couldn't we communicate perfectly well with only simple sentences in normal sequence? The answer is *NO*.

 ## INVERTED SENTENCE PATTERNS FOR EMPHASIS

There are several reasons that we need all these patterns and types. First, and most importantly, they give you options. These choices allow you to stress, or emphasize, some points more than others by the way you put the sentences together. These choices also allow you to make very clear to your reader the exact relationship between ideas.

Look at this sentence, for example:

According to demographers, Vermont is the most rural state in America.

Now look at the effect if we invert the sentence, thereby withholding the name of the state until the end:

Demographers say that the most rural state in America is Vermont.

Note how our interest builds as we wait to find out the identity of the state.
The use of inverted sentences to build interest and suspense is also typical in awards

ceremonies. At the Academy Awards, for example, the person announcing the award opens the sealed envelope, reads the card inside silently, and then proclaims, "The winner of the award for Best Picture of the Year is . . .!" As in the previous example, the inverted sentence pattern here is clearly more effective than the normal sequence would be.

 ## COMPOUND AND COMPLEX SENTENCES FOR CLARITY

As we said, being able to choose among sentence types and patterns also helps the writer to express ideas as clearly as possible. Simple sentences are clear and direct. Because they contain one main thought, well-written simple sentences are easy for the reader to understand. Hence most business writing is dominated by simple sentences. Sometimes, however, simple sentences cannot adequately express an idea. In these cases the writer has the option of using other types of sentences that will convey the precise idea involved. Look at these two sentences, for example:

I was the most qualified applicant.
I was offered the position.

These two simple sentences are clear. As simple sentences, however, they cannot express the idea that my being offered the position was the result of my being the most qualified. To express this idea we must combine the two statements by using either a coordinate or a subordinate conjunction.

I was the most qualified applicant, so I was offered the position.

The same is true of these two sentences:

I was the most qualified applicant.
I was not offered the position.

To express the contrast between the two ideas, we must combine them into one sentence.

I was the most qualified applicant, but I was not offered the position.

In each example the two coordinating conjunctions do more than link the two independent clauses. They clarify the relationship between the clauses.
Of course we could also choose to express these relationships as complex sentences.

Because I was the most qualified, I was offered the position.
Although I was the most qualified, I was not offered the position.

Coordinating conjunctions and subordinating conjunctions thus serve the same purpose of linking two clauses together and showing the relationship between them. They also show the relative importance of the clauses. In a compound sentence the writer suggests that the two independent clauses are of equal importance. In a complex sentence the writer suggests that the information in the independent clause is more important than that in the dependent clause.
The following chart reviews common conjunctions and the relationships between clauses they express.

COORDINATING CONJUNCTIONS

Coordinating Conjunction	Use
and nor or	Introduce ideas that *add to* or *reinforce* the idea in the preceding clause
but yet	Introduce ideas that *contrast with* the idea in the preceding clause
for	Introduces an idea that is a *cause of* the idea in the preceding clause
so	Introduces an idea that is a *result of* the idea in the preceding clause

SUBORDINATING CONJUNCTIONS

Subordinating Conjunction	Use
after as soon as since	Introduce relationships in *time*
although though	Introduce ideas that *contrast with* the idea in the independent clause
as . . . as more than	Introduce a *comparison* between the two clauses
as as if as though	Introduce the *manner of* the action in the independent clause
because as since	Introduce ideas that are a *cause of* the idea in the independent clause
if even if unless	Introduce *conditional* relationships
where wherever	Introduce the *place of* the action in the independent clause

 # COMBINING SENTENCES FOR CLARITY

The use of various types of sentences is also a mark of mature, precise thinking. The immature writer merely lists ideas; the mature writer clarifies the relationship of one idea to another. The technique of sentence combining involves putting two or more sentences together as a single sentence. Combining several simple sentences in a compound or complex sentence is often a good way to achieve clarity. Let's look at a few examples:

Montclair State College is located in Upper Montclair, New Jersey.
Montclair State College celebrated its diamond jubilee in 1984.

These are two *separate* statements about Montclair State College. They are not related causally to each other in any way. No subordinating conjunction like *although, because, since,* or *if* would be appropriate to express a relationship between them. Joining the two statements with the coordinating conjunction *and* would add nothing. As they are presently expressed, the ideas in each sentence receive equal weight. If we wanted to convey the sense of their relative importance, we could combine the two statements into a complex sentence by using the relative pronoun *which.* How we combined the two would depend on which we thought was more important. If the diamond jubilee celebration was more important, we would write the following:

Montclair State College, which is located in Upper Montclair, New Jersey, celebrated its diamond jubilee in 1984.

If we thought the college's location was more important, we would write the sentence this way:

Montclair State College, which celebrated its diamond jubilee in 1984, is located in Upper Montclair, New Jersey.

Now look at this pair of sentences:

Peter is a skilled mechanic.
Peter has opened his own repair shop.

These two sentences may have a causal relationship or they may not. How you decide to relate them—if you decide to relate them—will tell your reader what to think. Here are some possibilities:

Peter is a skilled mechanic and has opened his own repair shop.
Peter, who is a skilled mechanic, has opened his own repair shop.
Peter, who has opened his own repair shop, is a skilled mechanic.
Because Peter is a skilled mechanic, he has opened his own repair shop.

Sometimes the relationship between two statements seems quite evident. In these cases the relationship should be clearly expressed. Look at these two sentences.

Gabriella led her division in sales for four straight quarters.
Gabriella was named "Sales Representative of the Year."

For the sake of clarity these two statements should be combined into one. If you want to stress cause and effect, you would write the following:

Because Gabriella led her division in sales for four straight quarters, she was named "Sales Representative of the Year."

You could also make either statement a relative clause, thus giving additional stress to the remaining statement.

Gabriella, who led her division in sales for four straight quarters, was named "Sales Representative of the Year."
Gabriella, who was named "Sales Representative of the Year," led her division in sales for four straight quarters.

SIMPLE SENTENCES FOR CLARITY

Although it is true that complex sentences often convey complicated meanings more clearly than do several simple sentences, it is not true that complicated complex sentences are better sentences. The quality of your writing does not necessarily improve with complexity. In business, especially in reports, memos, and speeches, simple sentences are preferred. Look at this sentence.

> I was initially reluctant to invest in a computer because of the cost of a full system and my unfamiliarity with its operation, but as soon as I shopped for, selected, and bought one, I was glad I did, for my computer, with its word processing feature, has been invaluable in my work, and my children have spent hours enjoying the arcade games, which are among its many optional software packages.

This long compound–complex sentence is grammatically correct, but it is not an effective sentence. It is needlessly complicated. The meaning of this statement would be clearer if it were broken down into smaller sentences. Compare this revised version for clarity.

> I was initially reluctant to invest in a computer. I was concerned about the cost of a full system and my unfamiliarity with how to operate it. As soon as I bought one, however, I was glad I did. My computer, with its word processing feature, has been invaluable in my work. Moreover, my children have spent hours enjoying the arcade games, which are among its many optional software packages.

Here three simple sentences and two complex sentences express the ideas much more clearly and effectively.

VARIETY

The final reason for having so many sentence types and patterns is simply for the sake of variety. There is an old saying that variety is the spice of life. The same holds true for writing. Too much of the same thing can be dull and monotonous, whatever the subject. Hence one of the characteristics of effective writing is variety, and the skilled business writer takes care to vary sentence patterns and lengths.

Look at this job application letter.

Dear Ms. Zeitlin:

I am writing to apply for the position of administrative assistant in your personnel department. I saw the position advertised in The New York Times of Sunday, May 10.

I have enclosed my résumé with this letter. My résumé gives you a detailed account of my education, skills, and experience. I believe my education, skills, and experience qualify me for this position. I will graduate from Montclair State College with a Bachelor of Science degree in business administration. I took courses in Manpower Resources and Development, Wage and Salary Administration, and Personnel Research and Measurement. I believe these courses gave me an understanding of the concerns the human resources specialist must face. I have also learned about these concerns through my work experience. I was employed as a salesperson in Schmidt's Department Store for two years. I was in the men's clothing department. I am now the evening manager of the housewares department of Schmidt's Department Store. I believe I would be an asset to your company.

I will call your office on Monday, May 18. I will inquire about arranging a mutually convenient interview. I would be happy to provide you with any additional information. I may be reached at home at (201) 123-4567.

Sincerely,

Eduardo Vargas

There is nothing grammatically wrong with Eduardo's letter. The information it contains is impressive, but the letter is dull and repetitive. Almost all the sentences begin with the word *I*. All are simple sentences written in the normal sequence of subject–verb–object. All of the sentences are about the same length. In short, this is not an effective letter because it lacks variety.

Here is the same letter revised. Notice how sentence combining greatly improves this letter by adding variety to the sentence patterns.

Dear Ms. Zeitlin:

Please consider my application for the position of administrative assistant in your personnel department as advertised in The New York Times of Sunday, May 10.

My education, skills, and experience, which are detailed in the enclosed résumé, should qualify me for this position.

I will graduate from Montclair State College with a Bachelor of Science degree in business administration. My course of study included classes in Manpower Resources and Development, Wage and Salary Administration, and Personnel Research and Measurement, which gave me an understanding of the concerns facing the human resources specialist. This understanding has been complemented by my practical experience in retailing. Having worked both as a salesperson in men's clothing and as the evening manager in housewares at Schmidt's Department Store, I have firsthand knowledge of these concerns. The combination of educational background and work experience should, I believe, make me an asset to your company.

May I have the opportunity of an interview? I will call your office on Monday, May 18, to arrange a mutually convenient time. Please telephone me at (201) 123-4567 if you require any additional information.

Sincerely,

Eduardo Vargas

This revised version is much more effective than the first one. Eduardo has made the letter more interesting by varying his sentence lengths and patterns. Complex sentences are used as well as simple sentences, and the sentences do not always begin with the subject. The difference is not one of grammar or content, but style. Style is not *what* is said but the *way* it is said. Effective style in business writing demands variety. Make your writing interesting and effective by varying your sentences in length, pattern, and type.

Turn to Exercises 14.4 to 14.6.

 # THE PARAGRAPH

In the previous section we looked at some of the ways that different sentence patterns and types can be used to build effective messages. We noted particularly at the end of the section how you can add interest and effectiveness to your writing by varying your sentences in length, pattern, and type. In talking about writing more than one sentence, of course, we're talking about writing paragraphs.

Simply defined, a **paragraph** is a group of sentences on the same topic. Just as periods and capital letters signal the reader that the thought of one sentence is over and a new thought is about to begin, a paragraph signals that one subject has been completed and a new one is about to be introduced. Because paragraphs mark major divisions of thought, they serve as units on which the reader can focus. In business writing, most paragraphs tend to be short because short paragraphs are easier for a reader to read and understand than long, complicated ones. Long, complicated paragraphs should be broken down into separate subjects, each of which should be placed in its own paragraph.

Paragraphs can be organized in a variety of ways. The way that you will adopt will depend on your topic. One popular method is *chronological*. In this arrangement you organize your material according to a time sequence. Instructions on how to operate a machine, fill out a form, or find a place, for example, lend themselves to chronological organization. Another method of grouping is *spatial*. Using this method you group your material according to location. A description of how your office or sales floor is arranged, or the layout of the new mall would lend itself to spatial organization. A third and perhaps the most popular organizational principle is the *topical*. In this method you make a general statement and then support it with particular examples or illustrations. A report describing the results of market research or recommending various steps that should be taken to solve a problem could use a topical structure. This paragraph has been organized topically. It started with a general statement about the variety of ways a paragraph can be organized, then it described the ways and gave examples.

Sometimes in business writing, paragraphs are thought of in terms of their purpose. Eduardo's letter to Ms. Zeitlin, for example, follows what is commonly known as the AIDA formula. (AIDA stands for Attention–Interest–Desire–Action.) In the opening paragraph Eduardo attracts Ms. Zeitlin's *attention* by asking her to consider his application for the position of administrative assistant. The second paragraph is designed to develop her *interest* in Eduardo. In it he tells her that his education, skills, and experience make him a qualified applicant. The third paragraph develops his background and gives details of his education and experience. Its purpose is to increase Ms. Zeitlin's *desire* to speak with him about the position. The final paragraph is the *action* portion of the letter. Here Eduardo requests an interview.

Whatever principle of organization you use in writing a paragraph, the important thing is that you have one. Paragraphs are units of thought. They should contain one central thought that is the subject of the paragraph and around which the paragraph is logically organized. Like poorly written sentences, poorly constructed paragraphs can confuse the reader and convey a poor impression of the writer. Ineffective paragraphs have no place in the business world. The successful business writer knows how to write effective sentences, how to put these sentences together into effective paragraphs, and how to use these paragraphs to create effective messages.

We have been discussing how the parts of speech, sentence patterns, and sentence types can be used as tools to build the clear, effective messages that are so essential in the business world. The following pages present an overview of the seven qualities that are characteristic of effective business writing.

CHARACTERISTICS OF EFFECTIVE BUSINESS WRITING

CORRECT

The message should be grammatically correct. The ability to write grammatically correct sentences is assumed in the business world. Grammatical errors create a very bad impression of the writer, and they can be very distracting and annoying to the reader. The chief focus of this book has been to show you how to write messages that are grammatically correct and how to correct those that are not.

The concept of correctness extends beyond grammatical correctness. Not only should grammar and spelling be correct, but content must also be correct. A mechanically correct letter that contains the wrong date for an important meeting, specifies the wrong size or quantity for an order, or quotes an incorrect price is seriously flawed.

COURTEOUS

Business writing is always courteous. Good manners are a part of good business. *Please* and *Thank you* are important elements of business writing, whether they are expressly stated or only implied. Compare these pairs:

> Thank you for your order of five reams of letterhead stationery. (*Courteous*)
> We have received your order for five reams of letterhead stationery.

> Please return your payment in the enclosed envelope. (*Courteous*)
> Use the enclosed envelope when you return your payment.

CONSIDERATE

Courteous and considerate are related ideas, but they are not identical. Courteous refers more to word choice, to saying *Please* and *Thank you*. Considerate refers more to a general attitude, what is usually referred to in business writing as the "you-attitude." In other words the effective business writer always tries to think in terms of the reader and to see the situation from the reader's viewpoint. The considerate writer is tactful and does not alienate the reader.

> We have not received your check yet. (*Tactful*)
> You didn't send your check.

The considerate writer focuses on the reader's needs, not the writer's.

> You should receive your refund shortly. (*Considerate*)
> We mailed the refund check today.

> You will receive years of trouble-free service from our new MX 477 motor. (*Considerate*)
> After years of study and millions of dollars in research, our engineers have developed
> a motor that is more durable and dependable than any other motor we have ever sold.

Please send your check for $240 by August 15. In this way you will be able to protect your valuable credit rating. (*Considerate*)
We must have your check for $240 by August 15. If we don't receive it by then, we will take legal action.

COMPLETE

A message is complete when it contains all the information that it should contain. Just what that information is, of course, will depend on the nature of the message. For example, companies frequently are unable to fulfill a writer's request for information or products because the writer failed to include a return address. No matter how well written these requests are, they are incomplete and unsuccessful.

The announcement that fails to include the location or time, the order that fails to show color or size, the phone message that omits the area code—all are incomplete and ineffective. To be effective, a message must be complete. It must contain everything the particular situation requires.

The board meeting has been rescheduled for Tuesday, May 5, at 3:15 P.M. in Room 4. (*Complete*)
The time for next week's board meeting has been changed to 3:15 P.M.

CONCISE

When we say that a message is concise, we mean that it is no longer than it needs to be to achieve its purpose. A 30-page report is concise if it needs to be 30 pages to achieve its purpose effectively. A nine-word sentence is not concise if the same information could have been stated in six words. Conciseness does not necessarily mean brevity, however, for concise messages must still be effective. The following letter is brief, but it is not an example of effective business writing.

Dear Mrs. Baker:

We refuse.

Sincerely,

A concise message achieves its purpose without sacrificing clarity, completeness, courtesy, and consideration. The good writer does not cut these qualities from the message. The good writer simply eliminates unnecessary words. Look at these examples and notice how the prepositional phrase in the wordy sentence was turned into the verb in the concise sentence.

Wordy: These charges are in excess of those specified in the contract.
Concise: These charges exceed those specified in the contract.

Wordy: I am in agreement with you regarding the proposal.
Concise: I agree with you regarding the proposal.

Wordy: I have come to the conclusion that we must change our advertising strategy.
Concise: I have concluded that we must change our advertising strategy.

Here is a list of some of the lifeless and wordy expressions typically found in older business correspondence and the preferred modern equivalent. Eliminating these expressions from your writing will help to make it concise.

AVOID	PREFER	AVOID	PREFER
a check in the amount of	a check for	in the event that	if
at a later date	later	in view of the fact that	since, because
at the present time	now	subsequent to	after
despite the fact that	although	until such time as	until
due to the fact that	since, because	will you be kind enough to	please
in order that	so	with reference to	about

COHERENT

In a well-written business message everything "hangs together." The message is unified and well organized. Information that doesn't belong in the message is left out; information that does belong is included. The ideas are presented clearly so that the reader can understand them. These ideas are connected and follow logically from one another.

As we have seen, using coordinating and subordinating conjunctions to show the relationship between clauses is one method of achieving coherence.

> Your qualifications are excellent. Your qualifications do not meet our requirements. We are unable to offer you a position.
> Although your qualifications are excellent, they do not meet our requirements. Hence we are unable to offer you a position. (*Coherent*)

Irrelevant information is best omitted entirely. Where appropriate, it can be replaced by something more relevant.

> Ms. Baginski and Ms. Cruz met for lunch to discuss the contract, to review the proposal, and the dessert was delicious.
> Ms. Baginski and Ms. Cruz met for lunch to discuss the contract and to review the proposal. (*Coherent*)
> The panelists will be Richard Cowan, district representative of Armory, Inc.; Linda Grasso, director of sales for International Products; and Donna McCray, whose oldest daughter will graduate from Yale in June.
> The panelists will be Richard Cowan, district representative of Armory, Inc.; Linda Grasso, director of sales for International Products; and Donna McCray, district manager of New Haven Industries. (*Coherent*)

CLEAR

Clarity is a general quality that all good business writers constantly strive for. Effective business messages are clear, readable, and understandable. Clarity in writing is achieved through wise word choice, good sentence and paragraph construction, and the overall organization of the message. Vague pronoun references and dangling modifiers contribute to a lack of clarity. So do unfamiliar words, vague words, poorly constructed sentences that fail to emphasize what is important, and paragraphs that are poorly focused and lacking in unity. Most of the other characteristics of effective business writing, including correctness, conciseness, coherence, and completeness, contribute to clarity also. The sentences illustrating these qualities are also examples of clarity in business writing.

These seven qualities, often termed *The Seven C's,* are the characteristics of effective business writing. Whether you are writing a quick phone message, a brief memorandum, an important letter, or a lengthy report, it is important for you to keep these qualities in mind. As we have seen, when these characteristics are present, the result is effective business communication from which both the reader and the writer benefit. Thus not only in the composition exercises in the remainder of this text but also in all your writing, strive to make the characteristics of effective business writing characteristics of your writing too.

Turn to Exercises 14.7 to 14.11.

EXERCISE 14·1   SENTENCE TYPES

In the space to the right of each sentence, identify what type of sentence it is—simple, compound, complex, or compound-complex.

1. I quit and that's final!

1. _____

2. Even though the auditorium was large, it could not accommodate the huge crowd, and hundreds of people were turned away.

2. _____

3. We will not despair while there is still hope.

3. _____

4. Having forgotten his prepared remarks, he stood at the podium momentarily speechless.

4. _____

5. Ms. O'Neil read and edited the project proposal before sending it to the board of directors.

5. _____

6. Ms. O'Neil read and edited the project proposal before she sent it to the board of directors.

6. _____

7. Ms. O'Neil read and edited the project proposal, and then she sent it to the board of directors.

7. _____

8. She saw Carlos when she entered the room, but she didn't see me.

8. _____

9. I tried to call you earlier, but your line was busy.

9. _____

10. The waitress led us to our table, handed us copies of the menu, and brought us the wine list.

10. _____

11. The company is considering either remodeling the building or selling it and renting another one.

11. _____

12. I tried to speak with you about the contract last week, but you were out of town, so I had to complete the arrangements myself.

12. _____

13. Title VII of the Civil Rights Act of 1964 prohibits employment discrimination based on race, religion, color, sex, or national origin.

13. _____

14. Complete the form and return it in the enclosed envelope.

14. _____

15. Our production manager and our consulting engineer have informed me of some delays in retooling machines for your order, but this retooling will be completed soon, and your order will be shipped next week.

15. _____

EXERCISE 14·2   SENTENCE PATTERNS

In the space provided, write the number that correctly identifies the type of pattern each sentence follows. Use this key.

1. Subject–Verb
2. Subject–Verb–Direct Object
3. Subject–Verb–Indirect Object–Direct Object
4. Subject–Linking Verb–Subject Complement
5. Expletive–Verb–Subject
6. Question
7. Inverted Pattern

Then underline the subject of each sentence with one line; underline the verb with two lines.

1. I am delighted.   1. _____

2. She laughed uncontrollably for nearly a minute.   2. _____

3. We returned all four copies of the contract by registered mail early this morning.   3. _____

4. Jack gave Miss Vuksta his letter of resignation.   4. _____

5. There are a number of reporters waiting in the lobby.   5. _____

6. Why should I believe anything that you say?   6. _____

7. What a truly unique advertising concept this is!   7. _____

8. Following the heading "References" on the résumé is the phrase "Available upon
   request."   8. _____

9. When you prepare your résumé, list all your jobs in reverse chronological order,
   specifying your duties in each.   9. _____

10. Because Montclair State College believes that all its graduates should be com-
    puter literate, the college offers all students courses in the use of the computer. 10. _____

EXERCISE 14·3A   COMPOSITION: SENTENCE PATTERNS

Compose complete sentences on any topic according to the patterns specified in parentheses.

1.   (Subject–Verb) _____

_____

2.   (Compound Subject–Verb) _____

_____

3.   (Subject–Compound Verb) _____

_____

4.   (Subject–Verb–Direct Object) _____

_____

5.   (Subject–Compound Verb–Direct Object) _____

_____

6.   (Subject–Verb–Indirect Object–Direct Object) _____

_____

7.   (Subject–Linking Verb–Subject Complement) _____

_____

8.   (Expletive–Verb–Subject) _____

_____

9.   (Question) _____

_____

10.   (Inverted pattern) _____

_____

EXERCISE 14·3B   COMPOSITION: SENTENCE TYPES

Compose complete sentences in accordance with the directions in parentheses. Choose either your school or your job as the topic. All the sentences you write should relate to this topic. You may build different sentences from the same kernel sentence as was done in the text illustration, or you may compose unrelated sentences on the topic.

1.   (Simple sentence with one subject and one verb) _____

_____

2.   (Simple sentence with compound subject) _____

_____

3.   (Simple sentence with compound verb) _____

_____

4.   (Compound sentence with *and*) _____

_____

5.   (Compound sentence with *or*) _____

_____

6.   (Compound sentence with *but*) _____

_____

7.   (Complex sentence, natural order) _____

_____

8.   (Complex sentence, inverted order) _____

_____

9.   (Compound-complex sentence, dependent clause at the beginning) _____

_____

10. (Compound–complex sentence, independent clause at the beginning) _____

_____

EXERCISE 14·4 CONJUNCTIONS

Complete the following sentences by filling in the blanks with appropriate conjunctions suitable to the meaning of the sentence.

1. _____ I was leaving, it started to rain.

2. _____ sales have improved in recent months, our financial picture is still bleak.

3. _____ the doctor arrives, visitors must leave the patient's room.

4. I can hardly wait _____ I hear the results of the bar exams.

5. Dr. Zajac will notify us _____ she receives the report from the laboratory.

6. I tried to deposit my check this afternoon, _____ the bank was already closed.

7. _____ Miss Yeh is young, she is not immature.

8. The Personnel Department has functioned much more efficiently _____ Ms. Hoitsma was placed in charge.

9. I will arrive before 9:00 A.M. _____ I am not delayed.

10. _____ you have been a good customer, we would like you to have this small token of our appreciation.

EXERCISE 14·5 COMPLEX SENTENCES

Combine each of the following pairs of simple sentences into one complex sentence. Arrange the elements in whatever way seems to you to be most effective.

1. We do not carry Royex calculators. We feel Royex calculators are of poor quality. _____

    _____

2. Mr. Hartz was killed in an automobile accident this afternoon. He used to be a member of our department. _____

3. This ax handle is made of a new synthetic material. This synthetic material is ten times stronger than hickory. _____

    _____

4. The Birnbaum auditorium will accommodate 1,500 people. The auditorium would be an ideal location for our meeting. _____

    _____

5. My vacation is the week of March 15. I should be able to complete the project before April 1.

    _____

6. You will come to a fork in the road. You will see our offices on the right. _____

    _____

7. Gladys Stuehler graduated magna cum laude. She has received five job offers. _____

    _____

8. I own several credit cards. I do not carry much cash. _____

    _____

9. Some of our clients have requested additional information on the new bonds. I have prepared a brochure explaining the tax advantages available to purchasers of the new bonds. _____

    _____

10. Drilling for off-shore oil can be very expensive. Drilling for off-shore oil can also be very profitable. _____

    _____

EXERCISE 14·6 COMPOSITION: REVISING FOR VARIETY

The following letter from a former employee to her supervisor is a request for a recommendation. Revise it to achieve a greater variety in sentence length, pattern, and type. Write your revised letter in the space provided.

Dear Ms. Kreitling:

I worked in your department in 1982 and 1983. I worked as a salesperson in women's apparel. I enjoyed working for you during this period. I feel I learned a great deal about merchandising during this time.

I will graduate from Colorado State College in June of this year. I will graduate with a B.S. degree in business administration. I will be seeking employment soon in the area of marketing. I would like to use your name as a reference.

I intend to start sending out my résumés on March 15. I hope I will hear from you before then. I would like to bring you up to date on my activities. I am enclosing a copy of my résumé.

I want to thank you for your help.

Sincerely,

Meagan Terry

COMPOSITION: PARAGRAPH ORGANIZATION

Write a paragraph on a topic that interests you. Limit your paragraph to one main idea. Use either a chronological, spatial, or topical pattern of organization. You may wish to write a rough draft and revise it before writing your finished paragraph in the space below.

_____

_____

_____

_____

_____

_____

_____

_____

_____

_____

_____

EXERCISE 14·8   REVISING SENTENCES TO MAKE THEM COURTEOUS AND CONSIDERATE

Revise the following statements to make them more courteous and considerate. Write your revised sentences in the spaces provided.

1.   Fill out the attached card and return it right away. _____
_____

2.   I have received your letter of March 23. _____
_____

3.   We allow customers to charge their purchases on their VISA or MasterCard accounts. _____
_____
_____

4.   We are offering a series of holiday vacations to the Caribbean. We will permit people to reserve seats for a deposit of $25. _____
_____

5.   The instructions clearly specify that the coils of the coffee maker should be kept dry. You failed to follow the instructions. When you washed the coffee maker, you immersed it in water and ruined it. _____
_____

EXERCISE 14·9   REVISING TO ACHIEVE COHERENCE AND CLARITY

Rewrite the following passages to improve their coherence. Get rid of information that is irrelevant. Add suitable information if the sentence requires it. Reorganize and clarify ideas wherever you need to. Write your revisions in the spaces provided.

1. I have $10,000 to invest, and municipal bonds are tax free. _____

_____

_____

2. The two new members of the faculty are Dr. Audrey Fazekas, who received her degree from the University of Texas, and Dr. David Fernandez, who grew up in Portland. _____

_____

_____

3. Armand was not a very good student. Ms. Nanwani found him to be an intelligent and conscientious employee. Armand received frequent raises. _____

_____

_____

4. I have held a variety of jobs. In high school I worked as a busboy at the Chateau Monique. They served exotic food. I had an accident and broke my arm there one summer. When I was in junior high school, I had a paper route. I either walked or rode my bike. During the summers while I was in college, some days I made ice cream and somedays I sold it. I worked for a small ice cream company. As a high-school senior I sold encyclopedias door to door. I own a set of World Book encyclopedias now. After college I came to work for World Business Products. I work here now.

_____

_____

_____

_____

_____

_____

_____

_____

EXERCISE 14·10A SUBSTITUTING ACTIVE VERBS FOR VERB PHRASES

Substitute strong active verbs for verb phrases in the following sentences to make these sentences more concise. Write your revisions in the space above the lines.

1. We are in agreement that a strike authorization vote is needed.

2. Ms. Geils has done a survey of the owners of wood stoves.

3. The personnel director will give consideration to your application.

4. Mr. Odets is supposed to make a record of all incoming calls.

5. An independent auditor will do an analysis of our record keeping procedures.

EXERCISE 14·10B TRITE AND WORDY EXPRESSIONS

Revise the following paragraph to eliminate trite and wordy expressions. Write your changes in the space above the line.

Due to the fact that we have no openings at the present time, we are unable to schedule you for an interview. When a position becomes available at a later date, we will be in contact with you with reference to this position. Until such time as a position becomes available, will you be kind enough to complete the enclosed forms for our files in order that we may keep your application active.

EXERCISE 14·11   COMPOSITION: WRITING AN EMPLOYMENT HISTORY

Sometimes on a job application form you are asked to provide a brief employment history in paragraph form. Write your employment history below. Where have you worked? When? What were your titles? What were your duties?

As you write your description, keep in mind the material you have studied in this chapter. Try to develop interest through variety of sentence types and patterns. Make sure that your paragraphs are organized logically and that they demonstrate the seven characteristics of effective business writing we discussed. You will probably want to write a rough draft and revise it before writing your finished paragraphs in the space below.

15

PUNCTUATION I
THE PERIOD, THE QUESTION MARK,
THE EXCLAMATION POINT

PERIOD, QUESTION MARK, EXCLAMATION POINT

Can you read this?

marksofpunctuationtellthereaderwhentopause

Now, try it this way:

Marks of punctuation tell the reader when to pause.

What a difference a few spaces make. These spaces make a sentence easier to read because they break a long, unclear sequence of letters into easy-to-understand words. Similarly, marks of punctuation make sentences easier to read because they break an unclear sequence of thoughts into easy-to-understand ideas.

If you want your writing to say exactly what you mean, you must punctuate correctly and carefully. Improper punctuation can be not only confusing but also misleading. For example, notice how a single comma completely changes the meaning of these sentences:

Ellen, our new employee is an old friend of mine.
Ellen, our new employee, is an old friend of mine.

In the first sentence the writer is telling Ellen about the new employee. In the second sentence, Ellen is the new employee.

Because the meaning of a sentence can depend on how it is punctuated, in business you must be able to punctuate perfectly. The next five chapters will show you how.

 THE PERIOD (.)

The period is the most basic mark of punctuation. You are probably already very familiar with the rules for using it.

 RULE 1

Place a period at the end of a sentence that makes a statement.

The microscopes will be delivered by Friday.

309

Note 1: Review what you learned in Chapter 2 concerning the correct use of the period at the end of a complete sentence and the avoidance of sentence fragments and run-on sentences.

Note 2: When typing, space twice after the period before starting the next sentence.

Please pay the bill.   It is long overdue.

 ## RULE 2

Place a period at the end of a sentence that states a command or makes a request.

Bring it here.
Order the goods immediately.
Will you put it here, please.
May we hear from you before Friday.

The last two commands, worded as questions for the sake of politeness, are known as polite requests. Such requests end with a period, not a question mark. To distinguish between a direct question and a polite request, ask yourself whether the response expected is a verbal one or an action. When an *action* is expected, the statement is really a polite request and should end with a period.

 ## RULE 3

Use the period after a condensed expression that stands for a full statement or command.

Yes.   No.   Next.   Wait.   Good luck.   Congratulations.

Often, condensed expressions are answers to questions. As such they are acceptable sentence fragments, their meanings completed by the context of the question.

(When will you complete your report?) By the end of the week.
(Do you mind staying late tonight?) No, not at all.

 ## RULE 4

Place a period after an abbreviation.

Mr.	Dr.	N.Y.C.	r.p.m.
e.g.	J. Gordon Jones, Jr.	Ph.D.	Co.

Note 1: When a sentence ends with an abbreviation, use only one period.

Address the letter to Fulton Boyd, Esq.
The shipment goes to Morris Van Lines, Inc.

But: The plant is open for inspection all day (9:00 a.m. to 5:30 p.m.).

Note 2: Miss is not an abbreviation. *Mr., Ms., Mrs., Messrs.,* and *Mmes.* are abbreviations.

Dear Miss Smith: Dear Ms. Smith:

Note 3: Abbreviations composed of a series of lowercase letters should be typed with no space after each period. Space only after the final period; then use a single space unless you are starting a new sentence, in which case you use a double space.

The price quoted is f.o.b. Detroit.
We received a c.o.d. shipment from the Denver warehouse.
The package arrived c.o.d. I was unable to pay for it.

Note 4: Abbreviations composed of capital letters should be typed with a single space after each period. Pay particular attention to this spacing in typing the abbreviations in a person's name.

The C. P. A. examination is scheduled for early June.
Our new chairman is J. P. Roberts.

Note 5: Abbreviations are sometimes written in solid capital letters, without periods or spaces. Consult a dictionary when you are unsure of the correct abbreviation.

YMCA   VA   NATO   FHA

Note 6: The Appendix contains a listing of the official United States Post Office abbreviations for the fifty states. In business correspondence avoid abbreviating the names of states except in addresses and tabulations. Avoid abbreviating the names of cities also.

Note 7: Don't confuse a contraction and an abbreviation. A contraction that is written with an apostrophe does not require a period. The following are contractions:

Gen'l   Gov't   Rec't   Sec't   Sup't

The following numbers are considered contractions and do not require periods: 1st, 2nd (2d), 3rd (3d), 4th, 5th . . . 10th . . . 23rd . . . 100th . . . etc.

 ## RULE 5

Use a period to separate cents from dollars in a money amount.

$2.58 $10.10 $4,372.27

Note 1: Do not put a period after a dollar amount if no cents are indicated.

$2 $10 $4,372

But: $2.00 $10.00 $4,372.46

RULE 6

Use the period as a decimal point and in percentages.

.0   .06   .006   3.1416

Our studies indicate that 24.2 percent of purchasers are delinquent in their payments.

Note: Do not space after the period used in a dollar amount, a decimal, or a percentage.

 ## RULE 7

Use periods in tabulations or outlines. In tabulations, when a list is numbered or lettered, put a period after each number or letter. Do not put a period or other mark of punctuation after the items in the tabulation unless each item is a full sentence.

Basic to our way of life are these fundamental rights:
  1. Freedom of speech

2. Freedom of assembly
3. Freedom of religion
4. Freedom of the press

Note 1: When a list is written as a part of a sentence, you may enclose clarifying numbers or letters in parentheses. In this case, do not use a period with the numbers or letters, but punctuate as if they were not present.

Basic to our way of life are these fundamental rights: (a) Freedom of speech, (b) Freedom of assembly, (c) Freedom of religion, and (d) Freedom of the press.

In preparing an outline, put a period after the letter or number used to mark the first four division levels. Here is a part of the outline used to prepare this text:

I.   The Forms of Pronouns
    A.   Personal Pronouns
        1.   Nominative Case
            a. Subject
            b. Subject Complement

THE QUESTION MARK (?)

RULE 1

Use a question mark at the end of a direct question. In typing skip two spaces after the question mark at the end of a sentence.

```
Can they deliver by May 15?  I doubt it.
```

Note 1: Sometimes the question comes at the end of a statement, in which case a comma comes before it.

You did order the materials, didn't you?

Note 2: Sometimes a sentence is worded like a statement when it is actually a question. The writer must show his or her intention by the final mark of punctuation.

The car is in good working order?
The meeting has been postponed?
Only four people attended the meeting?

Note 3: Remember, a polite request ends with a period, not a question mark.

Won't you come in, please.
Will you please let us hear from you soon.

Note 4: Be wary of run-on sentences when using the question mark.

Right: Will you be at the banquet? We certainly hope so. *Not:* Will you be at the banquet, we certainly hope so.

Note 5: Do not use a question mark at the end of a sentence that refers indirectly to a question; use a period.

Direct Question: Do you know when the new models will be available?
Indirect Question: He wonders if you know when the new models will be available.
Direct Question: When will the new models be available?
Indirect Question: I wonder when the new models will be available.

Note 6: Don't be deceived by the length of a question. No matter how long a direct question may be, end it with a question mark.

Are you certain that we can expect delivery of the order by January 14 despite the newspaper's report that a strike may be called by the union at midnight on December 31?

Note 7: Although the question mark usually ends a sentence, it may be used in the middle of a sentence that contains a series of closely related questions. After each such question mark, skip one typewritten space and start the next word with a lowercase letter.

Can you name four Presidents? four Vice Presidents? four Chief Justices?
What would be our unit price if we purchase six gross? twelve gross? twenty gross?

 ## RULE 2

Use a question mark enclosed in parentheses to express doubt or uncertainty.

Jorge claims it will take less than 30(?) minutes to complete the procedure.
The message read: "Robert Ambertson(?) called. Will call back."
Joyce paid over $15,000(?) for her car.

 # THE EXCLAMATION POINT (!)

Use the exclamation point after a word or group of words that expresses strong feeling or emotion.

Hurrah!   Wait until you test drive the new Chevrolet!
Never!   What a marvelous film!
Watch out!

As with the period and question mark, space twice after an exclamation point before starting the next sentence.

No! I will not resign.

In business writing you should use exclamation points sparingly. Save them for that infrequent thought that really commands the emphasis the exclamation point provides.

 # PROGRAMMED REINFORCEMENT

S1 A period is used at the end of a sentence that makes a _____ or gives a command.

R1 statement

S2 Is this a statement or a command? **Put it down.** _____

R2 command

S3   Punctuate the following, placing a period at the end of each sentence and capitalizing initial letters of the sentences. **book sales are increasing this is particularly true of paperbacks**

R3   **Book sales are increasing. This is particularly true of paperbacks.**

S4   A period is placed after an abbreviation. If a sentence ends with an abbreviation, it has (one, two) period(s). Place periods where necessary: **The shipment is being sent c o d to Global, Inc**

R4   **one; . . . c.o.d. to Global, Inc.**

S5   In writing a dollar amount when no cents are indicated, a period (is, is not) used.

R5   is not

S6   In typing allow _____ blank space(s) after the period at the end of a sentence; allow _____ blank space(s) after each period in an abbreviation like c.o.d.; allow _____ blank space(s) after each period in an abbreviation like M. B. A.

R6   two; no; one

S7   A question mark is used after a (direct, indirect) question. It is not used after a(n) (direct, indirect) question.

R7   direct; indirect

S8   A question mark is not used after the following sentence because it is really a polite _____. **Won't you please be seated.**

R8   request

S9   There may be several questions in one sentence. How would you punctuate this? **Can you think of two advertising slogans four new jingles three eye-catching phrases**

R9   **Can you think of two advertising slogans? four new jingles? three eye-catching phrases?**

S10   A question mark enclosed in parentheses in the middle of a sentence is used to express _____.

R10   doubt or uncertainty

S11   In typing, leave _____ space(s) after a question mark at the end of a sentence; leave _____ space(s) after a question mark in the middle of a sentence.

R11   two; one

S12   The punctuation mark used after words that show strong feeling or emotion is the _____.

R12   exclamation point

S13   Use periods, question marks, and exclamation marks as needed: **What a break I got a ten percent raise did you**

R13   **What a break! I got a ten-percent raise. Did you?**

Turn to Exercises 15.1 to 15.5.

EXERCISE 15·1A   USING THE PERIOD

Cross out all incorrect punctuation in the following paragraphs and insert all necessary periods and capitals.

this morning we received a request to submit a bid on the equipment specifications for the new vocational school now being erected in Erie, Pennsylvania

it is our policy, as you know, to work only through our regular dealers if you would ask your representative to contact our Erie dealer, we would be delighted to prepare a bid

hand tools are our specialty, and we hope you will let us work with you in that area the large machine equipment, of course, is out of our line because of your long experience in this field, you should have no trouble in submitting a complete bid

*   *   *

we appreciate the information that you gave us in your letter of October 17

the purchasing agent for the Board of Education in Erie has given us permission to submit a bid on the equipment list for the new school since the bid must be submitted on or before November 19, it is necessary for us to work rapidly

some time ago you stated that there might be price changes after November 1 while we understand that increasing demands are being placed on the tool industry, still we must request a definite guarantee from your company that the prices in effect now will apply to the Erie school contract if it is awarded to our company may we hear from you before the end of the week

EXERCISE 15·1B   THE PERIOD

Insert periods wherever necessary in the sentences below. Show a capital letter if a new sentence follows.

1. I will be there at 8 P.M. I will see you then

2. Volunteer your services that is the way to help

3. Will you open the door, please my hands are full

4. My friend Ralph J Hobart, who has both an MBA and a CPA advised me to invest in IBM

5. Mrs M Franklin Smith, Jr, lives in Pittsburgh, Pennsylvania

6. Dr Frances R Jackson, DDS, ordered these drills to be sent c o d

7. John R Boyd, Esq, was officially listed as *Sup't of Arsenals* and later as *Sec'y of War*

8. He gained $245 on his first venture but lost $15,324 later

9. Washington, DC, is north of Raleigh, North Carolina

10. The merchandise went to Cap't Johnson of Wallace Lines, Inc

11. We stayed at the YMCA in St Louis, Missouri

12. Mrs Johnson asked Miss Smith to visit at noon

13. Norman Wells III received his BA from Yale and his PhD from Harvard

14. Won't you please be seated, Ms Barrett

15. The US 4th Army Brigade is being transferred from Ft Dix, New Jersey, to Guam aboard the *USS Enterprise*

16. We spent over half our monthly income on food (295 percent) and housing (252 percent) last year

17. Will you please add Mr and Mrs K D Davidson to the mailing list

18. In his dictation he often uses abbreviations such as *eg, ie,* and *etc*

19. Our office is open from 9:00 a m to 4:30 p m

20. Ms Brady asked Mr Chun if the mail had arrived yet

EXERCISE 15·2A THE QUESTION MARK AND EXCLAMATION POINT

At the end of each of the following sentences, place a question mark, an exclamation mark, or a period, whichever is correct.

1. Did you send the letter
2. Please mail it at once
3. Won't you come in, please
4. Why wasn't it filed at once
5. That's a fine idea
6. The director asked many questions
7. Who is there
8. I am not sure who filed the letter
9. Will you be kind enough to visit us
10. Why not take a chance
11. Why
12. Can we doubt his sincerity
13. That is the $64,000 question
14. Amazing
15. What an amazing discovery
16. Did you see the shipment
17. Have they acknowledged our order
18. Wonderful
19. Won't you please consider our offer
20. This is wonderful news, isn't it

EXERCISE 15·2B THE QUESTION MARK, PERIOD, EXCLAMATION POINT

Put question marks, periods, or exclamation points wherever necessary; show a capital letter if a new sentence follows.

1. Can you be there this evening
2. Will you please tell him to call me when he returns
3. Wow what a terrific sales campaign
4. Why don't you use a carbon it will help
5. Since our last order, have prices risen
6. Why was he discharged he was doing a good job
7. Are you sure that all figures have been carefully examined and checked
8. She asked me where you are going tonight
9. Can you name three generals three admirals three air chiefs
10. Where is she going, I wonder
11. May I help you

12. The weather is unusually cool, is it not, for this time of year

13. How much does it cost $30 $40 $50

14. Did you forget your appointment at 2 p m

15. There is no reason to keep these files, is there

16. Common abbreviations such as Mr, Ms, a m, p m, and c o d frequently appear in business correspondence

17. Wait don't leave yet

18. Will these contracts reach R M Benbrook, Esq, before 5 p m

19. Have the two incorrect charges, $16 73 and $25 72, been removed from my charge account

20. Have you seen the latest figures on the GNP

21. Wasn't that Louise J Hicks, M D

22. Would you like us to ship your order c o d

23. Do you know the difference in meaning between the abbreviations *i* e and e g

24. What do you expect to be doing in 5 years in 10 years in 20 years

25. Is Mr H R Gunderson a member of the SEC

EXERCISE 15·3   TERMINAL PUNCTUATION

Insert periods, question marks, exclamation marks, and capitals wherever appropriate in the following letter.

Dear Customer Service Representative:

last May we ordered the new manual by George Wilson, Jr as yet we have not received it although it is already July 15 may we ask for an explanation

is the manual out of print or was our order simply misplaced if it is in stock, please ship it at once, cod if not, let us know when we can expect it

rush

Very truly yours,

EXERCISE 15·4   COMPOSITION: THE PERIOD, QUESTION MARK, EXCLAMATION POINT

Compose the sentences called for in parentheses.

1. (a compound sentence that is a command) _____

2. (a polite request) _____

3. (an acceptable sentence fragment that is not an exclamation) _____

4. (a statement that ends with a question) _____

5. (a compound sentence that is a question) _____

6. (an indirect question) _____

7. (a sentence with a series of closely related questions) _____

8. (an exclamation) _____

EXERCISE 15·5   COMPOSITION: WRITING INSTRUCTIONS

Most college students hold a variety of part-time jobs and summer jobs during their years in school. A typical responsibility for these students is to train their replacements.

Pretend that you are leaving either your current or a previous job. You have been asked to train your replacement, who is completely unfamiliar with your areas of responsibility and how to fulfill them. Select one of these responsibilities and write a set of detailed instructions on how to perform it. Write your instructions in the space below.

16

PUNCTUATION II
THE COMMA

COMMAS IN SERIES, COMMAS WITH COMPOUND
SENTENCES, COMMAS WITH INTRODUCTORY
ELEMENTS

 THE COMMA (,)

The comma is the most frequently used mark of punctuation. There are many rules for using commas, but all of them can be seen as aspects of six basic rules. Rather than memorize a long series of rules covering specific occasions, familiarize yourself with the six basic rules presented in this and the following chapter.

 RULE 1: SERIES

Use commas to separate words, phrases, or clauses listed in a series. Each of the following sentences illustrates this use of the comma in a different instance.

1. Our new offices are located in a towering, ultramodern, air-conditioned skyscraper.
2. The Electrex Meter has been carefully, precisely, and painstakingly assembled for maximum sensitivity.
3. Wool, cotton, linen, or silk will be used in the manufacture of this dress.
4. This data management program automatically bills, posts, and maintains an inventory control.
5. The Armed Forces are ever-alert on the land, in the air, and on the sea.
6. In this course your objectives are to write, to speak, and to think clearly.
7. That our opponents are aggressive, that they are clever, and that they are ruthless must be recognized.
8. Turn the ignition key, gently press the gas pedal, and push the starter button.

Note 1: Examine all the sentences above. The first sentence illustrates a series of coordinate adjectives not linked by a coordinating conjunction. All the rest contain a conjunction before the final item in the series. Notice that a comma has been placed before each of these conjunctions.

Some authorities say that this final comma is optional. We believe it is preferable to include it, however, because sometimes the absence of this final comma could confuse a reader. Look at this sentence, for example:

For the next class meeting our economics professor assigned readings from texts by O'Leary and Kuntz, Friedman, Modolo and Nowak.

Did Modolo and Nowak each write a textbook, or did they, like O'Leary and Kuntz, co-author one? If you make it a habit always to place a comma before the conjunction that precedes the last item in a series, you will avoid the possibility of confusing your reader.

Note 2: Often you may be undecided whether to place a comma after the last item in a series. You can solve this problem by testing the last item as though it were alone in the sentence and not part of a series. For example:

1. Our offices are located in a towering, ultramodern, air-conditioned (, ?) skyscraper.

    Test: Our offices are located in an air-conditioned skyscraper. (Needs no comma.)
    Therefore: . . . *a towering, ultramodern, air-conditioned skyscraper.*
    The technical rule is: When a series of adjectives modifies a noun, no comma should be placed after the final adjective.

2. The Electrex Meter has been carefully, precisely, and painstakingly (, ?) assembled.

    Test: The Electrex Meter has been painstakingly assembled. (No comma)
    Therefore: . . . *carefully, precisely, and painstakingly assembled.* Technically: When a series of adverbs modifies a verb (or other part of speech), do not put a comma after the last adverb.

3. Wool, cotton, linen, or silk (, ?) will be used in the manufacture of this dress.

    Test: Silk will be used . . . (No comma)
    Therefore: *Wool, cotton, linen, or silk will be used* . . . Technically: When you have a compound subject, do not use a comma to separate the last item in the subject from the predicate.
    Note 3: Occasionally a series will be written with coordinating or correlative conjunctions between all items in the series. In this type of series, leave out the commas.

    The Electrex Meter has been carefully and precisely and painstakingly assembled.
    Wool or cotton or linen or silk will be used.

    Note 4: Be careful not to separate adjectives that are not in series. Look at this sentence:

    Try our new cleansing cream.

New is an adjective and *cleansing* is an adjective, but they are not in series. *New* modifies the word-group *cleansing cream,* not just the noun *cream.* Here are other examples:

    We are looking for an intelligent, pleasant, enthusiastic young teller. (*Young teller* is treated as a word-group.)
    The government's objectives are secure national defense and rapid national growth. (*National defense* and *national growth* are treated as word-groups.)

Note 5: Sometimes pairs of words or phrases will be listed in series. In these instances, use commas to separate the pairs from one another.

    To write and speak well, to think and act rigorously, and to live and fight courageously are your ideals.

Note 6: Many firm names are composed of a series of names. Be sure to separate the names with commas in precisely the format used on the firm's official letterhead. For example:

    Merrill Lynch, Pierce, Fenner & Smith
    Batten, Barton, Durstine & Osborne

As a general rule a comma is not placed before the ampersand (&) that often precedes the last name in a series.

Note 7: Frequently a long list will be ended with the abbreviation *etc.,* meaning *and others.* A comma should be placed before the *etc.* and should also be placed after the period unless it ends the sentence. (Some authorities consider this second comma optional.)

Never write *and etc.* since this would mean *and and others,* which is redundant.

Generally, do not use the abbreviation *etc.* when you can find a more explicit, less vague ending for the series. Do not use the abbreviation *etc.* when the series has been begun with *for example* or a similar phrase setting forth the incomplete nature of the lists because this too would be redundant.

> **Permissible:** The candidates expressed their views on farm policy, foreign relations, fiscal management, labor relations, etc.
> **Improved:** The candidates expressed their views on farm policy, foreign relations, fiscal management, labor relations, and other vital national issues.
> **Never:** The candidates expressed their views on vital national issues such as farm policy, foreign relations, fiscal management, labor relations, etc. (Leave out the *etc.* and the sentence becomes correct; or leave out the phrase *such as.* You can't have both.)

Note 8: When typing, allow a single space after the comma.

 # PROGRAMMED REINFORCEMENT

	S1 **I ordered pens, pencils, erasers, and paper.** This sentence illustrates the use of the comma with words in a _____.
R1 series	**S2** Do you place a comma before the word **and** in this sentence? **I sent back the bills, the invoice ? and the statements.** Answer: _____.
R2 Yes	**S3** If coordinate conjunctions (like **and**) connect all the words in a series, you (do, do not) place a comma before each conjunction. For example: **We polished, and waxed, and buffed each desk.**
R3 do not (Correct: **We polished and waxed and buffed each desk.**)	**S4** When you have a series of adjectives you (should, should not) place a comma after the last adjective. For example: **We offer fast, accurate, efficient ? service.**
R4 should not (**We offer fast, accurate, efficient service.**)	**S5** When you have a series of adverbs you (should, should not) place a comma after the last adverb. **This letter has been quickly, accurately, and efficiently ? typed.** _____
R5 should not	**S6** You (should, should not) place a comma after the last item in a compound subject. **Filing, typing, and posting ? are my best skills.** _____
R6 should not	**S7** Punctuate this sentence: **Courage fortitude and wisdom are the strengths of the nation.**
R7 **Courage, fortitude, and wisdom are the strengths of the nation.**	

S8 Adjectives that are not in series (should, should not) be separated by commas. Punctuate the following correctly:
1. **She wore a ranch-dyed mink coat.**
2. **We wish to inform you of our new credit policy.**
3. **We are seeking an intelligent responsible energetic young accountant.**

R8 should not; 1. no commas; 2. no commas; 3. **intelligent, responsible, energetic young accountant.**

S9 As a general rule a comma (should, should not) come before the ampersand (&) in a company name. Punctuate the following sentence correctly: **Doyle Doakes & Dorner is an old respected legal firm.**

R9 should not
Doyle, Doakes & Dorner is an old, respected legal firm.

S10 If a series ends with the abbreviation *etc.*, a comma (should, should not) precede the *etc.* A comma (should, should not) follow *etc.* if it does not end the sentence. Punctuate the following sentence correctly: **Towels linens draperies etc. are located on the third floor.**

R10 should; should; **Towels, linens, draperies, etc., are located on the third floor.**

Turn to Exercise 16.1.

RULE 2: COMPOUND SENTENCES

Use a comma to separate two complete thoughts that are connected by a coordinate conjunction (*and, but, or, nor, for*) or by the connectives *so* and *yet*. In other words, place commas between all independent clauses in a compound sentence.

Our offer was made in good faith, and we trust that you will give it full consideration.
We are not prepared to act now, nor will we be prepared for many months.

Note 1: Note that in each of these examples the comma comes before the conjunction. There is no comma after the conjunction because the conjunction is part of the final clause.

Note 2: In a short sentence composed of two independent clauses connected by *and* or *or*, you may omit the comma if the meaning of the sentence is clear. As a rule of thumb, you may leave the comma out if either part of the sentence has five or fewer words.

Your order arrived and we shipped it immediately.
Pay the bill or return the merchandise.

If two independent clauses are connected by *but* or *yet*, include the comma no matter how short the parts of the sentence.

We are ready to deal with you now, but we won't be forever.
They were not expected, yet they came.

Note 3: Remember that a comma by itself is insufficient to join two independent clauses into a compound sentence.

Wrong: We must change our advertising appeal, we may lose a large part of the market.

This error is known as a *comma fault*. To correct it, use a semicolon, use a comma plus a coordinate conjunction, or make two separate sentences.

Right: We must change our advertising appeal; we may lose a large part of the market.
Right: We must change our advertising appeal, or we may lose a large part of the market.
Right: We must change our advertising appeal. We may lose a large part of the market.

If you have forgotten about comma faults, review run-on sentences in Chapter 2.

Note 4: Three or more complete thoughts (independent clauses) may be joined in a series in a single compound sentence. In this instance only the final clause requires a comma and coordinate conjunction; the preceding clauses may be separated with only a comma.

He came, he saw, and he conquered.
Plan your campaign, put it into operation, and guide it to a successful conclusion.

Note 5: Don't confuse a compound sentence composed of two or more complete thoughts with a sentence that contains a compound predicate composed of two or more predicates. In this latter type of sentence, do not use commas to separate the parts of the compound predicate. Look at the next two sentences:

We carefully set up our booth at the fair and arranged the displays attractively. (One subject: *We.* Compound predicate: *set up . . . and arranged.*)
We carefully set up our booth at the fair, but the public did not attend in large numbers. (Two complete thoughts: *We set up . . . The public did not attend.*)

 # PROGRAMMED REINFORCEMENT

S11 When coordinate conjunctions connect long independent clauses, you (do, do not) use a comma. Punctuate the following sentence correctly: **I have not completed the filing but I will do so before lunch.**

R11 do; . . . **filing, but** . . .

S12 In a compound sentence the comma comes (before, after) the conjunction. Punctuate this sentence correctly: **She may not be a fast typist but she is an accurate one.**

R12 before; . . . **typist, but she** . . .

S13 In a short sentence composed of two independent clauses connected by *and* or *or*, you (may, may not) leave out the comma. Punctuate the following correctly:
1. **She is a fast typist and she is accurate.**
2. **Come yourself or send a representative.**

R13 may; 1. no commas needed; 2. no commas needed

S14 In a short sentence composed of two independent clauses connected by *but* or *yet*, you (may, may not) omit the comma. Punctuate the following correctly:
1. **She is a slow typist but she is accurate.**
2. **They were invited yet they refused.**

R14 may not; 1. . . . **typist, but** . . . 2. . . . **invited, yet** . . .

S15 Add commas where necessary in these sentences:
a. **I will go but you can't.**
b. **I will go and you can too.**
c. **I will go or you can.**
d. **I don't want to go yet I will.**

R15 a. . . . **go, but** . . .
b. **no comma**
c. **no comma**
d. . . . **go, yet** . . .

S16 To connect two independent clauses to create a compound sentence, you cannot use a comma by itself. You must either use a _____ or a _____ followed by a _____ _____ such as **and, but, or, nor,** or **yet.**

R16 semicolon; comma; coordinate conjunction

S17 You should not confuse a compound predicate with a compound sentence. The following is an example of a compound _____: **We will take the assignment and start as soon as possible.**

R17 predicate

S18 The following is an example of a compound _____ _____: **We will take the assignment, but you may have it if you like.**

R18 sentence

S19 Punctuate the following sentences correctly:
1. **I know we have met before but I don't remember your name.**
2. **Mr. Taylor knew they had met before but was unable to remember her name.**

R19 1. . . . **before, but I** . . .
2. no commas

Turn to Exercise 16.2.

 # RULE 3: INTRODUCTORY ELEMENTS

Use a comma to separate various introductory elements from the rest of the sentence.

Part A. Dependent Clauses

As you have learned, a complex sentence consists of a dependent clause and an independent clause. For example:

We have worked hard since the order arrived.

This complex sentence is in natural sequence because the independent clause (*We have worked hard*) precedes the dependent clause (*since the order arrived*). Here are other examples of complex sentences in the natural sequence:

We have started retooling since you placed the order.
They ran to congratulate him as soon as they heard the news.
She left the theater because she failed to get the part.

Frequently, however, the sentence may be inverted and the dependent clause placed at the beginning to give it greater emphasis. When a sentence begins with a dependent clause, use a comma to separate the dependent clause from the independent clause. This comma shows that the sentence is inverted.

Since you placed the order, we have started retooling.
As soon as they heard the news, they ran to congratulate him.
Because she failed to get the part, she left the theater.

Here are other examples of dependent clauses in inverted sentences. In studying these sentences, ask yourself what makes the first clause dependent and the second independent.

Although you agree, we cannot accept.
After she heard our reply, she reconsidered.
As I arrived, he left.
As long as you try, you are certain to succeed.
As soon as I hear from him, I will notify you.
Before you leave, drop in.
However unhappy you may feel, don't despair.
If you have an extra catalog, please send it to us.

Part B.   Verb Phrases

Introductory phrases containing verb forms should be set off from the rest of the sentence by a comma.

After hearing our reply, she reconsidered.
Before leaving, drop in.
Within the short amount of time allotted to us, I think we have accomplished much.
To gain access to the hall, try the back door.

Punctuate introductory modifiers that consist solely of a verbal the same way.

Perplexed, he put down the receiver.
Gasping, he raced toward the departing train.

Part C.   Prepositional Phrases

Short introductory prepositional phrases of up to four words usually are not followed by a comma. For example:

On June 27 we received your offer.
In our previous correspondence we thoroughly discussed the various proposals.
At the last meeting a new president was elected.

If the sentence begins with a long prepositional phrase or other kind of phrase, however, a comma should be used to separate the phrase from the rest of the sentence.

At the last meeting of the board of trustees, a new president was elected.
In our previous correspondence with the three parties involved, we thoroughly discussed the various proposals.

Part D.   Transitional Expressions and Interjections

As you learned in Chapter 13, there are many transitional phrases that can serve as connectives to join two independent clauses. These phrases are always preceded by a semicolon and followed by a comma.

Our sales are increasing everywhere; for example, Denver sales are up nearly 40 percent.

If this sentence were rewritten as two separate sentences, *for example* would be an introductory element and would still be followed by a comma.

Our sales are increasing everywhere. For example, Denver sales are up nearly 40 percent.
Her work is not perfect. In fact, it contains a large number of errors.

As you also learned in Chapter 13, a mild interjection or exclamation may begin a sentence. When it does, it is followed by a comma.

Well, at least I tried.   Yes, we will attend.
Oh, that's all right.   No, I cannot accept your offer.

PROGRAMMED REINFORCEMENT

S20 **We will stand with you if you wish.** This is an example of a _____ sentence because it contains an _____ clause and a _____ clause.

R20 complex; independent; dependent

S21 **We will stand with you if you wish.** **If you wish** is a _____ clause. The natural sequence of a complex sentence is for the dependent clause to come _____ the independent clause.

R21 dependent; after

S22 When a complex sentence follows the natural sequence (independent clause first), you (should, should not) place a comma after the independent clause.

R22 should not

S23 When a complex sentence is in inverted sequence (dependent clause first), you (should, should not) place a comma after the dependent clause.

R23 should

S24 Place commas in the following sentences as needed:
a. **In case you are opposed we'll stand with you.**
b. **They celebrated when they learned of our victory.**
c. **Whenever you are in town drop in.**

R24 a. . . . **opposed, we'll** . . .
b. no comma
c. . . . **town, drop in.**

S25 Place commas in the following sentences as needed:
a. **On our way to town we passed the new store.**
b. **The revised plans have been completed and approved but we won't break ground for a month.**
c. **While you were out Ms. Johnson phoned.**

R25 a. no comma
b. . . . **approved, but** . . .
c. . . . **out, Ms. Johnson phoned.**

S26 Short introductory prepositional phrases are usually (followed, not followed) by a comma. A comma (is, is not) used, however, to separate long introductory phrases from the body of the sentence. Place a comma in each of the following sentences where necessary:
a. **In June prices fell.**
b. **At the meeting we discussed this problem at length.**
c. **To get the best possible results from this equipment follow the directions closely.**

R26 not followed; is;
a. no comma
b. no comma
c. . . . **equipment, follow** . . .

S27 Transitional expressions and interjections used as introductory elements should also be followed by commas. Place commas where necessary in these sentences:
a. **Oh you don't say.**
b. **Well you are probably right.**
c. **Anton is not dependable. For example he missed this morning's conference.**

R27 a. **Oh, you** . . .
b. **Well, you** . . .
c. **For example, he** . . .

Turn to Exercises 16.3 to 16.6.

EXERCISE 16·1   SEPARATING ITEMS IN A SERIES

Place commas in the following sentences wherever necessary.

1. We will leave by car train or plane on Friday.

2. The successful teacher is friendly alert interesting and self-confident.

3. Our store deals in radios TV sets stereos video cassette recorders and similar products.

4. We have correspondence from you dated May 3 May 18 June 6 and July 15.

5. You will not be able to resist our newest model when you see its long low streamlined appearance.

6. Newspapers magazines books and periodicals—all will be on sale this week.

7. Our rates are $40 for a room without bath $50 for a room with bath and $75 for a two-room suite.

8. We deal in state bonds county bonds municipal bonds industrial bonds railroad bonds etc.

9. We deal in state county municipal industrial and railroad bonds.

10. She is seeking a secure challenging well-paying position in insurance.

11. We sell the finest kerosene benzene and alcohol lamps on the market.

12. The properties available are in Detroit St. Louis Cleveland and New York.

13. For lunch we offer roast beef salad and bread and butter.

14. The firm of Webber Price & Beamon is well known in the advertising world.

15. Would you be willing to spend a few dollars for a chance to break into a fast-growing profitable interesting respected profession?

16. Fame fortune and esteem—these were their goals in life.

17. Their firm deals in the finest silks and cottons and woolens and linens.

18. The box is neither lightweight nor presentable.

19. I can see now the lovely green lawn the broad gravel walk the giant shade trees and the perfect model of a colonial walk.

20. The new skyscrapers have been luxuriously ornately and decoratively designed.

21. That modern novelists are frank that they are imaginative and that they are perceptive are recognized facts.

22. Ask questions politely listen to details carefully and follow instructions intelligently.

23. Tact wisdom and diplomacy—these are marks of an enlightened intelligent foreign policy.

24. Please try our new furniture polish in either pine or lemon scent.

25. To plan and design carefully to purchase and order wisely and to build and construct sturdily are necessary steps.

26. She found three old manual adding machines in the storeroom.

27. He planned to invite laborers farmers storekeepers teachers etc. to his rally on tax reform.

28. The core curriculum includes courses in English mathematics history philosophy and foreign languages.

29. The work-experience portion of your résumé should indicate when you held the job what your job title was who your employer was and what your responsibilities and your accomplishments were.

30. Normally found in a letter of acceptance of a job offer are statements that formally accept the position voice appreciation for the offer confirm the details of the offer and express anticipation of doing good work.

EXERCISE 16·2A   SENTENCE ERRORS

This is a review exercise on run-on sentences and sentence fragments. Proofread the following letter, crossing out each error and writing in your correction. If you need to, review the material on run-on sentences and sentence fragments in Chapter 2.

Dear Ms. Brandt:

The Drake Hotel is a comfortable and well-managed manor. Situated on 80 gorgeous acres in the rolling hills of Bell Harbor. From the heart of Baltimore it can be reached by train or automobile. In less than an hour. Although it is near the city. It is far enough removed for rest and quiet.

Majestic old trees and attractive walks add to the beauty of the grounds the extensive lawns reach to the shore of Chesapeake Bay fishing and boating are always in season.

If you can possibly arrange your vacation to fall in August you will find the Drake Hotel grounds at their loveliest flowers are in full bloom and the shade trees are at their lushest. Of course some of our regular guests prefer the fall when the trees are ablaze with color. And the ground is covered with a thick carpet of fallen leaves.

We extend to you and your friends. A cordial invitation to visit us.

                    Yours sincerely,

EXERCISE 16·2B   COMPOUND SENTENCES

Place commas wherever necessary in the following sentences.

1. Our letters haven't been very serious but underneath their semi-jesting tone runs the feeling that we will eventually get your business.

2. It was inspected it was tested it was tortured but it didn't fade or shrink.

3. Last month we were pleased to send you one of our publications and we hope that it has satisfactorily answered your questions.

4. Booklets and showroom demonstrations are interesting but actual performance on the job is the most convincing.

5. An excellent pool is available for those who like to swim and a beautiful 18-hole course is open for those who like to play golf.

6. Every lesson in the manual is easy and every principle is outlined in complete detail.

7. He phoned but was unable to speak with her.

8. Forgive my curiosity but where have you been?

9. Your offer was received and was carefully considered by the board.

10. You have not written us for many weeks nor have you bothered to pay your bills.

11. We tried but we failed.

12. They tried and they succeeded.

13. She's staying but I'm leaving.

14. I have money invested in state county and municipal bonds so much of my interest income is tax free.

15. Let us eat drink and be merry for tomorrow we shall die.

16. Cheryl ran off the mimeographed copies Arnold collated them and Anita stapled and distributed them.

17. Our principal plant is in Newark our regional distribution office is in Saddle Brook and our national offices are in New York.

18. We will leave immediately after lunch on Friday for the seminar begins at 8:30 a.m. on Saturday.

19. Our sale on computer accessories ends this Saturday so now is the time to save money while purchasing those items you really want.

20. Arizona's income tax is progressive but it is less graduated than in some other states and it does not produce nearly so much revenue as the state's sales taxes.

EXERCISE 16·3   INTRODUCTORY ELEMENTS

Commas are missing in some of the following sentences. Place commas wherever necessary.

1. We have continued to operate at capacity despite the recession.

2. Despite the recession we have continued to operate at capacity.

3. Because of his long experience Jorge Padron is a valued employee.

4. In spite of your advice I accepted the offer.

5. Because of your fine credit record we are writing to offer you preferred-customer status with our store.

6. We have accomplished much since we started.

7. As soon as the clock struck five the staff left the office.

8. Because some employees took extended coffee breaks management was irritated.

9. They will not bargain unless you do so in good faith.

10. Since we started much has happened.

11. We should have an answer in less than an hour.

12. In my opinion municipal bonds are an excellent investment.

13. With the right combination of luck and wisdom we should succeed.

14. If you are willing to make the initial investment you will be amply repaid.

15. With few exceptions everything is proceeding as planned.

16. Through Cathy's efforts we have more than matched our goal.

17. Of course not everyone will agree.

18. Well if you insist I will chair the committee.

19. No I don't mind.

20. Yes I'll accept the motion as amended.

21. Utterly exhausted the arbiter recessed the negotiations.

22. During the strike there will be shortages of some items.

23. Having been soundly defeated in the New Hampshire primary the candidate withdrew from the race for President.

24. Unless sales increase dramatically in the fourth quarter we will suffer our first annual loss since 1970.

25. Angry and frustrated Tanya resigned.

EXERCISE 16·4   ITEMS IN A SERIES, INDEPENDENT CLAUSES, INTRODUCTORY ELEMENTS

Insert commas in the following sentences wherever necessary.

1. After mastering BASIC Connie went on to learn PASCAL FORTH and FORTRAN.

2. The four basic kinds of computer keyboards are calculator-style typewriter-style membrane and detachable.

3. I want you to learn to write to compose to correct and to dictate letters effectively.

4. The two sides bargained far into the night but they were unable to reach an agreement.

5. Hoping to find a secure challenging and well-paying position in banking Meredith sought the assistance of the college's job placement service.

6. We have made a good start but we have a long way to go.

7. Distraught the father of the injured girl rushed into the emergency room and demanded to see the attending physician.

8. With a Sears credit card you can take advantage of special sales even though you may be short of cash.

9. I'm quitting and that's final.

10. Although Astrid studied for weeks in preparation for the final examination she failed it so she had to take Calculus I again the following year.

11. Purolator Federal Express United Parcel and Airborne—these are all reliable companies.

12. In selecting companies to which to send job application letters Karen consulted *Moody's Manual of Investment Standard & Poor's Register of Corporations Directors and Executives* and the *Dun & Bradstreet Middle Market Directory.*

13. Shahla Alyce Bob and Murray have indicated their willingness to serve but no one else has expressed any interest in the committee.

14. Before returning to New York Mr. Tanaka plans to visit our Los Angeles office on Monday and our San Francisco office on Tuesday.

15. In the meantime Ms. Pickl will be in charge so there should be no delay in production.

16. Incidentally should I make the necessary arrangements or will you do it?

17. To conceive an idea put it into operation and see it through to completion takes intelligence perseverance and dedication.

18. Having worked in Farmingdale's for several years I know the types of sales promotions they normally run but this promotion is a new one.

19. If I can be of any further assistance please feel free to call on me.

20. The manuscript for the new and expanded edition of the textbook must be revised and resubmitted to the developmental editor by April 1.

EXERCISE 16·5 COMPOSITION: ITEMS IN A SERIES, INDEPENDENT CLAUSES, INTRODUCTORY ELEMENTS

Compose complete sentences according to the directions in parentheses.

1. (Write a sentence with three adjectives in a series.) _____
_____

2. (Write a compound sentence that contains one comma.) _____
_____

3. (Write a compound sentence that contains two commas.) _____
_____

4. (Write a sentence that begins with a dependent clause.) _____
_____

5. (Write a sentence that begins with a short prepositional phrase.) _____
_____

6. (Write a sentence that begins with a long prepositional phrase.) _____
_____

7. (Write a sentence that begins with a verb phrase used as a modifier.) _____
_____

8. (Write a sentence with three adverbs in a series connected by *and*.) _____
_____

9. (Write a sentence that begins with a mild interjection.) _____
_____

10. (Write a sentence that contains *etc.*) _____
_____

EXERCISE 16·6   COMPOSITION: WRITING A REQUEST FOR INFORMATION

A common type of message in business is the letter requesting information.

Think of some major item (for example, an expensive camera, stereo equipment, a home computer) you would like to buy. Think of all the features of the item that are important to you. What information do you need to have before you make this important purchase? Write to the manufacturer asking for this information. Ask for the names of dealers in your area. Don't forget to include your return address. Write your request letter in the space below.

17

PUNCTUATION III
MORE ON THE COMMA

COMMAS WITH NONESSENTIAL EXPRESSIONS, COMMAS WITH QUOTATIONS, COMMAS USED TO AVOID CONFUSION

In the last chapter you learned three of the six basic rules for using commas. These first three rules covered using commas in a series, in compound sentences, and with introductory elements. This chapter will present the remaining rules.

 RULE 4: NONESSENTIAL EXPRESSIONS

Use commas to set off expressions that could be left out without destroying the sentence or changing its meaning. This rule covers a variety of situations. We will examine these situations separately. Don't forget, however, that they are all part of this one general rule.

Part A

Use commas to set off the name of a person directly addressed.

Ms. Rivera, we think that you are the best candidate.

We can omit *Ms. Rivera* and still have a complete sentence: *We think that you are the best candidate.* Therefore, we set off *Ms. Rivera* with a comma.

Notice that the name of the person addressed is set off with commas no matter where it appears in the sentence.

Ms. Rivera, we think that you are the best candidate.
We think, Ms. Rivera, that you are the best candidate.
We think that you, Ms. Rivera, are the best candidate.
We think that you are the best candidate, Ms. Rivera.

Note 1: Use commas when you address someone directly with a term other than his or her name.

You, my friend, are in for a surprise.
Let me tell you, fellow alumni, what the committee has done.

Note 2: This rule applies only to the name of a person directly addressed. If you are talking about someone, don't set off the name with commas.

Chris is a good manager.
Chris, you are a good manager.

Part B

Use commas to set off an expression that explains a preceding word.

1. Mr. Phillips, president of Acme Steel, is here.

President of Acme Steel merely explains who *Mr. Phillips* is. We could leave it out and still have a full sentence unchanged in meaning.
Leave out: *president of Acme Steel*
Remainder: *Mr. Phillips is here.*

2. The Pacific Ocean, the largest body of water on earth, must be protected by a vast naval system.

Leave out: *the largest body of water on earth*
Remainder: *The Pacific Ocean must be protected by a vast naval system.*

3. We will send Ms. Jurek, our representative, to visit your office.

Leave out: *our representative*
Remainder: *We will send Ms. Jurek to visit your office.*

4. The company, having been dormant for years, is finally reawakening.

Leave out: *having been dormant for years*
Remainder: *The company is finally reawakening.*

5. Our firm will show you how, merely by changing your circulars, you can double your business.

Leave out: *merely by changing your circulars*
Remainder: *Our firm will show you how you can double your business.*
Look at this sentence, however:

6. Butter that is rancid is sickening.

Leave out: *that is rancid*
Remainder: *Butter is sickening.*
We don't actually mean that butter is sickening. Leaving out *that is rancid* would change the meaning of the sentence. *That is rancid* is essential to the meaning of the sentence. Therefore, it *should not* be set off by commas.

7. Butter, which is in great demand, is selling well.

Leave out: *which is in great demand*
Remainder: *Butter is selling well.*
Do we mean to say that *butter is selling well?* Yes. Therefore, the use of commas is proper since the expression *which is in great demand* is not necessary to the meaning of the sentence.

8. Air that is polluted is bad for you.

Leave out: *that is polluted*
Remainder: *Air is bad for you.*
We don't mean that *air is bad for you.* Only *polluted air* is bad for you. Therefore, *that is polluted* should not be set off with commas because it is necessary to the meaning of the sentence.

9. The people in our office, who won the prize, will get a bonus.

    Leave out: *who won the prize*
    Remainder: *The people in our office will get a bonus.*
    The use of commas here is correct if all the people in the office won the prize. The remainder tells us that all the people in the office will get bonuses. Suppose that the people in our office won a bowling contest against another office. Then the use of commas in this sentence is correct.

    Suppose, however, there was a bowling contest in which some people in the office won and others did not. In such a case we would not use commas.

    The people in our office who won the prize will get a bonus.

    In this case, *who won the prize* is essential to the meaning of the sentence since it tells us exactly which people get bonuses.

    Examine these last few example sentences again:

    Butter that is rancid is sickening.
    Butter, which is in great demand, is selling well.
    Air that is polluted is bad for you.
    The people in our office who won the prize will get a bonus.

    Each of these sentences contains a clause that begins with a relative pronoun—*that, which,* or *who*. These clauses are known as **relative clauses**. It is around these clauses that we sometimes put commas and sometimes do not, depending upon our meaning.

    When a relative clause is essential to our meaning, it is called a **restrictive clause**. For example, in the sentence *Butter that is rancid is sickening*, the clause *that is rancid* is a restrictive clause because it restricts, or limits, the type of butter we are talking about to one type: *butter that is rancid.*

    When a relative clause is not essential to our meaning, it is called a **nonrestrictive clause**. For example, in the sentence *Butter, which is in great demand, is selling well*, the clause *which is in great demand* is a nonrestrictive clause. It does not restrict our meaning to any one type of butter—all butter is selling well.

    Here is a simple test for determining whether a clause is essential (restrictive) or nonessential (nonrestrictive). First read the sentence the way it stands. Then delete the clause and reread the sentence. Did the meaning of the sentence change? If it did, the clause is essential and should not be set off with commas. If the meaning is still the same, the clause is nonessential and should be set off with commas.

    Sentences 6 to 9 demonstrate that restrictive clauses are not set off with commas because they are essential to the meaning of a sentence; nonrestrictive clauses are set off with commas because they are not essential to the meaning of a sentence. Even if you forget the technical names for these clauses, the important point is that you remember how to test to see if a clause or phrase is essential to a sentence.

    Note: In choosing between *which* or *that* at the beginning of a relative clause, use *that* if the clause is restrictive; use *which* if the clause is nonrestrictive. Look at Sentences 6 to 8 to see how this has been applied.

    Let's examine a few more examples of using commas to set off explanatory matter.

10. My son, Alan, is attending college.

    The commas around *Alan* lead to the inference that Alan is an only son.
    Leave out: *Alan*
    Remainder: *My son is attending college.* (This is correct if he is an only son.)
    If Alan has any brothers, however, the commas should be left out because we are restricting the meaning to this one son. His brothers may be in high school or grade school.

My son Alan is attending college.

Technically, in this sentence Alan is known as an **appositive**, which is a noun placed next to another noun to identify or explain it. In this sentence *Alan* identifies or explains the noun *son*. In the first sentence *Alan* is a *nonrestrictive appositive*; in the *second*, a *restrictive appositive*. See the discussion of names in apposition in Chapter 3.

11. Jackson Polk, of Harvard, will address the meeting.

If there is also a Jackson Polk at Yale, you would leave the commas out to restrict your meaning to the Polk at Harvard. Similarly, notice why commas are left out from the following sentences:

My friend George has written of you often.
The philosopher Locke expressed the rights of man.
The year 1933 ushered in the New Deal.
The word *togetherness* is overused nowadays.
The candidate expressing honest ideals despite widespread public disapproval of them will often win out.

Study each of the following sentences to see why various elements have been considered explanatory and have, therefore, been set off with commas.

Ergonomics, the study of how people relate to their environment, is a new science.
The new management trainees, especially Mr. Dawson and Ms. Lawrence, are highly motivated.
Our organization, like any young business, is eager to explore new markets.
These figures, all of which have been carefully checked, point to a disastrous conclusion.
We discussed a number of possibilities, none of which proved workable.
The candidate, realizing that the election was lost, conceded defeat.

This last sentence could be written: *Realizing that the election was lost, the candidate conceded defeat.*

In either sentence, *realizing that the election was lost* is a **participial phrase** modifying the subject *candidate*. You learned about participles and participial phrases in Chapter 9. Pick out the participial phrase in these sentences:

Fighting for his life, he lashed out viciously.
The architect, seeing the finished building, was elated.
We ordered rather late, counting on immediate service.

Each of the participial phrases in these sentences could be left out without changing the basic meaning of each sentence. Accordingly, they are set off with commas because they are merely explanatory phrases.

Look at this sentence, however:

Prices rising at a rapid pace are a sure sign of inflation.

Here we have the participial phrase *rising at a rapid pace*. Can it be left out from our sentence? No. This phrase is essential to the meaning of the sentence. It is acting like a restrictive clause and, therefore, should not be set off with commas. In fact, it really is a restrictive clause in disguise. What this sentence really says is this: Prices *that are rising at a rapid pace* are a sure sign of inflation.

Note: Remember, when you start a sentence with a participial phrase, be sure to follow it immediately with the subject to which it refers. Otherwise you will have a dangling participle.

Right: Checking our inventory, we noted a shortage.
Wrong: Checking our inventory, a shortage was noted.

If this isn't clear, go back and reread the discussion of dangling participles in Chapter 9.

 # PROGRAMMED REINFORCEMENT

S1 In general, commas (are used, are not used) to set off expressions that can be removed from the sentence without changing its meaning.

R1 are used

S2 Commas should be used to set off words of direct address. Punctuate these sentences:
a. **Tell me Amir are you staying late?**
b. **I beg you my friends to stop arguing.**

R2 a. **Tell me, Amir, . . .**
b. **I beg you, my friends, to stop arguing.**

S3 Commas are used to set off an expression that explains a preceding word. Circle the expression that should be set off by commas: **Betty the new employee is an old friend of mine.**

R3 **Betty, the new employee, is an old friend of mine.**

S4 A group of words that is not essential to the meaning of the sentence should be set off by commas. Are commas used correctly in these sentences?
a. **My typewriter, which is not new, works beautifully.**
b. **Gasoline, that is mixed with water, is useless.**

R4 a. Yes
b. No

S5 **Gasoline that is mixed with water is useless.** The word **that** is a relative pronoun. The clause **that is mixed with water** is called a _____ clause. If we leave out the relative clause from this sentence, what remains? _____ _____. This (has, has not) changed the meaning of our sentence.

R5 relative; **Gasoline is useless;** has

S6 Because leaving out **that is mixed with water** from the sentence in S5 changes its meaning, we know that this clause **restricts** our meaning to only one type of gasoline. It is therefore called a _____ clause.

R6 restrictive

S7 A restrictive clause is a relative clause that (is, is not) essential to the meaning of a sentence.

R7 is

S8 Because a restrictive clause is essential to the meaning of a sentence, we (can, cannot) treat it as being merely explanatory. Accordingly, we (do, do not) set it off with commas.

R8 cannot; do not

S9   **My typewriter, which is brand new, does not work very well.** The clause **which is brand new** is a _____ clause that (is, is not) essential to the meaning of our sentence.

R9   relative; is not

S10   If we leave out **which is brand new** from the sentence in S9, the remainder is: _____ _____ This (has, has not) changed the meaning of our sentence.

R10   **My typewriter does not work very well.;** has not

S11   Since omitting **which is brand new** does not change our meaning, it is a _____ clause. It is merely explanatory and, hence, (should, should not) be set off with commas.

R11   nonrestrictive; should

S12   There are two types of relative clauses—restrictive and nonrestrictive. A _____ clause is merely explanatory and should be set off with commas; a _____ clause is essential to the meaning of a sentence and should not be set off with commas.

R12   nonrestrictive; restrictive

S13   **Rising from his chair, he greeted the visitors. Rising** is the present participle of the verb **to rise.** The phrase **rising from his chair** is a _____ phrase.

R13   participial

S14   When a participial phrase (is, is not) essential to the meaning of a sentence, it should be set off with commas.

R14   is not

S15   Insert commas where necessary in these sentences:
   a. **Having made his position clear Mr. Mooney sat down.**
   b. **The person who is considerate of others will never lack friends.**
   c. **The order being processed is the one I want.**
   d. **Our representative having read her report left at once.**

R15   a. . . . **clear, Mr. Mooney** . . .
   b. no commas
   c. no commas
   d. **Our representative, having read her report, left at once.**

Turn to Exercises 17.1 to 17.3.

Part C

Use commas to set off a word, phrase, or clause that interrupts the natural flow of a sentence. By *interrupt* we mean that it forces you to pause. Here is a list of commonly used words, phrases, and clauses that should be set off with commas when they interrupt the natural flow of a sentence.

accordingly	however	notwithstanding
again	indeed	otherwise
also	meantime	personally
besides	moreover	respectively
consequently	namely	still
finally	naturally	then
furthermore	next	therefore
hence	nevertheless	too
as a rule	if any	of course
as you know	in fact	on the contrary
at any rate	in brief	on the other hand
by the way	in the first place	that is
I believe	in other words	to be sure
for example		

Look at these examples:

We are certain, then, that you will comply with our request.
The test results will, I believe, confirm my position.
Familiarity, it has been said, breeds contempt.
Mr. Morgan, by the way, used to work in our Pittsburgh office.
I am convinced, however, that she is innocent of the charges.

Note 1: The expressions listed above are not always set off with commas. When such an expression does not interrupt the natural flow of the sentence, you do not set it off with commas. For example:

However expensive the remodeling, we will go through with it.
If he is otherwise occupied, we will return later.
We therefore feel that you must act with caution.
But: We feel, therefore, that you must act with caution. (Here the placement of *therefore* makes you pause.)

Part D

Use a comma to set off a question that is added to a statement.

You sent the letter, did you not?

Leave out: *did you not?*
Remainder: *You sent the letter.*

Lovely day, isn't it?

Leave out: *isn't it?*
Remainder: *Lovely day.* (It is a lovely day.)

You will do as we ask, won't you?

Leave out: *won't you?*
Remainder: *You will do as we ask.*

Part E

Use a comma to set off a contrasting expression within a sentence—an expression that usually starts with *not, seldom,* or *never.*

Mr. D'Angelo has gone to Chicago, not to St. Louis.

Leave out: *not to St. Louis.*
Remainder: *Mr. D'Angelo has gone to Chicago.*

Our board meets often in private, seldom in public.

Leave out: *seldom in public.*
Remainder: *Our board meets often in private.*

We have always enjoyed high attendance, never low, during Easter.

Leave out: *never low.*
Remainder: *We have always enjoyed high attendance during Easter.*

Part F

The abbreviation *Jr., Sr.,* or *Esq.* (Esquire) at the end of a personal name is considered explanatory. So too are *Inc.* and *Ltd.* at the end of a company name. Always place a comma before each of these abbreviations. Always place a comma after each of these abbreviations unless it is possessive or it ends the sentence, in which case one period is all you need.

George Henry Smathers, Jr., is our newly elected president.
Enclosed is a letter from Robert G. Cyrus, Esq., our attorney.
Johnson and Johnson, Inc., recently published its latest quarterly earnings.
Johnson and Johnson, Inc.'s earnings are very impressive.

If you use the title *Esq.* after an attorney's name, do not write *Mr.* before the name. *Robert G. Cyrus, Esq.,* or *Mr. Robert G. Cyrus* is correct. Never: *Mr. Robert G. Cyrus, Esq.*
College degrees or honorary awards listed after a person's name are similarly set off with commas.

Elizabeth C. Ramsey, LL.D., Ph.D., has joined our faculty.
Kent Smith, D.F.C., is your Flight Commander.

Note: Roman numerals following a person's name—Pope John Paul II or Queen Elizabeth II—are not set off by commas.

Queen Elizabeth I of England came to the throne in 1558.
King Henry VIII had six wives.
Robert W. Jackson III will head this new operation.

Part G

The year written after a month and a date should be set off with commas because it is an explanation of which month and day.
Frequently, the careless writer leaves out the second comma that should follow the year in the middle of a sentence.

The Declaration of July 4, 1776, is still our guiding beacon.

If the name of the day as well as the date is used, use commas to set off the explanatory material.

The meeting on Tuesday, August 18, is scheduled for noon.
The meeting on August 18, Tuesday, is scheduled for noon.

If no day of the month is given, usage is divided on whether the year should be set off with commas. Although a comma frequently is used, it is not needed and hence is better left out.

Right: In October, 1975, sales increased nearly 30 percent.
Preferred: In October 1975 sales increased nearly 30 percent.

In military date style, preferred by some organizations, no commas are used.

Sales for the week ending 15 October 1975 were up 30 percent.

Part H

The name of a state or country after a city should be set off with commas because it identifies the particular city.

When in Rome do as the Romans do—and this means Rome, Italy, and Rome, Georgia, too.

When a street address is written out in a sentence, use commas to separate the various elements. Note that a comma is placed *after* the zip code number but not before it.

Mrs. Porter has lived at 2234 Peachtree Street, Atlanta, Georgia 30013, for seven years.

 # PROGRAMMED REINFORCEMENT

S16 Use commas to set off words, phrases, or clauses that interrupt the natural flow of a sentence. Punctuate these sentences correctly:
  a. **He told me that his new firm however did not check references.**
  b. **They do on the other hand conduct extensive interviews.**
  c. **I know of one interview for instance that lasted over three hours.**

R16 a. . . . **firm, however, did not** . . .
  b. . . . **do, on the other hand, conduct** . . .
  c. . . . **interview, for instance, that lasted** . . .

S17 **Not very good, is it?** In this sentence a comma is used to set off a _____ that is added to a statement.

R17 question

S18 **I want a winning sales campaign, not another losing one.** In this sentence a comma is used to set off a _____ _____ expression added to a statement.

R18 contrasting

S19 Punctuate the following correctly:
a. **Ron is very persuasive isn't he?**
b. **You will be able to complete this project on schedule won't you?**
c. **I want results not promises.**
d. **She is seldom late never absent.**

R19 a. . . . **persuasive, isn't he?**
b. . . . **schedule, won't you?**
c. . . . **results, not promises.**
d. . . . **late, never absent.**

S20 The abbreviations *Jr., Sr.,* and *Esq.* at the end of a personal name (are, are not) considered explanatory and (are, are not) set off by commas.

R20 are; are

S21 College degrees and honorary awards following a person's name (are, are not) set off by commas. The year written after a month and date (should, should not) be set off by commas.

R21 are; should

S22 Punctuate the following correctly: **On May 24 1982 Lawrence O'Brien Jr. received his B.S. degree from Montclair State College. His father Lawrence O'Brien Sr. and his only uncle Terence O'Brien Esq. attended the ceremony.**

R22 **On May 24, 1982, Lawrence O'Brien, Jr., received his B.S. degree from Montclair State College. His father, Lawrence O'Brien, Sr., and his only uncle, Terence O'Brien, Esq., attended the ceremony.**

Turn to Exercise 17.4.

 RULE 5: QUOTATIONS

Use a comma to set off a short quotation from the rest of the sentence.

He said, "I will not budge an inch."
The Golden Rule says, "Do unto others as you would have others do unto you."
"Send the bills at once," he threatened, "or there will be trouble around here."

Note 1: When the quotation is not direct and not in quotation marks, no comma is necessary.

She said that she would not budge.
The Golden Rule says that we should do unto others as we would have them do unto us.

Note 2: When the quotation is not a complete thought in itself but is built into the structure of the sentence, or when the quoted material is used as the subject, or as the subject complement of the sentence, or as a restrictive appositive, then leave out the comma even though you use quotation marks.

He said he was "very tired." (predicate adjective)
The slogan "Slavery is freedom" aroused considerable controversy. (restrictive appositive)
"Do unto others as you would have others do unto you" is the Golden Rule. (subject)
The Golden Rule is "Do unto others·as you would have others do unto you." (subject complement)

Note 3: When a comma ends a direct quotation, always place the final comma inside the final quotation marks.

Right: "Send your payment or suffer the consequences," he threatened.
Wrong: "Send your payment or suffer the consequences", he threatened.

If the quoted material ends with a question mark or exclamation point, use this mark inside the quotation marks and omit the comma.

"Who will help me?" he asked.
"Wow!" she exclaimed.

If the quoted material ends with a period, substitute a comma for the period:

"We are pleased to submit our payment," the letter stated.
But: The letter stated, "We are pleased to submit our payment."

RULE 6: AVOIDING CONFUSION

Use commas in special instances to avoid confusion within a sentence.

a. Use a comma to separate words that otherwise might be misread.

Note how the comma helps the reader in the following sentences:

Ever since, we have been increasing sales.
On second thought, of all our employees she is the most ambitious.
Only three days before, he came to New York.

b. Use a comma to separate a word that is repeated twice in succession or any two sets of figures in succession.

It has been a long, long time.
Whatever happened, happened fast.
I bowled 123, 158, and 185 on successive evenings.
But note: I need two 20-cent stamps.

c. Use a comma to indicate that a word or phrase has been left out.

This election we polled 14,372 votes; last election, 12,991. (The words *we polled* are left out of the second clause.)
America gained twelve gold medals; Sweden, six; Britain, four; France, two. (The verb *gained* is left out.)

d. Use commas to separate large numbers into units of three digits.

The auditorium contains 1,420 seats.
The official attendance at yesterday's game was 57,742.
The corporation's losses for the year were staggering: $2,124,377,000.

Exceptions: The following kinds of numbers are written without commas.

calendar years	1984
telephone numbers	(201) 893–4000
street addresses	24873 Pomona Street
zip codes	60120
decimal numbers	3.14159
page numbers	p. 1243
serial numbers	425–34892–06106
invoice numbers	No. 4398063
contract numbers	No. 736418

e.   When you invert the normal order of a person's name and put the last name first, separate the names with a comma.

John Paul Jones becomes *Jones, John Paul*

f.   Use a comma after the salutation in personal letters.

Dear Jim,   Dear Mom and Dad,

Use a comma after the complimentary close of personal, informal, and formal letters except when using the open punctuation letter style.

Sincerely,   Respectfully,   Cordially yours,
Very truly yours,   Sincerely yours,

REVIEW OF COMMON COMMA ERRORS TO AVOID

1.   Do not separate a subject from its predicate–verb by a comma if the predicate comes immediately after the subject.

   Right: An inefficient, unreliable worker should be discharged.
   Wrong: An inefficient, unreliable worker, should be discharged.

2.   Do not separate a predicate from its object by a comma if the object comes directly after the predicate.

   Right: Dale Carnegie wrote *How to Win Friends and Influence People.*
   Wrong: Dale Carnegie wrote, *How to Win Friends and Influence People.*

3.   Do not place the comma after the coordinate conjunction when it joins clauses in a sentence. Always place the comma before the conjunction.

   Right: She applied for the position, but she did not get it.
   Wrong: She applied for the position but, she did not get it.

4.   Do not use a comma to separate the two parts of a compound subject, a compound predicate, or a compound object when they are connected by *and, or,* or *but.*

   Right: The men and the women proved equally capable. (Compound subject)
   Wrong: The men, and the women proved equally capable.

Right: I typed or filed from nine to five. (Compound predicate)
Wrong: I typed, or filed from nine to five.

Right: They shipped autos and tractors from the warehouse. (Compound object)
Wrong: They shipped autos, and tractors from the warehouse.

5. Do not use a comma to set off a reflexive pronoun (a pronoun ending in *self*) used for emphasis.

    Right: Ms. Diaz herself will give the report.
    Wrong: Ms. Diaz, herself, will give the report.

6. Do not use a comma before *than* in a comparison.

    Right: It is wiser to fail than not to try at all.
    Wrong: It is wiser to fail, than not to try at all.

7. Do not use a comma after a prepositional phrase at the beginning of a sentence unless the phrase is very long.

    Right: On June 15 my vacation will start.
    Wrong: On June 15, my vacation will start.

 # PROGRAMMED REINFORCEMENT

S23 A comma is used to set off a short direct quotation from the rest of the sentence. Punctuate this sentence, adding a capital letter where necessary: **She said leave the bill of lading here.**

R23 **She said, "Leave the bill of lading here."**

S24 **She said to leave the bill of lading here.** This sentence does not contain quotation marks because it is an _____ _____ quotation.

R24 indirect

S25 No comma is used before a quotation that is not a complete thought but is a necessary part of the sentence. Is this sentence punctuated correctly? **Frank said he was "bushed, battered, and fatigued."**

R25 Yes

S26 When a comma ends a direct quotation, it is placed (inside, outside) the quotation marks. Punctuate the following sentence correctly: **"I intend to ask for a raise" Joe declared.**

R26 inside; **"I intend to ask for a raise," Joe declared.**

S27 A comma is used to substitute for which of the following when it ends the quoted material?
a. period
b. question mark
c. exclamation point

R27 a. period

S28 Punctuate the following quotations correctly.
a. **"Hooray" she exclaimed**
b. **"May I go too" he asked**
c. **"Here is the report you requested" she said**

R28 a. **"Hooray!" she exclaimed.**
b. **"May I go too?" he asked.**
c. **"Here is the report you requested," she said.**

S29 Use commas where necessary to avoid confusion within a sentence. Place a comma where necessary in the following sentences:
a. **Just the week before I had left for the Coast.**
b. **Ever since our orders have been increasing.**

R29 a. **. . . before, I . . .**
b. **. . . since, our . . .**

S30 Use a comma to separate words repeated in succession. Place commas where necessary in the following sentences:
a. **We have been through hard hard times together.**
b. **This will be a cold cold winter.**

R30 a. **. . . hard, hard . . .**
b. **. . . cold, cold . . .**

S31 Use a comma to indicate that a word or phrase has been left out. What omitted words are indicated by the commas in these sentences:
a. **This week we made four sales; last week, three.**
Answer: _____
b. **The Billing Department has twenty computer terminals; the Shipping Department, twelve.**
Answer: _____

R31 a. **we made**
b. **has**

S32 Insert commas where needed in these sentences:
a. **Last year we closed in August; this year in July.**
b. **He excels in bookkeeping; she in stenography.**

R32 a. **. . . year, in . . .**
b. **. . . she, in . . .**

S33 Rewrite each of the following complimentary closes, showing proper capitalization and punctuation:
a. **yours truly**
b. **sincerely yours**
c. **very truly yours**

R33 a. **Yours truly,**
b. **Sincerely yours,**
c. **Very truly yours,**

S34 Insert commas where necessary:
a. **Since we saw you last Mr. Jackson we have built a new plant that is the largest in the East.**
b. **Naturally if you insist we will have to agree won't we?**

R34 a. **Since we saw you last, Mr. Jackson, we have built a new plant that is the largest in the East.**
b. **Naturally, if you insist, we will have to agree, won't we?**

Turn to Exercises 17.5 to 17.9.

EXERCISE 17·1   SETTING OFF NAME OF PERSON ADDRESSED

Fill in all missing commas in the following sentences.

1. Thank you Ms. Shin for your prompt reply to our questionnaire.

2. We have directed Mr. James Koenig of our credit department to discuss terms of payment with you.

3. They are being shown this week Mrs. Watson.

4. Mr. Adams we have learned that you will soon enjoy delivery of your new car.

5. I have looked further Mr. Garnier into the Gray lumber situation.

6. Lisa Martin says that economic conditions will remain favorable.

7. Madam does the approach of warm weather suggest sending your furs to storage?

8. Is it the fault of this store that your account remains inactive Mrs. Pulaski?

9. Mr. Bianco's inspection of our floor equipment was unexpected.

10. January sales now being held throughout the store offer you exceptional values Miss Wu.

EXERCISE 17·2 SETTING OFF EXPLANATORY EXPRESSIONS

Insert commas wherever proper in the following sentences.

1. Our representative from New Orleans Ms. A. J. Johnson is in town.

2. Asia the largest of the continents is becoming a major focus of international trade.

3. Our new location the corner of Sixth Avenue and 42nd Street offers free parking.

4. Our attorney Mr. G. A. Rivera will call at your office tomorrow.

5. It is my pleasure to introduce H. Colin Phillips our president and cofounder.

6. Would you enjoy living in a residential park a veritable winter wonderland of over 500 acres of high healthy beautifully wooded fertile land Ms. Solokov?

7. We advise you to see either Ms. R. J. Urwanda director of the bureau or Mr. P. T. Sullivan her assistant.

8. The speakers were Margaret Hilary Brittingham professor of applied economics and John Rogers Jr. professor of political science.

9. The Mississippi America's longest river flows into the Gulf of Mexico.

10. Realizing his position George resigned.

11. George realizing his position turned in his resignation.

12. Rushing to catch the bus he tripped and sprained his ankle.

13. Forgetting her prepared speech she stood before the audience dumbfounded.

14. While attending the convention last month I met an old friend.

15. After hearing the good news I decided to sell my shares in the company.

EXERCISE 17·3A   NONRESTRICTIVE CLAUSES

Each of the following sentences involves a nonrestrictive clause—that is, a relative clause that should be set off with commas. Place commas where necessary.

1. This morning we received a report from Mr. Kozol who is our representative in New York.

2. Wellington chalk which is hard and long-lasting is the most economical for school use.

3. Mr. Anthony Como who is president of the National Savings Association sent a copy of his latest address.

4. Our creditors all of whom have been most patient will be pleased to hear of our latest plans to repay our debts.

5. The manufacture of this equipment which is the finest ever made is a painstakingly exact process.

6. Ergonomics which is the study of the relationship of employees to their physical environment is important in the design of today's business office.

7. Our office furniture all of which we bought last year is ergonomically designed for maximum comfort.

8. The new executive assistant who was trained at business school is the best we've ever had.

9. The luggage which was engraved with her initials was presented to Ms. Phillips.

10. The park which is noted for its old trees was established in 1889.

EXERCISE 17·3B   RESTRICTIVE CLAUSES

Each of the following sentences has an explanatory expression that should NOT be set off with commas because to do so would change the meaning of the sentence. Underline each such restrictive clause.

1. The proprietor who does a poor job does not last long in business.

2. The advertisement that catches the eye is the one that is most effective.

3. Medicine is a profession that satisfies a person's desire to serve others.

4. The information that I want is in the ledger in Room 27.

5. Anyone who works hard can succeed.

6. Only those who are geniuses gain acclaim as musicians.

7. A rumor that we heard yesterday is disturbing.

8. The ledger that is in Room 27 contains the information I want.

9. We observed a downward trend that is most unsatisfactory.

10. Lawyers who represent themselves have fools for clients.

EXERCISE 17·3C   COMMAS AND EXPLANATORY EXPRESSIONS

Each of the following sentences includes an explanatory expression. Place commas around those expressions that should be set off with commas; underline those expressions that should not.

1. Any baked goods that are not sold today should be removed from the shelves.

2. Your fall order which we received last week has been filled.

3. The person who works the hardest isn't always the most successful.

4. John Pollack who was tried for larceny was acquitted.

5. Deliver only those posters that you consider best as soon as possible.

6. The letter that was sent to her came back unopened.

7. This work which I feel sure you will enjoy is not very difficult.

8. Furniture that is ergonomically designed is more comfortable than conventional furniture.

9. Our book is printed in large type that is easy to read.

10. That woman who spoke to you at such great length yesterday is back.

11. This business which you have merely sampled these past months can provide ample excitement for a lifetime.

12. The Mr. Heinz who manages the bank called while you were out.

13. Mr. Oglethorpe is a man who knows every facet of this business.

14. The order which we have been awaiting for weeks was delayed again.

15. She is the applicant whom I would hire.

16. My teacher Mary Ann Lewis was an inspiring influence.

17. I myself have much to learn.

18. The poet Milton composed his greatest work after he became blind.

19. Our business like any other new business will benefit from exposure.

20. These data all of which are interesting do not change our prediction about the direction the market will take.

21. Knowing that sales are the lifeblood of an organization we invest considerable time and money in training our sales staff.

22. The new executives who lead our top organizations have youth and vitality.

23. They shipped the merchandise in June assuming you wanted it for the July sale.

24. A sales letter that creates a strong desire to buy brings maximum results.

25. His brother Albert is more imaginative than his brothers William and Thomas.

EXERCISE 17·4A   COMMAS AND INTERRUPTING ELEMENTS

This exercise gives you practice in using commas to separate words such as *therefore* from the body of the sentence. Place commas wherever they are needed in the following sentences.

1. It is however unnecessary for you to reply at once.

2. Feel free of course to take as much time as you need.

3. Naturally we were shocked to hear of the loss.

4. It is nevertheless imperative that your representative contact us at once.

5. We feel on the other hand that your client is entitled to partial reimbursement.

6. As we understand the situation the failure was entirely the fault of your agent.

7. To be very frank we were satisfied with neither the lamps the shades nor the fixtures.

8. It is in our opinion impossible to predict the outcome at this moment.

9. The costs of complete retooling however are extremely high.

10. No one naturally can be blamed for such an innocent mistake.

11. As a rule commas should set off nonessential information.

12. I believe for example that a brusque answer does much harm and little good.

13. We feel therefore that an immediate decision is essential.

14. No they did not report on time.

15. Well none of us is perfect.

EXERCISE 17·4B   COMMAS AND QUESTIONS ADDED TO STATEMENTS

This exercise gives you practice in using commas to set off questions that are added to statements and to set off opposing ideas beginning with not. Place commas wherever necessary in the following sentences.

1. You received our catalog didn't you?
2. We will send you east not west.
3. This isn't easy is it?
4. We always judge a person by accomplishments not by promises.
5. We offered you this line last year didn't we?
6. You can do the job can't you?
7. Look for facts not opinions.
8. In managing employees one should be courteous and considerate not rude and authoritarian.
9. This is easy isn't it?
10. We hold most meetings in the morning few in the afternoon.

EXERCISE 17·4C   MISCELLANEOUS USES

This exercise concerns commas used in abbreviations and commas used with dates and geographical names. Place commas and periods in the following sentences wherever necessary.

1. Amy D. James is our new president.
2. We have received a letter from Morris C. Cohen Esq our attorney.
3. Frances Kearney LL.D. Ph.D. will support our fund drive.
4. Jack Kent Inc well-known publishers will give a cocktail party at the St. Regis.
5. Eleanor C. Squires Ltd our Canadian firm is quite active.
6. September 3 1912 was the date of the founding of the company.
7. The affair last Wednesday August 17 was a huge success.
8. The issue for July 1964 is a particularly interesting one.
9. John Gillespie III has lived at 373 Ocean Avenue San Francisco California for five years.
10. Roberto L. Ramirez Jr. was born on Tuesday August 29 1978 in Detroit Michigan.

EXERCISE 17·5   DIRECT QUOTATIONS

Place commas in the following sentences wherever necessary.

1. She said "This is ridiculous."
2. "I will not resign" the chairperson said "nor will I alter my position."
3. "Why" I asked "doesn't he admit he was in error?"
4. "This is the worst job I have ever seen" she fumed.
5. I told the buyer "Either you accept our offer, or we will take our business elsewhere."
6. "Send the check to my office" was written on the top of the memo.
7. "Who punched the clock at 5 P.M.?" she asked.
8. "Eureka!" he shouted at the top of his lungs "I have the solution."
9. Ms. Roberts said that she would return in about an hour.
10. The vice president stated "I'll be in about noon."

EXERCISE 17·6   MISCELLANEOUS USES

Place commas wherever necessary in the following sentences.

1. Last year our stockholders averaged $6000 each in profits.
2. On July 15 1984 the workers in our plants numbered 6475.
3. The contract dated 4 August 1976 is still valid.
4. They have lived at 1220 Keystone Avenue Springfield Illinois for eight years.
5. Despite poor January sales our overall net profit for the past year was over $250000.
6. We addressed the letter to Mrs. Lou Swanson 5202 South Spruce Lane Madison Wisconsin.
7. Since our last visit in December 1984 we have reconsidered your $800000 expansion plan.
8. We have reviewed your books for the month of July 1985 and we find a $3257.50 discrepancy with our figures.
9. On December 1 1986 we expect you to deliver 50000 tons of No. 10 steel to our warehouse at 1614 Bruce Avenue Pittsburgh Pennsylvania.
10. Please change my address in your listings from Ms. Polly Jones 616 Almond Street New Orleans Louisiana to Ms. Polly Mayer 327 Cypress Avenue Miami Beach Florida.

11. Ever since we have avoided telephoning.

12. Only three hours before we saw him alive.

13. It has been a long long process of waiting.

14. Whoever spoke spoke in vain.

15. Last year's gross sales totaled $48176395500.

16. Last year the department received two promotions; the year before none.

17. Our best years for gross sales were 1978 1980 1981 and 1985.

18. We have located a copy of invoice No. 39486 but we are unable to find a copy of the other one.

19. Alexander Pope wrote "Whatever is is right."

20. For a while longer work periods between breaks will be necessary.

EXERCISE 17·7   COMPOSITION: EXPLANATORY EXPRESSIONS, INTERRUPTING ELEMENTS, OTHER USES OF THE COMMA

Compose complete sentences according to the directions in parentheses.

1. (Write a sentence that contains the name of a person directly addressed.) _____

2. (Write a sentence that contains a restrictive clause.) _____

3. (Write a sentence that contains a nonrestrictive clause.) _____

4. (Write a sentence that contains a participial phrase modifying the subject.) _____

5. (Write a sentence that contains *however* as an interrupter.) _____

6. (Write a sentence that contains *of course* as an interrupter.) _____

7. (Write a sentence that contains a question added to a statement.) _____

8. (Write a statement that contains a contrasting expression beginning with *not, seldom* or *never*.) _____

9. (Write a sentence that contains a short quotation.) _____

10. (Write a sentence that contains a verb repeated twice in succession.) _____

EXERCISE 17·8   PERIOD, QUESTION MARK, COMMA

Insert commas, periods, or question marks wherever necessary in the following letter.

Dear Ms. Hwang:

Your letter and the booklet "Computerized Records Systems" reach us at a time when our records management is a matter of great concern This booklet therefore has received our careful attention

Since our office force was reduced last year the increased volume of business during the past year has intensified the urgency of our records-management problem Though we have been considering the use of fully computerized systems for a long time we are not yet convinced that such a large outlay of money would be cost efficient Nevertheless something must be done to relieve the pressure of our work load which continues to grow

Will you have your representative Mr. Omar call on Monday May 10 at ten o'clock to evaluate our system and to present the advantages of your program We are particularly interested in the relative merits of aperture cards microfiche and ultramicrofiche compared to the various forms of microfilms

We would like Mr. Omar to examine our ordering billing and shipping procedures as well as our overall system of information storage and retrieval Above all we want him to meet the supervisors and staff of our records department and after he forms an impression of them we would like him to submit a written report of his recommendations with respect to personnel This would seem to be a reasonable approach wouldn't it

Are you aware of the many many new products that are being offered by our company to customers throughout North Central and South America Since January 1984 we have been involved in a $30000000 expansion of our product line Because this expansion succeeded despite great odds today we stand first in sales volume in this field and we intend to maintain this position

Our problem is to manage our records more efficiently and that I believe is exactly what your firm can help us achieve We look forward therefore to Mr. Omar's visit

Sincerely

EXERCISE 17·9 COMPOSITION: WRITING AN ORDER LETTER

Most of the time when you order a product from a magazine, there is an order form for you to use. For those times when there is no preprinted form, you will need to write an order letter.

Pick a catalogue or magazine that contains products of interest to you. Write a letter in which you order two or three of the items you particularly want. Remember to specify quantity, size, style, color, product number, or whatever other specific information is appropriate. Be sure to indicate the total cost of your order, how you intend to pay for it, and where and when you want it delivered. Write your letter in the space below.

_____

_____

_____

_____

_____

_____

_____

_____

_____

_____

_____

_____

_____

_____

_____

_____

_____

_____

_____

_____

PUNCTUATION IV
THE SEMICOLON AND COLON

THE SEMICOLON, THE COLON

 ## THE SEMICOLON (;)

The purpose of a **semicolon** in a sentence is to mark a major pause or break. It indicates a greater pause than a comma, although not quite so great a pause as a period. As you will see, the semicolon usually is used to separate independent clauses, although it may also separate phrases. Hence you must be able to recognize clauses and phrases to use the semicolon correctly. Because you can recognize clauses and phrases in a sentence, you should have no trouble with the four rules that govern the use of the semicolon.

 ### RULE 1

Use the semicolon to separate two closely related *complete thoughts* that are not separated by a coordinate conjunction (*and, but, for, or, nor*). In other words, semicolons can be used to connect two or more independent clauses to create a compound sentence.

Prices rose; wages fell. (The semicolon implies a relationship between the two events.)

Prices rose, but wages fell. (The conjunction *but* expresses the relationship.)

Prices rose. Wages fell. (The period does not necessarily imply any relationship.)

Never: Prices rose, wages fell. (This is a run-on sentence.)

Right: To err is human; to forgive, divine.
Right: Mail the enclosed card now; you will receive your gift by return mail.

You have now studied three ways to connect the two independent clauses in a compound sentence:

1. Use a coordinate conjunction (*and, but, or, nor, for, so, yet*) preceded by a comma.
2. If one of the clauses is very short (five or fewer words), you may leave out the comma and use a coordinate conjunction by itself.
3. You may leave the coordinate conjunction out and use a semicolon by itself.

There is one more way to connect the clauses in a compound sentence:

4. If each clause is very long, and if one or more of the clauses contains commas within itself, then you may use a coordinate conjunction preceded by a semicolon instead of a comma. The semicolon used in this manner helps the reader follow a complicated sentence without confusion. For example:

Naturally, having heard of the offer, he rushed to the employment office; but, despite his haste, he found that the job had already been filled.

Employing every means at her disposal, the U.S. Ambassador, Shirley Temple Black, attempted to befriend the inhabitants of that small, underdeveloped nation; and her efforts were ultimately rewarded by success, which was justly earned.

The American is noted for friendliness and innocence; the Englishman, for formality and reserve; and the Frenchman, for explosiveness and warmth.

Note: When typing a sentence, space only once following the semicolon before starting the next word.

RULE 2

Use the semicolon to separate two complete thoughts (independent clauses) that are connected by a conjunctive adverb or transitional phrase such as *accordingly, also, consequently, further, hence, however, indeed, in fact, moreover, nevertheless, then, therefore, thus, whereas.*

The deadline has passed; accordingly, we are canceling our order.

The odds were insurmountable; nevertheless, we fought on.

Please give us your exact measurements; then we can tailor-fit the suit to your dimensions.

The doors open at six; however, you will be admitted at five.

I know you will be satisfied; in fact, I guarantee it.

Remember, a comma always follows such transitional phrases and conjunctive adverbs of more than one syllable.

If you need to, review the discussion of conjunctive adverbs in Chapter 13.

RULE 3

Use the semicolon to separate a series of items when the items themselves contain commas. The semicolon is used in this way to prevent confusion by clearly indicating the main divisions between the items in the series.

Our new board of directors is composed of Rodney G. Jones, president; Augustus E. Smythe, vice president; and Ormand Cole, Jr., secretary-treasurer.

The totals are 3,728; 2,142,709; and 36,016.

Note: In each of the cases governed by these three rules, the semicolon separates items of equal grammatical rank. That is, clauses are separated from clauses, phrases from phrases, numbers from numbers. Don't use a semicolon to separate items of unequal grammatical rank, such as a clause and a phrase, or an independent clause and a dependent clause.

RULE 4

Use a semicolon before an expression or its abbreviation such as *for example (e.g.), namely (viz.), that is (i.e.), to wit,* when this expression introduces a list or explanation. Always use a comma immediately following each of the above expressions.

He had one credo; namely, do unto others as you would have them do unto you.

There are many fine potential locations for the convention; for example, New York, Chicago, Los Angeles, or Honolulu.

If the list or explanation occurs in the middle of the sentence rather than at the end, use dashes rather than semicolons.

Many fine potential locations—for example, New York, Chicago, Los Angeles, or Honolulu—are available for the convention.

The semicolon is an extremely useful mark of punctuation if it is not overused. The danger comes when it is used to string together a series of separate thoughts into long, complicated sentences. It is frequently better and clearer to break such sentences into shorter sentences by the use of the period or to subordinate one clause to another to express their relationship more accurately.

 # PROGRAMMED REINFORCEMENT

	S1 The mark of punctuation used to indicate a major pause or break is the _____.
R1 semicolon	**S2** The semicolon indicates a (greater, weaker) pause than a comma.
R2 greater	**S3** The semicolon indicates a (greater, weaker) pause than a period.
R3 weaker	**S4** A semicolon (can, cannot) be used to connect two or more independent clauses to create a compound sentence.
R4 can	**S5** There are four ways that the independent clause in a compound sentence may be connected: a. You may use a _____ conjunction like **and** or **but** preceded by a _____. b. If one of the clauses is very short, you may omit the _____ and use the _____ _____ by itself. c. You may omit the conjunction and use a _____ _____ by itself. d. If the clauses are long and contain commas, you may use a coordinate _____ preceded by a _____ instead of a comma.
R5 a. coordinate; comma b. comma; coordinate conjunction c. semicolon d. conjunction; semicolon	**S6** Punctuate using a semicolon: **The storm affected business many firms were forced to close.**
R6 . . . **business; many** . . .	**S7** Use a semicolon in the following sentence: **There is no question but that personal contacts are sometimes valuable in business but in the long run, I think, success depends far more on ability than on any other factor.**
R7 . . . **in business; but in the long run** . . .	

S8 **Our firm is only ten years old; nevertheless, we have established an excellent reputation.** A semicolon is used here because a _____ plus a conjunctive adverb like **nevertheless** (is, is not) strong enough to join the two clauses. If the word **nevertheless** were replaced by the coordinate conjunction **but,** a comma (would, would not) be strong enough.

R8 comma; is not; would

S9 Lists introduced by expressions such as **namely, that is, for example,** and their respective abbreviations _____, _____, _____, are generally preceded by semicolons.

R9 viz.; i.e.; e.g.

S10 Punctuate this sentence: **The sales representative omitted three cities namely Spokane, San Diego, and Oakland.**

R10 . . . **three cities; namely, Spokane** . . .

S11 Dashes, not semicolons, should set off a formal list that occurs in the middle of a sentence. Punctuate the following two sentences:
a. **Only three possibilities namely stupidity carelessness or misinformation can explain this outrageous mistake.**
b. **Only three possibilities can explain this outrageous mistake namely stupidity carelessness or misinformation.**

R11 a. . . . **possibilities— namely, stupidity, carelessness, or misinformation—can** . . .
b. . . . **mistake; namely, stupidity, carelessness, or misinformation.**

S12 Punctuate the following: **Here are the receipt numbers: 6,352 4,008 and 6,927.**

R12 . . . **numbers: 6,352; 4,008; and 6,927.**

Turn to Exercise 18.1.

 # THE COLON (:)

As you have seen, the purpose of the semicolon is to serve as a separator, separating elements within a sentence. The purpose of the **colon** is different: it directs the reader's attention to what follows.

 ## RULE 1

Use the colon to introduce a quotation of one long sentence or of two or more sentences regardless of length. Use a comma to introduce a quotation of one short sentence or part of a sentence.

Senator Hillis replied as follows: "I know the importance of this investigation, but I cannot become party to such a circus."
She said simply, "I accept."

A colon is also used to introduce a quotation of any length when the introduction comments directly on the quotation or when the quotation is attributed to something inanimate.

> The manager's reply was swift and decisive: "You're fired!"
> The report concluded: "The continued prosperity of our organization depends on implementing these proposals immediately."

 ## RULE 2

Use the colon to formally introduce a list or idea. Generally, a formal introduction includes a word or phrase such as *as follows, the following, these, this, thus.*

> Erect the desk as follows: Attach the legs to the side panels; then nail the side panels to the top.
> The following invoices are unpaid: No. 3721, No. 3723, and No. 3746.
> The real problems are these: the price in Britain, the shipping cost, and the tariff.

Note 1: As the examples above indicate, the word following the colon is capitalized when a complete sentence follows the colon. It is not capitalized when less than a complete sentence follows the colon.

Note 2: In some sentences, the formal introductory expression (*as follows, namely,* etc.) is left out but clearly understood. In such a sentence use a colon or a dash.

> We have three real problems: the price in Britain, the shipping cost, and the tariff.
> We missed three trains: the 5:15, the 6:07, and the 7:03.

Or:

> We missed three trains—the 5:15, the 6:07, and the 7:03.

Note 3: Do not use a colon when the list immediately follows the verb or a preposition.

> The reasons he succeeded are his great initiative, perseverance, and cleverness. (*But:* These are the reasons he succeeded: his great initiative, his perseverance, and his cleverness.)
> Send copies of the report to Ms. Rudy, Ms. Becker, and Mr. Brewton.

Note 4: Do not use a colon when another sentence comes between the introductory sentence and the list.

> Representatives from the following companies will be on campus this week. Students interested in interviews should contact the Job Placement Service.

IBM	Exxon	The Tandy Corporation
American Cyanimid	Standard Oil	Johnson and Johnson

 ## RULE 3

Use the colon in various sections of the business letter.

1. After the salutation except in open punctuation.

> Dear Ms. Ruiz:
> Gentlemen:

2. Following the words *attention* and *subject* in the attention and subject lines.

    Attention: Mr. Joseph Cardin
    Subject: Account No. 7318

3. Between the dictator's and typist's initials at the end of a letter. (If the person who signs the letter also dictates it, only the typist's initials are used.)

    KDS:jb

    Note 1: Colons also appear in interoffice memorandums in the sender, receiver, and subject lines, which are normally preprinted.

    TO: English Department Faculty

    FROM: Keith Slocum for the Elections Committee

    SUBJECT: Results of English Council Elections

 RULE 4

Use the colon to separate elements in various other situations.

1. Time

    Use the colon to separate hours from minutes when the time is expressed in figures.

    6:43 A.M.   5:06 P.M.

    Note 1: On a timetable the colon is often replaced with a period.

    6.43 A.M.   5.06 P.M.

2. Titles

    Use the colon to separate a title from a subtitle.

    (book) *Business English: A Worktext with Programmed Reinforcement*
    (speech) "American Marketing Strategy: Responding to International Pressures"

3. Biblical citations

    Use the colon to separate chapter from verse in a biblical reference.

    Genesis 1:26   John 1:14

4. Mathematical ratios

    Use the colon to separate parts of a mathematical ratio.

    $3:15 = 10:x$

5. Bibliographical citations

    Use the colon to separate the place of publication and the name of the publisher in footnotes and bibliographies.

Keith Slocum, *Business English*, 3rd ed. (Indianapolis: Bobbs-Merrill, 1985), p. 234.

Note: Space twice after the colon before starting the next word, but do not use any space when the colon appears as part of a number.

 # PROGRAMMED REINFORCEMENT

	S13 The semicolon and the colon (do, do not) serve the same basic purpose.
R13 do not	**S14** While the semicolon acts as a separator, the purpose of the colon is _____.
R14 to direct the reader's attention to what follows	**S15** To introduce a quotation of one long sentence or of two or more sentences regardless of length use a _____. To introduce a quotation of one short sentence or part of a sentence, use a _____.
R15 colon; comma	**S16** Punctuate the following sentences correctly. a. **Ms. Jacobs said "I accept your offer."** b. **Ms. Jacobs said "I accept your offer, but only with the understanding that I be allowed to withdraw at the end of the year, or at the completion of the project."**
R16 a. **Ms. Jacobs said, "I accept. . . ."** b. **Ms. Jacobs said: "I accept. . . ."**	**S17** The punctuation mark you use before a formal list introduced by the words *as follows* or *the following* is the _____.
R17 colon	**S18** If the formal introductory expression such as *namely* or *the following* is left out but clearly understood, a colon (may, may not) be used.
R18 may	**S19** If the list immediately follows the verb or a preposition in a sentence, a colon (should, should not) be used.
R19 should not	**S20** Punctuate the following sentences correctly. a. **I have one main objection to your proposal It won't work.** b. **My most difficult subjects are accounting and calculus.** c. **These are my two most difficult subjects accounting and calculus.** d. **Send invitations to Marc, Bill, Betty, and Ruth.**
R20 a. **proposal:** b. no additional punctuation needed c. **subjects:** d. no additional punctuation needed	

S21 Show which of the following items in a business letter should properly be followed by a colon.
a. the date
b. the salutation
c. the complimentary close

R21 b.

S22 Colons can also be used to separate various elements in a variety of situations. In which of the following is a colon properly used?
a. To separate hours from minutes in an expression of time
b. To separate pounds from ounces in weight
c. To separate the title from the subtitle in a book
d. To separate the city from the state in an address
e. To separate chapter from verse in a biblical reference

R22 a., c., e.

S23 Punctuate the following correctly: **Please ship these items to us before the 6 30 mail pickup three dozen spools two dozen balls of twine a gross of envelopes.**

R23 **Please ship these items to us before the 6:30 mail pickup: three dozen spools, two dozen balls of twine, a gross of envelopes.**

S24 When typing, leave _____ blank space(s) after a colon that introduces a formal list or a quotation; leave _____ blank space(s) after a colon that separates hours from minutes.

R24 two; no

Turn to Exercises 18.2 to 18.6.

EXERCISE 18·1   THE SEMICOLON

Place a semicolon in each of the following sentences wherever one is needed. Add other punctuation where necessary.

1. We have not received payment for your last two shipments consequently we have delayed filling your current order.

2. This is a coincidence we were just speaking of you.

3. There are two reasons for our decision namely your determination and your perseverance.

4. To be perfectly frank I am sorry to see them go but I know that try as you might you had no alternative but to fire them.

5. The market went up for some stocks others however declined in value.

6. All of us were concerned about the employment picture for the year as presented by the government but following your advice we felt it our duty to remain calm and subsequent events have proved the wisdom of that advice.

7. Our membership includes Diego Sanchez the eminent painter Jules Hirsh the famous caricaturist and Cynthia Price the well-known columnist.

8. She had one principle namely to do unto others before they did unto her.

9. The manager spoke to the staff about staying late however it was to no avail and the work was not completed in time.

10. During the meeting George said that he appreciated the committee's desire that he should assume the role of chairman that he would of course consider the offer but that he did not feel under the circumstances that he could accept the position.

11. The only branches that registered losses were Wilmington Delaware Cleveland Ohio and Newark New Jersey.

12. The new word processors were ordered three weeks ago they should arrive by the end of next week.

13. Your account is now several months past due therefore we are unable to grant you further credit.

14. My three sons were born on August 16 1977 April 10 1980 and December 9 1981.

15. The random access memory (RAM) temporarily stores programs and data in the computer the read-only memory (ROM) permanently stores programs data or languages.

EXERCISE 18·2 **THE COLON**

Place a colon in each of the following sentences wherever one is needed. Add other punctuation where necessary.

1. We have recorded your order as follows one slide projector six carousels one screen one metal table.

2. This was his reply "My only regret is that I have but one life to give for my country."

3. At precisely 456 P.M. our plane departs.

4. The following is stock on hand 3000 No. 10 envelopes, 2500 No. 13, and 1500 No. 17.

5. This is what she said "No amount of money could ever repay you for the fine unselfish job you did on behalf of your nation."

6. The letter began with this statement "Dear Sir I wish to thank you for your help."

7. A conference call was arranged among the author the developmental editor and the acquisitions editor.

8. The problems we must face are these avoiding nuclear war upholding liberty developing free societies.

9. We listed three stock prices $5.52 $5.59 $6.01.

10. The following furniture was ordered three tables three desks four chairs and four sofas.

11. For graduation all students are required to complete courses in English mathematics accounting and computer science.

12. This file contains basic writing supplies stationery envelopes pens ink and stamps.

13. Only four people failed to attend the meeting Fred Rogers Marc Spade Al Rosen and Margaret Fisk.

14. Have you read his latest book *Building an Empire The Art of Creative Investment*

15. To   Laura Brunson Personnel Records
    From   Joanne Himes Central Services
    Subject   Employee Promotions
    The following employees are being considered for promotion Please forward their records by November 1
       Julio Cruz   Bud Cravitz   Lisa James   Mary Lewitz

EXERCISE 18·3   PUNCTUATION REVIEW

This exercise involves the use of the colon, semicolon, comma, and period. Insert these marks wherever proper in the following sentences.

1. We offer a choice of three cabinets the stately Classical the functional Colonial or the streamlined Modern

2. Once again we are extending the time however in the future there will be no further extension

3. Standing up in the Assembly Patrick Henry shouted "Give me liberty or give me death"

4. The workday begins at 8 30 A M it ends at 5 00 P M

5. The traits that I most admire in a person are these honesty wisdom and perseverance

6. During the past few months which have been especially hectic I inspected the following divisions the Tennessee factory the Missouri offices and the Louisiana warehouse

7. Therefore we are pleased to be able to extend this invitation but bear in mind that much as we would prefer that it be otherwise this must be our last offer

8. You Ms Lopez have already received our final offer henceforth we shall not bother you again

9. To err is human to forgive divine

10. Since our last report we have restudied the figures you submitted but despite our attempts to reconcile them the surplus figures do not coincide

11. I will be unable to keep my 10 30 A M appointment however I will be able to keep my afternoon appointments

12. The possible meeting dates are as follows Tuesday November 8 Wednesday November 16 and Tuesday November 29

13. The final sentence read "These measures will insure a steady growth for our company both now and for years to come"

14. I missed the 7 15 train consequently I was late for the interview

15. Professor Simonson requires that all research papers contain the following parts title page outline introduction body conclusion and bibliography

16. Copies of the proposal should be sent to Mr Duffey Mr O'Hare Ms Snyder and Mr Olson

17. Our employees are all experienced accountants in fact most are CPAs

18. Both Mr Mattuck and Mrs Slater share a common characteristic they value professional success above all else

19. The members of the panel are Lydia Evans sales representative Allied Sales Robin Samuels marketing director Datatech Inc and Louise Fletcher director of sales Easton Products Ltd

20. It was our understanding that the new modular furniture would be identical with the furniture we presently own that it would be delivered by United Express prior to December 15 and that we would be billed on the regular terms of 2/10 net 30

EXERCISE 18·4   SEMICOLON AND COLON

The following memorandum is written without any punctuation. Insert all necessary punctuation marks.

TO   Maxine Tranter
FROM   Kim Oh
DATE   November 3 1984
SUBJECT   Sites for Marketing Conference

Here is the information you requested

Three hotels are potential sites for our conference namely The Hilton The Biltmore and The Plaza All three have conference facilities more than sufficient for our needs The Hilton can accommodate 2172 The Biltmore 2647 The Plaza 2645.

Each has modern conference facilities including ballrooms and seminar rooms moreover each offers excellent dining and entertainment for conference participants

Only the Biltmore however would be able to arrange an 8 30 P M preconference session I believe this is an important consideration accordingly I recommend The Biltmore as our conference site

EXERCISE 18·5 COMPOSITION: SEMICOLON AND COLON

Compose complete sentences according to the following directions.

1. (Write a sentence using a colon and the phrase *the following.*) _____

_____

2. (Write a sentence using a semicolon followed by *for example.*) _____

_____

3. (Write a sentence using a semicolon followed by *and.*) _____

_____

4. (Write a sentence using a semicolon followed by *however.*) _____

_____

5. (Write a sentence using a colon followed by a quotation.) _____

_____

EXERCISE 18·6 COMPOSITION: WRITING A THANK-YOU LETTER

When people have been especially kind or helpful to you, it is always appropriate to send them a note of appreciation.

Assume that you have just accepted a job offer. You are very happy because this position seems to be everything you were seeking in employment. One of your former teachers, at your request, wrote a letter of recommendation for you. You know the letter helped you get the job because the personnel director mentioned during your second interview how favorably she was impressed by it. Write your former teacher a thank-you letter. Write your letter in the space below.

_____

_____

_____

_____

_____

_____

_____

_____

_____

_____

19

PUNCTUATION V
OTHER MARKS OF PUNCTUATION

QUOTATION MARKS, THE APOSTROPHE, THE
HYPHEN, ELLIPSES, THE UNDERSCORE,
PARENTHESES, BRACKETS, THE DASH

The primary purpose of the marks of punctuation we have discussed so far has been to show major divisions of thought. The period, question mark, and exclamation point are **end-of-sentence** or **terminal punctuation.** They mark the fundamental units of thought in the language. Semicolons, colons, and commas, known as marks of **internal punctuation,** show divisions *within* sentences. The marks of punctuation set forth in this chapter are also marks of internal punctuation. These marks are not used to show divisions of thought. Instead, they perform a variety of more specialized functions.

QUOTATION MARKS (" ")

RULE 1

Use quotation marks to enclose a direct quotation. A direct quotation repeats the exact words of what was originally said or written.

> In your letter of July 9 you state: "Our records indicate that shipment was made on June 15 via Universal Shippers, Inc."

Do not use quotation marks around an indirect quotation. An indirect quotation is a rewording of the original statement. It is frequently introduced by the word *that.*

> In your letter of July 9 you write that the shipment was sent via Universal Shippers on June 15.

Note 1: Use a colon to introduce a direct quotation of one long sentence or of two or more sentences regardless of length.

> The President declared: "In a time of peril such as this we must jealously guard our liberties and defend our national integrity against all encroachments."

Use a colon when the introduction comments directly on the quotation, whatever its length.

> The President's reply was firm and direct: "I am confident of victory."

Use a comma to introduce a direct quotation of one short sentence or of part of a sentence.

The President said, "I am confident of victory."

Note 2: When a complete statement is quoted and ends the sentence, the period is placed inside the final quotation marks.

Patrick Henry shouted, "Give me liberty or give me death."

When a complete statement is quoted but does not end the sentence, a comma is placed inside the final quotation mark.

"Give me liberty or give me death," shouted Patrick Henry.

When a complete statement being quoted is broken into more than one part, enclose each part in quotation marks. Do not start the second part with a capital. Note the use of commas.

"Send us the bill," he wrote, "and we will mail you a check by return mail."

Note 3: When recording the direct conversation of two or more persons, place the statements of each person in separate quotation marks and in separate paragraphs.

The chairman shouted, "Order! Order in the house!"
"I will not be silenced," answered Lutz, jumping up from his seat with arms waving wildly.
"Friends," interrupted Obeji, "let us now look at this matter in a calmer frame of mind."

Note 4: If a quotation consists of more than one sentence, the quotation marks go at the beginning and at the end of the entire statement. If the single quotation is more than one paragraph, the quotation marks go at the beginning of each paragraph, but at the end of only the *last* paragraph.

The letter read: "We are making this offer just this week. Note that it is being made together with our sale of daytime dresses. We are sure you will like our selection.
"Any time during the morning that is best for you will be best for us. Will you come?"

Note 5: Use single quotation marks (apostrophes on the typewriter) to indicate a quotation within a quotation.

I said, "I believe in the old saying, 'Haste makes waste.'"

Note 6: When typing quotation marks, do not skip a space after the beginning quotation mark or before the closing quotation mark.

RULE 2

Use quotation marks around the titles of minor works such as poems, short stories, one-act plays, lectures, songs, sermons, and articles or chapters in magazines, newspapers, and books. The name of a magazine, newspaper, or book is written either in italics (indicated by underlining the name) or in all capital letters rather than with quotation marks.

Mr. Landers was interviewed for the article "A Look at Ten Top Executives" in *Corporate Management Monthly.*

Did you read "The Automated Electronic Office of the Future" in *The Wall Street Journal*?

For Friday the instructor assigned Chapter 12 of *Administrative Office Management*, "The Use of Tests to Select Office Workers."

LIFE is doing a series on "The Universe."

Note: Capitalize the first letter of each important word in the title. Capitalize articles, short conjunctions, and short prepositions when they occur at the beginning of the title, but not when they occur in the middle.

 RULE 3

Quotation marks may be placed around words used in unusual senses, coined phrases, or colloquial expressions.

My "Uncle" George is actually an old friend of my father.

We feel that this textbook is "user-friendly."

Carmen Huerta led a workshop on how to "nail down" a sale.

Do not use quotation marks to apologize for expressions. If the words are appropriate, they can be used without quotation marks. If they are inappropriate, they should not be used at all.

 RULE 4

Combining quotation marks and other punctuation can give a great deal of trouble unless you are careful. Pay close attention to these simple rules.

1. Always place a final *period* or *comma* inside the quotation marks.

   He said, "Let the chips fall."

   "Give me the statistics," she retorted, "and I'll have the answers in a minute."

2. Always place a final *colon* or *semicolon* outside the quotation marks.

   Here is a partial list of causes cited in "The Rising Cost of Living": higher wages, increased tariffs, lower rates of productivity growth.

   The encircled troops were told, "Surrender or die"; they chose to fight on.

3. The *question mark, exclamation point*, and *dash* are placed inside the quotation marks when they relate specifically to the quoted material.

   "Will you join me?" she asked.

   "Wow!" was all he could say.

   "Our flight position is—" were the pilot's last recorded words.

4. The *question mark, exclamation point*, and *dash* are placed outside the quotation marks if they relate to the entire sentence.

   Did you read our article, "The Higher Light"?

   Congratulations on your latest article, "How to Invest"!

   "To be or not to be . . ."—Shakespeare.

PROGRAMMED REINFORCEMENT

S1   Quotation marks (should, should not) be placed around direct quotations. They (should, should not) be placed around indirect quotations.

R1   should; should not

S2   Punctuate the following, inserting capitals if necessary. **Tell me he said why I haven't heard from you have you been ill**

R2   **"Tell me," he said, "why I haven't heard from you. Have you been ill?"**

S3   (Circle one.) In a direct conversation between two people: a. the entire conversation is put into one paragraph beginning and ending with quotation marks; b. a separate paragraph with beginning and ending quotation marks is used for quote of each speaker.

R3   b.

S4   In a single quotation consisting of several paragraphs, quotation marks are put at the _____ of each paragraph but at the end of only the _____ paragraph.

R4   beginning; last

S5   Titles of books are usually underlined or printed in capitals, but titles of articles and less important materials are written with _____ marks.

R5   quotation

S6   Punctuate this sentence: **The French expression nouveau-riche may be translated as the newly arrived.**

R6   **The French expression "nouveau-riche" may be translated as "the newly arrived."**

S7   The _____ and the _____ are always placed inside the closing quotation marks; the _____ and the _____ are always placed outside the closing quotation marks.

R7   comma; period; colon; semicolon

S8   The question mark, exclamation mark, and dash are placed inside or outside the closing quotation marks depending on whether they relate specifically to the material being quoted or to the entire sentence. If they relate specifically to the quoted material, put them (inside, outside) the closing quotation marks. If they relate to the sentence as a whole, put them _____ the closing quotation marks.

R8   inside; outside

S9   Punctuate these sentences, adding capitals if needed:
a. **Why haven't I seen you before he asked**
b. **She exclaimed this is preposterous**
c. **Do you recall his words give me liberty or give me death**

R9   a. **"Why haven't I seen you before?" he asked.**
b. **She exclaimed, "This is preposterous!"**
c. **Do you recall his words: "Give me liberty or give me death"?**

Turn to Exercise 19.1.

THE APOSTROPHE (')

 ## RULE 1

Use the apostrophe to indicate that a letter or letters have been left out in a contraction. Do not place a period after a contraction as you would after an abbreviation. Notice where the apostrophe goes and what letters it replaces in the following contractions:

aren't	I'll	he's	who's
can't	he'll	I'm	Gen'l
couldn't	she'll	it's	Gov't
isn't	they'll	they're	Nat'l
weren't	we'll	we're	Sec'y

An apostrophe is also used to show that numbers in a year have been left out.

Representatives from the classes of '08 and '10 were present at the '63 Homecoming.

 ## RULE 2

Use the apostrophe to form the possessive case of a noun. Form the possessive of a singular noun and irregular plural noun by adding apostrophe s ('s). Form the possessive of a regular plural noun by adding only an apostrophe.

A teacher's success depends upon a student's efforts.
John's office called, but Ramon's line was busy.
Keypunch operators' skills will determine their success.
Knox's Toy Store will begin carrying children's clothing in the fall.

See the discussion of possessive nouns in Chapter 3.
Remember, the possessive form of a *pronoun* does not take an apostrophe: *hers, its, ours, yours, theirs.*

Is this book hers?
Yours truly,
The firm sent its representative.

It's is a contraction of *it is; its* is a possessive pronoun.

If this room is to remain orderly, it's essential that everything be returned to its place after use.

 ## RULE 3

Use the apostrophe to form the plural of letters, numbers, and abbreviations made up of separate letters.

Mississippi has four *i*'s, four *s*'s, and two *p*'s.
This month we ordered a new shipment of No. 107's.
There are three Y.M.C.A.'s in this city.

The plural of words being used simply as words usually is formed just by adding *s*. However, if a particular plural formed this way might appear confusing, add apostrophe s ('s).

We want no *ifs, ands,* or *buts.*   He uses six *I*'s in his very first sentence.

Note: Many writers use *'s* to form plurals only when necessary for clarity. See Chapter 3.

THE HYPHEN (-)

RULE 1

Use the hyphen to divide a word that cannot be completed at the end of a line.

> She said that it would be impossible to com-
>   plete the project on schedule.

The rules for word division are presented in detail in Chapter 20.

RULE 2

There are certain expressions that should always be hyphenated:

1. Compound words that begin with *self*, such as *self-conscious, self-evident, self-assurance, self-respect, self-confident.*
2. Compound words that begin with *ex, pro,* or *anti* when followed by a word beginning with a capital letter. For example: *ex-President, ex-Senator, pro-American, pro-United Nations, anti-Communist* (but *exspouse, prolabor, antislavery*).

RULE 3

As you learned in Chapter 5, there are other expressions that are sometimes hyphenated and sometimes not—expressions such as *up to date, high class, first rate, high grade, well informed.* These expressions are **compound adjectives**. Whenever a compound adjective comes before the noun it modifies, it should be hyphenated.

> We have an up-to-date system.
> Our store caters to a high-class clientele.
> We deal in first-rate goods.
> We need a well-informed public.
> She competed in the hundred-yard dash.

When a compound adjective comes after the noun it modifies, do not hyphenate it.

> Our system is up to date.
> Our clientele is high class.
> Our goods are first rate.
> Our public is well informed.
> She ran a race of one hundred yards.

Note 1: Do not use a hyphen after an adverb ending in *ly* even if it precedes the noun:

> highly trained athlete
> brightly decorated hall
> widely heralded appearance
> oddly strange mixture

Note 2: Observe this sentence: *We are short of ten- and twenty-dollar bills.*
Note the hyphen after *ten.* This sentence really says: *We are short of ten-dollar bills and twenty-dollar bills;* hence the use of the hyphen after *ten.* Here are similar examples:

> They stock half-, three-quarter-, and seven-eighth-inch bolts.
> He swam in the 50-, 100-, and 220-yard free-style races.
> They produced 24-, 32-, 64-, and 128-page versions of the book.

Note 3: When writing out numbers, hyphenate compound numbers from twenty-one through ninety-nine. Do not hyphenate hundreds, thousands, or millions. Look at these examples:

> Our goal is ten out of thirty-seven.
> One-hundred thirty-seven attended the seminar.
> On the amount line of a check, $137,645 is written as "One hundred thirty-seven thousand six hundred forty-five dollars."

The rules for expressing numbers are presented in Chapter 20. As you will learn, in most business situations numbers are expressed as figures rather than as words.

 # ELLIPSES (. . .)

Ellipses are a series of dots used in the middle of a direct quotation to show that part of the quotation at that point has been left out. Three dots are used at the beginning of, or in the middle of, a quoted sentence. If the material left out is at the end of a sentence, a fourth dot representing the period is added. Do not use more or fewer dots than these.

> If a man has freedom enough to live healthy . . . he has enough.—Goethe.
> According to Immanual Kant: "Freedom is that faculty which enlarges the usefulness of all other faculties. . . ."

Ellipses are also used to show the end of an unfinished thought.

> If economic conditions don't improve soon . . .

In typing ellipses, space after each period.

 # THE UNDERSCORE (___)

Use the underscore to show words that would be italicized in print. This includes titles of works published separately such as books, magazines, periodicals, and newspapers.

> The New York Times has been highly critical of Mr. Newcomb's new book, How to Succeed in the Marketplace.

Use the underscore to emphasize individual words in a sentence or to set off words used as nouns under discussion in a sentence.

> This offer will never be repeated.
> The words affect and effect are frequently confused.

 # PARENTHESES ( )

 ## RULE 1

Use parentheses to enclose expressions that are completely incidental, explanatory, or supplementary to the main thought of a sentence.

> There is no possibility (so I am told) that this deal will go through.
> You have already learned (see Chapter 3) about nouns.

Note 1: When a sentence ends with an expression in parentheses, place a period after the parentheses. For example:

You have already learned about how to avoid sentence fragments (see Chapter 2).

Note 2: When a complete sentence appears in parentheses as part of another sentence, as in the above examples, it is not started with a capital letter nor finished with a period. When a sentence in parentheses is an independent thought, it is started with a capital letter and ended with appropriate punctuation inside the closing parenthesis:

I have told the Director that you will have the goods delivered by Tuesday. (Kay, please don't let us down.) He will accept shipment no later than then.

Note 3: Do you place punctuation inside or outside the final parenthesis? If the punctuation relates only to the material in parentheses, place the punctuation inside.

His latest article ("Lost Opportunities") is certain to receive an award.
When using a telescope, never (Never!) look directly at the sun.

If the punctuation relates to the whole sentence and not specifically to the material in parentheses, place the punctuation outside the closing parenthesis mark.

No matter where we have traveled (in the United States and Canada at least), we have never found a better hotel.

Note 4: In some instances it is correct to use either dashes or parentheses, whichever you prefer:

Right: This offer (and it is our final offer) is too good to be refused.
Right: This offer—and it is our final offer—is too good to be refused.

Notice how the dashes set off the parenthetical statement more sharply than do the parentheses and thus emphasize it, whereas the parentheses tend to deemphasize it.

 ## RULE 2

Parentheses are used to enclose numbers or letters itemizing a list that is part of running text.

Practice serves to (a) improve your coordination, (b) increase your speed, and (c) develop your strength.

Note 1: If you had tabulated this list, you would write it as follows:

Practice serves to accomplish the following:
a. improve your coordination
b. increase your speed
c. develop your strength

 ## RULE 3

Numbers frequently are written out in both words and figures in formal documents. Parentheses are usually placed around the figures. For example:

The total fee for our service shall be Six Hundred Dollars ($600).
We acknowledge receipt of your order for three hundred (300) barrels of crude oil.

Note 1: In spelling out a dollar amount in a legal document, capitalize each word in the figure and capitalize the word *Dollar.* The figure in parentheses appears after the word *Dollar: Six Hundred Dollars ($600).*

Note 2: In spelling out a quantity of material, do not capitalize the numbers or the unit of measurement, and place the figures in parentheses before the name of the unit of measure: *three hundred (300) barrels.*

 # BRACKETS [ ]

Brackets are used in a printed direct quotation to show material that is not part of the quotation but that has been inserted by the editor for purposes of explanation or correction. They are seldom used in business writing.

> The minister referred to a favorite adage, "The exception proves [tests] the rule."
> "The succession of Scotland's James V [VI] to the English throne in 1603 was remarkably trouble free."

Brackets also are used as a substitute for parentheses within parentheses.

> David Johnson's newest book (*Writing for the World of Business* [the chapters on report writing are especially good]) has been praised by many business executives.

 # THE DASH (—)

 ## RULE 1

Use the dash to indicate a major break in the continuity of thought.

> The large house—and it was very large—was completely demolished by the fire.
> I know—or should I say, I feel—that you will do well.

 ## RULE 2

Use the dash to emphasize an explanatory phrase.

> We want to tell you about our product—the Schenley car.
> Mario—the only experienced member of our staff—has just resigned.

Note 1: Properly used, the dash is an effective tool to catch the reader's eye. If you use the dash too often, however, you destroy its effectiveness and leave a sloppy, difficult-to-read page. The good writer uses the dash only for special emphasis.

Note 2: The dash is frequently used to set off an explanatory phrase that contains one or more commas.

> Several states—especially Illinois, Ohio, and New Jersey—would be ideal locations in which to build another plant.

Note 3: Don't leave out the second dash. If an explanatory phrase starts with a dash, it also should end with a dash—not with a comma.

> **Wrong:** Several states—especially Illinois, Ohio, and New Jersey, would be ideal locations in which to build another plant.

RULE 3

Use the dash after an expression such as *namely* or *that is* when this expression introduces a list in tabulated form.

> We are aware of three contributing factors; namely—
> 1. the bad weather
> 2. the rise in prices
> 3. the shortage of labor

 RULE 4

Use a dash before a word used to sum up a preceding series.

> Experience, integrity, commitment—these were the qualities the candidate stressed in every campaign speech.
> Charlotte Reynolds, Seth Eisenberg, Anne Wichowski—any one of these people would be an excellent supervisor.
> The bad weather, the rise in prices, the shortage of labor—all these factors contributed to our present problem.

 RULE 5

Use a dash before the name of the author after a quotation.

> Unbroken happiness is a bore; it should have ups and downs.—Moliere

Note 1: In business the correct way to make a dash on a typewriter is by striking the hyphen twice, leaving no space before or after this dash.

> The officers of the company--the president, vice president, and secretary-trea-
> surer--have approved the plans for merger.

 PROGRAMMED REINFORCEMENT

S10 An apostrophe is used to indicate letters that are left out in contractions. Insert apostrophes in the following contractions: **cant; shouldnt; wont; youll; Id**

R10 can't; shouldn't; won't; you'll; I'd

S11 You use an apostrophe to show possessive (nouns, pronouns), but you do not use an apostrophe to show possessive (nouns, pronouns).

R11 nouns; pronouns

S12 Rewrite each of the following words as a possessive. **Laura our company it their businesses**

R12 Laura's; ours; company's; its; theirs; businesses'

S13 The apostrophe is often used to form the plural of letters and numbers. Write these correctly: **All the t s were uncrossed in letters of the 1820s and 1830s.**

R13 t's; 1820's; 1830's

S14 Compound words or expressions beginning with **self,** are always hyphenated; those beginning with **anti, pro,** and **ex** only some times. Write these expressions correctly: **selfrespect antiRussian proAmerican exofficio**

R14 self-respect; anti-Russian; pro-American; ex-officio

S15 Adjective phrases such as **up to date** or **first class** are hyphenated when they come before the noun they modify; they are not hyphenated when they come after the noun. Insert hyphens where proper:
a. **We use up to date methods.**
b. **This dinner was first class.**
c. **I speak from first hand experience.**
d. **They shipped low grade ore.**
e. **The ore they shipped was low grade.**
f. **Listen to WXYZ for up to the minute market analysis.**

R15
a. **up-to-date**
b. **none**
c. **first-hand**
d. **low-grade**
e. **none**
f. **up-to-the-minute**

S16 When the adjective phrase contains an adverb ending in **ly**—for example, **highly trained**—you generally do not hyphenate even when the phrase comes before the noun. Insert hyphens where proper:
a. **He is a highly skilled worker.**
b. **We need a well informed citizenry.**
c. **The truth is self evident.**
d. **We enjoyed a sincerely interested audience.**
e. **They held a five day reunion.**

R16
a. **none**
b. **well-informed**
c. **self-evident**
d. **none**
e. **five-day**

S17 When writing out numbers, hyphenate compound numbers from twenty-one to ninety-nine. Do not hyphenate hundreds, thousands, or millions unless the entire number immediately comes before the noun it modifies. Insert hyphens in the following numbers:
a. **six million four hundred eighty two thousand nine hundred fifty five**
b. **a nine hundred fifty five dollar deficit**

R17
a. **six million four hundred eighty-two thousand nine hundred fifty-five**
b. **a nine-hundred-fifty-five dollar deficit**

S18 The dots that show that material has been left out from a direct quotation are known as _____.

R18 ellipses

S19 An ellipse at the beginning or in the middle of a quotation is indicated by _____ dots; at the end, by _____ dots.

R19 three; four

S20 The underscore is used to show words that would be italicized in print. Which of the following should be underscored?
a. the title of a magazine
b. an article in a magazine
c. the name of a newspaper
d. the title of a book
e. the title of an essay
f. a word to be emphasized

R20 a. c. d. f.

S21 Parentheses are used to enclose expressions that are completely incidental to the main thought of a sentence. Often instead of using parentheses you may use _____.

R21 dashes

S22 When a sentence ends with a statement in parentheses, place the final period (inside, outside) the parentheses. For example: **Turn to Lesson 4 (page 37)**

R22 outside; **(page 37).**

S23 **Foreign affairs, the cost of living (which is rising) national defense, and civil rights are major political issues.** In this sentence a comma should be placed (inside, outside) the closing parenthesis mark.

R23 outside

S24 In formal documents, a number often is written out and also is expressed by a figure in parentheses. In the following two sentences, which words should be capitalized?
a. **The contract calls for payment of two hundred dollars ($200).**
b. **The invoice calls for two hundred (200) tons.**

R24 a. **Two Hundred Dollars**
     b. no capitals

S25 Insert parentheses in the following sentences:
a. **If I understand the truth at least insofar as it is possible to ever know the truth, Robinson has violated our trust.**
b. **Under said Agreement Licensee pays a royalty of fifteen percent 15%.**

R25 a. **the truth (at least insofar as it is possible to ever know the truth), Robinson . . .**
     b. **. . . percent (15%).**

S26 Insert dashes in the following sentences:
a. **The truth at least I think it's the truth is that Robinson has violated our trust.**
b. **We are proud of that symbol of free enterprise the New York World's Fair.**
c. **To be or not to be Shakespeare.**

R26 a. **The truth—at least I think it's the truth—is . . .**
     b. **. . . free enterprise— the New York World's Fair.**
     c. **To be or not to be— Shakespeare.**

S27 The preferred way to make a dash on a typewriter is to strike the _____ twice, leaving no space before or after the dash.

R27 hyphen

Turn to Exercises 19.2 to 19.7.

EXERCISE 19·1A   QUOTATION MARKS AND OTHER PUNCTUATION

Insert all necessary punctuation in each of the following sentences. Capitalize where necessary.

1. The instructor told the class the ability to communicate effectively is essential for success in today's business world

2. Who manufactures these he asked

3. The president spoke with authority saying you may be certain that our firm adheres only to the highest standards of business ethics

4. His essay business ethics is a classic

5. Did you receive any compensation for your article the high-tech battle between Japan and the United States

6. She asked an important question how can we justify our own failure to help them

7. Of all the people I know he said none is more just than your father Arthur Robinson

8. Try our new air conditioner the ad stated it will bring cool comfort to your home or office

9. The enclosed booklet make your own weather will show you how to maintain your volume of business during these hot summer months

10. How are sales for your latest book make your fortune

11. In your letter you write that the cost per unit will soon increase

12. Shakespeare wrote the evil that men do lives after them the good is oft interred with their bones

13. Marie Antoinette never said let them eat cake

14. Get out of my office he bellowed

15. Let us know by Friday she wrote whether you will accept the offer

16. He accused his competitor of being a blind pig-headed mule

17. Rush help or—were the last words we heard before we lost contact with them

18. Great was all she could shout

19. Did you read the book how to double your money

20. I wonder mused Anna why he's doing this

Punctuate the following memorandum correctly.

TO   Julie Gregg

FROM Mike Flanders

RE   Martin Manufacturing Co. Project

We received a letter from Modern Offices Inc that reads as follows

We have your letter of June 15 in which you enclosed the specifications for the safe equipment to be installed in the new offices of the Martin Manufacturing Company

We will be glad to send you pictures and details of Western safes that meet these requirements

It would be more convincing however to have you and your customer visit us in Cleveland May we therefore extend an invitation to you and your customer to come to Cleveland at our expense

Please let us know when it will be most convenient for you and we will make the necessary hotel reservations

Cordially yours

In view of the invitation extended to us in this letter I think we should very seriously consider sending a representative to inspect the Western safes in Cleveland.

EXERCISE 19·2A   THE APOSTROPHE

In the space provided, write the correct word.

1. (It's, Its) a wonderful opportunity for you.   1. _____

2. Is this (yours, your's)?   2. _____

3. (Your, You're) offer is most interesting.   3. _____

4. The (women's, womens') coats are on the second floor.   4. _____

5. (There, They're) are three reasons for this decision.   5. _____

6. Give them (their, they're) due.   6. _____

7. (They're, Their) fed up with this type of bickering.   7. _____

8. The class of (63, '63) held a reunion recently.   8. _____

9. The company sent (its, it's) form letter.   9. _____

10. Salary is only one measure of a (persons, person's) success.   10. _____

11. This is your handwriting, (is'nt, isn't) it?   11. _____

12. Her handwriting is so poor that I can't tell her (as, a's) from her
    (is, i's).   12. _____

EXERCISE 19·2B   POSSESSIVES AND CONTRACTIONS

If the sentence is correct, mark C in the space provided. If it is incorrect, use the space above the sentence to indicate the necessary changes.

1. I can'nt understand the failure of their companys rep to visit any of our shops.   1. _____

2. Our figures for the past half years sales reflect the concentration of our outlets
    in the citys prime market area.   2. _____

3. Their's is a very enviable position to be in, isn't it?   3. _____

4. Im certain that its still not too late to open an IRA.   4. _____

5. Lings Clothing Store features the best in mens, womens, and childrens wear.   5. _____

6. We're looking forward to seeing you and you're family at the Class of 78
    Reunion.   6. _____

7. Who's going to take care of the billings while we're on vacation?   7. _____

8. The director of the medical records department says she'll locate that patients'
    records herself.   8. _____

9. I'm unable to tell whether these letters of her's are Us or Is.   9. _____

10. Well save $20,000 by implementing the recommendations in Ms. Hennessy's
    report on forms management.   10. _____

EXERCISE 19·3   COMPOUND WORDS

In this exercise some compound words are written as one word; others are hyphenated. Still others are written as two separate words. Below is a list of compound words written separately. In the space provided, write them correctly. Consult your dictionary if necessary.

1.	self evident	1.	_____
2.	letter head	2.	_____
3.	ex president	3.	_____
4.	self control	4.	_____
5.	vice chairman	5.	_____
6.	mother in law	6.	_____
7.	all right	7.	_____
8.	can not	8.	_____
9.	not withstanding	9.	_____
10.	real estate	10.	_____
11.	ex governor	11.	_____
12.	type written	12.	_____
13.	editors in chief	13.	_____
14.	over due	14.	_____
15.	post card	15.	_____
16.	self conscious	16.	_____
17.	any body	17.	_____
18.	vice president	18.	_____
19.	no one	19.	_____
20.	some thing	20.	_____

EXERCISE 19·4   PARENTHESIS, DASH, HYPHEN, ELLIPSES, UNDERSCORE, BRACKETS

Insert all necessary punctuation in the following sentences.

1. It is self evident at least it should be so to a reasonable person that our economic outlook is brightening.

2. Please look at our advertisement you can find one in this month's issue of New Era to see what we mean by an efficient layout.

3. You should be able to collect the facts and we mean all the facts with little trouble if you apply yourself.

4. And the Licensee hereby agrees to pay Licensor on the first day of each month commencing on January the first Nineteen hundred and eighty five the sum of Two Hundred Dollars $200.

5. As you have already learned see Chapter 5 a pronoun should agree in person and number with its antecedent.

6. We are interested I might say very interested in your assessment of the conference.

7. As a result of our long experience never forget we have been in business for over a hundred years we feel it our duty to advise against purchase of this stock.

8. Our representative Ms. Paula Perrier didn't you meet her at our last convention will be glad to assist you.

9. This chance and it's your very last chance is a fine opportunity.

10. Practice to a listen carefully b speak clearly c make your point.

11. Reading writing speaking these are the skills all students must master.

12. The phrase non sequitur literally means it does not follow.

13. The New York Times The Wall Street Journal and The Washington Post these are her daily sources of information.

14. I wish I could help you but was all she could say.

15. I refuse wrote President Harry Thorndyke to compromise my principals sic of honesty and integrity.

EXERCISE 19·5   COMPOSITION: MARKS OF PUNCTUATION

The following sentences contain errors in punctuation. Correct these errors and then in the space provided explain the reasons for the corrections you made. Use complete sentences.

1. Juan responded, "I believe in the old saying, "Neither a borrower nor a lender be."" _____

_____

_____

2. The article, *The Latest in Compact Computers,* in this month's *Office Administration and Auto-mation* is very informative. _____

_____

_____

3. Increasing levels of responsibility, variety of experience, and opportunity for advancement: these are the features I seek in a position. _____

_____

_____

4. Have you heard the commercial that ends, "At Sims a well educated consumer is our best customer?" _____

_____

_____

5. The housing industry is again experiencing a period of growth, see chart on opposite page, and this growth should continue through the remainder of the year. _____

_____

_____

EXERCISE 19·6A   PUNCTUATION

This is a review exercise on punctuation. Insert all punctuation marks that have been left out in the following passage.

HOW BANKS OPERATE

The ordinary idea of a bank is of an institution in which one deposits money for safekeeping and withdraws it as it is needed There are many people who think of a bank in no other terms who give no thought to the manner in which a bank profits by these operations.

The two fundamental concerns of a bank are borrowing and lending money When you deposit money in a bank whether it is in a checking account a savings account a certificate of deposit or an individual retirement account IRA you are lending it money The bank in turn lends this money or a part of it to others at a rate of interest that is higher than that which you receive The difference is the profit made by the bank Such an institution must keep a surplus on hand with which to accommodate your withdrawals or the checks that you issue

As a general rule a checking account balance draws no interest Depositors receive services for the use of their money A savings account however draws a small rate of interest a certificate of deposit a larger rate The bank profits by lending your money at a higher rate than it pays

Another commonly used service of a bank is provision of storage facilities for money securities important papers jewels and other valuables These are guarded in what is known as a safe deposit vault a place that is rented for a certain sum per year for this purpose

A bank sells service It hires borrows money and it rents lends money When the customer hires money he or she has to pay the rent which is interest The customer also has to provide collateral or security which may be sold in case the money is not repaid

In addition a bank offers many other services to its clients or customers It collects drafts checks and coupons from bonds it pays checks issued by depositors it extends credit and it acts as trustee administrator executor and guardian It advises clients with regard to the investment of money in securities land or business of any kind In short it is usually able to advise and assist in all kinds of financial transactions

EXERCISE 19·6B   PUNCTUATION

The following letter is written with no punctuation marks and with most capital letters omitted. Insert all punctuation marks. Where a letter should be capitalized, cross out that letter and write the capital letter above it.

Randall and Peck Inc

35 Draper Avenue

Elgin Illinois 60120

Ladies and Gentlemen

the following is a well known fact as boredom goes up productivity goes down the enclosed booklet let muzik work for you will show you how to create a more pleasurable working environment that will reduce employee fatigue and boredom and as a result help increase employee productivity

whether your business operates in a small office or a huge plant Muzik Makers Inc can supply you with the prerecorded music that is right for you this music specifically selected for your particular needs can calm employee nerves reduce fatigue due to work strain and lessen work monotony as a result your employees attitudes toward their jobs will improve they will be absent and tardy less often when they arent bored they make fewer and less costly errors

as you will learn from the booklet the kind of work your employees perform will determine the type of music classical numbers semiclassical numbers show tunes or popular tunes that should be played you will also learn why whatever music you select should not be played continuously as you will see we recommend an on for 15 minutes off for 15 minutes cycle to give your employees the greatest psychological lift you will also learn why we recommend music be played especially at high fatigue periods namely midmorning midafternoon and immediately before lunch and quitting time

heres what one satisfied subscriber to Muzik had to say

morale at our plant in Tucson was very low before we subscribed to your service productivity was down absenteeism was up employee turnover was very high im happy to report that after using your service for three months we have seen the situation improve dramatically the change in employee attitudes has been remarkable employee absenteeism tardiness and turnover have fallen the quality of work has improved productivity has increased overall business volume and profits have grown we owe it all to your service as far as im concerned no business should be without Muzik its fantastic

why not take the advice of this successful business person and the thousands who say the same bring Muzik into your office and let Muzik work for you you wont be sorry you did

Sincerely,

EXERCISE 19·7   COMPOSITION: WRITING A CLAIM LETTER

No business wants to make mistakes, but, at some time or another, every business does. When this happens, the customer writes a claim letter seeking an adjustment to correct an error in shipment or an improper billing or to request replacement of goods received in a damaged condition.

Assume that you have been a regular subcriber to *Today's World* magazine for six years. Last year you renewed your subscription for three more years. You still have your canceled check as proof. Recently, however, you have received a series of messages from the publisher urging you to renew your subscription promptly before it expires. Write to the subscription department asking them to correct this error. The address is *Today's World*, Subscription Department, 123 45th Street, Omaha, Nebraska. Write your letter in the space below.

_____
_____
_____
_____
_____
_____
_____
_____
_____
_____
_____
_____
_____
_____
_____

20

ELEMENTS OF STYLE

CAPITALIZATION, WORD DIVISION, NUMBERS

In the preceding chapters we have discussed the correct use of the parts of speech and marks of punctuation. As you have seen, errors involving these topics can result not only in ungrammatical constructions, but also in a lack of clarity, and even a breakdown in meaning. In this chapter we are going to look at capitalization, word division, and the expression of numbers. We have called these topics **elements of style**. **Style** refers to the particular manner in which an idea is expressed rather than the idea itself. The decision to write "Southern Missouri" or "southern Missouri," "fifty dollars" or "$50" is a choice of style. The meaning is not affected.

This does not mean that either choice is equally acceptable. As you will see, there are certain customs people have agreed on involving when to use capital letters, how to divide a word at the end of a line, and how to express numbers. We call these agreed-upon methods of expression **conventions**. One such convention, as you know, is to begin every sentence with a capital letter. Another is to capitalize a person's name. A third is to express phone numbers in figures rather than words. You would undoubtedly find a message that did not observe these conventions very distracting and even confusing.

There are many other conventions that the careful business writer knows and observes in business correspondence. The reader expects it. A writer's failure to follow these conventions could distract or confuse the reader. As a business writer, you want your reader to concentrate on the message itself, not the form in which it is expressed. Hence it is important to know and practice the stylistic conventions that most business writers observe.

Many of the conventions presented in each section are well known to you. You have used them automatically for years. Focus on those with which you are less familiar.

 ## CAPITALIZATION

 ### RULE 1

Capitalize the first word of every sentence (including this one). Capitalize a word or the first word of a phrase used as a sentence substitute.

Yes.   Next.   Not on your life.

 ### RULE 2

Capitalize the first word of a direct quotation that is a complete sentence.

He said, "This job must be improved upon."
"This job," he said, "must be improved upon."

When quoting an expression that is not a complete sentence, do not capitalize the first word.

He said that this job "must be improved upon."

RULE 3

Capitalize the first word after a colon when it introduces a complete sentence or series of complete sentences.

> He made the following declaration: "This job must be improved upon."
> She suggested three additional reasons for the declining sales figures: 1) Remodeling of the mall has created congestion and inadequate parking; 2) a truckers' strike has resulted in a shortage of some popular items; and 3) nearby competitors have introduced innovative advertising and promotional schemes to attract customers.

RULE 4

Capitalize the first word of each line of poetry.

> My mind to me a kingdom is;
> Such present joys therein I find
> That it excels all other bliss
> That earth affords or grows by kind.
>   —Sir Edward Dyer (1540–1607)

RULE 5

Capitalize each amount when spelled out in formal or legal documents, as follows:

> Eighty-seven Dollars and Twenty-four Cents
> Sixty-four Thousand Dollars

RULE 6

Capitalize the first word in the salutation of a letter plus all nouns and titles in the salutation.

Dear Ms. Chang: Dear Professor Turner: My dear Sara,
Ladies and Gentlemen:

Note: "My dear" is appropriate for personal letters, but it is not used in business correspondence.

RULE 7

Capitalize only the first word in the complimentary close of a letter.

Sincerely yours,   Yours sincerely,   Very truly yours,

RULE 8

Capitalize the pronoun *I* and the interjection *Oh*. Unless you are writing advertising copy, you will seldom if ever have occasion to use *Oh* in business writing.

I'm due for a raise and, Oh, can I use it.

RULE 9

Capitalize the first letter of each important word in the title of a work of art or literature. Do not capitalize articles (*a, an, the*), short conjunctions, and short prepositions that occur in the middle of the title.

Have you read *How to Win Friends and Influence People?*
Washington's "Farewell Address" was his greatest speech.
She entitled her talk, "Russia, the Modern Dilemma."
Have you ever seen the painting "The Blue Boy"?
My latest book, *Delegating Power Throughout the System,* is on sale.

 ## RULE 10

Capitalize the following letters and abbreviations:

1. college degrees (*e.g.,* B.A., M.A., Ph.D.)
2. radio and television stations (*e.g.,* WNCN and WNET)
3. initials standing for proper names (*e.g.,* J.F.K. and F.D.R.)
4. abbreviations for proper nouns (*e.g.,* D.C. [District of Columbia])
5. two-letter state abbreviations such as IL (Illinois) and VT (Vermont). A complete list of these abbreviations is included in the Appendix.
6. abbreviation for number (No.):
Serial No. 486290
License No. S5506 87335 77923
Social Security No. 158-38-4654

Note: Do not use No. with invoices and models:

Invoices 24, 25, and 26; Model K35b25

Note: Do not capitalize the following abbreviations:

1. *a.m.* and *p.m.*: 9 a.m., 4 p.m. (In word processing, however, AM and PM are also acceptable.)
2. p. or pp. to indicate page numbers: p. 35, pp. 35–38.

 ## RULE 11

Capitalize all proper nouns and their derivatives. A proper noun refers to a specific person, place, or thing. For example:

George Washington   Canada   Toyota

The derivatives of proper nouns are also capitalized:

Canadian border   Shakespearean drama   Victorian England

Descriptive names that are often substituted for real proper nouns should also be capitalized.

Honest Abe (Abraham Lincoln)   the Windy City (Chicago)
the Sultan of Swat (Babe Ruth)   the Big Board (New York Stock Exchange)
the Big Apple (New York City)

Because company names, product names, and trade names are all proper nouns, business correspondence is full of proper nouns. Although you should have no difficulty knowing when to capitalize most of them, some of the rules are a bit tricky. The guidelines listed below will help you solve the capitalization problems of proper nouns that you may face when you are in the office. Study them carefully.

GUIDELINES ON CAPITALIZATION OF PROPER NOUNS

 ## GOD AND SACRED WORKS

Capitalize all nouns and pronouns that refer to God, the *Bible*, books of the *Bible*, and other sacred works.

God, the Father	the Trinity	*Talmud*
Koran	Book of Job	Ecclesiastes

> The Holy Scriptures tell us that God created the world in six days and that He rested on the seventh day.

 ## MONTHS AND DAYS

Always capitalize the names of months of the year, days of the week, and holidays.

> Classes begin on the last Monday in August, nearly one week before Labor Day.

 ## SEASONS

Never capitalize the names of seasons except in the rare instance when the season is being personified (*i.e.*, referred to as though it were a living being).

> Our fall order was not delivered until winter.
> Old Man Winter won't stop our snow tires from giving you perfect traction.

 ## DIRECTIONS

a. When the name of a direction refers to a specific section of the country or of the world, it then becomes a proper noun and it should be capitalized.

> The West is concerned about water development.
> The Southwest is growing rapidly in population and industry.
> The Mississippi flows through the North and the South.

b. When the name of a direction is used to refer to a point on the compass, it should not be capitalized.

> The plane circled twice, then headed west.
> Philadelphia is southwest of New York.
> The Mississippi flows from north to south.

c. *Eastern, Southern, Western,* and *Northern* are capitalized when used as part of the name of a major world division such as a hemisphere, a continent, or a nation. They are not capitalized when used as part of the name of a minor world division such as a state, a county, or a city.

> During recent years considerable economic consolidation has occurred in Western Europe.
> This particular sales territory includes eastern New York, northeastern Pennsylvania, and northern New Jersey.

d. Names derived from a particular geographical locality are capitalized.

> Southerner   Northerner

GEOGRAPHIC TERMS

A geographic term such as *river, ocean, mountain,* or *valley* may or may not be capitalized. The decision depends on its use in the sentence. Learn these three simple rules.

a. Capitalize a geographic term such as *river* when you use it as part of the name of a particular river or other geographic designation:

Hudson River   Pacific Ocean   Bear Mountain
Death Valley

b. Do not capitalize a geographic term such as *river* when it is placed before the name of the river:

  The river Jordan   The valley of the river Nile

  Exception: The word *mount* is capitalized when it precedes the name of the mountain.

Mount Everest   Mount Rainier   Mount Whitney

c. Do not capitalize a geographic term such as *river* when you use it in the plural.

  Missouri and Mississippi rivers   Appalachian and Rocky mountains
  Atlantic and Pacific oceans

 POLITICAL DESIGNATIONS

Political designations such as *state, city,* or *county* are always capitalized when they are a part of the specific name of the area.

Oklahoma City   New York State   Bucks County

When a political designation such as *state, city,* or *county* is written before the specific name, it may or may not be capitalized, depending upon its meaning in the sentence.

  The state of Nevada is famed for its scenic beauty.
  The State of Nevada has concluded its appeal to the United States Supreme Court.

 BUILDINGS

Similar rules govern the capitalization of words such as *building, highway, tunnel,* and *revolution.* Generally, capitalize such a word when you are using it as part of a specific name.

Biltmore Hotel   Empire State Building   French Revolution
Lincoln Highway

  But:

  French and American revolutions   Pan Am and Chrysler buildings
  Coventry and Grand hotels

 HISTORIC PERIODS AND EVENTS

Capitalize the names of historic events, periods, and documents, and well-known political policies.

the Revolutionary War   the Declaration of Independence
the Sixties   the New Deal
the Renaissance   the Monroe Doctrine

FAMILY RELATIONSHIPS

Capitalize words that show family relationships when the word precedes the person's name or is used in place of the person's name. Do not capitalize such a word when it is preceded by a possessive pronoun.

Aunt Martha   My father is visiting us this weekend.
My aunt   When is Mother coming?
We sent Aunt a card.

 TITLES

Usage varies regarding when to capitalize such titles as *president, treasurer, director,* etc. The practice in newspapers and magazines, for example, is to capitalize them as seldom as possible. The following guidelines are followed by most business writers.

1. The titles of high-ranking government officials and people in religious office are capitalized when they come before a name, follow a name, or replace a name.

   President Abraham Lincoln was assassinated in 1865.
   Abraham Lincoln, President of the United States, was assassinated in 1865.
   The President of the United States was assassinated in 1865.
   The Secretary of State met with the Russian Premier.
   The Pope visited the United States several years ago.
   Similar views were expressed by Archbishop Cardinal Cody.
   The featured speaker was Ella Grasso, Governor of Connecticut.
   While in London we saw the Prime Minister.
   The Vice President succeeds to the Presidency in the event of the death or resignation of the President.

2. The titles of business people are capitalized when they precede the name. They are not capitalized when they follow a name, replace a name, or are used in apposition to a name.

   Have you met Vice President McGee?
   We conferred with District Manager Alfredo Avilla regarding the proposal.
   Jane McGee, vice president of Allied Sales, met with us.
   We conferred with the district manager, Alfredo Avilla, regarding the proposal.
   The vice president met with us.
   We conferred with the district manager.
   The president of Allied Sales also serves as chairman of the board.

 ORGANIZATIONS

Do you capitalize the name of an organization, such as *company, association, commission,* or *department*?

a. These words are capitalized when they are part of the names of specific organizations:

   Business Department   National Association of Manufacturers
   American Steel Company   Sales Department

b. These words are capitalized when they are used as substitutes for the complete names of specific organizations.

   We in the Company take pride in our latest production record.
   The Association welcomes you to its vast membership.
   The Department has been awarded a trophy for outstanding employee cooperation.

But: There is a company in Denver with a fine production record.
A new association is being formed by lumber dealers across the continent.
Which department handles this problem?

Note: Although departments and divisions of your own company are capitalized, those of other organizations are not.

their sales department
his credit division
Refer the matter to their claims department for appropriate action.

 GOVERNMENT AGENCIES AND POLITICAL PARTIES

Capitalize the names of specific governmental agencies.

United States Senate	Air Force	Board of Elections
Court of Appeals	Police Department	Council of Foreign Ministers

Capitalize the names of political parties. *Party* may or may not be capitalized:

Democratic Party   Republican party

 FORMER TRADEMARKS

Certain words are derived from proper nouns but are not capitalized because they are now used as common nouns or as other parts of speech. You can make a fascinating study of former trademarks that have been deprived of their claim to a capital letter because the courts held that the words had become part of our everyday language. Here are a few examples:

aspirin	cellophane	escalator
shredded wheat	thermos bottle	

 SCHOOL SUBJECTS

Do not capitalize the name of any school subject or course of study except for a language or a specifically described course.

This year I am going to study shorthand and typing.
But: I added Shorthand IV and Advanced Typing to my schedule.
I am studying English, but not Spanish or mathematics.

Note: Capitalize the words *high school* and *college* only if the specific title of a particular school is used.

I went to Riverhead High School and then spent three years at college.

 PROGRAMMED REINFORCEMENT

S1 In which of the following should the first word *not* be capitalized? (a) a sentence; (b) a word or phrase used as a sentence substitute; (c) a direct quotation that is a complete sentence; (d) a direct quotation that is not a complete sentence; (e) the first word of each line of poetry;

R1 d.

S2   Which of the following should be capitalized in a salutation?
(a) the first word; (b) all nouns; (c) all titles; (d) all words

R2   a., b., c.

S3   What is the proper form for the following salutations?
a. **dear mom,**
b. **dear mr. bond:**
c. **ladies and gentlemen:**
d. **ms. olga stavros, project director**

R3   a. **Dear Mom,**
b. **Dear Mr. Bond:**
c. **Ladies and Gentlemen:**
d. **Ms. Olga Stavros,
Project Director**

S4   In the complimentary close of a letter, which words are capitalized? (a) none; (b) only the first; (c) all
Write the proper form of each of the following complimentary closes: **sincerely, yours truly, very truly yours,**

R4   b. **Sincerely, Yours truly,
Very truly yours,**

S5   College degrees, radio stations, and initials standing for proper names and nouns as well as important words in the titles of works of art and literature are capitalized. The abbreviations *a.m.* and *p.m.* are not. What is the correct capitalization of the following: **paula warner, ph.d., will discuss her recent book, <u>how to insure your future success,</u> this evening at 9 p.m. on radio station wvkc.**

R5   **Paula Warner, Ph.D., will discuss her recent book, <u>How to Insure Your Future Success,</u> this evening at 9 p.m. on radio station WVKC.**

S6   Proper nouns refer to a (general, specific) person, place or thing. Proper nouns (should, should not) be capitalized.

R6   specific, should

S7   Which of the following are normally capitalized?
a. days of the week
b. months of the year
c. seasons of the year

R7   a. and b.

S8   Correctly capitalize the following sentence: **This spring, classes will resume in april on the tuesday after easter.**

R8   **This spring, classes will resume in April on the Tuesday after Easter.**

S9   Which of the following is correct? (Check one)
a. All directions are capitalized.
b. No directions are capitalized.
c. Directions are capitalized only when they refer to a specific section of the country or world.

R9   c.

S10   Circle the direction(s) you would capitalize in this sentence: **The plant was located in the south about three miles east of Atlanta.**

R10   **South**

S11   *Eastern, southern, western,* and *northern* are capitalized only if they refer to major world divisions. They are not capitalized if they refer to a minor or local geographical division. Which words should be capitalized in these sentences?
     a. **Poland is part of eastern Europe.**
     b. **He works in northern Oregon.**

R11   **Eastern**

S12   A name derived from a particular geographical locality is capitalized. **She is a Southerner, but I am a Northerner.** Which words should be capitalized in this sentence: **I am a new englander who was born in the south.**

R12   **New Englander; South**

S13   Geographical terms such as *river, ocean, mountain,* or *valley* are capitalized when are used as part of a name. They are not capitalized when they precede the name. The word *mount* is an exception; it is capitalized even when it precedes the name of the mountain. Which words should be capitalized in these sentences:
     a. **the islands of the pacific and the valleys of the appalachians date back millions of years.**
     b. **The hudson river, which empties into the atlantic ocean, separates New York from New Jersey.**
     c. **The view of the pacific ocean from mount fuji is magnificent.**

R13   a. **Pacific; Appalachians**
       b. **Hudson River; Atlantic Ocean**
       c. **Pacific Ocean; Mount Fuji**

S14   Political designations such as *state, city,* or *county* are capitalized when they are part of the actual name of the area. Which of these are correct?
     a. **New York City is the largest city in America.**
     b. **Washington State borders on Canada.**
     c. **Dade county is in Florida.**

R14   a. and b.

S15   Words like *hotel, highway, tunnel,* or *revolution* are capitalized when they are part of the proper name. Circle any errors in this sentence: **The Plaza hotel can be reached by the Lincoln tunnel or the George Washington bridge.**

R15   **Hotel; Tunnel; Bridge**

S16   Which of the following names should be capitalized?
     a. historic events
     b. historic periods
     c. historic documents
     d. well-known political policies
     e. all of the above

R16   e.

S17   Words that show family relationships are capitalized
     a. when the word precedes the person's name
     b. when the word is used in place of the person's name
     c. when the word is preceded by a possessive pronoun

R17   a. and b.

S18 Which words should be capitalized in these sentences?
  a. **My mother lost her savings in the great depression.**
  b. **When is father coming home?**
  c. **I understand that uncle eddie is an authority on the policies of the new deal.**

R18 a. **the Great Depression**
  b. **Father**
  c. **Uncle Eddie, the New Deal**

S19 In business, titles of high-ranking government officials are capitalized
  a. when they precede the person's name
  b. when they follow the person's name
  c. when they are used in place of the person's name
  d. all of the above

R19 d.

S20 Titles of people in business are capitalized
  a. when they precede the person's name
  b. when they follow the person's name
  c. when they take the place of the person's name
  d. when they are used in apposition to the person's name
  e. all of the above

R20 a.

S21 Which words should be capitalized in the following sentences?
  a. **The president and the secretary of state greeted the chinese premier at the white house.**
  b. **The corporate vice president met privately with the treasurer.**
  c. **Wendell Tyler, our chairman of the board, is the older brother of senator Ralph Tyler.**

R21 a. **The President and the Secretary of State greeted the Chinese Premier at the White House.**
  b. **correct as written**
  c. **Wendell Tyler, our chairman of the board, is the older brother of Senator Ralph Tyler.**

S22 Names of organizations such as *company, association,* or *department* are capitalized when they are part of the name of a specific organization. They are also capitalized when used as substitutes for the complete names of specific organizations. Which words should be capitalized in these sentences?
  a. **The association welcomes you as a new member.**
  b. **An association of publishers may be formed.**
  c. **June Spencer, president of the business education association, spoke at the meeting.**

R22 a. **Association**
  b. **none**
  c. **Business Education Association**

S23 School subjects are not capitalized, except for languages or specifically described courses. Circle the subjects incorrectly capitalized in this sentence: **He studied Mathematics, English, Advanced Algebra II, and Typing in school.**

R23 **mathematics; typing**

S24 The words *high school* and *college* are not capitalized unless they are part of a specific school name. Which words should be capitalized in this sentence? **After graduating from Jefferson high school, she decided to work rather than go on to college.**

R24 **High School**

S25 As a review, circle the words you would capitalize in these sentences:
   a. **My employer, karl schmitz, started the olympic printing company in the summer of 1964 in the southern part of new england.**
   b. **After moving the plant from the mohawk valley to get hudson river power, he was elected president of the printers association of america.**
   c. **Ms. desai then taught a course in english at newark college of engineering for students with high school diplomas.**

R25 a. **Karl Schmitz; Olympic Printing Company; New England**
   b. **Mohawk Valley; Hudson River; Printers Association of America**
   c. **Desai; English; Newark College of Engineering**

Turn to Exercise 20.1.

WORD DIVISION

When a word cannot be completed at the end of a line, it is divided by a **hyphen**.

> He was surprised to discover just how diffi-
> cult it was to find replacement parts.

The trend in letter writing in business today is to avoid the use of word divisions whenever possible. Your guiding rule when typing copy, therefore, should be to divide words only when it is absolutely necessary to do so to maintain a reasonably even right margin. A line of type that is five spaces longer is acceptable in business practice.

Observe the following rules about word division whether you are using a typewriter or word processor:

1. When dividing a word, type a hyphen at the end of the first line, not at the beginning of the second.
2. Divide words only between syllables. Consult your dictionary to see how words are properly divided (syllabicated).
3. You may not divide one-syllable words. For example, *walked, punched, thought,* and *through* may not be divided.
4. You should not divide a two-syllable word of five or fewer letters. For example, *again, ago, also,* and *elate* should not be divided.
5. A two-syllable word may not be divided if one of the syllables consists of only one letter. The word *consists* may be divided into *con-sists.* The word *arouse* may not be divided into *a-rouse.*
6. When the middle syllable of a word is a single vowel, that vowel should come at the end of the first line, not at the beginning of the second. The word *hesitate* (hes-i-tate) should be divided as *hesi-tate,* not *hes-itate.* So, too, *accompaniment* should be divided as *accompani-ment* rather than *accompan-iment.* However, when the single vowel is part of the suffixes *able, ible,* or *ity,* then divide the word before the vowel: *reli-able, forc-ible, secur-ity.*
7. Do not divide a proper noun, a contraction, an abbreviation, or a number.

ACCEPTABLE	UNACCEPTABLE	UNACCEPTABLE
Kathleen J. Kazmark	Kathleen J. Kazmark	Kath- leen J. Kazmark
Cleveland, Ohio	Cleve- land, Ohio	
May 24, 1945	May 24, 1945	
Serial No. 756-89354	Serial No. 756- 89354	
4321 N. Valley Road	4321 N. Valley Road	43- 21 N. Valley Road

8. If possible, do not divide a word if it is the last word of a paragraph or a page.
9. Do not end more than two successive lines with a divided word.
10. Carry over at least three letters to the second line.

| **Correct:** | shortly | lux-ury | con-sumer |
| **Incorrect:** | short-ly | luxu-ry | consum-er |

11. Divide hyphenated compound words only at a point where a hyphen naturally occurs.

sister-in-law   self-control   above-mentioned

12. As a general rule, divide words between double letters unless the word is derived from one that ends in a double letter (*small*). In the latter case, the word is divided after the root word.

small-est   stuff-ing   excel-lence
woo-ing   rub-ber   win-ning

PROGRAMMED REINFORCEMENT

S26 In business correspondence when is it appropriate to divide a word?
a. whenever it is convenient
b. only when absolutely necessary
c. never

R26 b.

S27 A hyphen is used to divide a word at the end of a line. The hyphen is placed (at the end of that line, at the beginning of the next line).

R27 at the end of that line

S28 Words may be divided (a) only between syllables, (b) anywhere that is convenient.

R28 a.

S29 Words of only one syllable (may, may not) be divided. Words of fewer than six letters (may, may not) be divided.

R29 may not; may not

R30   **through, rely, able, straight**

S30   Circle the words that should *not* be divided. **through thorough rely reliance ability able straight**

R31   may not; may not

S31   You (may, may not) divide a word so that only one letter is left at the end of the first line. You (may, may not) carry over only one or two letters to the next line.

S32   Circle the words in the following list that should not be divided: **hardness emerge afraid reserve surely hardly emergent handily batted**

R32   **emerge; afraid; surely; hardly**

S33   When a middle syllable is composed of a single letter (like the **e** in **plan-e-tary**), that letter should be placed at the end of the first line, not at the beginning of the second. Place a slash (/) to show where you should break these words: **cal-o-rie cap-i-tal cat-a-log cel-e-brate log-i-cal**

R33   **calo/rie; capi/tal; cata/log; cele/brate; logi/cal**

S34   Circle which of the following may be divided.
(a) proper nouns;   (d) numbers;
(b) contractions;   (e) none of the above
(c) abbreviations;

R34   e.

S35   Where may hyphenated words be divided?
a. only where the hyphen occurs
b. anywhere that conforms with the normal rules of word division

R35   a.

S36   In most cases words are divided between double letters. If the word is derived from one that ends in a double letter, however, the word is divided after the root word. Use a slash (/) to indicate where each of the following words should be divided: **billing smallest running excellent follow innate**

R36   **bill/ing small/est run/ning excel/lent fol/low in/nate**

S37   Use one or more slashes (/) to indicate where to break the following words. If you should not break a word, put a circle around it: **a-dopt ad-u-late af-firm-er a-gent a-gree-ment al-ler-gy al-ler-gic al-le-vi-ate**

R37   **adopt; adu/late; af/firmer; agent; agree/ment; al/lergy; al/ler/gic; al/le/vi/ate**

Turn to Exercises 20.2 and 20.3.

 NUMBERS

The expression of numbers, like capitalization, is a matter of convention, and not all authorities agree completely on what these conventions are. The general trend in business writing today is to express numbers as figures, rather than as words, whenever possible. Numbers written as figures are shorter and more easily understood than those written in words. Numbers that appear in invoices, purchase orders, billing statements, sales slips, and so forth are always written as figures. In sentences, however, numbers are sometimes expressed in figures and sometimes in words. The following guidelines explain the generally agreed-upon conventions for the expression of numbers in business communication.

1. As a rule, indefinite numbers are expressed in words and specific numbers are expressed in figures.

    Over two hundred people attended the conference.
    There were 206 people at the conference.

2. In general, the numbers from one to ten are spelled out. Numbers above ten are expressed as figures.

    The committee consists of six members and one alternate.
    There are 36 full-time members of our department.
    There are 427 parking spaces in Lot A.

    Note 1: Page numbers in a book are always expressed in figures: p. 6, p. 125, pp. 42–45.
    Note 2: For ease of reading, round numbers in millions or billions are expressed in a combination of figures and words.

    The proposed legislation would raise an estimated $2 billion.
    Over 6.5 million people voted in the last statewide election.

    Note 3: Numbers in formal invitations and announcements are expressed in words.

    . . . on Saturday, the twenty-eighth of December, nineteen hundred and seventy-four.

3. Numbers that appear at the beginning of a sentence should be spelled out. If the number is long, reword the sentence to avoid awkwardness.

    Avoid: 27 employees were promoted recently.
    Use: Twenty-seven employees were promoted recently.

    Avoid: 337 people attended the retirement dinner.
    Acceptable: Three hundred thirty-seven people attended the retirement dinner.
    Preferred: There were 337 people in attendance at the retirement dinner.

4. Sometimes several numbers appear in the same sentence or paragraph. In such cases, to ensure uniformity, observe the following guidelines.

    a. Numbers performing a similar or related function should be expressed in the same way. They should all be expressed as the largest number is expressed.

    Three students were absent from class on Monday, four more were absent on Wednesday, and a total of ten were absent on Friday.
    Only 5 of the 74 people surveyed were opposed to the proposal.

    b. When numbers are performing different or unrelated functions, a mixed style is acceptable. Follow the guidelines presented above.

    The three surveys were administered to 73 personnel over a period of five months.

    c. When two numbers appear consecutively without any intervening punctuation, the shorter or less complicated number is expressed in words.

There are 24 twelve-page contracts to read and sign.
We printed 500 forty-page pamphlets this morning.
She bought eighteen 89-cent refills.

5. Indefinite amounts of money are expressed in words; exact amounts are expressed in figures.

Total sales in our department last week exceeded nine thousand dollars.
Total sales in our department last week were $9,345.

Note: Some writers always use figures in expressing amounts of money. They would write "Total sales in our department last week exceeded $9,000."

When expressing whole dollar amounts, do not include the decimal point and zeros except for purposes of uniformity.

Right: These cassettes cost $12 each.
Wrong: These cassettes cost $12.00 each.

Right: This appliance has a wholesale price of $67.50 and a retail price of $125.00.
Wrong: This appliance has a wholesale price of $67.50 and a retail price of $125.

In legal documents both words and figures are used. The words are all capitalized and the figures are placed in parentheses.

Seven Hundred Thirty Dollars ($730)

6. The time is written in figures when *a.m.* or *p.m.* follows, but in words when *o'clock* follows.

The meeting began promptly at 9 a.m. and concluded at 11 a.m.
Ms. Hitashi was in conference from 10:00 a.m. until 2:45 p.m.
Ms. Hitashi was in conference from ten o'clock that morning until nearly three o'clock that afternoon.

Note: As the above examples illustrate, when expressing time on the hour, you should leave the colon and zeros out except for purposes of uniformity.

7. In the writing of street addresses, building numbers (except for the number One) are written as figures. Street names of ten and below are written as words; street names above ten are written in figures.

The company's general offices are at One Congress Plaza.
Our local branch office recently moved from 125 Third Street to 47 39th Street.

When a compass direction separates a house number from a street number, current practice is to leave out the *th*.

Their address is 431 North 17 Avenue.

8. Figures are used to express numbers in the following situations.

a. market quotations

Our stock closed this week at 23½.

b. dimensions

The opening measures 6 inches by 8 inches.

c. temperatures

At noon the temperature was 7 degrees (or 7°).

d. decimals

These machine parts have a tolerance of .005 inch.

e. pages and divisions of a book

The charts appear on pp. 214–217 of Vol. 3.

f. weights and measures

These canisters weigh less than 20 pounds, but they will hold 125 gallons of fuel.

g. identification numbers

The newscaster on Channel 5 reported that, because of the accident, Route 80 was closed at Exit 39.

9. tables

SIZE OF FRESHMAN CLASS, 1982–1985

Year	Number	Percentage	Cumulative Percentage
1982	1652		
1983	1567	−5.3	
1984	1480	−5.6	−10.6
1985	1391	−6.0	−16.0

10. phone numbers

Please call us at (201) 893-4000 for further information.

11. dates

The contract was signed on August 16, 1977.
The contract was signed on 16 August 1977.

12. percentages

The local bank is offering mortgage rates of 11 percent.

PROGRAMMED REINFORCEMENT

S38 In business writing, numbers are usually expressed in figures; within sentences, however, numbers may be expressed in words. As a rule in sentences, indefinite numbers are expressed in (words, figures) and specific numbers are expressed in (words, figures).

R38 words; figures

S39 Generally, numbers from one to ten are expressed in _____; numbers above ten are expressed in _____.

R39 words; figures

S40 Are the numbers in the following sentences expressed correctly? Write *yes* or *no* after each sentence.
a. **There are 346 full-time employees on our payroll.** _____
b. **We employ about 200 part-time employees.** _____
c. **I must complete 3 more reports before the end of the month.** _____
d. **I processed 17 requests for reimbursement today.** _____

R40 a. Yes b. No c. No d. Yes

S41 For ease of reading, round numbers in millions and billions are expressed (a) completely in words; (b) completely in figures; (c) in a combination of figures and words. Revise the following sentence to make it easier to read.
Total profits over the three-year period rose from $137,000,000 to four hundred seventeen million dollars.

R41 c. **Total profits . . . rose from $137 million to $417 million.**

S42 Numbers that appear at the beginning of a sentence should be expressed in (words, figures). Awkward sentences should be recast. Revise the following sentences.
a. **12 people in our division are ill with the flu.**
b. **One thousand four hundred and eighteen students were admitted to this year's freshman class.**

R42 words;
a. **Twelve people in our division are ill with the flu.**
b. **There were 1418 students admitted to this year's freshman class.**

S43 When several numbers appear in the same sentence or paragraph, those performing a similar function should be expressed in the same way. Numbers performing unrelated functions may be expressed differently. Revise the following sentences where necessary.
a. **Copies of the 4 reports were distributed to all 85 employees in less than 2 days.**
b. **Only 3 of the 61 people in our division were not recommended for a full salary increment.**

R43 a. **Copies of the four reports were distributed to all 85 employees in less than two days.**
b. **Correct as written.**

S44 Indefinite amounts of money are expressed in (words, figures); exact amounts of money are expressed in (words, figures).

R44 words; figures

S45 Revise the following sentences where necessary.
a. **I have exactly $93.46 in my checking account.**
b. **I have less than $100 in my checking account.**

R45
a. Correct as written
b. **I have less than one hundred dollars in my checking account.**

S46 An expression of time is written in (words, figures) when *a.m.* or *p.m.* follows; it is written in (words, figures) when *o'clock* follows. Which of the following are correct?
a. **I will finish this report before 5 o'clock.**
b. **I will finish this report before five o'clock.**
c. **It's ten p.m. Do you know where your children are?**
d. **It's 10 p.m. Do you know where your children are?**

R46 figures; words; b and d are correct

S47 Write *words* or *figures* to show how to express the following in street addresses.
a. building numbers _____
b. street names of ten and below _____
c. street names above ten _____

R47
a. figures
b. words
c. figures

S48 Words are used to express numbers in which of the following situations?
a. page numbers   b. dimensions
c. temperatures   d. decimals
e. phone numbers   f. dates
g. percentages   h. all of the above
i. none of the above

R48 i.

Turn to Exercises 20.4 to 20.7.

EXERCISE 20·1A   CAPITALIZATION

Below is a series of excerpts taken from business correspondence. If the capitalization is correct as it appears, place a C in the answer space. If the capitalization is incorrect, in the answer space write the word or words as they should appear.

1. She felt that management "wanted nothing changed . . . ."   1. _____

2. He said, "the report erroneously stated . . . ."   2. _____

3. He said that the report "erroneously stated . . . ."   3. _____

4. Leah explained: "first, I want to say . . . ."   4. _____

5. dear Mrs. Benson: 5. _____

6. Yours truly,   6. _____

7. Very Truly Yours,   7. _____

8. . . . my other text, *Business Spelling And Word Power,*   8. _____

9. "My employer," she began, "Is one . . . ."   9. _____

10. . . . Three hundred dollars ($300) . . .   10. _____

11. Ladies and gentlemen: 11. _____

12. . . . the book *Corruption throughout the System* . . .   12. _____

13. . . . social security no. 158-58-8558   13. _____

14. . . . at 7:00 P.M. the following evening   14. _____

15. . . . found on P. 26 of your text   15. _____

16. . . . Janice's PH.D. exams . . .   16. _____

17. . . . radio station WFLN   17. _____

18. . . . Leonardo's "the Last Supper"   18. _____

19. . . . this morning at 6:30 a.m.   19. _____

20. Bernice said, "I can't, but, oh, I wish . . . ."   20. _____

Some words that should be capitalized are not capitalized. Other words that should not be capitalized are capitalized. Cross out all incorrect letters and write the correct form above each.

1. The Medlock tool co. appreciates the Information it received from you on October 17.

2. Our Local board of education is seeking bids on the new School.

3. The Dade county vocational institute has a new superintendent, samuel Jones.

4. Allen and Bianca, inc., received your Order for the Fall line early in September.

5. Mr. Robert c. Phillips, chairman of the Firm of Phillips and sons, intends to open up the northwest as its newest market.

6. The Carlsbad and lenox Hotels are located South of Main street.

7. The new England Advertising Agency of Bemis, Baumer, and Beard offers exceptional coverage as far South as Northern New Jersey.

8. The chevrolet is a popular car in the south.

9. The Southern part of texas is hottest in the summer.

10. The ohio river flows from East to West.

11. Every person of spanish descent should know some spanish.

12. The united nations building is near the east river.

13. The united states supreme court is our highest tribunal.

14. The department Supervisor of stern's Department Store spoke yesterday.

15. It is unnecessary to italicize words like platonic or pasteurize.

16. She graduated from High School and went to Yale university.

17. The river nile is longer than the hudson river.

18. Our vice President is brushing up on her french by vacationing in Southern France this summer.

19. We have inquired of our Attorney, ms. lynn s. sauer, to ascertain our Rights against the Omega insurance co.

20. The assistant director of The Lakeland hotel is Michael Mccallum, jr.

21. The president left the white house at Noon and rushed to the airport via the Expressway.

22. The Bookkeeper passed her c.p.a. Examination.

23. The u. s. s. president Pierce is in its Berth in liverpool, england, awaiting its scheduled crossing of the atlantic ocean next summer.

24. The american society for the prevention of cruelty to animals is known as the a. s. p. c. a.

25. According to mr. James a. vulcan, secretary of the american association of manufacturers, the northwest is a fertile field for expansion; however, secretary Vulcan warns against too great reliance upon the federal government. He feels that congress will not make any substantial Appropriations during its Spring session.

EXERCISE 20·2A   WORD DIVISION

This exercise involves the use of the hyphen to divide words at the end of a line. Assume that each of the following words comes at the end of a line. In the spaces provided, write the two parts into which the word should be divided. Consult your dictionary if necessary.

1. problem
2. narrate
3. amount
4. hopeful
5. message
6. natural
7. question
8. inert
9. innate
10. legible
11. consumer
12. manager
13. idea
14. straight
15. planning
16. smallest
17. sofa
18. dwelling
19. swiftly
20. luxury
21. modem
22. suggest
23. program
24. abound
25. self-fulfillment

EXERCISE 20·2B   WORD DIVISION

Cross out any word or words in each of the following groups of words that is divided incorrectly or that does not follow preferred word-division style. In the answer space, write the correct division of each word you crossed out. If there are no errors, write C in the answer space. The / represents the place where the hyphen should be placed.

1.	adminis/tration	depend/able	employ/er	1. _____
2.	confi/dent	ef/fect	indeb/tedness	2. _____
3.	sug/gest	a/bound	coopera/tive	3. _____
4.	twel/fth	ap/proval	volun/teer	4. _____
5.	bul/letin	ac/cess	practi/cal	5. _____
6.	bus/iness	a/lign	per/sonal	6. _____
7.	pro/gress	ho/tel	question/naire	7. _____
8.	alumi/num	mor/tgage	bu/reau	8. _____
9.	com/fort	al/ready	conven/ience	9. _____
10.	adequ/ate	ship/ped	recog/nize	10. _____
11.	remit/tance	doc/ument	occa/sion	11. _____
12.	in/voice	grad/uate	cour/tesy	12. _____
13.	differ/ence	ter/ritory	ob/serve	13. _____
14.	corpor/ation	physi/cian	spel/ling	14. _____
15.	represen/tative	justi/fy	begin/ning	15. _____
16.	pre/paration	recom/mendation	con/nection	16. _____
17.	organi/zation	condi/tion	mod/ern	17. _____
18.	cas/ual	tele/phone	import/ant	18. _____
19.	sister-/in-law	nota/tion	manage/ment	19. _____
20.	defin/ite	ap/point	lei/sure	20. _____

EXERCISE 20·2C **WORD DIVISION**

Rewrite each item below to show the preferred word or word-division ending for the end of the line. If the item may not be divided, rewrite it in full.

1. January

2. Chicago, Illinois

3. November 17, 1984

4. Mr. Andrew R. Cooper

5. 138-48-9760

6. modification (last word on a page)

7. economical (last word in a paragraph)

8. UNICEF

9. Minneapolis

10. 245 Main Street

1. _____

2. _____

3. _____

4. _____

5. _____

6. _____

7. _____

8. _____

9. _____

10. _____

EXERCISE 20·3 COMPOSITION: WORD DIVISION

For each of the following words in parentheses, show how you would divide the word at the end of a line and explain why you would divide it that way. Use complete sentences.

1. (business)

   _____
   _____
   _____

2. (counselor-at-law)

   _____
   _____
   _____

3. (satisfy)

   _____
   _____
   _____

4. (beginning)

   _____
   _____
   _____

5. (adaptable)

   _____
   _____
   _____

EXERCISE 20·4A   **NUMBERS**

Assume that the following items appear in business correspondence. If they are wrongly expressed, write the correct form in the space provided. If they are expressed correctly, write C in the space.

1. approximately two hundred people   1. _____

2. exactly two hundred and fourteen people   2. _____

3. only 3 committee members   3. _____

4. a department of 42 full-time faculty   4. _____

5. nearly 14,500,000 voters   5. _____

6. p. six in your text   6. _____

7. over $47,000,000,000 annually   7. _____

8. need 36 20-cent stamps   8. _____

9. Four thousand Dollars ($4,000)   9. _____

10. 8 o'clock   10. _____

11. six p.m.   11. _____

12. reviewed 20 twelve-page contracts   12. _____

13. located at One Lexington Avenue   13. _____

14. located at 134 7th Ave.   14. _____

15. a temperature of eight degrees   15. _____

16. a tolerance of three one-thousandths of an inch   16. _____

17. Exit 15 on Route 6   17. _____

18. November twenty-fourth   18. _____

19. twelve percent   19. _____

20. November 22nd   20. _____

21. an annual salary of $26,500   21. _____

22. 6th Avenue   22. _____

23. nearly 3/4 of our employees   23. _____

24. only $.79 each   24. _____

25. Twelfth Street   25. _____

EXERCISE 20·4B   NUMBERS

Each of the following sentences contains one or more errors in the expression of numbers. Cross out all errors and make the necessary corrections in the space above them.

1. One reliable authority estimates that nearly 72,000,000,000 documents are created each year.

2. Standard office stationery measures eight-and-one-half inches by eleven inches.

3. You may use either the small No. 6¾ business envelope or the large No. ten envelope.

4. If a reduction ratio of forty-two to one is used, three hundred and twenty-five standard pages can be recorded on a single sheet of microfiche.

5. On December fourteenth Alba submitted three receipts for out-of-pocket expenses: $17.25, 89 cents, and $3.

6. By 3 o'clock that afternoon Jo's temperature had dropped to ninety-nine point eight degrees.

7. Her 20 supporters took seats in the 1st, 3rd, and 4th rows.

8. The new director of operations is not yet 40 years old, but she has nearly 10 years of administrative experience.

9. Fewer than 3,000,000 people voted in the last state election.

10. Chapter Twenty, entitled "Report Writing," begins on page four hundred.

11. These three styles cost seventy-five cents, eighty-nine cents, and $1.09 respectively.

12. Go to the store on Twelfth Avenue and purchase four more eight-inch diskettes.

13. 146 leases must be renewed by June first.

14. Of the proposed twenty-two chapters in the book, two have yet to be written and six more require substantial revision.

15. He appended Schedule Thirty-four Sixty-eight to IRS Form Ten Forty and mailed his return before the April fifteenth deadline.

16. Most retailers operate on a markup of 100%.

17. Did you say 6th Street or 16th Street?

18. The drawer measured twelve inches by eighteen inches by three inches.

19. Figure Two appears on p. eight.

20. I must raise $1,700,000 by 2 o'clock tomorrow.

21. The Business Department comprises ten assistant professors, eleven associate professors, and six full professors.

22. I waited for the doctor from eleven-thirty a.m. until one-fifteen p.m.

23. Almost 400 people waited in front of the theater on 15th St. for nearly 2 hours hoping to see him.

24. Our company operates a small fleet of 8 6-cylinder and 4 8-cylinder trucks.

25. The 4 surveys were administered to 65 employees during a period of 3 months.

EXERCISE 20·5 COMPOSITION: NUMBERS

Each of the following sentences contains an error in the expression of numbers. Correct the error and then explain the correction you made. Use complete sentences.

1. I have only twenty-five dollars to spend, but the least expensive model costs $39.95. _____
_____
_____

2. Don't miss the 1 o'clock train because the next one doesn't come until 4. _____
_____
_____

3. Our current address is Three West Sixty-fourth Street, but we will soon be moving to Thirty West
Seventieth Street. _____
_____

4. We have already distributed all 1000 12-page brochures. _____
_____
_____

5. 217 burglaries were reported in this area last month. _____
_____
_____

5. Only five of the 15 people questioned could identify the candidate by name. _____
_____
_____

7. The new tax is expected to raise in excess of $1,300,000,000 in the first two years. _____
_____
_____

8. The maximum seating in this restaurant is one hundred eighty-five. _____
_____
_____

CAPITALIZATION, WORD DIVISION, EXPRESSION OF NUMBERS

The following letter is written without any capital letters. Cross out each lowercase letter that should be capitalized and write the capital letter above it. Also correct any errors in the expression of numbers and word division. If a word is incorrectly divided, divide it correctly. Do not change any words that are correctly divided.

may 17, 19xx

mr. sean murphy

127 fourteenth street, apt. twelve

new york, new york 10010

dear mr. murphy:

are you one of the many new york city businesspeople who would like to spend a few days or a few weeks in the country, but whose busi-ness interests demand that you not venture far from manhattan? the ho-tel gramatan in the hills of westchester county, midway between the scen-ic hudson river and long island sound, offers you a most inviting home twenty-three miles and 38 minutes from grand central terminal, the heart of the shopping and theater district.

the hotel is of moorish design, and the wide spanish balconies encircling it are literally "among the tree tops."

accommodations are on the american plan, with rates considera-bly less than the cost of equivalent accommodations in town: single room and board, $450 per week and upward; large room and private bath with board for two people, $690 per week and upward. our exceptional dining facilities, with seating for over 200 people, are open from six a.m. to 11:30 p.m.

the hotel offers an excellent golf course, 8 of the best ten-nis courts in westchester county, a string of fine saddle horses, and 100's of miles of good country roads for motoring and driving.

charlotte vandermere, drama critic of <u>the</u> <u>new</u> <u>york</u> <u>times</u>, visited the hotel gramatan in july of last year. upon her return to new york, she wrote the following in her column, "going on in new york": "the hotel gramatan is one of the finest hotels i have ever visited. its european cuisine is excel-lent."

why don't you take a drive up the scenic hutchinson river park-way to exit seventeen and visit the gramatan some time this fall?

very respectfully yours,

EXERCISE 20·7   COMPOSITION: WRITING A COMPLAINT LETTER

Sometimes problems are not so simple and easy to correct as the error regarding the magazine subscription in the previous chapter. Still, when you feel you have been treated very badly or when a product or service does not meet reasonable expectations, you have every right to expect the company to make some sort of adjustment or, at the very least, offer you an apology. Just remember that no matter how angry you are, a moderate, reasonable tone is more likely to elicit a favorable response than an angry one.

Write your own complaint letter about some problem you've recently experienced (e.g., discourteous treatment by salespeople, poor service, merchandise of inferior quality). Tell the company to whom you are writing what happened, why you are unhappy, and what you want them to do. Write your letter in the space below.

21

GLOSSARY OF PROPER USAGE
WORDS FREQUENTLY CONFUSED OR MISUSED

So far we have discussed how to use the eight parts of speech correctly, how to compose and punctuate grammatically correct sentences, and how to apply the rules covering accepted styles for capitalization, word division, and the presentation of numbers. In this chapter we are going to discuss the correct use of words that many people frequently confuse or misuse. When these words are not used correctly, serious writing problems can result.

To begin, look at the following sentence. It contains a number of errors. How would you correct it?

> Mr. Ortega whom is our principle stockhold-
> er is anxious to have purchased shares in
> two other companys, however he lacks sufficient
> capitol.

Write your corrected version here:

_____

_____

_____

Here is the preceding sentence with all corrections made. Compare your version with it.

> Mr. Ortega, who is our principal stockholder,
> is eager to purchase shares in two other
> companies; however, he lacks sufficient capital.

You probably corrected the errors in punctuation, word division, pronoun case, noun plural, and verb tense. Did you also change *principle* to *principal*, *anxious* to *eager*, and *capitol* to *capital*? The difference in each case is not a matter of *spelling*, but *meaning*. *Principal* and *principle*, for example, are *homonyms*. They sound alike, but they are spelled differently and have different meanings. They are not interchangeable. In this sentence *principal* (meaning *primary*) is the correct word. *Principle* (meaning a *rule* or *standard*) is wrong. Similarly, *anxious* and *capitol* are incorrect. Each is spelled correctly, but in the context of the sentence, each is the wrong word. Looking the word up in the dictionary to be sure you have spelled it correctly is of no value if it is the wrong word in the context of the sentence. Hence in studying and using the pairs of words presented in this chapter, you must concentrate on the *meaning* of each word.

In our sample passage, if *principle*, *anxious*, and *capitol* are not corrected, the passage actually says this:

> Mr. Ortega, who is our fundamental rule or doctrine stockholder, is very worried to purchase shares in two other companies; however, he lacks sufficient building where the legislature meets.

Clearly, writers who misuse words this way convey a very poor impression. If you received a memo or letter that contained this passage, how would you feel about the writer? Would you think the writer was careful? reliable? competent? Would you want that writer to work for you?

The incorrect choice of words can harm the writer in other ways. For instance, when Carole opened her new bathroom and kitchen boutique, she wrote and distributed a sales leaflet describing some of her featured merchandise. She particularly called people's attention to some beautiful table linens with "complimentary placemats." She was delighted at the number of people who came into the store in response to her flier. She was not delighted to learn that most people had come in to obtain their free placemats. Carole should have written "complementary placemats."

Misusing words in this fashion also affects the reader. It is distracting for a reader to stop to correct an error, mentally supplying the correct word in place of the word that is there. A reader cannot concentrate on the writer's message when he or she has to put up with such interruptions.

Sometimes the writer's intended meaning itself can be unclear. Then the reader is simply confused. For example, suppose you received a report recommending the purchase of more "stationary cabinets." Would you think that the writer meant cabinets that stayed in one place as opposed to ones that were on wheels? Or would you think the writer obviously meant cabinets to hold writing supplies and had written the wrong word? Suppose you received the following instruction: "Please appraise your staff." What would you do? Would you evaluate your staff? Or would you think the writer wanted you to tell them something and had mistakenly used "appraise" instead of "apprise"?

As you can see, the incorrect substitution of one word for another can affect both the writer and the reader in significant ways. It also can have a more general effect on the quality and precision of our language. For example, there is a very useful distinction between *disinterested* (neutral, impartial) and *uninterested* (indifferent to, uncaring). Many people use *disinterested* when they mean *uninterested*. If enough people fail to make the distinction, in time the word *disinterested* will mean *uninterested*. It will no longer mean *neutral*. Similarly, if we continue to say *anxious* when we really mean *eager*, in time *anxious* will come to mean *eager*. The sense of anxiety this word should properly convey, in contrast to eagerness, will be lost. We express ideas through language. When we lose a word, we lose some of our language. We lose some of our capacity for expressing ideas.

Thus in writing or editing you must be conscious not only of the rules of grammar and punctuation but also of the proper selection of words. Remember, this is not a question of spelling; it is a matter of meaning. You must know what the words mean and in what situation to use them.

This chapter presents an alphabetical list of those words that many people confuse or misuse. Each word is defined and illustrated so that you can see clearly the context in which it is used correctly. Because the errors that result from the misuse or confusion of these words can be easily corrected, we have not included any Programmed Reinforcement in this chapter.

 # 1.   ACCEPT/EXCEPT

Accept is a verb meaning *to consent to, agree to* or *to take willingly, to receive.*

I am pleased to accept your offer.
I accept your decision.
Will you accept a collect call from Mr. Ishi Takai?

Except is normally a preposition meaning *with the exclusion of, other than, but.*

All the packages except one have arrived.

Except is also used as a conjunction meaning *if it were not for the fact that.*

I would buy this personal computer except it costs too much.

2.   ACCESS/EXCESS

Access means a passage, a way, a means, or admittance. It can be used as a noun or a verb.

Notice: Driver does not have access to safe.
Joe will not have access to his inheritance for another two years.
All branch officers may access the central data bank.

Excess refers to an amount or degree beyond what is normal or required.

The chef trimmed the excess fat from the steaks.
One should never do anything to excess.

3.   ADAPT/ADOPT/ADEPT

Adapt and *adopt* are verbs. When you *adapt* something, you change or adjust it for a new situation or purpose.

These plans can be adapted to fit your needs.
This text can be adapted to a variety of teaching situations.

When you *adopt* something, you take it and use it as your own.

We will adopt your proposal.
Your instructor adopted this book for your course.

Adept is an adjective. When you are *adept,* you are very skillful or expert in what you do.

Marie is adept in designing merchandise displays.

4.   ADVICE/ADVISE

Advice is a noun meaning *opinion, counsel.*
Advise is a verb meaning *to offer advice, to counsel.*

I need your advice.
What is your advice regarding this problem?
What do you advise me to do?

In business writing, *advise* is also often used to mean *to inform, to notify.*

Please advise me of your decision regarding this contract.
Please advise me when you receive the shipment.

5.   AFFECT/EFFECT

Affect is a verb usually meaning *to influence.*

This new government regulation will affect our annual sales.
I hope I can affect your decision.

Effect is usually used as a noun meaning *result.*

Her speech had the desired effect.
What will be the effect of this new government regulation on our annual sales?

In plural form *effects* can also mean *belongings* or *property.*

She kept her personal effects in the top drawer of her desk.

Effect can also be used as a verb meaning *to bring about.*

We intend to effect a few minor changes in company policy.
The report affected (influenced) the board's policy.
The report effected (brought about) the board's policy.

 ## 6.   AIN'T

Ain't is a nonstandard contraction of *am not.* Some people also use it to mean *are not, is not, has not,* and *have not. Ain't* is not standard English usage and is always unacceptable.

I'm not going. (Not: I *ain't* going.)
He isn't going. (Not: He *ain't* going.)
I'm doing rather well, am I not? (Not: . . . *ain't* I?)

 ## 7.   ALLOT/ALOT/A LOT

Alot is a common misspelling of *a lot.*
The phrase *a lot* is colloquial and vague. Avoid it. Choose a word or words that are more precise.

Vague: We received a lot of phone calls this morning.
Better: We received nearly fifty phone calls this morning.
Wrong: I like my job alot.
Right: I like my job a lot.
Better: I like my job more than any other I've had.

The verb *allot* means *to assign a share, to allocate.*

The manager told us to allot no more than three days to this assignment.
Allot each distributor four cases.

 ## 8.   ALL RIGHT/ALRIGHT

Alright is a common misspelling of *all right,* which means *all correct.* There is no such word as *alright,* just as there is no such word as *alwrong.* All *right* and *all wrong* are two words.

She got the questions on the first part of the exam all right.
She got the questions on the last part of the exam all wrong.

All right may also be used to mean *yes* as well as *acceptable, satisfactory.*

All right, I'll go.
Although I had hoped for a reproduction of higher quality, this one is all right.

Although such uses of *all right* are common, some people feel that they are inappropriate in formal writing. These people would prefer the following:

Yes, I'll go.
This reproduction is acceptable.

9.   ALLUDE/ELUDE

The verb *allude* means to make an indirect reference.

During his lecture, Professor Jacobs alluded to Shakespeare's *Hamlet.*
Your committee report alludes to several problems but fails to suggest any possible
    solutions.

In cases like these, do not use *elude,* which means *to escape notice or detection.*

The bank robber eluded the police.
The bookkeeping error eluded the auditor.

10.   ALLUSION/ILLUSION

An *allusion* is an indirect reference.

During his lecture, Professor Jacobs made an allusion to Shakespeare's *Hamlet.*

An *illusion* is a deceptive impression or false image.

It would be an illusion to believe that sales will continue at their present rate during the
    winter months.

Elusion is the act of eluding or evading. This word is used very rarely. There is no such
word as *illude.*

11.   AMOUNT/NUMBER

The word *amount* refers to things in bulk or mass.

The amount of land available for industrial development in this town is limited.
Newspapers recycle a large amount of newsprint every day.

Use *number* for things that can be counted as individual items.

A number of employees are home ill with the flu.
The number of acres available for industrial development is limited.

12. ANGRY/MAD

Do not use *mad* to imply anger or peevishness. *Mad* means *insane*. Dogs go mad and froth at the mouth; people simply get angry.

Right: I am angry at his impertinence.
Right: A mad person may be confined to an asylum.
Wrong: She is mad at him because he snubbed her.

Turn to Exercise 21.1.

 ## 13. ANXIOUS/EAGER

Anxious is an adjective derived from the noun *anxiety*, meaning *worry*. An anxious person is someone who is perplexed, concerned, or disturbed. *Eager* comes from *eagerness*, meaning *enthusiasm, interest, desire*. An eager person, therefore, is enthusiastic.

Right: I am angry at his impertinence.
Right: I am anxious about my mother's health.
Wrong: I am anxious to see my friend tomorrow.

(If you were worried, not eager, you would say: *I am anxious about my friend's reaction to me tomorrow.*)

 ## 14. APPRAISE/APPRISE

Appraise means *to estimate, to make an evaluation of, to judge*.

The bank will appraise our property on Second Avenue later this week.

Do not confuse *appraise* with *apprise*, which means *to notify, to inform*.

Right: Please apprise me of your decision.
Right: We will apprise you of the results of the bank's appraisal.
Wrong: Please appraise me of your decision.

 ## 15. AWHILE/A WHILE

Awhile and *a while* frequently are confused.
Awhile is an adverb meaning *for a short time*.

Stay awhile and have lunch with us.
Wait awhile until the rain stops.

The adverb *awhile* is never preceded by *for, in* or *after*. These three prepositions are used with the noun phrase *a while*, which means *a period of time*.

Right: Stay for a while and have lunch with us.
Wrong: Stay for awhile and have lunch with us.
Right: Wait for a while until the rain stops.
Wrong: Wait for awhile until the rain stops.

Sometimes *a while* is not preceded by a preposition.

Right: They picked up the mail a while ago.
Wrong: They picked up the mail awhile ago.

 ## 16.   BEING THAT/BEING AS

There is no such conjunction as *being that* or *being as.* They are nonstandard phrases for *since* or *because.*

Right: Since you don't want to go, I'll go alone.
Wrong: Being that you don't want to go, I'll go alone.
Right: Because he is ill, I'll stay late.
Wrong: Being as he is ill, I'll stay late.

Seeing as how is also a nonstandard phrase for *since* or *because.*

Right: Since she isn't here, I'll come back tomorrow.
Wrong: Seeing as how she isn't here, I'll come back tomorrow.

 ## 17.   CAN/MAY

Be careful to use *can* and *may* properly.
Can means *is capable of.* In other words, *can* refers to physical ability. *May* means *has permission to.* In other words, *may* refers to consent.

May I leave work an hour early? (Will you give me permission to leave early?)
Can you spare me? (Are you capable of getting along without me?)
May we have the car tonight?
I understand the car is being repaired. Can we have it by tonight?

 ## 18.   CANVAS/CANVASS

Canvas, a noun, is used to make sails and tents.

Joan received a set of canvas luggage for her birthday.

Canvass, a verb, means to go through a district or area soliciting votes for a candidate or orders for a product.

Volunteers for Miller canvassed the Third Precinct.

 ## 19.   CAPITAL/CAPITOL

Capital has various meanings. In business you will use it to refer to *wealth* or *assets.*

Do we have sufficient capital for such a major investment?

Capital is also used in the following senses:

Begin every sentence with a capital letter.

Do you believe that capital punishment is a deterrent?
Trenton is the state capital of New Jersey.

The building where the legislature meets, however, is called the *capitol*.

Ms. James has an important meeting at the capitol in Trenton.

Although *capitol* is often written with a small *c* when it refers to a state building, it is always written with a capital C when it refers to the home of the United States Congress.

From Trenton, Ms. James will fly to Washington to meet with Senator Williams at the Capitol.

20.   CITE/SITE/SIGHT

The word *sight*, referring to *the ability to see*, does not pose any problems.

Ralph Thomas has lost the sight in one eye.

But *cite* and *site* are often confused. *Cite* is a verb meaning *to quote an authority, to refer to, to acknowledge.*

Miss Roberts cited several famous economists for support.
I can cite four leading authorities who feel as I do.

Site is a noun referring to a *location or plot of ground where something is located.*

The building site for the new bank has already been determined.
She cited Mr. Tyler as an authority on the evaluation of potential building sites.

21.   COARSE/COURSE

Coarse is an adjective meaning *rough, crude, not fine.*

Begin sanding the table with coarse sandpaper.

Course is a noun with a variety of meanings including *a way* or *path* or *direction taken, part of a meal,* and *a series of study in school.*

What should be our course of action?
The main course at the banquet featured duck in orange sauce.
Larry is taking a course in technical writing in the evening division at the college.

22.   COMPLEMENT/COMPLIMENT

The word *complement* refers to something that *completes a whole.* If two items *complement* each other, they are *complementary*.

Two angles the sum of which is 90 degrees are complementary angles.
When performed properly, these two jobs are complementary.
This proposed writing program would complement our existing training program.

The word *compliment* refers to *praise* or to *something given free of charge.*

I want to compliment you on the excellent quality of your work.
Please accept this gift with our compliments.
During December a complimentary calendar will be mailed to all our customers.

23.   COMPOSE/COMPRISE

Compose means *to make up, to create.* The whole is *composed* of its parts. *Comprise* means *to include.* The whole *comprises* its parts. Many people use *comprise* where *compose* would be correct.

> **Right:** The college is composed of six different schools.
> **Right:** The college comprises six different schools.
> **Wrong:** The college is comprised of six different schools.

Turn to Exercise 21.2.

24.   CONFIDANT/CONFIDENT

A *confidant* is a person to whom secrets are entrusted. The feminine form of *confidant* is *confidante.*

> In addition to the president only Mr. Spiers, who was the president's confidant, knew of the takeover bid.

When you are *confident,* you are assured, certain.

> I am confident we will complete this assignment ahead of schedule.
> Ms. Canter is my confidante; I am confident she can be trusted.

25.   CONTINUAL/CONTINUOUS

When something is *continual,* it happens *over and over again.*

> The manager was forced to fire John because of his continual absences.

When something is *continuous,* it is *unbroken, occurring without interruption.*

> A settlement was reached after over twenty-four hours of continuous negotiations.

26.   COUNCIL/COUNSEL/CONSUL

When you ask someone for *advice,* you are seeking *counsel.* If someone advises or *counsels* you, he or she is acting as your *counselor.* A lawyer is a counselor.
A *council* is a legislative or advisory body. Its members are *councilors.*

> **Wrong:** Mary saw her councilor to discuss her course schedule for the spring semester.
> **Right:** Mary saw her counselor to discuss her course schedule for the spring semester.
> **Right:** He counseled her to take an additional writing course.
> **Right:** She is a member of the student council.

A *consul* is an official appointed by a government to live in a foreign city to look after his or her country's business interests and citizens living or visiting there. The offices of the consul are known as the consulate.

Most foreign countries send one or more consuls to New York.

27. DISCREET/DISCRETE

These two words are very similar in spelling, but they are quite different in meaning. When you are *discreet*, you show good judgment. *Discreet* is related to the word *discretion*.

A good attorney is always discreet in handling a client's affairs.

Discrete means *separate and distinct*. A person may be *discreet*, never *discrete*.

Separate the applications into five discrete units.

28. DISINTERESTED/UNINTERESTED

The prefix *dis* means *away from* or *apart*. *Disinterested* persons are interested, but their interest is away from or apart from the issue. They are impartial, fair, interested but aloof. A judge should always be *disinterested*, but never *uninterested*. The prefix *un* means *not*; *uninterested* means *not interested*.

Right: I want a disinterested arbiter to make the decision.
Right: I am uninterested in impressing people.
Wrong: He yawned at his desk showing he was disinterested in the work.

29. EMINENT/IMMINENT

The word *eminent* means *outstanding* or *distinguished*.

The eminent economist Dr. Michelle Fisher addressed the meeting.

The word *imminent* means *impending, about to happen*.

Financial collapse seemed imminent.
The arrival of the eminent professor was imminent.

30. ENVELOP/ENVELOPE

The word you will usually use in business writing is *envelope* (remember the final e), the folded paper container for letters.

A postage-paid envelope is enclosed for your convenience.

Don't confuse *envelope*, a noun, with the verb *envelop*, which means *to wrap up, cover, or surround*.

Does the fog envelop the harbor every morning?

31. FORMALLY/FORMERLY

Formally, meaning in accordance with certain rules, forms, procedures, or regulations, is an adverb derived from the adjective *formal.* Don't confuse it with *formerly,* derived from the adjective *former* and meaning in the past, some time ago.

> I don't believe we have been formally introduced.
> Gerald R. Ford was formerly President of the United States.
> Scott Foremann, formerly the fraternity treasurer, was formally sworn in as the new president.

 ## 32. GOT/HAS GOT/RECEIVED

Do not use *has got* to indicate possession.

> **Right:** She has a fine idea. (*Not:* She has got a fine idea.)
> **Right:** What have you in your file? or What do you have in your file? (*Not:* What have you got in your file?)

Do not use *got* when you mean *received.*

> **Right:** We received the package this morning. (*Not:* We got the package this morning.)
> **Right:** I received permission to take the rest of the day off.
>   *Or,* I have permission to take the rest of the day off. (*Not:* I got permission to take the rest of the day off.)

 ## 33. HEALTHFUL/HEALTHY

Healthful means good for the health, producing or contributing to good health. *Healthy* means being well, having good health. People are not *healthful,* they are *healthy.* They become *healthy* by eating *healthful* foods, doing *healthful* activities, and living in a *healthful* climate.

> Lynne is very healthy; she exercises regularly and eats only healthful foods.

 ## 34. IMMIGRATE/EMIGRATE

The difference between *immigrate* and *emigrate* is one of direction. When you *immigrate,* you come into a country of which you are not a native (note the *i*'s in *immigrate* and *into*). When you *emigrate,* you leave a country for residence in another (note the *e*'s in *emigrate* and *leave*).

> Ms. Liebowitz's ancestors immigrated to America in the early 1900s.
> They emigrated from Germany.

Turn to Exercise 21.3.

 ## 35. IMPLY/INFER

Many people confuse these two verbs, often using *infer* when they really mean *imply.* *Imply* means *to suggest without stating.*

Although he didn't say so, Mr. Slegle implied that he would retire next year. What do you mean to imply by that remark?

Infer means *to deduce, to conclude from evidence.*

>**Right:** I inferred from Mr. Slegle's statement that he would retire next year.
>**Right:** What should I infer from that remark?
>**Wrong:** Although he didn't say so, Mr. Slegle inferred that he would retire next year.

Remember: The speaker or writer *implies*, the listener or reader *infers*.

36.   INTERSTATE/INTESTATE/INTRASTATE

Interstate and *intrastate* frequently are confused. *Interstate* means *between* states; *intrastate* means *within* a single state.

>The Interstate Commerce Act covers all transactions taking place from state to state. Each state has exclusive control over its intrastate affairs.

Intestate refers to something totally unrelated. It means *having made no valid will.*

>Serious legal problems can result when a person dies intestate.

37.   KINDLY/PLEASE

Kindly has been overworked in business writing. Don't say *kindly* when you mean *please.*
Don't say: Kindly send us your payment in the enclosed envelope.
Say: Please send us your payment in the enclosed envelope.
Although *kindly* should be avoided in this sense, when it acts as an adjective or adverb in another way, its use is acceptable.

>The doctor's kindly manner reassured the patients.

38.   LEAD (VERB)/LEAD (NOUN)/LED (VERB)

Don't incorrectly substitute the present tense of the verb *to lead* (rhymes with *need*) for the past tense *led* (rhymes with *red*).

>**Right:** She led the company in sales last week.
>**Wrong:** She *lead* the company in sales last week.

Just remember that *lead* as a verb is pronounced like *need.* Do not confuse *led,* the past tense, with the noun *lead* (also pronounced like *red*) meaning *the metal used for plumbing.*

>**Right:** The waiter led us to our table.
>**Right:** He has led a virtuous life.
>**Right:** He may lead his class in marks.
>**Right:** The lead was mined as an ore.

39. LEND/LOAN/BORROW

Lend and *borrow* are both verbs. *Lend* means *to give someone else your property temporarily*. *Borrow* means *to accept someone else's property temporarily*.

Right: Will you lend me your typewriter?
Right: I'd like to borrow your typewriter.
Wrong: Will you borrow me your typewriter?

Loan is a noun. A *loan* is the thing that is lent.

Right: I need a loan of $500. Will you lend it to me?

Many people also use *loan* as a verb. Although this used to be grammatically incorrect, the use of *loan* as a verb is so common that it is now generally accepted. Although either *loan* or *lend* may be used as a verb, however, the careful business writer prefers *lend*.

Preferred: Will you lend me your typewriter?
Acceptable: Will you loan me your typewriter?

 ## 40. LET/LEAVE

Leave (left) means *to go away*. It should not be confused with *let*, meaning *to allow* or *permit*.

Right: Let me work alone.
Wrong: Leave me work alone.
Right: You should have let him go.
Wrong: You should have left him go.

Note: *Leave* and *let* are interchangeable when they are followed by a noun or pronoun and *alone*. Thus *Leave me alone* and *Let me alone* are both correct, but each has a different meaning. *Leave me alone* suggests politely that you go away. *Let me alone* suggests (more brusquely) that you should stop irritating me.

 ## 41. LOSE/LOOSE

The verb *lose* is always pronounced *looz*. It means *to suffer loss*. This is quite different from *loose*, pronounced like *moose*, which means *free, not close together*, or as a verb, *to untie, to make free*. Just remember that *lose* means a loss, with one *o* in each word; *loose* means *free*, with a double vowel in each word.

Right: Did you lose your books?
Right: I will lose my temper soon.
Right: The animals broke loose.
Right: Let's pull the loose ends together.
Wrong: You will loose your wallet if it sticks out of your pocket.

42. MAYBE/MAY BE

Maybe (one word) is an adverb meaning *perhaps.*

Maybe we can have lunch together.
Maybe I'll see you at the convention.

May be (two words) is a verb form expressing possibility.

It may be that I'll see you at the convention.
Ms. George may be delayed in traffic.

 ## 43. NOWHERES/SOMEWHERES/ANYWHERES

These are not words in standard English. The correct words are *nowhere, somewhere,* and *anywhere.*
Remember: Leave off the *s* at the end.

Right: He could find it nowhere.
Right: Somewhere over the rainbow, skies are blue.
Right: Put the machine anywhere that's convenient.

 ## 44. PERSONAL/PERSONNEL

Personal is an adjective and refers to a particular person.

She keeps her personal effects in the top drawer of her desk.
Don't let your personal affairs interfere with your work.

Personnel refers to the employees of a business and usually acts as a noun.

All personnel in this section are asked to observe the "No Smoking" ordinance.
Mr. Rich handles all problems involving personnel.

Sometimes *personnel* also serves as an adjective.

She resigned from her job in the personnel office for personal reasons.

 ## 45. PRECEDE/PROCEED/PROCEEDS

Precede and *proceed* are frequently confused. *Precede* means *to be or go before in importance, position, or time.*

A great deal of discussion preceded the merger.
A brief meeting of the board in executive session will precede the general meeting.

Proceed means *to go forward, to carry on.*

After the demonstrators were removed from the auditorium, the senator proceeded
  with his speech.
You may proceed with the repair work once the estimate has been approved.

Proceeds is a noun. It is always used in a plural form and refers to *money received from the sale of merchandise.*

Today's proceeds will be donated to the United Way.
A determination of the total proceeds must precede any discussion of how to proceed with their distribution.

46. PRESCRIBE/PROSCRIBE

Prescribe means *to order as a remedy.* The medicine you pick up at the pharmacy is your prescription.

The doctor prescribed a mild sedative for the patient.

To *prescribe* also means *to set down as a rule.*

All store employees must adhere to the standards prescribed in the employees' manual.

To *proscribe* means *to forbid* or *to inhibit.*

The manual proscribes jeans and T-shirts for all sales staff.

Turn to Exercise 21.4.

47. PRINCIPAL/PRINCIPLE

Principle is a noun meaning *fundamental truth* or *integrity.*

She is a woman of unswerving principles.
He does not understand the principles of effective office management.

Principal has a wide variety of meanings. As an adjective it means *chief; main; first; highest or foremost in rank, degree, importance.*

His failure to attend class regularly was the principal reason for his poor performance on the final exam.
Salary is not my principal concern.

As a noun *principal* refers to *the chief administrator of a school* and *the sum of money on which interest is calculated,* among its variety of meanings.

The speaker today is the principal of the local grade school.
The principal plus interest will be due in ninety days.

48. REGARDLESS/IRREGARDLESS

There is no such word as *irregardless. Regardless* is all that you need.

Regardless of the weather, we will leave on time.
These stocks will maintain their value regardless of the market.

49. RESPECTFULLY/RESPECTABLY/ RESPECTIVELY

Some writers make the error of substituting *Respectably (in a decent fashion)* for the proper letter closing—*Respectfully (full of respect)*. *Respectively* is also quite unrelated; it means *in proper sequence* or *in order*.

Right: Please answer soon. Respectfully yours, . . .
Right: He spoke respectfully (full of respect) to the minister.
Right: He was dressed respectably (in a decent fashion) for the occasion.
Right: I want Maria and Janos respectively to address the group. (In the named sequence or order.)
Right: Roosevelt, Truman, and Eisenhower respectively had their impacts on the American people.

 ## 50. STATIONARY/STATIONERY

Although these two words are spelled almost identically, they have very different meanings.
Stationary means *in a fixed position*.

This machine must be stationary; bolt it to the floor.

Stationery refers to writing paper and envelopes.

Our office stationery is high-quality bond paper.

Memory Aid: stationAry refers to plAce; stationERy refers to papER.

 ## 51. STAYED/STOOD

Do not confuse *stayed* with *stood. Stayed* is the past tense of *stay*. It means *remained*.

I should've stayed in bed.
We stayed late to complete the job.

Stood is the past tense of *stand*.

The soldier stood at attention throughout the ceremony.
I don't know how he stood the strain.

 ## 52. TEACH/LEARN

Do not confuse the words *teach* and *learn*. To *teach* means *to give knowledge to someone else*. To *learn* means *to receive knowledge from someone or something*.

The teacher teaches the class.
The class learns from the teacher.

53.   THAN/THEN

Do not use *then,* meaning *at that time* or *later* (an adverb), when you want to use the conjunction *than,* which shows a comparison.

Right: She is bigger than I.
Right: If you ask, then I will answer.
Wrong: She is older *then* I.

 ## 54.   THEIR/THERE/THEY'RE

Because these three words all sound the same, they are often confused. Learn to distinguish among them. *There* is an adverb or an expletive. The pronoun *their* is the possessive form of *they. They're* is a contraction of *they are.*

There were four people in the office.
I wish you had been there.
They're very happy with the quality of our product.
Their endorsement should help our sales.
They're holding their meeting there tonight.

 ## 55.   THIS HERE

These expressions are all nonstandard:

Wrong: This here book is interesting.
Wrong: That there desk is beautiful.
Wrong: These here books are heavy.
Wrong: Those there desks are light.

The word *here* or *there* in the above sentences is unnecessary and should be left out.

Right: This book is interesting.
Right: That desk is beautiful.
Right: These books are heavy.
Right: Those desks are light.

 ## 56.   TWO/TOO/TO

Two is a number—2.

Send me two pairs of shoes.
They ordered two dozen shirts.

To is a preposition.

I am going to another department.
He rose to his feet.

To is also part of the infinitive.

I want to go at once.

To err is human.

Too is a word that intensifies the meaning of something. It means *more than* or *also.*

I want to go too.
There is too much work.
Our inventory is too large.

To help you choose between *to* and *too*, remember that the double *o* in *too* intensifies the word. So use *too* when you want to intensify your meaning.

 ## 57. WE'RE/WERE/WHERE

These three words are often misused, usually through carelessness and haste rather than ignorance of their correct meanings. *Remember:*
We're is a contraction for *we are.*

Did you say that we're invited to the celebration?

Were is a past tense form of the verb *to be.*

Were we invited to the celebration?

Where refers to place.

Where is the celebration?

Turn to Exercises 21.5 to 21.7.

EXERCISE 21·1A   ITEMS 1 TO 12

In the space provided, write the correct word.

1. I refuse to (accept, except) shipment.   1. _____

2. I think we can (adapt, adopt, adept) this part to fit our machine.   2. _____

3. When I want your (advice, advise), I'll ask for it.   3. _____

4. As the new supervisor, Ms. Juacinto plans to (affect, effect) major changes in her department.   4. _____

5. Is it (alright, all right) to leave early this afternoon?   5. _____

6. There is an (accessive, excessive) amount of waste under the present system.   6. _____

7. Everyone (accept, except) Mr. Kowalski will be at this afternoon's conference.   7. _____

8. The company is about to (adopt, adapt, adept) a new policy regarding profit sharing.   8. _____

9. What do you (advice, advise)?   9. _____

10. What has been the (affect, effect) of this reorganization on corporate profits?   10. _____

11. (Alright, All right), you may go.   11. _____

12. Miss Agronski is very (adapt, adept, adopt) in writing effective résumés.   12. _____

13. All donations will be gratefully (accepted, excepted) and acknowledged.   13. _____

14. Do we need to change these plans or can we (adapt, adopt, adept) them in their present form?   14. _____

15. What is your (advice, advise)?   15. _____

16. How has this reorganization (affected, effected) corporate profits?   16. _____

17. Some of these forms are damaged, but most are (all right, alright).   17. _____

18. President Hoffman is fond of (alluding, eluding) to Benjamin Franklin.   18. _____

19. I like her (alot, a lot, allot).   19. _____

20. I don't have (access, excess) to that information.   20. _____

21. The (amount, number) of coal is limited.   21. _____

22. Don't be (mad, angry) with me.   22. _____

23. Don't allow this sale to (elude, allude) you.   23. _____

24. (Alot, A lot, Allot) of people are out sick with the flu.   24. _____

25. José can (access, excess) the main data bank for that information.   25. _____

26. A large (amount, number) of people have expressed an interest in our new IRA.   26. _____

27. He liked the new designer's clothes so much, he seemed to be (mad, angry) about them. 27. _____

28. Her sense of power is only an (allusion, illusion). 28. _____

29. (Alot, A lot, Allot) each person ten tickets. 29. _____

30. Never show that you are (angry, mad) if you are kept waiting for an interview. 30. _____

EXERCISE 21·1B   ITEMS 1 TO 12

In the space provided, show whether these sentences are correct (C) or incorrect (I). If the sentence is incorrect, cross out the error and write your correction in the space above the error.

1. Will you except a little advice? 1. _____

2. Let's adopt a more flexible policy in this area. 2. _____

3. My broker's advise is to sell that stock. 3. _____

4. The importation of foreign steel has effected our country's steel industry. 4. _____

5. I ain't seen no one around here for weeks. 5. _____

6. Some of the sentences in this exercise are alright. 6. _____

7. Congressman Schmidt proposed a tax on excess profits. 7. _____

8. All except the Fowlers have excepted the invitation. 8. _____

9. Ain't we going to leave before noon? 9. _____

10. A special password is required to gain excess to these computer files. 10. _____

11. Ms. Neprash has no allusions about the difficulty of the job she faces. 11. _____

12. The new CEO intends to effect significant changes on all levels of our corporate structure. 12. _____

13. The auditor detected an error that had illuded the bookkeeper. 13. _____

14. I've told the store manager to alot only ten square feet of floor space to this display. 14. _____

15. What is the total amount of acres here? 15. _____

16. He appeared to be angry, so a psychiatric examination was requested. 16. _____

17. This book makes illusions to numerous authoritative studies. 17. _____

18. This program can be easily adapted to fit your needs. 18. _____

19. What is the amount of usable square feet on this floor of the building? 19. _____

20. The good salesperson never gets mad with the customer. 20. _____

EXERCISE 21·1C   ITEMS 1 TO 12

Select from the following words the one that correctly fits into the blank in each of the sentences below.

accept	adapt	advise	a lot	allude	amount
except	adept	affect	alot	elude	number
access	adopt	effect	all right	allusion	angry
excess	advice	allot	alright	illusion	mad

1. We cannot _____ any returns on sale merchandise.

2. We must _____ our sales campaign to the changing market conditions.

3. Ms. Dubrowski sought legal _____ before signing the contract.

4. He tried for days to _____ the process server.

5. A large _____ of customers have complained about our new returns policy.

6. Roberta was _____ with her assistant.

7. The _____ of the new taxes was immediate.

8. Only three employees have _____ to those files.

9. The contest is open to anyone _____ employees of the station and their immediate families.

10. The responses to the survey were in _____ of 35 percent.

11. Our company will _____ a new payroll plan in January.

12. The policies of the Federal Reserve Board _____ our entire economy.

13. Do not _____ more than two days to complete this assignment.

14. The light, modular furniture created the _____ of spaciousness.

15. The _____ of recordkeeping required by the government is overwhelming.

EXERCISE 21·1D   COMPOSITION: ITEMS 1 TO 12

Complete each of the following sentence starters in a meaningful fashion.

1. The effect _____

2. Allot _____

3. Please accept _____

4. My advice _____

5. The number _____

6. The amount _____

7. We can adapt _____

8. An illusion _____

1. He was (anxious, eager) to get started on the project.   1. _____

2. Please (appraise, apprise) me when you reach your decision.   2. _____

3. She is late for work once in (awhile, a while).   3. _____

4. (Can, May) you reach the top shelf if you stretch?   4. _____

5. Most of my (capital, capitol) is tied up at present.   5. _____

6. The comptroller is always (citing, siting) statistics.   6. _____

7. He was (anxious, eager) about the hospital report.   7. _____

8. The bank (appraised, apprised) the property at $90,000.   8. _____

9. Wait (awhile, a while) until she returns.   9. _____

10. (Can, May) we be excused from the exercises?   10. _____

11. I'll meet you on the steps of the (capital, capitol) at noon.   11. _____

12. The committee surveyed the proposed (cite, site) for the new
industrial complex.   12. _____

13. One should be (anxious, eager) about the effects of smoking.   13. _____

14. The jeweler (appraised, apprised) the diamond.   14. _____

15. After (awhile, a while) you won't feel so disappointed.   15. _____

16. Springfield is the (capital, capitol) of Illinois.   16. _____

17. Muriel's (cite, site, sight) is beginning to fail.   17. _____

18. The branch manager (complimented, complemented) her staff on
the high quality of their work.   18. _____

19. Our curriculum is (composed, comprised) of a wide variety of
courses.   19. _____

20. Rub the inside of the fowl with (coarse, course) salt.   20. _____

21. For your pledge of $50, Channel 13 will send you this sturdy (canvas,
canvass) totebag.   21. _____

22. Marta received two (complimentary, complementary) tickets to
next Saturday's matinee.   22. _____

23. Multiplex International (comprises, composes) several dozen
separate companies.   23. _____

24. We will, of (course, coarse), keep you informed.   24. _____

25. The candidate's supporters (canvased, canvassed) the ward.   25. _____

EXERCISE 21·2B   ITEMS 13 TO 23

In the space provided, show whether these sentences are correct *(C)* or incorrect *(I)*. If the sentence is incorrect, cross out the error and write your correction in the space above the error.

1. I am anxious to get a fresh start in my job.   1. _____

2. The jeweler appraised the buyer of the diamond's value.   2. _____

3. For awhile the outcome was in doubt.   3. _____

4. We feel that, seeing as how you are so intelligent, you will do a good job.   4. _____

5. Can we now discuss this report?   5. _____

6. What is the capitol of Oregon?   6. _____

7. Can you cite any examples?   7. _____

8. Sit down and rest a while.   8. _____

9. Being that there is a shortage of word processors, we can get excellent jobs.   9. _____

10. Can our class tour your plant next Thursday?   10. _____

11. Our capitol expenditure in this expansion program is greater than we had anticipated.   11. _____

12. Can you site any examples?   12. _____

13. His abilities exactly compliment hers.   13. _____

14. One international airline reminds its customers that European tours are comprised of people.   14. _____

15. Sherri has enrolled in a full-time course of study at the university.   15. _____

16. The canvass tent has been treated with fire-retardant chemicals.   16. _____

17. My complements to the chef!   17. _____

18. Our curriculum comprises a wide variety of courses.   18. _____

19. Otto's language was often coarse.   19. _____

20. The Girl Scouts will soon canvas the neighborhood selling cookies. 20. _____

EXERCISE 21·2C   ITEMS 13 TO 23

Select from the following list of words the one that correctly fits into the blank in each of the sentences below. Then write the word in the blank.

anxious	awhile	can	capital	sight	compliment
eager	a while	may	capitol	coarse	compose
appraise	being that	canvas	cite	course	comprise
apprise	since	canvass	site	complement	

1. Our company has invested heavily in _____ improvements this year.

2. Pauline bought three pairs of _____ shoes.

3. Ms. Schniller left for the airport _____ ago.

4. _____ we have the courtesy of a reply?

5. Has the committee decided on a _____ for the new hospital?

6. We often _____ Miss Kim for her attention to detail.

7. Heidi is always able to _____ the latest statistics to support her position.

8. We are _____ to be of any assistance.

9. Many a successful business deal is completed on the golf _____.

10. Our new word processing equipment will _____ our secretarial services.

11. Please _____ me of the results of the bidding.

12. The architect specified _____ bricks for the exterior of the building.

EXERCISE 21·2D   COMPOSITION: ITEMS 13 TO 23

Complete each of the following sentence starters in a meaningful fashion.

1. I am anxious _____

2. She will appraise _____

3. Can _____

4. May _____

5. The capital _____

6. The site _____

7. A course _____

8. A complimentary _____

EXERCISE 21·3A   **ITEMS 24 TO 34**

In the space provided, write the correct word.

1.   There was a (continual, continuous) stream of applicants all day.   1. _____

2.   What (council, counsel) would you offer me regarding high-risk investments?   2. _____

3.   A good judge must be (disinterested, uninterested) in the case before the court.   3. _____

4.   His arrival was (eminent, imminent).   4. _____

5.   Dr. Bahmani was (confident, confidant) she would be promoted.   5. _____

6.   Can I trust you to be (discreet, discrete) about this matter?   6. _____

7.   John is (continually, continuously) late for his appointments.   7. _____

8.   If you need legal advice, consult a (councilor, counselor).   8. _____

9.   His failure shows he was (disinterested, uninterested) in the work.   9. _____

10. Professor Khanna is an (eminent, imminent) authority in her field.   10. _____

11. Please enclose a self-addressed stamped (envelop, envelope) with your request.   11. _____

12. Amar was not permitted to speak at the meeting because he had not been (formally, formerly) recognized. 12. _____

13. Doris is remarkably (healthy, healthful) for a person her age.   13. _____

14. Ms. Kraus's ancestors (immigrated, emigrated) from Germany.   14. _____

15. All the candidates said they were (confident, confidant) of victory in the forthcoming election.   15. _____

16. A person to whom secrets are entrusted is a (confident, confidant).   16. _____

17. Ms. Douma rearranged the office into five (discreet, discrete) work areas.   17. _____

18. The smell of gas seemed to (envelope, envelop) the area.   18. _____

19. Dr. Stefanchik (got, has got, received) her degree from Stanford.   19. _____

20. Mr. Markovitz has served as his country's (council, counsel, consul) in New York for more than ten years. 20. _____

21. Mr. Smythe (has, has got, received) a slight cold.   21. _____

22. Ms. Olefskie and I have never been (formally, formerly) introduced.   22. _____

23. I like to vacation at a resort where the climate is (healthy, healthful).   23. _____

24. People who (immigrated, emigrated) to this country from Europe often found homes in the big cities.   24. _____

25. Professor Pai was (formally, formerly) a colleague of mine at the University of Pennsylvania.   25. _____

EXERCISE 21·3B   ITEMS 24 TO 34

In the space provided, show whether these sentences are correct (C) or incorrect (I). If the sentence is incorrect, cross out the error and write your correction in the space above the error.

1. Good writing requires continuous practice.   1. _____

2. Rita Perez heads our local advisory counsel.   2. _____

3. Dr. Taylor is widely esteemed for her eminent achievements in chemical research.   3. _____

4. Sarah was asked to serve on the advisory counsel.   4. _____

5. Janet made an appointment to see her councilor about her class schedule.   5. _____

6. Ms. Li was selected as the referee because she was uninterested in the two sides presented.   6. _____

7. A distinct shift in company policy is eminent.   7. _____

8. The foreign dignitaries met with their country's counsul.   8. _____

9. Have you got the time?   9. _____

10. For maximum effect, music in the office should alternate with periods of silence; it should not be played continually.   10. _____

11. Following the successful interview, Helen was confidant she would be offered the position.   11. _____

12. Because one of the committee members was not discrete, word of the committee's recommendation spread quickly through the building.   12. _____

13. A window envelop does not need to be addressed because the inside address of the letter appears through the window.   13. _____

14. At the next meeting she will be formerly inducted as an officer.   14. _____

15. Most people consider yogurt to be an especially healthy food.   15. _____

16. Ellis Island was the processing station for Europeans who emigrated to America.   16. _____

17. Ms. Vuksta served as Mr. Walencik's confidante on all important matters.   17. _____

18. Although the closing of the plant had been predicted, a feeling of utter disbelief continued to envelop the town.   18. _____

19. He has not got a good reason for his absences.   19. _____

20. Our offices were formerly located in what is now a developmental laboratory.   20. _____

EXERCISE 21·3C   ITEMS 24 TO 34

Choose from the following list of words the one that correctly fits into the blank in each of the sentences below. Then write the word in the blank.

confidant	consul	discrete	imminent	got	immigrate
confident	continual	disinterested	envelop	formerly	emigrate
council	continuous	uninterested	envelope	healthful	received
counsel	discreet	eminent	formally	healthy	

1. Sales representatives who are _____ in the products they represent are unlikely to succeed.

2. Dr. Kohn is _____ late for his appointments.

3. The _____ has decided to deny your request.

4. Professor Wolfson is an _____ authority on ergonomics.

5. We _____ her application this morning.

6. She introduced Tullio as her "trusted friend and _____."

7. A heavy fog may still _____ the area.

8. Brendan Byrne was _____ the Governor of New Jersey.

9. I may look _____, but I feel terrible.

10. In the summer months people from the cities seem to _____ to the shore.

11. The station provided _____ election coverage.

12. Ms. Raczynski's announcement of her candidacy appears _____.

13. I am _____ this new marketing strategy will succeed.

14. A No. 10 _____ measures 4⅛ by 9½ inches.

15. The attorney was not always _____.

EXERCISE 21·3D   COMPOSITION: ITEMS 24 TO 34

Complete each of the following sentence starters in a meaningful fashion.

1. I am confident _____

2. The consul _____

3. She was formally _____

4. A continuous _____

5. The eminent _____

6. A disinterested _____

7. A discreet _____

8. The healthful _____

In the space provided, write the correct word.

1. It is possible to (imply, infer) a great deal from your report.   1. _____

2. The (lead, led) in this pencil is too soft.   2. _____

3. I had to (lend, loan, borrow) money from my boss to get home.   3. _____

4. She won't (let, leave) me finish my work.   4. _____

5. What are you (implying, inferring) by that statement?   5. _____

6. Joyce (lead, led) all the students in her class.   6. _____

7. (Lend, Loan, Borrow) me your book until tomorrow.   7. _____

8. (Let, Leave) us explain the problem as we see it.   8. _____

9. What she means to (imply, infer) by that remark is quite clear.   9. _____

10. Because he died (interstate, intrastate, intestate), the distribution of his estate was affected.   10. _____

11. (Kindly, Please) complete and return the enclosed form by March 30.   11. _____

12. (Maybe, May be) I'll be able to complete this project on schedule after all.   12. _____

13. I (may be, maybe) able to complete this project on schedule, but I doubt it.   13. _____

14. All trading between states is controlled by federal regulations affecting (interstate, intrastate, intestate) commerce.   14. _____

15. The dentist worked on the (lose, loose) tooth.   15. _____

16. My (personal, personnel) affairs should not concern you.   16. _____

17. Let us (proceed, precede) to the next item of business.   17. _____

18. There are certain (prescribed, proscribed) procedures we must follow in all hiring.   18. _____

19. Ms. Querijero's résumé (maybe, may be) in this file.   19. _____

20. Do not (lose, loose) your head in an emergency.   20. _____

21. Never allow your (personal, personnel) bias to affect your professional judgment.   21. _____

22. Our supervisor (proceeds, precedes) every announcement with a cough.   22. _____

23. The Administrative Sciences (Personal, Personnel) Advisory Committee recommended Professor Peters for tenure.   23. _____

24. The sign on the store door (prescribed, proscribed) tank tops and bare feet, so we could not enter.   24. _____

25. The (proceeds, precedes) from the sale will be donated to charity.   25. _____

EXERCISE 21·4B   ITEMS 35 TO 46

In the space provided, show whether these sentences are correct (C) or incorrect (I). If the sentence is incorrect, cross out the error and write your correction in the space above the error.

1. Most advertisements infer things they do not actually say.   1. _____

2. Georgette lead her region in sales for the fourth straight quarter.   2. _____

3. The bank agreed to loan the money.   3. _____

4. They should not have left her go.   4. _____

5. What is implied by this gap in time in Mr. Mihn's résumé?   5. _____

6. I don't like to lend money from anyone.   6. _____

7. If you would leave me be, I would not be so irritable.   7. _____

8. Firms involved in interstate highway construction must observe federal specifications.   8. _____

9. The pediatrician's kindly manner helped all her patients feel at ease.   9. _____

10. May be I will and may be I won't.   10. _____

11. We proceeded according to her directions.   11. _____

12. That rattle seems to come from a lose bolt in the chassis.   12. _____

13. Put the package down anywheres.   13. _____

14. One local restaurant still proscribes anything other than coats and ties for men at dinner.   14. _____

15. Representative Fenwick never let her personnel views affect her performance in public office.   15. _____

16. I would precede as we originally planned.   16. _____

17. Ms. Roberts is in charge of all matters concerning office personal.   17. _____

18. If we don't receive some abatement in taxes, we will be forced to move our business somewheres else.   18. _____

19. Operating solely between Buffalo and Albany, Northern New York Trucking is an interstate trucking firm.   19. _____

20. The correct method for dealing with delinquent accounts is proscribed on p. 37.   20. _____

Choose from the following list of words the one that correctly fits into the blank in each of the sentences below. Then write the word in the blank.

implied	kindly	let	borrow	may be	proceed
inferred	please	leave	lose	personal	proceeds
interstate	lead	lend	loose	personnel	prescribed
intrastate	led	loan	maybe	precede	proscribed
intestate					

1. Commerce within state boundaries is an _____ matter.

2. The remainder of the order _____ included in tomorrow's shipment.

3. A severe diabetic, Mr. Stagi is _____ all forms of sweets.

4. Pencils actually contain graphite, not _____.

5. President Reagan _____ that he would seek re-election long before his official announcement.

6. If this advertising campaign fails, we will _____ their account.

7. _____ reply by Friday.

8. _____ she'll meet us at the airport.

9. Dr. Heinemann _____ complete bedrest for her patient.

10. I _____ from what you said that you weren't happy here.

11. Mr. Zatorski _____ the call for a change in policy.

12. Miss Gil asked her parents to _____ her the money for the down payment.

13. _____ me tell you what kind of person Monique is.

14. All our office _____ records are fully computerized.

15. A buffet luncheon will _____ the awards ceremony.

Complete each of the following sentence starters in a meaningful fashion.

1. How will the proceeds _____

2. It may be _____

3. She implied _____

4. I infer _____

5. The personal _____

6. They will proceed _____

7. He prescribed _____

8. The interstate _____

EXERCISE 21·5A   ITEMS 47 TO 57

In the space provided, write the correct word.

1. Ms. Kaspriski (stayed, stood) at the office until well after dark.

     1. _____

2. Our bitter experience has (taught, learned) us to avoid risky deals.

     2. _____

3. Claire does not know the first (principal, principle) of effective leadership.

     3. _____

4. Who is (their, there, they're) representative?

     4. _____

5. There are (to, too, two) many people in the office force.

     5. _____

6. It was a mistake to leave my last job; I should have (stayed, stood) there.

     6. _____

7. When students do not like a teacher, the teacher will find it difficult to (teach, learn) them.

     7. _____

8. Flo completed the work and (than, then) went home.

     8. _____

9. (Their, There, They're) financial picture is much better (than, then) ours.

     9. _____

10. Would you come (to, too, two), please?

     10. _____

11. I wish I could be (their, there, they're).

     11. _____

12. (That, That there) car is for sale.

     12. _____

13. We still owe nearly all of the (principal, principle) on our home mortgage.

     13. _____

14. MCI's long-distance rates are lower (than, then) AT&T's.

     14. _____

15. I would refuse their offer (regardless, irregardless) of the salary.

     15. _____

16. She correctly closed the letter "(Respectfully, Respectably, Respectively) yours."

     16. _____

17. We need another carton of (stationary, stationery).

     17. _____

18. The attorney listened with (respectful, respectable, respective) attention to her opponent's arguments.

     18. _____

19. Mona is enrolled in "(Principals, Principles) of Office Management)" this semester.

     19. _____

20. (Where, Were, We're) going to the symposium next week.

     20. _____

EXERCISE 21·5B   ITEMS 47 TO 57

In the space provided, show whether these sentences are correct (C) or incorrect (I). If the sentence is incorrect, cross out the error and write your correction in the space above the error.

1. The officer stayed at attention until the ceremony was over.   1. _____

2. Experience is the best learner.   2. _____

3. She keyboards faster then any other employee.   3. _____

4. Their planning a retirement party for Mr. Louis.   4. _____

5. Is this here terminal broken too?   5. _____

6. Send the two packages by first class mail.   6. _____

7. He studies harder then she.   7. _____

8. Their was nothing we could do.   8. _____

9. Send those there two letters by Federal Express.   9. _____

10. They picked up their checks and then went to the bank.   10. _____

11. Who is your school's principle?   11. _____

12. Irregardless of your feelings in the matter, we must go on.   12. _____

13. James Tate was second in sales in his firm, a highly respectful
    position.   13. _____

14. We're you able to attend last year's conference?   14. _____

15. Our new stationery is ivory.   15. _____

16. We have to raise our prices regardless of the consequences.   16. _____

17. Use both hands to keep the wood stationery while the machine is
    in operation.   17. _____

18. Our firm's principle concern is always a satisfied client.   18. _____

19. Were were you?   19. _____

20. All extra stationary is kept in this supply cabinet.   20. _____

EXERCISE 21·5C   ITEMS 47 TO 57

Choose from the following list of words the one that correctly fits into the blank in each of the sentences below. Then write the word in the blank.

principal	respectably	stationery	learn	there	two
principle	respectfully	stayed	than	they're	we're
regardless	respectively	stood	then	to	were
irregardless	stationary	teach	their	too	where

1. I would buy this development property _____ of the asking price.

2. We _____ unable to deliver the package before 10 a.m.

3. There is a fundamental _____ of economics here that you fail to understand.

4. Our company recycles all old _____ for message pads.

5. She finished the typing; _____ she did the proofreading.

6. _____ sorry for the delay.

7. I cannot argue with _____ analysis of the situation.

8. We paid 14 percent interest on the _____.

9. Chevrolet, Chrysler, and Ford _____ led the year in total automobile sales.

10. It won't take very long for me to _____ you how to operate a CRT.

11. There are _____ many companies competing for the same share of the market.

12. _____ experts in time and motion analysis.

13. The defendant answered all the judge's questions _____.

14. These smaller machines are portable, but these larger ones are _____.

15. This report is more difficult to write _____ I had expected.

EXERCISE 21·5D   COMPOSITION: ITEMS 47 TO 57

Complete each of the following sentence starters in a meaningful fashion.

1. To _____
_____

2. Two _____
_____

3. Too _____
_____

4. Where _____
_____

5. The principal _____
_____

6. A stationary _____
_____

7. She stayed _____
_____

8. The principle _____
_____

EXERCISE 21·6   WORDS CONFUSED AND MISUSED

The following letter contains many errors. Cross out all incorrect words and write the correct forms above them.

Dear Ms. Lenczyk:

Enclosed is a copy of the "Guide to the Annual Exposition of Office Equipment." Kindly except it with our complements.

Like our representative told you awhile ago, this Annual Exposition, to be held at the state capitol armory, promises to be even better then last year's. The Exposition will be comprised of displays by every major manufacturer and distributor of office equipment and supplies in this here region. It will be proceeded by a special display entitled "The Office of the Future."

Irregardless of your business you will find all the equipment your office needs. The amount of items on display will not be equalled anywheres else. Here is your opportunity to test, compare, and choose between many different models of every variety of office equipment.

Talk with the representatives of each participating company. Leave them evaluate your needs and advice you as to which machines can compliment your present equipment and which could be adopted to fit your individual requirements. In addition, imminent specialists will be present to appraise you of the principle developments in office management techniques. You can talk with them about your particular concerns. There council will be free.

Do not leave a special opportunity as this pass, for if you loose this chance, you maybe mad with yourself later. We are confidant you will not be disinterested in the equipment on display. Being that this Annual Exposition is so special, we urge you to register now before it is to late to reserve your ticket. If you have not already sent in your deposit, please do so right away. Return your check in the enclosed envelop. We're anxious to see you there.

Respectably yours,

No company likes to receive complaints, but customer complaints are a fact of business life. Most companies take them seriously and try to solve customers' problems in any reasonable way possible.

Pretend that you are the customer service representative for the company to whom you wrote the complaint letter in Exercise 20.7. How would you answer it? Would you grant the claim? Reject it? Offer some alternative solution to the one proposed in the complaint letter? Assume whatever seems to you to be a reasonable position for your company to take. Write your answer in the space below.

22

PROOFREADING

PROOFREADERS' MARKS, HOW TO USE
PROOFREADERS' MARKS, SUCCESSFUL
PROOFREADING

 PROOFREADERS' MARKS

When Ergo-Tech Associates received a request from Ms. Carol Okada for some information about their modular office furniture and equipment, they sent her a booklet and the letter on page 464.

If you were Ms. Okada, how would you respond to this letter? Would you trust Ergo-Tech Associates to redesign your office? Of course you wouldn't—unless you had money to throw away.

In business the impression you create can be very important. Careless dress and behavior at an employment interview can cost you a job. How you present yourself in print can have similar importance. A sloppy résumé and cover letter can cost you an interview and possible position. An inaccurate report with misspellings and typographical errors can cost you a raise or promotion. A slipshod, hastily thrown together sales letter can cost you a client. The modular work stations designed by Ergo-Tech may be excellent. The sloppy and careless sales letter from Ergo-Tech's sales manager, however, conveys a very negative impression about the company and, by extension, about its product. Would you let a company that presents such an image of itself have control over the design of your office? Or would you, like Ms. Okada, seek another company with which to do business?

The final step in producing effective business correspondence is careful proofreading. This is the step that is all too often performed hastily or even ignored. Careful proofreading would have found and eliminated the errors in Mr. Ostrowski's letter—and might have secured a new client for the company. This chapter will show you how to proofread carefully and accurately.

In every one of the previous chapters you have been asked to correct sentences or paragraphs. In each case you crossed out any errors you found and wrote your corrections in the space above them. Your corrected copy for the first paragraph of the final letter in the preceding chapter looked like this:

Enclosed is a copy of the "Guide to the Annual Exposition of Office Equipment."
~~Kindly except~~ Please accept it with our compl*i*ments.

When you made these corrections, you were being an editor, proofreading and correcting written material. A professional editor would have done exactly the same thing. When an editor sees a word that is incorrect, he or she draws a line through it and writes in the correct word above it.

Writers, editors, printers, and business people in general have a great many other alterations they may wish to make in a piece of writing from the rough-draft stage to that of finished final copy. They indicate these changes through the use of a commonly agreed-upon set of symbols. These symbols, known as **proofreaders' marks**, are a shorthand way of indicating what corrections need to be made in a piece of writing before it is printed in its final form.

463

ERGO-TECH ASSOCIATES

**1273 Fairway Drive
Hackensack, NJ 07605
(201) 123-4321**

June 15, 198___

Ms. Carol Okada
Mgmt. Services, Inc.

281 E. Normal Ave.
Morristown, NJ 07960

Dear Ms OKada:

We are plaesed to be sending you a copy ofour booklet "The Office of
the Future—Today". Which you requested on june 12.

Our patented modular wrok stations are designed to insure individual
individual privacy and promote increased efficeincy. 6 typical
installations are shown on pages 26-thirty-one. You will also by be
intrested in the drawings of typical office layouts we have designed on
pages 34-40. Our designers surveys indicate that office arrangements
incorporating our modules can affect savings of up to 30%.

After reading the booklet you can have questions about the design of
your offices. Our agent in you're area is Ms. Joan Fyzee, 93 1st
1st Street, Parsippany NJ 07054 (phone 987-6543). Ms. Fyzee can give
you farther information on design, costes, and installaition—All
without any olbigation on your part.

Why not contact her today. A cord or letter phone call to Ms. Fyzee
can be the frist step in giving you the office of the future—today.

Very truely yours,

John Ostrowski

John Ostrowski
Sales Manager

Why should you learn and use these particular symbols when you are editing and proofreading? First, using proofreaders' marks lets you edit your own or someone else's writing very efficiently. For example, instead of writing "all the letters in this word should be capitalized," you simply underline the word three times. Instead of writing "begin a new paragraph here" or "do not begin a new paragraph here," you simply write "¶" or "no ¶." Second, if anyone else who is familiar with proofreaders' marks looks at the copy you have edited, he or she will know what you mean. And third, of course, you will be able to interpret material edited by others.

In this chapter we're going to present the standard proofreaders' marks most writers use when editing a manuscript or other piece of writing. The exercises will give you the chance to use and interpret these symbols in a variety of business situations. When you complete this chapter, you should have a good working knowledge of the process of proofreading. You'll be able to interpret proofreaders' marks correctly when you see them on edited copy, and you'll be able to proofread your own or someone else's writing accurately and confidently.

The chart on the inside of the front and back covers presents the common proofreading marks and shows how they are used. Professional editors and printers also use a number of additional specialized marks to indicate changes in size and style of typeface. These marks do not concern us here.

Do not try to memorize this chart. Just look at what the marks mean and how they are used. You will become proficient in the use of these marks by using them. Refer to the chart freely as you work through the exercises that follow. After you've used the marks for a short while, you'll feel more comfortable with them. You'll discover as you work through the exercises at the end of the chapter that you won't need to refer to the chart so frequently. Soon you will be using proofreaders' marks automatically.

HOW TO USE PROOFREADERS' MARKS

Let's take some exercises from the previous chapters to see how we would correct them using the proofreaders' marks. Look first at this sentence from Exercise 19.1A.

The instructor told the class the ability to communicate effectively is essential in todays business world

Here is the same sentence with editor's corrections.

The instructor told the class the ability to communicate effectively is essential in today's business world.

Here is the corrected copy:

The instructor told the class, "The ability to communicate effectively is essential in today's business world."

Now look at this passage from Exercise 2.4B.

No two people are alike, one person jumps to a conclusion without careful consideration of all available information. Another examines each fact. Checks every claim. Profits from the experience of others, and then makes a decision.

This is the passage with editor's corrections.

No two people are alike, one person jumps to a conclusion without careful consideration of all available information. Another examines each fact, Checks every claim, Profits from the experience of others, and then makes a decision.

Here is the corrected copy:

No two people are alike. One person jumps to a conclusion without careful consideration of all available information. Another examines each fact, checks every claim, profits from the experience of others, and then makes a decision.

As editor, how would you correct this sentence?

Did you receive any compensation for your recent article the high-tech battle between japan and the U.S.

Make your corrections right on the page. Now compare your corrections with the edited sentence below.

Did you receive any compensation for your recent article the high-tech battle between japan and the U.S. ?

How would you correct this sentence?

Ms Saleem left the following message I will be unable to keep my 1030 a m appointment however I will be able to keep my afternoon appointments

Here is the sentence with editor's corrections:

Ms. Saleem left the following message: I will be unable to keep my 10:30 a.m. appointment; however, I will be able to keep my afternoon appointments.

What corrections would you make in the following passage?

The semicolons prupose in a sentnece are too mark a maajor pause or break, it indicates a pause greater than a comma though not quiet so great so great a pause asa period.

Compare your edited version with the one that follows.

The semicolon's prupose in a sentnece are too mark a maajor pause or break, it indicates a pause greater than a comma, though not quiet so great so great a pause asa period.

This is how the corrected passage would appear.

The semicolon's purpose in a sentence is to mark a major pause or break. It indicates a greater pause than a comma, though not quite so great a pause as a period.

Notice that we made two basic kinds of corrections. We corrected the punctuation and grammar of the passage. Errors of this type are often referred to as **substantive errors.** We also corrected various **typographical errors** such as transposed letters, extra letters, and repeated words. As an editor you must be alert for both kinds of errors.

Here is a passage from the beginning of Chapter 3 in rough manuscript form with many intentional errors. It has been edited in preparation for being set into print.

Nouns are eihter concreteor abstract. Concrete Nouns name particular things which can be experiencd by one of the senses. Things that can be seen, felt, heard, tasted, of or smelled. Abstract nounsname qualities and concepts.

Based on these corrections, the printer would print the passage this way:

Nouns are either *concrete* or *abstract*. *Concrete nouns* name specific things that can be experienced by one of the five senses—things that can be seen, felt, heard, tasted, or smelled. *Abstract nouns* name qualities and concepts.

Suppose, however, the manuscript had not been edited. If the printer set up the unedited passage without making any corrections, it would look like this:

Nouns are eihter concreteor abstract. Concrete Nouns name particular things which can be experiencd by one of the senses. Things that can be seen felt, heard, tasted, or or smelled. abstract nounsname qualities and conceptts.

EDITING PRINTED AND SINGLE-SPACED COPY

Authors who are reading page proofs of their work must make editorial corrections from copy like this. In rough copy, the manuscript is typed double spaced. Any corrections can be written directly above the error because there is enough room to make corrections right in the text itself. In print, however, there is no longer enough room. In these cases you should write the corrections in the margin. If you must make several corrections in a line, write them next to each other in the order in which they occur and separate them by a perpendicular line. You may use both margins. Do not draw a line to where the correction should go. Instead, place a caret (∧) in the text to show where the correction is to be made.

There are two principal reasons for indicating corrections in this way.

1. There simply is not enough room on the copy itself to write the corrections. Trying to insert all corrections in the copy would result in an unreadable mess.
2. A printer who is going to make corrections reads down the margin looking for errors that must be corrected. The printer no longer is interested in reading through the copy, wasting time reading what does not need to be corrected and perhaps overlooking what does. Corrections in the margin are clear to see, and that's all the printer looks for.

This is how you would edit this typeset copy. Note that the proofreading marks are the same as those you used before. Only their position (in the margin) is different.

Although you may not be editing galleys and page proofs very often, you will no doubt be proofreading single-spaced letters and memos. The same procedure applies. Do not try to crowd your corrections into the body of the letter. Instead, write them in the margin where they can be seen. Remember: Be sure to write them *directly opposite* the line to which they refer. Do not draw a line from the margin to the place of correction; simply insert a caret where the correction is to be made.

The letter from Ergo-Tech Associates with which we began the chapter is on page 468. It made a poor impression then. Now proofread it, showing all the corrections that need to be made when the letter is retyped so that it will make a good impression.

ERGO-TECH ASSOCIATES

**1273 Fairway Drive
Hackensack, NJ 07605
(201) 123-4321**

June 15, 198___

Ms. Carol Okada
Mgmt. Services, Inc.

281 E. Normal Ave.
Morristown, NJ 07960

Dear Ms OKada:

We are plaesed to be sending you a copy ofour booklet "The Office of
the Future—Today". Which you requested on june 12.

Our patented modular wrok stations are designed to insure individual
individual privacy and promote increased efficeincy. 6 typical
installations are shown on pages 26-thirty-one. You will also by be
intrested in the drawings of typical office layouts we have designed on
pages 34-40. Our designers surveys indicate that office arrangements
incorporating our modules can affect savings of up to 30%.

After reading the booklet you can have questions about the design of
your offices. Our agent in you're area is Ms. Joan Fyzee, 93 1st
1st Street, Parsippany NJ 07054 (phone 987-6543). Ms. Fyzee can give
you farther information on design, costes, and installaition—All
without any olbigation on your part.

Why not contact her today. A cord or lettex phone call to Ms. Fyzee
can be the frist step in giving you the office of the future—today.

Very truely yours,

John Ostrowski

John Ostrowski
Sales Manager

Compare your editing with the edited copy on page 469.
The letter in final form is found on page 470. It projects a positive image of the company, the kind of image to which Ms. Okada is likely to respond favorably. This letter will help convince her that Ergo-Tech Associates can provide her office with the modular work stations she needs. The difference between this letter and the original letter is the result of careful editing and proofreading.

ERGO-TECH ASSOCIATES

**1273 Fairway Drive
Hackensack, NJ 07605
(201) 123-4321**

June 15, 198__

Ms. Carol Okada
Mgmt. Services, Inc.
281 E. Normal Ave
Morristown, NJ 07960

Dear Ms. Okada:

We are pleased to be sending you a copy of our booklet "The Office of the Future—Today," Which you requested on june 12.

Our patented modular work stations are designed to insure individual individual privacy and promote increased efficiency. 6 typical installations are shown on pages 26 thirty-one. You will also by be intrested in the drawings of typical office layouts we have designed on pages 34-40. Our designers surveys indicate that office arrangements incorporating our modules can affect savings of up to 30%.

After reading the booklet you can have questions about the design of your offices. Our agent in you re area is Ms. Joan Fyzee, 93 1st 1st Street, Parsippany NJ 07054 (phone 987-6543). Ms. Fyzee can give you farther information on design, costs, and installaition—All without any obigation on your part.

Why not contact her today, A cord or letter phone call to Ms. Fyzee can be the first step in giving you the office of the future—today.

Very truly yours,

John Ostrowski

John Ostrowski
Sales Manager

SUCCESSFUL PROOFREADING

As you've seen, learning proofreaders' marks and their meanings is not hard to do, it just takes a little time. Learning how to use them correctly is a skill that you can master with a little practice. Successful proofreading, however, requires real effort. You must concentrate on

ERGO-TECH ASSOCIATES

**1273 Fairway Drive
Hackensack, NJ 07605
(201) 123-4321**

June 15, 198___

Ms. Carol Okada
Management Services, Inc.
281 East Normal Avenue
Morristown, NJ 07960

Dear Ms. Okada:

We are pleased to send you a copy of our booklet "The Office of the
Future—Today," which you requested on June 12.

Our patented modular work stations are designed to insure individual
privacy and promote increased efficiency. Six typical installations are
shown on pages 26-31. You will also be interested in the drawings on
pages 34-40 of typical office layouts we have designed. Our designers'
surveys indicate that office arrangements incorporating our modules
can effect savings of up to 30 percent.

After reading the booklet, you may have questions about the design of
your offices. Our agent in your area is Ms. Joan Fyzee, 93 First Street,
Parsippany, New Jersey 07054 (phone 987-6543). Ms. Fyzee can give
you further information on design, costs, and installation—all without
any obligation on your part.

Why not contact her today? A card or phone call to Ms. Fyzee can be
the first step in giving you the office of the future—today.

Very truly yours,

John Ostrowski

John Ostrowski
Sales Manager

what you're doing, reading slowly and carefully. If you proofread hastily because you're in a
hurry or because you don't care or because you're certain that there are no errors, you will do
a poor job. A poorly edited letter to a close friend may not be very important. Careless
proofreading of a letter to a potential customer or client could be serious, however, and a
widely circulated company report with uncorrected errors could seriously damage the
company's image. Important documents should be proofread carefully several times.

No matter how carefully you have proofread a piece of finished copy, you may still have overlooked something. That's why it is always a good idea to proofread something important one more time. When the manuscript for a textbook is set in print, for example, it is usually proofread by both the printer and the publisher. Then the author carefully proofreads the galleys or page proofs, and all these corrections are incorporated into the final copy, which is then printed and bound. The author then proofreads the finished text after publication, looking for printing errors that went unnoticed prior to publication. These corrections are then made in the text when it goes into a second printing.

Usually, students and teachers who use the text find one or two printing errors that have somehow still gone unnoticed.

Accurate and successful editing and proofreading demand your full attention. You must concentrate and take your time to do the best job you possibly can. Your goal is to make the final copy as good as you can make it because it is a direct reflection on you. A sloppy job of proofreading says to the reader that you are sloppy and indifferent. Clean, correct final copy says you are careful and conscientious, that you care about and take pride in doing things right. Careful proofreading can be your personal mark of excellence.

In the exercises you have been completing throughout this text you have been looking for errors that you know are present. You have even known what particular kinds of errors to look for in each exercise. In a normal editing situation, however, you don't know if there are any errors—in fact, you hope there aren't. Nor do you know what kinds of errors in particular to watch for. Any kind of error might be present anywhere. Accordingly, the best way to proofread something is to do it slowly and carefully, and do it more than once. Read through the material the first time with particular attention to the overall context. Do the sentences make sense? Is the vocabulary accurate? Are there any words missing or incorrectly repeated? Are there any grammatical errors? Then reread the copy much more slowly, focusing on the details. Is each word spelled correctly? Is all punctuation accurate and complete? Are proper nouns capitalized in accordance with standard business usage? Are numbers expressed correctly? Are words divided properly? Are all the lines aligned correctly? Do the headings of a report appear in the correct place and are they centered when they are supposed to be? If it is a business letter, is it positioned attractively on the page, with balanced margins? The list of such specifics could go on. Many people recommend that in this second stage of proofreading you read backwards, from right to left. This will force you to concentrate on each word so that you will catch errors in typing and spelling you might otherwise miss. You must, of course, read the material in the correct order to catch most other kinds of errors. Overall, the best general advice remains the same: *Take your time.*

SUMMARY OF PROOFREADING TECHNIQUES

1. Read through material for sense. Make sure all information is complete.
2. Check grammar.
3. Check spelling. (Use a dictionary!)
4. Check punctuation.
5. Check elements of style (capitalization, word division, expression of numbers).
6. Check overall format and appearance of material.

EXERCISE 22·1A   IDENTIFYING PROOFREADERS' MARKS

Write the letter from Column 2 that best describes the change shown by the entry in Column 1.

COLUMN 1	COLUMN 2	ANSWERS
1. bus̯ness	a. delete and close up	1. _____
2. _Business_ English	b. add space	2. _____
3. busŞiness	c. keep as it was	3. _____
4. Ɓusiness	d. insert letter	4. _____
5. busn̯i̯ess	e. move as shown	5. _____
6. Business#English	f. delete	6. _____
7. business english	g. italicize	7. _____
8. business ~~business~~	h. capitalize	8. _____
9. <del>business</del> English	i. make letter lowercase	9. _____
10. (English) business	j. transpose	10. _____

EXERCISE 22·1B   USING PROOFREADERS' MARKS

Make the changes in Column 1 called for in Column 2.

COLUMN 1	COLUMN 2
1. She said, Please be seated.	insert quotation marks
2. tothe bank frommy broker	add a space
3. note References	capitalize entire word
4. she will ~~probably~~ attend	restore word
5. The rules of language	start new paragraph
6. The rules of language	align to the left
7. Ave. 8	spell out
8. She said, "Please be seated"	insert period
9. due to the fact that it is already noon	change "due to the fact that" to "because"
10. because it is noon	insert "already" between "is" and "noon"
11. an up to date résumé	insert hyphens
12. The New York Times	italicize
13. Budget Director	lowercase capitals
14. The work however was completed	place commas around "however"
15. Were willing to help.	insert apostrophe
16. because already it is noon	move "already" to between "is" and "noon"

EXERCISE 22·2   PROOFREADING A BIBLIOGRAPHY

Often a business report ends with a **bibliography,** which is an alphabetical list of works cited or consulted. Proof-read the following bibliographical entries so that, when retyped according to your corrections, they will duplicate the bibliography printed at the end of the exercise.

References

Allen, Fred t. Ways to Improve Emlpoyee Communication. Nations Business, Sept. 1975, pp 54-56.

Benet, James C. "The Communication Need of business executives. The Jurnalof Business Communication.
  Spring 1971, pp. 5-11.

Forbes, Malcom. "Howto write better business letters," Newsweek, 18 October 1984.

"The Farther Adventures of English, the Wall Street Journnal, February 14, 1980, p. 20, col 2

Morse Peckham. "Humanistic Education For Business Exutives." Phila.: Univ. of Pennsylvania Press, 1906.

McCauley, Rosemary and Kieth Slocum. Business Spelling and Word Power. 2nd Ed. INdianappolis Bobbs Merrill Educational publishing, 1983

                         REFERENCES

Allen, Fred T. "Ways to Improve Emlployee Communication." Nation's Business, September 1975, pp. 54-56.

Bennet, James C. "The Communication Needs of Business Executives." The Journal of Business Communication, 8 (Spring 1971), 5-11.

Forbes, Malcolm. "How to Write Better Business Letters."Newsweek, 18 October 1984, pp. 34-35.

"The Further Adventures of English." The Wall Street Journal, 14 February 1980, p. 20, col. 2.

McCauley, Rosemarie and Keith Slocum. Business Spelling and Word Power. 2nd ed. Indianapolis: Bobbs-Merrill Educational Publishing, 1983.

Peckham, Morse. Humanistic Education for Business Executives. Philadelphia: University of Pennsylvania Press, 1960.

EXERCISE 22·3   PROOFREADING AN EDITED MANUSCRIPT

Below is a portion of the manuscript for a magazine article that offers advice on the job search process. Proofread this unedited copy so that when the passage is printed, it will look like the finished copy printed at the end of the exercise.

Interveiw Followup

    Most interviewers will bring a job interview toa close by telling you when the co. intends to make a decission. Youll here from us by the ned of the Month.

    If the co. has not notifyed you by then you can call the interviewer to enquire aboutthe progress or status of youre aplication. if a decision has not not been made yet you will have brouhgt your name back to the attention of the interviewer; if the company has made a decision, andyou have not been selected you will knwo w here you stand. And can concentrate your eforts on other companies.

Interview Follow-up

    Most interviewers will close a job interview by telling you when the company intends to make a decision: "You'll hear from us by the end of the month." If the company has not notified you by then, you may call the interviewer to inquire about the "progress" or "status" of your application. If a decision has not yet been made, you will have brought your name back to the interviewer's attention. If the company has made a decision and has not selected you, you'll know where you stand and can concentrate your efforts on other companies.

EXERCISE 22·4   PREPARING A MANUSCRIPT FOR THE PRINTER

The following passage is from a manuscript for a textbook on office procedures. Proofread these paragraphs taken from the chapter on word processing. Prepare them for the printer by marking all corrections. Be alert for occasional grammatical errors as well as typographical errors.

Useing a earpeice anda foot control device,, the the transcriptionist listens tothe materail that have been dictated on the media (a tape or disk. And simultaneous keyboardes the infromation in mailable form,

The automatde electronis typewriter which the typist normally uses. Offers a numbre of features not foundon conventional typewriters. Known as "text editors them typewriters provide fro the storage of evry keystroke. they allow the tyipist to recall and playbback the material is any changes are required. Or extra copys is needed. With a text editore a typist can corect errores simply by by back spacing. And retyping the cirrect letter or letters or letters. Some texteditors has a CRT screen cathode ray tube—similar to a tv screen). On these machines, a typist can set up a hole page on the screeen for any changes and correctiones befor printning a final or hard copy. This here hard copy is played back at typing rats ranging form one hundred eighty to 550 wpm. If the transcriptionist has key boarded the material correctly this copy is error-free.

EXERCISE 22·5   PROOFREADING A PAGE PROOF

The following passage is from a page proof of a textbook on data processing. Proofread it to show the printer what changes need to be made before the book is printed.

For phases make up the data processing cycle input procesing stroage and out put. Input de vices take teh the information form the source docment. And convert it into a fromat that can b'e red by the computer. the heart of the system is the centarl procesing unit the *CPu*. This devise comprising the logic uint andthe controll unit, monitors all the processing it does this through a program Which is simply a set fo insturctiones telling the computer what to do. These Instructiones are communicated through one of sevral porgramming languages. Sotrage refers to computer memmory. which is of too types Main storage, stored within teh cpu itsel f and auxiliary storage, stored on other mediums such as magnetic tapes or diskes. The output stage is

the final final stage. hear infromation form the computer memory are presented in a form a person can use. Such as printed infromation(printouts) visual display (terminal access, and microflim.

EXERCISE 22·6 INTERPRETING PROOFREADERS' MARKS

Retype the following edited memorandum in accordance with the directions indicated by the proofreaders' marks.

TO: All Office Personnel

FROM: Maureen Hoeffler, Personel (Mgr.) sp

DATE: May 15, 198__

SUBJECT: misue of office supplies

During the passed ③ months our expenses has increased allmost 20% because PERCENT

of the mis use ofoffice supplys and equipment. Such unnecessary expenses must stet

be eliminted accordingly, as of today the following policies will be observed:

Office Tempreture: Office tempreture willreman constant during the winter

months at 68° and at 72° during the summer months. (lc)

Lights: No unecessary lights will be left on. Please turn off all lights

underscore as you leave a individual unoccupied office. This includs the

Rest rooms.

Telephone Usage: No personal long-distance calls will be permitted local calls cap

will not be restricted.

Supplies: 1. office supplies are tobe used for business pruposes] ds

only.

2. The copy machine is not to be used for personal matters

is there are a machine available for you're use at a charge

of 10¢ a copy.

While I realize that this will be inconvenient for some of you Im sure you will

all do your part to see that this office runs economicly as well as efficiently.

Thank you for your cooperation.

CORRESPONDENCE FOR EDITING

In the last group of exercises you used your proofreading skills to edit material in preparation for its being typed or printed in final form. While you needed to correct a few errors in grammar and usage, you focused most of your attention on typographical and printing errors.

In this section you are going to apply your editing skills to more substantive errors. The following letters do not contain typographical or printing errors. Instead they contain many intentional errors in grammar, usage, punctuation, and elements of style. These are the kinds of errors involved in the editing exercises at the ends of the previous chapters. In each of these exercises you proofread a letter that illustrated the problems discussed in that chapter. The exercise at the end of Chapter 10, for example, focused on the correct use of adjectives.

In real life, of course, possible errors in grammar, usage, and punctuation in a given piece of writing are not confined to one particular type of problem. Any kind of error may be present.

The six letters in this section, representing various kinds of letters that you might meet in your work, contain a number of random errors. As such, they provide you with a more realistic editing challenge than do the editing exercises at the ends of the other chapters. In addition, because these letters involve many of the topics discussed in prior chapters, they give you a good indication of how well you have mastered the material you have studied in *Business English*.

EXERCISE 22·7   AN INVITATION TO SPEAK TO A GROUP

The following draft contains many intentional errors. Correct all the errors using the appropriate proofreaders' marks.

Dear Ms. Tkaczenko;

Each Spring the members of Future Business Leaders of America sponsors a lecture series, which are intended to acquaint it's membership with aspects of business. Our meeting for March is about the role of the Advertising Agency in marketing and I was writing to you to ask if you would address the group. I heard you speak at a group of students during Career Day in Lincoln High School two year's ago, I was so impressed that I saved the program and wrote to your company Ad-Vance Associates asking for additional information. Since I'm responsibly for establishing the spring series of programs I'm delighted to have the opportunity to ask if it will be possible for me to hear you again?

Because many of our members are interested in Writing, we would particularly like to be hearing about the ways the advertising copywriter goes about creating a successful campaign. What decisions goes into planning such a campaign. What are the people involved. What roles do they play. If you were able to appear and would address yourself to these and similar topics we are most grateful.

Because we are a nonprofit organization which is supported only by a nominal budget from the student government association we have been unable to offer you any honorarium for appearing. What we can offer you are a interested and appreciative membership for your audience—some of which may theirselfs wish to eventually join your rapidly-growing company when they graduate, and enter the world of advertising and marketing.

Respectably Yours,

EXERCISE 22·8   A RESPONSE TO A
LETTER OF COMPLAINT

The following draft contains many intentional errors. Correct all the errors using the appropriate proofreaders' marks.

Dear Mr. Montoya:

Our district manager has passed your letter of the fourth on to me. As you describe it, the service, that you received at our Route 25 station, is not hardly the kind of service you should expect from Petro. You have every reason to be offended with the attendants actions and Petro apologizes for it. We had spoke to the station owner after we receive your letter. He and myself feel badly about this incident; and I can assure you that neither him nor his associates wants these kind of incident to happen again.

Getting good night shift employees is a continuous problem for Petro and other dealers. Frankly, some of these employees are careless about the performance of his dutys. Our personal department is working hard to solve this problem. I hope however you won't let this one experience color your perspective on the vast majority of our employees and the quality of their service. Petro had always made it a company policy that the customers happiness comes first—thats implicit in our motto. Please accept once again my apologys for this unfortunate incident, and my assurance that an incident of a similar nature will not never happen again.

Please don't be angry at us. We value your patronage, and hope that you will continue to purchase our products. As you may know, Mr. Montoya we have recently been promoting our products and service through a series of free premiums available at participating dealers throughout Northern New Jersey. In case you have been unable to obtain one of these marvelous car thermometers, I have enclosed one with this letter. We believe it is the bestest dashboard thermometer available on the market today. Kindly except it with my complements. And my desire that you continue to be a happy Petro user.

Sincerely,

EXERCISE 22·9   A FINAL REQUEST FOR PAYMENT

The following draft contains many intentional errors. Correct all the errors using the appropriate proofreaders' marks.

Dear Mr. Ford:

On January, seventh, you purchased a microwave oven in our housewares department. It is now may and the charge of $379.24, has yet to be paid. This is the fifth reminder we've been sending you regarding you're failure to pay the above amount.

We've asked you to pay a portion of your bill. To make arrangements for a series of payments. To come tell us why you are unable to meet your obligation; but you have failed to respond to any of our letters. Because you haven't made no effort to settle your account. We are forced to reluctantly conclude that you do not intend to pay this bill. If we have been wrong please submit the entire balance in full immediately. Providing you're check reaches us by May thirtieth we will take no further action. If we do not hear from you by then we are forced to turn this claim over to our attorney.

We re sure you don't want to face the additional court costs and attorney fees such a procedure will necessarily entail. Let alone the embarrassment. Won't you please remit now? While we at Wilson's are reluctant to take claims to this legal limit we feel that we have a duty not only to ourselves and our other customers to ensure that all debts due the store are collected, otherwise any outstanding debts would have to be passed on to all of our customers in the form of more higher costs. Which we are not going to leave happen. We have no alternative accordingly but to give you this final opportunity to settle your account if you do not we are forced to precede with legal action against yourself by referring this action to our legal councillor.

Very truly yours,

EXERCISE 22·10   A LETTER SOLVING A CUSTOMER'S PROBLEM

The following draft contains many intentional errors. Correct all the errors using the appropriate proofreaders' marks.

Dear Mr. Chuy:

I was sorry to learn from your letter of December 12 that the oak, sewing, center, that you ordered for your daughter's Birthday, was damaged so bad when it had arrived that you was unable to except it. I understand how much you must of been looking forward to surprising you're daughter with this lovely present and how disappointed you must of been. If I was in your position I know how I would have felt.

When we shipped the sewing center to you the American Transport company gave us a receipt acknowledging that we had packed the center perfect. Thereby absolving us of responsibility to any damage incurred in shipping. Thus we are not liable to damages to the sewing, center, the damage you speak of is there responsibility, not our's.

However, like I said, I understood your position. You have bought off us a sewing center which is damaged. You were right to refuse delivery.

We value you as a customer Mr. Chuy and want you to be satisfied. We don't want you to be annoyed by us. Therefore we are shipping you another center by Interstate Express. Although it may not reach your home before your daughter's birthday. I hope the beauty and quality of the oak, sewing center, will make up for the delay.

In order to spare you any farther inconvenience, the claim against American Transport will be preceded with by us.

I hope that these plans are satisfactory with you. Please tell me, if I can be of any further service. In the meantime, thank you for purchasing the sewing center and wish your daughter a very happy birthday.

Sincerely,

EXERCISE 22·11   A RESPONSE TO A CUSTOMER'S REQUEST

The following draft contains many intentional errors. Correct all the errors using the appropriate proofreaders' marks.

Dear Mrs. Agronski:

    We had just received your letter of August 28 accompanied by your your check for $37.50 for an Imperial Ice Cream Maker. We were glad to learn of your interest in the Imperial Ice Cream Maker; but we are sorry to inform you that we are unable to comply to your request. You see Mrs. Agronski although we are manufacturing the Imperial we do not sell them. Instead we distribute Imperial Ice Cream Makers to various retailers throughout the Country whom sell the Imperial to people in there communities such as yourself.

    We did this for two principle reasons.

    The first reason is because by selling the Imperial solely through retail outlets, the unit price of the Imperial can be kept low. The savings we realize in shipping charges by shipping the Imperial in bulk lots will be past on to our customers.

    Second, if a problem was to have arose, for example if the Imperial was to require servicing, it would be convenienter for our customers to have it repaired by they're local dealers rather then shipping it to our plant here in Buffalo.

    We are therefore returning your check along with the names of several retailers in your area that carry the Imperial. We are confident that whoever you choose to do business with, you will find them helpful and courteous.

    We are also enclosing a pamphlet Imperial Desserts which provides a collection of delicious recipes designed to be especially prepared in the Imperial. This pamphlet normally sells for two dollars, please accept it with our compliments. We hope it will make you owning the Imperial all the more enjoyable.

                     Sincerely,

A FORM LETTER TO CHARGE ACCOUNT CUSTOMERS

The following draft contains intentional errors. Correct all the errors using the appropriate proofreaders' marks.

Dear Stein's and Bartell's Customer:

Stein's and Bartell's Department Store are pleased to announce to all of its customers that we are now the exclusive distributor in the greater metropolitan area of the all new Great Cuisine Food Processor. The ultimate machine in it's field. Charles Crouton the imminent food critic for Professional Cooking Magazine calls it "the perfect processor".

Contrast the Great Cuisine to other food processors and quickly you'll see why the Great Cuisine is different than and superior too any of its competitors.

The Great Cuisine offers a choice between 10 different speeds not just 2. These multiple speeds permit controlled slicing and shredding. The Great Cuisine lets you slice soft vegetables at slow speed. Chop meat at medium speed. And grating parmesan cheese at high speed.

The Great Cuisine has a bowl capacity significantly larger then any food processor. In the Great Cuisine you can make three loaves of bread dough, in its competitors you only can make one. In the Great Cuisine you can chop over 2 pounds of meat at once, in its competitors you can't chop no more than a half a pound.

As other food processors the Great Cuisine has come equipped with the standard slicing disc shredding disc and steel knife. But the Great Cuisine offers a great many optional blades as well, a thin, slicing, disc, a thin, shredding, disc, a french fry blade, a julienne blade, a rippled cut blade, and most recently, a specially-designed blade for whipping cream. In addition the Great Cuisine offers two special attachments a juice extractor and potato peeler.

Everyone of the components of the Great Cuisine are made to meet the highest specifications and the manufacturer Cuisine Products Inc. offers the extensivist guarantee of any manufacturer of food processors today.

The Great Cuisine is truly most unique. Any one, who is serious about cooking, owe it to themselves to have the Great Cuisine in their home.

Remember you can't buy the Great Cuisine Food Processor nowheres else. And the price is surprisingly affordable—only three hundred dollars. Which of course you can charge on your Stein and Bartell card. But the amount of machines we have in stock are very limited. And we have all ready sat several aside to meet previous special orders. Thus you should plan to come in our store soon for a free demonstration of the new and exciting Great Cuisine, you won't be sorry you did.

Sincerely Yours,

FINAL PROOFREADING EXERCISES

Like the letters in the last section of exercises, the exercises in this final section contain various errors involving grammar, punctuation, usage, and elements of style. They also contain the kinds of printing and typographical errors described earlier in this chapter. These exercises thus provide you with a highly realistic editing situation. Be alert for and correct all substantive and typographical errors. As an editor your primary concern here is to concentrate on correctness rather than style of writing, but if you feel that a particular idea is expressed awkwardly or ineffectively, then rewrite it. After all, you're the editor.

EXERCISE 22·13   APPLYING FOR A JOB

The first step in applying for a job is usually to send the company in which you're interested a copy of your résumé, accompanied by a cover letter.

Your résumé is a summary of your background, experience, and qualifications. Its most important sections detail your education and your work experience. These are presented in reverse chronological order. Because you will be sending your résumé to many companies, you will want to create a clean, typed copy free of errors, which then can be photocopied. An alternative is to have your résumé professionally printed.

The purpose of your cover letter, also known as a letter of application, is to introduce yourself to the prospective employer. In it you highlight your qualifications and request an employment interview. You will want to develop a standard letter to accompany your résumé, but each letter should be individually typed and addressed to the appropriate person at the company to which you're applying. You will probably modify your standard letter somewhat to suit the requirements of specific openings. The next two exercises will give you practice in proofreading a job application letter and a résumé.

EXERCISE 22·13A   A JOB APPLICATION LETTER

The following letter contains many intentional errors. Correct all the errors using the appropriate proofreaders' marks. Then retype the corrected letter in final form.

Ms. Carole Raffello
Director of Personal
Hillside International Corporation
2743 7th Avenue
New York, NY 10010

Dear Ms Raffello::

Please, consider me for a position into Hillside International Corporations management trainee porgram. My qualifications include 4 years of College where I major in Business administrration plus experience in retail sales and management.

Because my father had owned and operated a small, retail, clothing store while I was growing up, while still a boy selling became of interest to me. When he sells his store two years ago I was certain I want to to make retailing my career. Thus I directed my four year course of studys at bloomfield state college toward this goal. Taking courses specific designed for the student int rested in retailing such as Retail management and Distribution of goods and services. I aslo took several courses in Writing given by the English department. Because I knew them would be valuable to myself in my choosed profession.

Because I recognize that being a retail manager require managing both goods but people; I tried and be active in various extra curricular activitys at Bloomfeild state. I was a active member of the local business fraternity Kappa Kappa Chi, of which I was elected secretary my final year.

I was also amember of The World Business Ass. And I was involved in the annual Red Cross blooddrive. Which I chaired in 1948.

Throughout my four years in High School and during the Summers of my first two year's in College I was working in my father's store. These last two years I have been purforming similar dutys in my position at Super Discount Distributors. Where I have been able to put in practice what I've been learned in my college courses.

My résumé is enclosed, it provides all the particulars of my training and experience as well as the names of Professors and employers who you can ask to evaluate my work in the classroom and on the job.

I am anxious to discuss my qualifications with you in greater detail at an interview at you're convenience. I look froward to hearing from you.

                            Sincerely,

                          Paul Kupczak

                          Paul Kupczak

EXERCISE 22·13B   A RÉSUMÉ

The following résumé is intended to accompany the previous job application letter. It has been set in print by the printer, but it contains many errors. Carefully proofread the résumé and indicate all the corrections the printer should make before running off 100 copies. Use the appropriate proofreaders' marks.

PAUL KUPCZAK
728 Middleton Ave.
Clifton, NJ 07014
(201) 555-1378

OBJECTIVE: Enrty level positionin retail management with ample opportunity for advancement.

EDUCATION: B.S., Bloomfield, state College, Bloomfeild, NJ 07047
                    Major: Business Admin. Concentration: Mgmt.
may 1985   GPA: 3.2 on a 4-point Scale
                    Courses include: Retail managemnt, Distribution of Goods and Services
                                      international marketing research
                                      Over seas Opreation Management
                                      Intrenational Bus. Principals
June 1981   Clifton, high school. Clifton, NJ 07014
                    Graduated top twenty percent of class

EXPERIENCE:

                    Kupczaks Clothing Store, Clifton, N.J.
(1977–1938)   <u>Cleark</u>. Responsibilitys included assisting customers, stockinng merchanside,
parttime   creating displays, and taking invrentory. Managed store in owners absence
(1983–present   Super Discount Distrributors. Little Fallls, NJ 07065
                    <u>Asst. Manager</u>. Promoted form salespersob. Evening maganer of outwear
                        department. Supervise 4 people. Responsibel for inventory control, to
                        process purchase orders creating displays, assisting customers. NTraining
                        and Supervise new part-time employees in the de½t.
                    Names "Employeeof the Month twice.

ACTIVITYS: KAppa Kappa CHI (busines fraternity) Secertary senior year
                    World Business Association
                    soccer team, intermural basketball
                    Chair Person, campus Red cross Blood Drive, 1948

Special Skiils: Reading and speak German fluent

REFERENCES: Dr. Eleanor Kruk, Department ofbusiness Admin.
                    Bloomfield State College, Bloomfield, NY 07047
                    Dr. Ernesto Del Toro, Dept, of English
                      Bloomfield State Colllege, Blomfield, NJ 07047
                      Ms. Doroty Choi; District Manager
                    Super Discount Distributers. 1 Westway Ave.
                      Little Falls, Nj 07065

EXERCISE 22·14   A SHORT REPORT

One of the most common forms of communication in business is the *report*. Some reports are short, informal presentations of only a few pages. Others are long, formal documents of multiple sections including title pages, tables of contents, introductions, bibliographies, charts, graphs, and appendices. Some reports, such as a company's annual report, are intended for people outside the organization. Others, such as a personnel report, are intended to stay within the organization. Some reports (e.g., an accident report) are written on preprinted forms. Others may be written in the form of a letter or memorandum. Progress reports, periodic reports, information reports, analytic reports, and recommendation reports are among the types of short reports frequently written in business. Each normally contains three parts: introduction, body, and conclusion. Each part may contain more than one section. The precise material contained in each part will vary depending on the nature of the report.

The following report is for in-house distribution, so the writer has decided to use a memo format. The introduction presents the problem. The body analyzes the causes of the problem and then recommends solutions to solve the problem. The conclusion provides a brief summary of the report.

Proofread and edit this report in preparation for final typing and distribution. Correct all errors in grammar, usage, punctuation, and style of presentation as well as all typographical errors. Indicate how you want the headings to appear, which indentations you wish to keep or remove, and how items should be aligned. Improve any passage that strikes you as awkward or ineffective.

Your instructor may ask you to retype the report in final form based on your edited copy.

TO: George Altounian, Vice-President for Personal
FROM: Barbara Weiskopf, Administrative Asst.
DATE: Janruary 15, 198_
SUBJECT: Employee Turnover

Background.

During the passed too years us at DataTech International have suffered an increasing turnover problem inour Operations Department. Although are slaries and benefits are competitive with other companys in our area, area, and our plant is modern and attractive. Fully one third of our clerks and operrators leave within the frist year of employment. Inotherwords, one in three people we hire today will not be with us one year from now. That there is a alarming statistic.

While we are still able to be attarcting highly-qualified people to be filling them vacancies. The costs to the company is real high. Total recruitment costs and training colst per new employee averages close to $2,000. Moreover our studies indicate that druing the weeks and monthes immediately proceding there decision to be leaving, the qualitty of wrok these people does drops as much as twenty% below the norm, The quality of their work also declines too. In addition, their is an incraese in lateness and tardiness, an increased absenteeisn, and a a general declinein morale, that effects affects the entire department. High employee turnover is a real severe prolbem that must be solved.

Results Of Interview.

In order to determine the causes of the alarming high turnover rate. I conducted a series of exit interviews. I asked them operators and claerks who left the company within the last 6 omnths, why they was leaving? Here is the results.

32 people left DataTechs Operations Department during the last 6 months.

488

Reason fr Leaving	No. of workers
heavy rush-hour traffic	15 (47%)
part-time employment preferred	10 (31)
personal reasons	7 (22%

Thus the overwhelming majority of employees, whom have left the company during the last six months have left due to the fact of two primary reasons. Only a few peoples have lefted for personel reasons. Indeed almost people I spoke to was satisfied with their jobes here. and with DataTech. The trafic and work conditions taht are causing them to leave cna be changed by us.

RECOMMENDATIONS

I recommend that the co. establish a flextime schedule for it's employees in the operation's department.

Our present workday for these employees is 830 am to 4:30 p.m.. This puts people in to the heart ofthe rush hour notonly coming but going. The extensive constrcution on many of the area roadways, which are leading into and away from DAtaTech, further increas the problm. We should expand our Operations Department workday by 2 hrs. from 7:30 a.m. to 5;30 P.M. with three overlapping shifts.

Shift A: 7:30 a.m. to 3:30 p.m.
Shift B   8:30 am to 4:30 p.m.
Shift C 9:30 a.nm to %:30 pm.

These staggered shifts will improve the trafficflow near the co. druing comm-uting time. People that work either the a or c shift will miss a great deal of rush hour traffic. We wll still have every one on duty during our peak hours of 10:00 to 3:00.

Second, I recommend that we establish a policy of of employing more parttime employees in the Operations' Departmnet. Here again the flexible scheule would allow for part time people to either work mornings (7:30 to Noon) or afternoons noon to 4:30 5 days per week. If the company does in fact extend its opeartions to saturday like we currently are considering. Then we could aslo establish a parttime schedule of Monday - Wednesday - Friday or Tuesday - Thrusday - Saturday for these employees. Present employees would be gave the option of selecting among a new part-time position or the full-time position they hold presently.

Summary

The problem of high-employee turnover in the Operations Dept. cannot hardly be ignored. The conpamy is loosing valuable trained people, the quality of owrk has suffered, and its expensive to keep hiring and replacing employees so frequent. The flexbime schedule, that I had outlined, will address the major causesfor leaving voiced by near 80% of them employees who of left the company within the past six months. If such a plan was in operation, three out of for poeple that has left the company would still be with us perhaps. The cost of such a plan would not be high, the potential savings are considerable. I believed that flextime would demonstrateto our employes our concern for they're wellbeing and happiness. It would increase morale. It would decrease costes. it would improve productivity. And it would enhance the overall profitpitcure of DataTech. I recommmend it for youre consideration to you.

EXERCISE 22·15   COMPOSITION: WRITING A BRIEF REPORT

As we said, the report is one of the most common forms of business communication, and the report offering recommendations to solve a particular problem is a common type of report.

Think of a problem at your school that needs to be corrected. Inadequate parking, the poor quality of cafeteria food, and unreasonable policies and procedures involving registration, for example, are nearly universal complaints at every school in the country. Select one of these or a different area of concern and think about how you would improve it. Present your recommendations in the form of a short report in memorandum format. Use the organization of the report in the previous exercise as a model.

APPENDIX A

THE DICTIONARY

Most people normally use a dictionary for two reasons: (1) to find out how to spell a word, and (2) to find out what a word means. Actually, a good dictionary can tell you a great deal more. Below is a typical entry from *Webster's New World Dictionary of the American Language*. The labels point out all the information the entry provides in addition to the definition and correct spelling. Refer to this sample entry as you read the following discussion.

SPELLING

The dictionary tells you the correct spelling of a word. Some words have more than one acceptable spelling. In such cases the dictionary lists each of these spellings. The first spelling given is the more common spelling and is the spelling you should prefer in business.

DEFINITION

Each entry provides a definition of the different meanings of the word. Sometimes these definitions are illustrated by sentences or partial sentences. The entry for *initiate* includes two such verbal illustrations.

Some dictionaries list definitions in order of the development of the word. Original meanings are shown first, and more recent meanings follow. Other dictionaries do not employ this historical approach. They list the most common meaning of the word first. It is helpful for the reader to know which method of arrangement was used.

SYLLABICATION

In most dictionaries one or more dots are used to indicate how a word is divided into syllables. If you want to know how a word may be divided at the end of a line of type, the dictionary will show you. *Initiate*, for example, would be divided as *initi-ate*, not *init-iate*. (The rules for word division are presented in Chapter 20.)

A dictionary entry also shows you whether a compound word is written as one solid word (officeholder), hyphenated (off-season), or as two words (office hours).

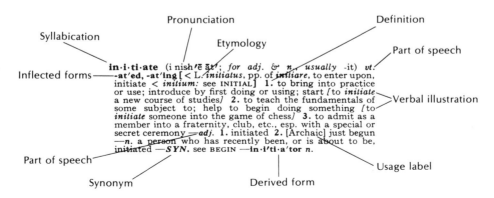

FIGURE A-1. Sample dictionary entry. (With permission from *Webster's New World Dictionary, Second College Edition.* Copyright © 1982 by Simon & Schuster, Inc.)

PRONUNCIATION

Immediately after the boldface entry of the word is an indication of how it is pronounced.

Stress marks show which syllables are **accented,** that is, spoken a bit more forcefully than other syllables. Often, as in the sample entry, a word contains several accents or stress marks. In these cases a heavy stress mark following a syllable indicates a strong stress; a lighter stress mark indicates a weak or secondary stress.

Initiate has two stresses. The second syllable receives the primary stress; the last syllable receives the secondary stress.

Special symbols called **diacritical marks** tell you how to pronounce each syllable. The *key words* at the bottom of each page show you how to pronounce each of these symbols. (These pronunciations are explained in full in the front of the dictionary.) Some words may be pronounced more than one way. In these cases the first pronunciation listed is the more common.

Initiate is pronounced in two ways, depending on how it is used in a sentence. When *initiate* is used as a verb (its normal use), the final syllable is pronounced ATE. When *initiate* is used as an adjective or a noun, the final syllable sounds like IT.

PARTS OF SPEECH

After the phonetic pronunciation of the word is a boldface label indicating what part of speech the word is. These are the labels typically used:

n.	noun	**prep.**	preposition
vt.	transitive verb	**conj.**	conjunction
vi.	intransitive verb	**pron.**	pronoun
adj.	adjective	**interj.**	interjection
adv.	adverb		

Our sample entry tells us that *initiate* is normally used as a verb, but it may also be used as an adjective and a noun.

As we have just seen, the pronunciation of *initiate* changes according to the part of speech it is being used as. Sometimes the spelling or meaning of a word may also differ depending on its part of speech. Thus it is important to read these labels carefully.

ETYMOLOGY

The material in brackets [ ] tells you the *etymology* or brief history of the word—where it comes from. Most words in English are derived from other languages. *Initiate,* the entry tells us, comes to us from Latin. Other words are derived from proper names. The word *boycott,* for example, originates from an Irish land agent, Captain C. C. Boycott, who was ostracized by his neighbors.

INFLECTED FORMS

As you know, nouns, verbs, adjectives, and adverbs can change forms grammatically. Nouns have singular and plural forms, verbs change tenses, adjectives and adverbs have positive, comparative, and superlative forms. We call these **inflected forms.** You have learned how to form the regular inflections of these parts of speech, and you know most irregular inflections. Dictionaries do not have enough room to show regular inflected forms, but they do show irregular inflected forms.

The inflected forms of *initiate* are not difficult, but the final e is left out in forming the past and present participles. Hence the entry shows *initiated* and *initiating.*

SYNONYM

A **synonym** is a word that means the same, or almost the same, as another word. Sometimes the entry for a word contains a list of synonyms. In our sample entry *begin* is listed as a synonym for *initiate.* The capital letters for *begin* indicate that further synonyms may be found under the entry for *begin.* This entry lists as synonyms *begin, commence, start, initiate,* and *inaugurate.* It also compares the slight differences in their meanings.

Some entries also include a list of **antonyms,** words that mean the opposite of a given word. The words *end, finish,* and *conclude* are listed as antonyms of *begin.* They are thus also antonyms of *initiate.*

USAGE LABEL

Some words are more appropriate in one situation than they are in another. For example, you might tell your friend that you "goofed," but in a business situation you would more likely say that you "made a mistake."

The dictionary indicates levels of usage for many entries. These usage labels tell the reader whether a word is appropriate in a given situation. Here are the typical labels. Words not identified by one of these labels are considered part of standard English and are appropriate for any occasion.

colloquial	Characteristic of informal writing and conversation.
slang	Not conventional or standard; used in very informal contexts.
obsolete	Occurs in earlier writings but is no longer used.
archaic	Occurs in earlier writings but rarely is used today.
poetic	Term or sense used chiefly in poetry, especially earlier poetry.
dialect	Term or sense is used only in certain geographical portions of the United States.
British, Canadian, Scottish, etc.	Characteristic of Great Britain, Canada, Scotland, etc.

One of the senses of *initiate* is labeled as *archaic.* You would not use the word in this sense in business writing.

OTHER INFORMATION IN AN ENTRY

In addition to all the information already described, some entries also include special information about grammar and usage. You can learn, for example, whether a noun is considered singular or plural, or which preposition is required with a specific word, or whether a word requires different prepositions depending on the situation.

The body of the dictionary also includes a variety of charts and tables. Lists of colleges and universities, historical and geographical information, proofreading symbols, and rules for punctuation, capitalization, expression of numbers, and similar material are usually provided in a series of appendices.

SUMMARY

As you can see, a dictionary contains a wealth of information. It can be your most useful aid to correct writing, spelling, and vocabulary building. Properly used, a good dictionary can be the most valuable reference book at your disposal. If you do not already own a good, up-to-date dictionary, you should purchase one for your personal reference library.

TYPES OF DICTIONARIES

There are three basic kinds or types of dictionaries. An **unabridged dictionary** is a large volume containing nearly all English words. *Webster's New International Dictionary,* for example, contains over 450,000 entries. Unabridged dictionaries are available in schools and libraries. Newspapers and businesses involved in publishing would use this kind of dictionary. Few people, however, really need a dictionary this large. For most people, an **abridged dictionary** is the appropriate choice.

There are two kinds of abridged dictionaries. A **pocket dictionary** usually contains about 75,000 entries. Pocket dictionaries are small and efficient, and many students carry them to class for quick checks of correct spelling. These dictionaries are too small to contain many of the features found in larger dictionaries, however, and they are inadequate for all your needs.

The second type of abridged dictionary is the **desk** or **college dictionary.** A good desk dictionary contains between 155,000 and 170,000 entries plus all of the extra features described above. It is an excellent reference source for the college student and the business person. A good college-level dictionary should be a part of your library. Here are four good ones: *The American Heritage Dictionary of the English Language; The Random House Dictionary of the English Language; Webster's New Collegiate Dictionary; Webster's New World Dictionary of the American Language.*

APPENDIX B

SPELLING

As we have seen, mistakes in grammar, punctuation, and usage can undermine your credibility as a writer. Mistakes in spelling can be even more damaging. Most people are very critical of spelling errors. If you make mistakes in spelling, your reader is likely to think you are (at best) careless or (at worst) uneducated and unintelligent. Because correct spelling is seen as being so important, your success in the business world will depend heavily on your ability to spell.

Correct spelling is not easy. English is a very diverse language. It has a German base to which have been added substantial borrowings from Latin, Greek, and French, plus a host of other languages, each with its own spelling conventions. Moreover, pronunciation is not necessarily much help in providing clues to the correct spelling of a word. Consider, for example, the following:

cough—rhymes with *off*
dough—rhymes with *sew* and *so*
rough—rhymes with *stuff*

This does not mean that learning how to spell is a hopeless task. It isn't. Spelling is a skill and, like other skills, it can be learned.

Despite the acknowledged inconsistencies in English spelling, there are more consistencies than inconsistencies. In fact, about nine out of ten words in English can be spelled correctly by following a set of spelling rules. Thus it is of great value to be familiar with these rules.

Dictionaries and spelling texts list these rules in detail. There are exceptions, but the rules cover far more words than there are exceptions. The following rules are particularly helpful because they apply to so many words and typical spelling problems. Furthermore, there are relatively few exceptions to these rules. Learn these six important rules and how to apply them. Once you do, you will be a more confident and successful speller.

DOUBLING THE FINAL CONSONANT

RULE

When adding a suffix that begins with a *vowel,* double the final consonant if:

1. The word ends in a single consonant (except *x*), and
2. This consonant is preceded by a *single* vowel, and
3. The word is pronounced with the accent on the *last* syllable.

Do not double the final consonant unless *all three* conditions are met.

This rule really is not so complicated as it may sound at first. Just take it step by step. Because so many spelling errors are the result of failing to follow this rule, and because so many words are covered by this rule, it is well worth knowing.

EXAMPLES

admit	admitted	admitting	admittance
begin	beginner	beginning	
commit	committed	committing	
control	controlled	controlling	controllable
drop	dropped	dropping	dropper
fit	fitted	fitting	fittest
equip	equipped	equipping	
forget	forgettable	forgetting	
occur	occurred	occurring	occurrence
regret	regretted	regretting	regrettable
stop	stopped	stopping	stoppage

Remember: Double the final consonant only when a word satisfies all three conditions. The final consonants of the following words are not doubled because the words do not meet all three conditions.

appear	appeared	appearing	appearance
box	boxed	boxing	
balloon	ballooned	ballooning	balloonist
concoct	concocted	concocting	concoction
credit	credited	crediting	creditor
differ	differed	differing	difference
index	indexed	indexing	
parallel	paralleled	paralleling	
register	registered	registering	
tax	taxed	taxing	taxable
visit	visited	visiting	visitor

There are a few exceptions to this rule. They include the following words:

cancellation	excellent	transferable
crystallize	gaseous	transference

WORDS ENDING IN *E*

RULE

Drop the final e from a word when adding a suffix beginning with a vowel (*ing, able, al, er,* etc.). Do not drop the final e from a word when adding a suffix beginning with a consonant (*ment, less, ly,* etc.).

As with the first rule, a great many spelling errors result from the failure to follow this rule. Learn it well.

EXAMPLES

achieve	achieved	achieving	achievement
advertise	advertised	advertising	advertisement
blame	blamed	blaming	blameless
complete	completed	completing	completely
excite	excited	exciting	excitement
forgive	forgivable	forgiving	forgiveness
hope	hoped	hoping	hopeful
measure	measurable	measuring	measurement
like	liked	liking	likely
move	moved	moving	movement
use	usage	using	useless

The few exceptions to this rule are frequently misspelled. Pay particular attention to the following:

argue	argument
nine	ninth
abridge	abridgment
awe	awful
true	truly
acknowledge	acknowledgment
due	duly
whole	wholly
judge	judgment

WORDS ENDING IN *CE* OR *GE*

RULE

Do not drop the final e from words ending in ce or ge when adding *able* or *ous*. The final e is retained to keep the c and g soft—like s and j.

EXAMPLES

acknowledge	acknowledgeable
advantage	advantageous
change	changeable

courage	courageous
manage	manageable
marriage	marriageable
outrage	outrageous
notice	noticeable
service	serviceable

WORDS CONTAINING *EI* OR *IE*

RULE

Write *i* before *e*,
Except after *c*,
Or when sounded like *a*,
As in *neighbor* or *weigh*.

Remembering the three parts to this verse will help you solve most spelling problems involving *ei* or *ie*.

Write *i* before *e*

achieve	client	niece
aggrieve	field	patient
audience	friend	relief
believe	grief	review
brief	lien	yield
cashier	mischief	

Except after *c*

ceiling	deceit	receipt
conceit	deceive	receive
conceive	perceive	

Or when sounded like *a*

beige	heir	surveillance
eight	neighbor	vein
feint	reign	weight
freight		

As with the other rules, there are some exceptions:

ancient	foreign	seize
caffeine	forfeit	sheik
conscience	height	sleight
counterfeit	leisure	sovereign
either	neither	sufficient
efficient	science	weird
financier		

PREFIXES AND SUFFIXES

RULE

When adding a prefix that ends with the same letter that begins the main word, include both letters.
When adding a suffix that begins with the same letter that ends the main word, include both letters.

EXAMPLES: PREFIXES

dis	+ similar	= dissimilar	mis	+ spell	= misspell
il	+ legal	= illegal	over	+ rule	= overrule
im	+ mature	= immature	un	+ necessary	= unnecessary
inter	+ regional	= interregional	under	+ rate	= underrate

accidental + ly = accidentally
actual   + ly = actually
cruel   + ly = cruelly
respectful + ly = respectfully

common + ness = commonness
even   + ness = evenness
mean   + ness = meanness
sudden + ness = suddenness

WORDS ENDING IN Y

RULE

Words that end in *y* preceded by a consonant usually change the *y* to *i* before the addition of any suffix, except suffixes beginning with the letter *i*.
Words that end in *y* preceded by a vowel do not change the *y* to *i* when a suffix is added.

EXAMPLES

Words ending in *y* preceded by a consonant:

accompany	accompanies	accompaniment	accompanying
apply	applied	application	applying
bury	buried	burial	burying
comply	complies	complication	complying
identify	identified	identification	identifying
notify	notified	notification	notifying
rely	relies	reliable	relying
study	studies	studious	studying
verify	verified	verifiable	verifying

Words ending in *y* preceded by a vowel:

annoy	annoyed	annoyance	annoying
convey	conveyed	conveyance	conveying
display	displayed	displays	displaying
employ	employable	employment	employing
survey	surveys	surveyed	surveying

Note that this rule applies to forming the plurals of nouns ending in *y*.

company	companies	attorney	attorneys
secretary	secretaries	boy	boys
variety	varieties	valley	valleys

There are a few exceptions to the rule:

day + ly = daily
gay + ly = gaily
lay + d = laid
pay + d = paid
say + d = said

MNEMONIC DEVICES

There are two basic ways to learn to spell the one word in ten not covered by a spelling rule or that is an exception to the rule. The first of these is to use some form of memory aid to help you remember the spelling. Such aids are called **mnemonic devices.** Word associations, sayings, visualizations—anything that can help you remember how to spell a word—can be effective mnemonic devices. Here are some examples:

stationERy → papER
stationAry → plAce
"I see *a rat* in sep*arat*e."
"*Br,* it's cold in Fe*br*uary."
"A good *secret*ary keeps an employer's *secret*s."

MEMORIZATION

The other way to learn how to spell a word is simply to memorize it. If the word does not conform to the spelling rules and you can't think of a useful mnemonic device, you will have to resort to rote learning. Simply commit the word to memory. Follow these three basic steps.

1. *See it.* Examine the word. Note distinctive letter sequences and common letter groupings.
2. *Say it.* Pronounce the word slowly and clearly. Then close your eyes and visualize the word as you say it and spell it.
3. *Write it.* Write the word several times, saying each letter as you write or type it. Write it several more times until the word is thoroughly familiar.

Remember, do not start your program of spelling improvement by memorizing lists of words. Rote memorization should be your *last* resort. First become familiar with the rules that govern the large majority of words in the language. Then develop mnemonic devices for as many troublesome words as you can that are exceptions to the rules. Then commit the remaining words that you need to know to memory. And remember the best rule of all: When in doubt, consult your dictionary.

400 FREQUENTLY MISSPELLED WORDS

The 400 words listed below are not the difficult, unusual words used in spelling competitions. Rather, they are common, everyday words that people use all the time and often fail to spell correctly. Because these are the words that are misspelled most often, if you master this list of words, you will have come a long way toward becoming a proficient speller.

Pay particular attention to the asterisked(*) words on the list. They are among the most frequently used words in business correspondence.[1] In writing in the business world you will use them often and will need to spell them confidently and without error.

absence	although*	brilliant	definite
abundant	amateur	business*	dependent
accede	among*	calendar	describe
accept	amount*	capital, capitol	description*
acceptance	analysis*	career	desirable
accessible	analyze	ceiling	desert, dessert
accident*	annoyance	certain	despair
accidentally	annual*	challenge	development*
acclaim	answer	changeable	different*
accommodate	apparent	choose, chose	difficult
accompaniment	appear*	cloths, clothes	dining
accomplish	appearance	collect	disappearance
accuracy	applies	column	dilemma
accurately	appreciate*	coming	disappoint
accuse	approach*	commercial	disastrous
accustom	appropriate*	committee*	discipline
achievement	approximately*	companies*	discuss*
acknowledgment	arguing	competition	discussion*
acquaintance	argument	completely	disease
acquire	arrange	concede	dissatisfied
across	article	conceive	disgusted
actually	athlete	connote	divide
adequately	attendance,* attendants	conscience	dominant
admitted	attitude	conscientious	dropped
admitting	auxiliary	conscious	due*
adolescence	bargain	considerably	during*
advantageous	basically	consistent	efficient
advertising*	beautiful	continuous	eligible
advertisement	becoming	controlling	embarrass
advice, advise*	before*	controversial	encourage
afraid	beginner	convenience*	entirely
against*	believe*	council,* counsel	environment
aggravate	believing	criticize	equipped
aggressive	benefit	curriculum	especially
alleviate	benefited	curious	exaggerate
almost	bigger	cylinder	excellent*
all right	boundary	daily	except
alphabetical	breath, breathe	deceive	existence
already	brief	decision*	expense*

---

1. Devern J. Perry, "The Most Frequently Used Words and Phrases of Business Communications" (Research report to the Delta Pi Epsilon Research Foundation, July 1982), Appendix C, pp. 1–42.

experience*
explanation
extremely
familiar
families
fascinate
favorite
February
fictitious
field*
finally
financially
foreign
fortieth
forty, fourth
forward*
freight
friend
fulfill
fundamentally
further*
generally
government*
governor
grammar
guard
happiness
hear, here*
height
hopeless
hoping
humorous
ignorance
imaginary
illusion
immediately*
immense
importance
incidentally
independent
indispensable
industrious
inevitable
influential
ingredient
initiative
intellect
intelligence
interest*
interference
interpret
interrupt
involve*
irrelevant
irresponsible
jealous
judgment
knowledge
laborer
laboratory
later, latter

led, lead
leisure
library
license
likely
literature
loneliness
loose, lose
losing
luxury
magnificence
maintenance*
manageable
maneuver
manner*
manufacturer
marriage
mathematics
meant
mechanics
medicine
miniature
minute
mischief
misspell
mortgage*
mysterious
naturally
necessary*
neighbor
neither
niece
ninety
ninth
noticeable
numerous
obstacle
occasionally
occurred
occurrence
off*
offered*
official
omitted
operate
opinion*
opportunity*
opposite
organization*
original*
paid*
pamphlet
parallel
paralyze
particular
pastime
peculiar
perceive
performance*
permanent
permitted

persistent
personal,* personnel*
persuade
physical*
piece
planned
pleasant
political
possession
possible*
practical
precede
preferred
prejudice
preparation
presence
prestige
prevalent
principal, principle
privilege
probably*
proceed
professor
prominent
psychology
pursue
quantity
quiet, quite
really
receipt
receive*
recognize
recommend
reference*
referring
regard*
relieve
religious
remembrance
repetition
representative*
requirement*
resistance
resources
responsible*
restaurant
rhythm
ridiculous
sacrifice
safety*
satisfying
scenery
schedule*
science*
secretaries
seize
separate
sergeant
serviceable
several*
shining

shoulder
significance
similar*
sincerely
site,* cite
source
speak, speech
specimen
stationary, stationery
stopped
straight, strait
strenuous
stretch
strict
substantial
subtle
succeed
success*
sufficient
summary*
supersede
suppose
surprise
syllable
symbol
symmetrical
synonym
temperament
temperature
technique
tendency
than,* then*
their,* there*
themselves
therefore*
thorough
though
through*
together*
tomorrow
transferred
tremendous
tried
truly
undoubtedly
unnecessary
until*
useful
using*
vacuum
valuable
varies
vegetable
view
weather, whether*
weird
were,* where*
wholly, holy
woman, women
writing
yield

Appendix C

PARTS AND STYLES OF THE BUSINESS LETTER

Business people communicate with others outside their organization primarily through the business letter. We have already seen that correct grammar, usage, and mechanics are essential to a successful letter. The overall impression that a letter creates is also determined by how it appears on the page. If the reader's attention is drawn to how the letter looks—to poor centering, an unusual or awkward format, an incomplete arrangement of information—rather than to the words themselves, the effectiveness of the message is undermined.

Business writers have developed several basic letter styles and parts that readers can expect to find in normal business correspondence. These standard styles and parts help the reader to focus on *what* the writer is saying rather than on *how* the writer says it. In this way the interests of both the writer and the reader are best served. The following pages describe the basic parts of the business letter and present models illustrating the four basic letter arrangements.

PARTS OF THE BUSINESS LETTER

1. LETTERHEAD (WRITER'S RETURN ADDRESS)

Most businesses use 8½-by-11 inch stationery with printed letterhead. The letterhead includes the name, address, and telephone number of the company. It may include the company logo or slogan as well.

Personal business letters should not be typed on company letterhead. They should be on plain paper or printed personal stationery. When plain paper is used, the writer's return address is typewritten just above the date.

2. DATELINE

The date is typed three spaces below the last line of the letterhead or 2 inches from the top edge of the paper, whichever is lower. The date is written in either of these forms: January 15, 1984 or 15 January 1984. Do not abbreviate the month or use the abbreviated form 1–15–84.

3. INSIDE ADDRESS

The inside address includes the name, title, and address (street, city, state, and zip code) of the person to whom the letter is being sent. If the letter is sent to a business or organization, then the name and address of the business or organization are used.

4. ATTENTION LINE

An attention line, typed two lines below the address, is used to name the particular person or department to whom you are directing the message. An attention line is used when the letter is addressed directly to a company. When the letter is addressed to a particular person by name or job title, no attention line is necessary.

5. SALUTATION

The salutation is typed two lines below the address block or attention line (if used). The salutation should agree in form with the inside address: *Dear Ms. Garcia* for a letter addressed to an individual; *Ladies and Gentlemen* for a letter addressed to an organization.

6. SUBJECT LINE

The subject line names the letter topic. It is usually typed at the left margin two lines below the salutation, though in some letter formats it may be indented or centered.

7. MESSAGE

The message is also referred to as the *body* of the letter. Most business letters are typed single spaced, with one blank line between paragraphs.

8. COMPLIMENTARY CLOSE

The complimentary close is typed two spaces below the last line of the letter. Depending on the nature of the message, the complimentary close may range from *informal (Sincerely, Cordially)* to *formal (Yours truly, Respectfully yours).*

9. COMPANY NAME

The company name may be used to show that the letter represents the views of the company as a whole and not just those of the individual writer. It is typed entirely in capital letters, two spaces below the complimentary close.

10. WRITER'S NAME AND TITLE

The writer's name is typed four lines below the company signature (if used), or the complimentary close. This allows the author enough space to sign his or her name. The author's title or department should be typed next to or below the typewritten name, depending on which placement appears more balanced.

11. REFERENCE INITIALS

The initials of the typist appear two spaces below the writer's name and title. The writer's initials, when used, appear before those of the typist. If the writer's name is typed on the signature line, the writer's initials are unnecessary.

12. ENCLOSURE NOTATION

The enclosure notation, typed two spaces below the reference initials, shows that some other materials are included with the letter. It reminds the typist to include these materials with the letter, and it reminds the recipient to look for them.

13. CARBON COPY NOTATION

The carbon copy notation tells the addressee that one or more other people will also receive a copy of the letter. The initials cc are typed one or two spaces below the enclosure notation (if used), followed by the name or names of the other recipients. Use of a colon after cc is optional.

14. POSTSCRIPT

A postscript may be used to add comments at the end of a letter. It allows the writer to express an afterthought or to give an idea special emphasis. The postscript is typed two lines below the carbon copy notation and begins PS: or PS.

15. SECOND AND SUCCEEDING PAGES

Most business letters are a single page. The second and succeeding pages of long business letters are typed on plain paper of the same quality as the letterhead (but without letterhead). The heading, typed seven lines from the top of the page, includes the name of the addressee, the page number, and the date.

Figure 1 illustrates all 15 parts of the business letter.

Very few business letters contain all the parts just described. The following basic parts are normally included in any business letter. The remainder are included only as needed or where preferred.

Letterhead or return address	Salutation	Signature
Dateline	Message	Reference initials
Address	Complimentary close	

LETTER STYLES

Four basic letter styles are used in business. They are 1) the full-block style, 2) the modified-block style, 3) the modified-block style with indented paragraphs, and 4) the simplified letter style. Each is illustrated below. Each may also be used for personal business letters.

PUNCTUATION STYLES

Punctuation style refers to the punctuation marks that are used after the salutation and complimentary close in a business letter. Two styles are commonly used. *Mixed punctuation* includes a colon after the salutation and a comma after the complimentary close. This is the style used by most organizations. In *open punctuation* no punctuation marks appear after the salutation or complimentary close. Figures C-2 and C-3 illustrate mixed punctuation. Figures C-1 and C-4 illustrate open punctuation. (A third style, *closed punctuation*, in which a comma or period appears after every line of the salutation and complimentary close, is now rarely used.)

---

① **COMMUNICO, INC.**
1423 Eighth Avenue
Philadelphia, PA 19104
(312) 654-3210

② September 20, 198___

Contemporary Designs, Inc.
③ 234 Baltimore Avenue
Haddonfield, PA 19205

④ Attention Ms. Beverly McKnight

⑤ Ladies and Gentlemen

⑥ SUBJECT: STYLE OF BUSINESS LETTERS

⑦ As you requested, I am sending you a group of letters that illustrate the four basic styles used in business correspondence. Each has special features which individual business writers prefer. For the sake of uniformity and to present a company image, however, you will probably want to select one particular style to be used by all your departments.

This letter illustrates the full block style. As you can see, all lines begin at the left-hand margin. Because this style is so efficient for the typist, it is widely used and preferred by many businesses.

Notice that open punctuation is also used in this letter. Although either open or mixed punctuation can be used with the full-block style, most businesses use open punctuation because it saves time and thus complements the full-block style.

FIGURE C-1.   The full-block style.

Although most people like the clean, businesslike appearance of the full-block style, some people object to this arrangement because everything is on the left and the letter can appear unbalanced. These people prefer one of the two modified-block styles.

---

(15) Contemporary Designs, Inc.
Page 2
September 20, 198___

In addition to the sample letters, I am enclosing descriptions of the standard parts of the business letter which you and Mr. Kupczak may find helpful.

(8) Sincerely yours

(9) COMMUNICO, INC.

Barbara Ravina

(10) Barbara Ravina, Consultant
Office Services Department

(11) alw

(12) Enc.

(13) cc Mr. Michael Kupczak

(14) PS. You may include a postscript with any of these letter styles.

FIGURE C-1.   The full-block style. (*continued*)

1.	Letterhead	9.	Company Name
2.	Dateline	10.	Writer's Name and Title
3.	Inside Address	11.	Reference Initials
4.	Attention Line	12.	Enclosure Notation
5.	Salutation	13.	Carbon Copy Notation
6.	Subject Line	14.	Postscript
7.	Message	15.	Second and Succeeding Pages
8.	Complimentary Close		

COMMUNICO, INC.
1423 Eighth Avenue
Philadelphia, PA 19104
(312) 654-3210

September 20, 198__

Contemporary Designs, Inc.
234 Baltimore Avenue
Haddonfield, PA 19205

Ladies and Gentlemen:

This letter illustrates the modified-block style. Some people also refer to it as the modified-block style with blocked paragraphs.

In this format the dateline, complimentary close, and signature block begin at the horizontal center of the page. All other lines begin at the left margin.

A letter arranged in this style is balanced visually toward the center of the page. Many people find this style more visually appealing than the full-block style. Because some of the lines begin in the middle of the page, however, it is less efficient to type than the full-block style.

The full-block letter contained all the parts of a business letter. This letter contains only those parts normally included in any business letter. The remaining parts are optional and are included only as needed or where preferred.

Sincerely,

COMMUNICO, INC.

Barbara Ravina

Barbara Ravina, Consultant
Office Services Department

alw

FIGURE C-2.   The modified-block style.

COMMUNICO, INC.
1423 Eighth Avenue
Philadelphia, PA 19104
(312) 654-3210

September 20, 198__

Ms. Beverly McKnight
Office Manager
Contemporary Designs, Inc.
234 Baltimore Avenue
Haddonfield, PA 19205

Dear Ms. McKnight:

This letter illustrates a variation of the modified-block style called the semiblock style or the modified block with indented paragraphs.

As you can see, it is identical with the modified-block style with one exception: the first line of each paragraph is indented (usually five spaces). While some writers like the appearance of this arrangement, many companies do not use it because it is less efficient to type than the other styles.

Notice that the mixed punctuation style is used in this and the modified-block letter. A colon follows the salutation and a comma follows the complimentary close. This is the punctuation style most often used with the modified-block letter arrangements.

Cordially,

COMMUNICO, INC.

Barbara Ravina

Barbara Ravina, Consultant
Office Services Department

BR:alw

FIGURE C-3.   The modified-block style with indented paragraphs.

COMMUNICO, INC.
1423 Eighth Avenue
Philadelphia, PA 19104
(312) 654-3210

September 20, 198___

Ms. Beverly McKnight
Office Manager
Contemporary Designs, Inc.
234 Baltimore Avenue
Haddonfield, PA 19205

THE SIMPLIFIED LETTER

Do you like this letter style, Ms. McKnight? It illustrates the simplified letter style developed by the Administrative Management Society. The easiest of all formats to set up and type, it contains the following characteristics:

1. It uses the full-block style with open punctuation.

2. It omits the salutation and complimentary close.

3. It includes a subject line typed all in capitals with two blank lines above and below it.

4. It includes the name and title of the author typed all in capital letters at least four lines below the body of the letter.

While some people prefer this letter because of its efficiency and simplicity, others feel that it seems unfriendly because the traditional salutation and complimentary close are omitted.

BARBARA RAVINA--CONSULTANT, OFFICE SERVICES DEPARTMENT

alw

FIGURE C-4.   The simplified letter.

APPENDIX D

COMMON ABBREVIATIONS

STATES AND TERRITORIES

	Common	Zip		Common	Zip		Common	Zip		Common	Zip
Alabama	Ala.	AL	Kentucky	Ky.	KY	Oklahoma	Okla.	OK			
Alaska	Alaska	AK	Louisiana	La.	LA	Oregon	Oreg.	OR			
Arizona	Ariz.	AZ	Maine	Maine	ME	Pennsylvania	Pa.	PA			
Arkansas	Ark.	AR	Maryland	Md.	MD	Puerto Rico	P.R.	PR			
California	Calif.	CA	Massachusetts	Mass.	MA	Rhode Island	R.I.	RI			
Colorado	Colo.	CO	Michigan	Mich.	MI	South Carolina	S.C.	SC			
Connecticut	Conn.	CT	Minnesota	Minn.	MN	South Dakota	S.Dak.	SD			
Delaware	Del.	DE	Mississippi	Miss.	MS	Tennessee	Tenn.	TN			
District of			Missouri	Mo.	MO	Texas	Tex.	TX			
Columbia	D.C.	DC	Montana	Mont.	MT	Utah	Utah	UT			
Florida	Fla.	FL	Nebraska	Nebr.	NE	Vermont	Vt.	VT			
Georgia	Ga.	GA	Nevada	Nev.	NV	Virginia	Va.	VA			
Guam	Guam	GU	New Hampshire	N.H.	NH	Virgin Islands	V.I.	VI			
Hawaii	Hawaii	HI	New Jersey	N.J.	NJ	Washington	Wash.	WA			
Idaho	Idaho	ID	New Mexico	N.Mex.	NM	West Virginia	W.Va.	WV			
Illinois	Ill.	IL	New York	N.Y.	NY	Wisconsin	Wis.	WI			
Indiana	Ind.	IN	North Carolina	N.C.	NC	Wyoming	Wyo.	WY			
Iowa	Iowa	IA	North Dakota	N.Dak.	ND						
Kansas	Kans.	KS	Ohio	Ohio	OH						

CANADIAN PROVINCES

Alberta	Alta.	New Brunswick	N.B.	Prince Edward Island	P.E.I.
British Columbia	B.C.	Newfoundland	Nfld.	Quebec	Que.
Manitoba	Man.	Nova Scotia	N.S.	Saskatchewan	Sask.
		Ontario	Ont.		

MONTHS OF THE YEAR

Jan.	January	May	May	Sept.	September
Feb.	February	June	June	Oct.	October
Mar.	March	July	July	Nov.	November
Apr.	April	Aug.	August	Dec.	December

COMPASS DIRECTIONS

E.	East	N.W.	Northwest	S.W.	Southwest
N.	North	S.	South	W.	West
N.E.	Northeast	S.E.	Southeast		

UNITS OF MEASURE

Length		Weight		Time		Electronic	
c.m.	centimeter	cg.	centigram	d.	day	a.	ampere
ft.	foot, feet	gm.	gram	hr.	hour	c.	cycle
in.	inch	gr.	grain	min.	minute	kc.	kilocycle
m.	meter	kg.	kilogram	mo.	month	kv.	kilovolt
mi.	mile	lb.	pound	sec.	second	kw.	kilowatt
mm.	millimeter	mg.	milligram	yr.	year	mc.	megacycle
yd.	yard	oz.	ounce	a.m.	before noon	v.	volt
				M.	noon	w.	watt
				p.m.	afternoon		

Standard Business Terms

abbreviated, abbreviation	abbr.
absolute	abs.
account	acct.
acknowledged	ack'd
acre	A
additional	addl.
adjective	adj.
ad libitum (at pleasure)	ad lib.
administration	adm.
Administrative Management Society	AMS
Administrator	Admr.
adverb	adv.
advertise	adv.
affidavit	afft.
against	vs.
agent	agt.
agreement	agmt.
also known as	a.k.a.
America, American	Am.
American Automobile Association	A.A.A.
American Bankers Association	A.B.A.
amount	amt.
and	&
and others	et al.
and the following pages	ff.
Anno Domini (in the year of our Lord)	A.D.
anonymous	anon.
answer	ans., A.
apartment	apt.
appendix	app.
approximate	approx., ap.
article	art.
as soon as possible	ASAP
Associated Press	AP
association	assn.
assorted	astd.
at	@
attention	attn., atten.
Attorney	Att., Atty.
Avenue	Av., Ave.
average	av., avg.
Bachelor of Arts	A.B., B.A.
Bachelor of Law	LL.B.
Bachelor of Science	B.S.
balance	bal.
bale(s)	bl.
bank	bk.
banking	bkg.
barrel	bbl.
Before Christ	B.C.
board	bd.
bill of lading	B/L
bills payable	B.P.
bills receivable	B.R.
bill of sale	B/S
Boulevard	Blvd.
branch office	B.O.
brother	Bro.
brothers	Bros.
brought forward	b.f.
building	bldg.
bulletin	bul.
bureau	Bu., Bur.
bushel	bu.
box	bx.
by authorization	P.P.
by way of	via
capital	cap.
Captain	Capt.
carbon copy	c.c., cc
care of	c/o
cartage	ctg.
carton	ctn.
catalog	cat.

cathode ray tube	CRT
Centigrade	C.
cents	c., cts.
certificate	cert., ct., ctf.
certificate of deposit	CD
Certified Administrative Manager	C.A.M.
Certified Professional Secretary	C.P.S.
Certified Public Accountant	C.P.A., CPA
chapter	chap., ch., C.
charge	chg.
chief executive officer	CEO
Christmas	Xms., Xmas
circa (about)	ca.
collect, or cash, on delivery	c.o.d., COD
Company	Co.
collection	coll.
Colonel	Col.
commerce	com.
commission	comm.
compare	cf.
continued	contd., cont., con.
copyright	©
Corporation	Corp.
correct	OK
cost, insurance and freight	c.i.f., CIF
cost of living adjustment	COLA
credit	cr.
creditor	Cr.
debit	dr.
degree	deg.,°
deliver	del.
department	dpt., dept.
destination	dstn.
dictionary	dict.
Director	Dir.
discount	dis.
distributor, distribution	dist.
division	div.
direct current	d.c., dc
ditto, the same	do.
doing business as	d.b.a.
dollar(s)	d., dls., dols.
dozen	doz.
Doctor	Dr.
Doctor of Philosophy	Ph.D.
Doctor of Dental Surgery	D.D.S.
Doctor of Divinity	D.D.
Doctor of Laws	LL.D.
Doctor of Medicine	M.D.
each	ea.
Editor	Ed.
electric	elec.
employment	empl.
enclosure	enc., encl.
end of month	e.o.m.
envelope	env.
Environmental Protection Agency	EPA
equal	eq.
Equal Employment Opportunity Commission	EEOC
errors and omissions expected	E. & O.E.
establish	est.
estimated time of arrival	ETA
Esquire	Esq.
et cetera, and so forth	etc.
example	ex.
exchange	exc., exch.
Executor	Exec.
expense, express	exp.
extension	ext.
Fahrenheit	F., Fahr.
Federal	Fed.
Federal Bureau of Investigation	FBI
Federal Communications Commission	FCC
Federal Deposit Insurance Corporation	FDIC

Federal Insurance Contributions	
Act	FICA
Federal Reserve Board	FRB
Federal Trade Commission	FTC
feminine	fem., f.
figure	fig.
first	1st (no period)
first class	A-1
folio	fo., fol., f.
footnote	fn., ftnt.
for example	e.g.
For your information	FYI
Fort	Ft.
forward	fwd.
fourth	4th (no period)
free alongside ship	f.a.s., FAS
free on board	f.o.b., FOB
freight	frt., fgt.
from	fr., fm.
gallon	gal.
General	Gen., Gen'l
General Headquarters	GHQ
general mortgage	gm
goods	gds.
Governor	Gov.
government	gov't
gram	g.
gross	gr.
Gross National Product	GNP
guaranteed	gtd.
half	hf.
hardware	hdw.
Headquarters	Hq.
height	ht.
health maintenance	
organization	HMO
Highway	Hwy., Hy.
history	hist.
Honorable	Hon.
horsepower	hp., hp
hospital	hosp.
hundred	C
hundredweight	cwt.
I owe you	IOU
illustration, illustrated	ill., illus.
improvement	imp., impr.
in the place cited	loc. cit.
in the same place	ib., ibid.
in the work cited	op. cit.
inches	in.
inclusive	incl.
Incorporated	Inc.
Individual Retirement Account	IRA
industrial, independent	ind.
inferior	inf.
initial	init.
in regard to	re
insurance	ins.
intelligence quotient	I.Q.
interest	int.
International	Int.
International Business Machine	I.B.M.
Interstate Commerce	
Commission	ICC
inventory	invt.
invoice, investment	inv.
Invoice Book	I.B.
Island, Isle	I.
italics	ital.
joint	jt.
Journal	J., Jr., Joun.
Junior	Jr.
Justice of the Peace	J.P.
karat	K., kt.
laboratory	lab.
language	lang.

large	la., lge.
latitude	lat.
leave	lv.
Ledger folio	L.f.
Legislature	Leg.
lesson	Les.
less-than-carload lot	l.c.l., LCL
let it stand	stet
letter	ltr.
letter of credit	L/C
library	lib.
Lieutenant	Lieut., Lt.
limited	Ltd.
line	l.
list price	L.P.
liter	L.
literature	lit.
location, local	loc.
longitude	long.
lumber	lbr.
machine	mch., mach.
Madam	Mme.
Mademoiselle	Mlle.
magazine	mag.
mail order, money order	MO
Major	Maj.
Manager	Mgr.
manufactured	mfd.
manufacturing	mfg.
manufacture	mfr.
manuscript(s)	ms., MS, mss., MSS
mark	mk.
market	mkt., mar.
masculine	m., mas., masc.
Master of Arts	M.A.
Master of Business	
Administration	M.B.A.
Master of Ceremonies	M.C.
Master of Science	M.S.
maturity	mat.
mathematics	math.
maximum	max.
medium	med.
memorandum	memo.
merchandise	mdse.
Mesdames	Mmes.
Messieurs	Messrs., MM.
metropolitan	met.
midnight	mid., mdnt.
military	mil.
miscellaneous	misc.
Miss or Mrs.	Ms.
Mister	Mr.
Mistress	Mrs.
money order	m.o.
Monsieur	M.
mortgage	mtg.
mount	Mt.
municipal	mun.
namely	viz.
namely or to wit	sc., scil., sct.
national	Nat., Natl.
net in 30 days	n/30
no good	n.g.
not available, not applicable	NA
not sufficient funds	N.S.F., N/S
Notary Public	N.P.
note well	n.b., N.B.
number	no., #
obituary	obit.
obsolete	obs.
Occupational Safety and Health	
Act	OSHA
opened	opd.
opposite	opp.
optional	opt.
ordinance	ord.
organization	org.

original	orig.	revised	rev.
out of stock	os	right	rt.
		road	rd.
Pacific	Pac.	route	Rt.
package	pkg.	rural free delivery	R.F.D.
page	p.	rural route	R.R.
pages	pp.		
paid	pd.	Sainte	Ste.
pair	pr.	Savings	Sav.
pamphlet	pam.	section	sec.
paragraph	¶, par.	Senate, Senator	Sen.
parcel post	p.p.	Secretary	Sec., Secy.
parenthesis	paren., par.	Securities Exchange	
parkway	Pkwy.	Commission	SEC
part	pt.	Senior	Sr.
patent	pat.	school	sch.
payment	payt.	shipment	shpt.
per annum	per an.	shipping order	SO
percent	%, pct.	signature	sig.
piece	pc.	signed	/S/
pint	pt.	singular	sing.
place	pl.	so, thus	sic
place of the seal	L.S.	square	sq.
Plaintiff	Plf.	standard	std.
population	pop.	steamship	SS.
port of entry	p.o.e., POE	stock	stk.
Post Exchange	PX	Street	St.
Postmaster	PM.	subsidiary	subs.
Post Office	P.O.	Superintendent	Supt.
postpaid	ppd.	supplement	supp.
postscript	P.S., PS	syndicate	synd.
pound sterling	£		
pound shilling pence	£s.d.	table	tab.
power of attorney	P/A	tablespoon	tbsp., T.
preferred	pfd.	teaspoon	tsp., t.
premium	pm., prem.	telephone	tel.
President	Pres., P.	temporarily	pro tem.
price	pr.	Territory	Ter.
principal	prin.	that is	i.e.
private branch exchange	PBX	the following	seq.
problem	prob.	the same	id.
Professor	Prof.	thousand	M
Profit and Loss	P & L, P/L	township	Twp.
pronoun	pron.	trial balance	T/B
public	pub.	Treasurer	Treas.
Publishing, Publisher	Pub.	Trust, Trustee	Tr.
purchase order	PO		
		United Nations	U.N., UN
quality	qly.	United Press International	UPI
quantity	qty.	University	Univ.
quart	qt.		
quarter, quire	qr.	very important person	VIP
question	Q.	vice president	V.P.
		video-display terminal	VDT
railroad	R.R.	volume	vol.
railway	Ry.		
ream, room	rm.	warehouse receipt	W.R.
receipt	rec't	waybill	W/B
receivable	rec.	week	wk.
received	recd., rcd.	weight	wt.
reference	ref.	which see	q.v.
Registered	®, rg., reg.	which was to be proved	Q.E.D.
Registered Nurse	R.N.	wholesale	whsle.
regular	reg.	Wide Area	
Reply, if you please	R.S.V.P.	Telecommunications Service	WATS
report	rep't	work	wk.
returned	rtd.		
Reverend	Rev.	zero-base budgeting	ZBB

INDEX